REAL-WORLD RESEARCH

REAL-WORLD RESEARCH

Sources and Strategies for Composition

Rai Peterson
Ball State University

Houghton Mifflin Company   Boston   New York

Senior Sponsoring Editor: Suzanne Phelps Weir
Senior Associate Editor: Janet Edmonds
Project Editor: Gabrielle Stone
Senior Production/Design Coordinator: Carol Merrigan
Manufacturing Manager: Florence Cadran
Senior Marketing Manager: Nancy Lyman

Cover Design: Rebecca Fagan
Cover Illustration: Tana Powell

Printed in the U.S.A.

Library of Congress Catalog Number: 99-71913
ISBN: 0-395-90126-X

123456789—DSG—03 02 01 00 99

Contents

Preface

Today, college is part of the real world. The "ivory tower" image of colleges and universities belongs to another age. As schools of higher education are increasingly held accountable by legislatures and the media for the measurable gains they bring to society, whatever boundaries did exist between "the real world" and that of the academy are dissolving. Televised college courses, Internet-based classes, service learning programs, and community-based educational initiatives have brought colleges to the world and vice-versa. Students don't "graduate into" society; they are immersed in it continuously. Contemporary college students are often experienced decision makers who have shouldered a good deal of responsibility already. Increasingly, students in higher education are simultaneously earning a living, raising children, and dealing with a host of other "real life" concerns.

Student research is valid and valued. Students use the same methods and materials employed by practicing professionals in nearly every field every day. (Many of today's fantastically successful high-technology companies were founded by college students!) *Real-World Research* recognizes the opportunities and possibilities available to college composition students. It encourages students to choose research subjects that fascinate them, to use respected primary and secondary sources, and to pursue research projects that are exciting to conduct and assess.

Real-World Research is a comprehensive text for first-year composition courses that require students to write a research paper. With an engaging tone, no-nonsense approach, comprehensive coverage, and helpful features, it demystifies the researching process. It offers practical suggestions, from organizing note cards to using World Wide Web search engines to staying calm during an interview. Unlike other texts, *Real-World Research* helps students uncover interesting topics, explore information and perspectives, develop a position, and complete successful academic work. It presents research as an exciting and rewarding process that we all use daily when reading a newspaper, watching a television news show, learning about products from advertising, trying a variety of solutions to everyday problems, getting to know people better, and so on. Research in all of its forms offers exciting opportunities for personal growth and public knowledge. By directing students to discover new and "relevant" information, this book demonstrates that research is entertaining and useful, as fascinating as it is necessary.

Our culture values research. Many professions involve a heavy research component. Some of the jobs in which we engage vicariously through prime-time television programs and movies involve complex research tasks. Trial lawyers, forensic pathologists, detectives, FBI agents, news producers, mystery writers, sports reporters, even talk show hosts perform research as part of their jobs. In academic settings, however, research is often divorced from its cultural context and relegated to lifeless test tubes and dusty back-issues of periodicals. It becomes prescribed and pretentious—an intimidating series of duties to be tediously performed and recorded. The spontaneity and serendipity of real-life research is exchanged for the rote task of replicating a standardized researching process. Most textbooks' research chapters make little mention of the various methods associated with different disciplines, or of engaging resources outside of typical library holdings.

■ Distinctions

The scope, approach, coverage, and features of *Real-World Research* are the significant areas of difference between it and other texts on how to write a research paper. Most research writing books are casebooks taken up during only that part of the semester when writing a research paper is studied. *Real-World Research*, by contrast, contains reading material and assignments that make it useful either as a primary text in a composition class, to be used throughout the semester, or as a supplemental text. It encourages students to pursue research assignments of varying complexity and duration and to try various modes of research in different academic fields. Because this book defines research broadly, it instructs students in how to seek out sources for reliable, original, authoritative data through exciting forms of research such as interviews and observation. Throughout, students are asked to analyze, synthesize, evaluate, develop, and present ideas.

■ Features

Real-World Approach and Emphasis
The tone of this book is empowering and encouraging. It introduces students to the mechanics of such real-world tasks as scheduling an interview, arranging to examine archival documents, obtaining assistance in understanding complex documents, and making contact with other computer users around the world. *Real-World Research* prompts students to contact government officials and offices, conduct interviews, and actually enter the milieu of their research paper topics. It prompts students to inquire into and report findings that are unique and that give a sense of purpose and audience to the college research project.

Interviews with Researchers
Real-World Research demonstrates the relevance of research to work-related tasks. Interviews with people in a variety of occupations, ranging from a

small business owner to a museum curator to a newscast writer, are included at the end of each chapter in Part One. The interviews provide students with in-depth illustrations of how research processes are critical in all dimensions of life. Each person interviewed explains each step in his or her researching process, from getting ideas to the final presentation of their work. Every interview is followed by suggested writing assignments.

Application Exercises

Each chapter ends with three exercises that ask students to apply the strategies and steps of the researching process discussed within the chapter. Some of these exercises require collaborative work. Others call for individual reflection or activity. The exercises are focused but flexible enough for students to adapt them to meet the needs of their individual research projects. A fourth exercise at the end of each chapter fosters "writing to know." It encourages students to conduct research and put their findings into writing immediately.

Research and Writing with Electronic Sources

Real-World Research encourages students to seek sources of information throughout their college reference library and to use the Internet to discover additional sources beyond the confines and limitations of the library. Strategies, tips, directions, and examples are provided.

Focus on Developing Arguments

The entire text helps students understand the relationship between gathering information from a variety of sources and developing and supporting a thesis. Chapter Ten, "Planning an Argument," presents a comprehensive, practical look at the elements and strategies of formal argumentation.

Student Writing

Research notes, drafts, and a final paper written by a real student are woven into most of the chapters in Part Two to illustrate the points and processes covered by the text. The final draft of this research paper is also used in Chapters Thirteen and Fourteen to provide students with detailed examples of the MLA and APA documentation formats. Six additional student research papers are included in Part Three of the book to illustrate different approaches to topic selection, research sources, and paper organization.

Alternative Media Presentations

Today's students may have opportunities to present their research findings in media that can extend and enhance their writing. Chapter Fifteen, "Creating Alternative Media Presentations," explores a variety of alternative formats, including public presentations, poster sessions, World Wide Web sites, and videos.

Internships and Careers

Part Four, which addresses searching for an internship, is especially relevant to students' research into career choices. Research techniques presented in the text are applied to the job search, particularly to finding available positions, gathering information necessary to write a knowledgeable letter of introduction and appropriate resume, and preparing for an interview.

Acknowledgments

I want to thank the following coinhabitants of the "real world" for their advice and assistance in the preparation of this manuscript: Donna Browne, Diane Calvin, Adrienne Jones, and Judy Koor from Bracken Library; Mary Alexander, Ann Bay, and Keith Melder from the Smithsonian Institution; Paula Nassen Poulos and Wynell Schamel from the National Archives; Helen Dalyrumple and Barbara Morland from the Library of Congress; Ruthie McIntosh from the Barbara Bush Foundation for Family Literacy; Myles Ogea from the MT Cup; Susanna Aaron from NBC; Matt Roberts and Rosemary Keenan from CBS; Dawna Kemper from First Merchants Bank; Karla Kirby from Ball Memorial Hospital; and the Delaware County, Indiana, Offices of the Assessor, Auditor, Clerk of Court, and Building Commissioner.

The following students provided responses to the text in draft form and contributed their manuscripts to this book: Kyle Parker, Cathy Bennett, Duane Clemens, Kim Craig, Lindsay Davis, Amanda Harry, Tad Hickel, Carole Kirsch, Kyle Keever, Catherine Meeker, David Meeker, Amanda Messersmith, Quinn Nguyen, Tim Peters, Kim Powers, Sam Scholl, Brian Seelig, Brent Thomas, and Travis Wilson.

I would also like to thank the following reviewers, who offered invaluable suggestions for changes and additions during development of the manuscript: Tiane Donahue, Northeastern University; Charles Elwert, University of Illinois; Mary A. Fortner, Lincoln Land Community College; Julia Galbus, University of Southern Indiana; Greg Garrett, Baylor University; Kim Brian Lovejoy, Indiana University–Purdue University at Indianapolis; Shirley Morahan, Truman State University; Joyce Neff, Old Dominion University; Kathleen G. Rousseau, West Virginia University; Eileen B. Seifert, DePaul University; Sandra Spencer, University of North Texas; Daphne Swabey, University of Michigan; and Judith Williamson, Sauak Valley Community College.

I sincerely thank my colleagues at Ball State University who make working unlike work at all, especially Bryan Byers, Joel English, Tom Koontz, Linda Hanson, Jamie Miles, Web Newbold, Carole Clark-Papper, Sarah Penning, Paul Ranieri, Becky Rickly, Barb Stedman, Joe Trimmer, and Jeff White, all of whom talked and thought about the pedagogy in this book with me. Today's lesson is brought to you by the letters JKL.

REAL-WORLD RESEARCH

PART ONE

Sources

Chapter One

Practicing Real-World Research

Discovery is the most engaging experience we know, and research is the activity that leads to discovery. Imagine that when you turn this page you discover a letter written by an infantryman at the Battle of Shiloh (see Figure 1.1). Imagine that somewhere in this book is buried the identity of an anonymous birth mother from your family tree. Imagine that the next sentence reveals which car has all the features you want and is within your budget. Imagine that when you put this book down, you could immediately begin testing an antibody that will arrest the AIDS virus. Imagine that at the conclusion of this chapter you could venture a plausible guess as to who informed Woodward and Bernstein on Watergate. Imagine that the information found herein could increase your appreciation of your favorite song, poem, film, novel, or play. Imagine that by closely reading these words, you might discover a discrepancy in a famous alibi, an untried solution to an ancient problem, or some new evidence that could reconcile evolution and creationism. Imagine the enthusiasm with which you would read on. That is the kind of self-sustaining excitement generated by an engrossing research project.

■ What Is Research?

Research is a generic term that can be used to describe a wide variety of learning and information-gathering activities. We engage in many forms of research every day: reading a newspaper, watching a television show, surfing the World Wide Web, learning about new products from advertisements, asking a colleague or teacher for advice, trying a variety of solutions to everyday problems, figuring out why an object broke and how to repair it, getting to know our friends better, and so on. Research is necessary, abundant, almost ubiquitous in our society. It is difficult to avoid researching on a very simple level: does this ice cream taste as good as a more expensive brand? What makes this room so inviting? Does that person's smile indicate empathy? Is it going to rain today? Will a cold battery start my car's engine if I turn off the radio and the air conditioner? Answering life's questions

My dear Brother,
                                   Flat Creek, MO
                                   Nov 6th 1861

I have just a few minutes to spare as it is now in the night & our company has orders to go out on a scout early in the morning to be away from camp several days.

We are 42 miles from Springfield where the Northern Army are encamped, their forces are variously estimated at from 48 to 60 thousand with from 100 to 120 (forces) or harmn.

I have never been able to ascertain the strength of our army. Col. Stone estimates the entire strength of the Southern Army here at 28 thousand. I think it is doubtful, but proud that we give them a fight or not. Nearby are the Missourians in this part of the state are against us and are acting as spies for the North.

If we do not get reinforcements we may have to fall back into Arkansas and Texas, but I hope this may not be for where large Armies pass the people are bound to suffer for they seach every thing as they go. We have too many horses & I am afraid many of them may starve this winter. My horse is in good order now & as gay as ever. We have had very good luck both with Men & horses. We have not had a single death in our regiment & very little sickness every thing considered. I am in fine health & good spirits. I am trying to put all my trust in Him who is all powerful in Heaven & Earth, thank God for his Goodness to me. All the boys in our Company are like brothers to me & treat me with all the kindness & respect I can wish. They are all well. We have had no very cold weather yet & no snow. John Laws has been quite unwell and when George Laws left us John went Bentonville to stay untill he recovered. He is now in better health than he has been in this Summer. Dr. Thomas & Andrew More are in good health.

Did Beord get the hogs from Mrs. Selvidge. I had so many things to think of I forgot to ask him. How did the potatoes turn out, & how are the hases doing. Did you get the corn, & the Rye for Ma. How are you all getting along. How is Ma, Elizabeth & my dear little Boys & girls & Lucy & Will & Jimmy & little Isham & Abe. You cant tell me too much about them in your next letter which I hope you will write as soon as you get this. I am uneasy about my poor little Pleasant, how is his health now. Does Ma seem low spirited. Comfort her all you can. The Lord is my refuge & my defense. Of Trust in him Isham, for he does all things well. How is Cousin Jums, Ann & the Girls. Give my love to them & tell me if Batillo has paid off his note & if Malergin has paid Elizabeth the amount of his notes. And if you have collected any money.

I dont wont you to pay a single debt now but keep every dollar you can get. I owe no one who is not able to do without it for a year or two & we may see our families suffer for bread if we dont save it. Dont let any one know that you get any money except G.W. Guys or Mr. Laws & tell them to say nothing about it. (They will prevent hard thoughts.) You may show this to Cousin Joms if you wish & to Mr. Guys and Laws. May the Lord keep you all.
                            Your brother, Edward

Figure 1.1 A letter sent back home from an infantryman during the Civil War.

consumes nearly all of our time. We rely on our researching ability to solve problems, to save time, to win the esteem of our coworkers and friends, and to educate and entertain ourselves every day.

Informal, Day-to-Day Research

You don't need a book to make a researcher of yourself; you have been conducting informal systematic research all of your life. Your enrollment in this course is the result of research. Some amount of research likely influenced your choice of which school to attend, whether or not you live in campus housing, the route or means of transportation you use to get to class, the clothing you choose to wear, and even the way you will read and record the ideas in this text.

When the outcome is personally useful, research scarcely seems like work at all. It is exciting to discover the features your next personal computer might incorporate, exhilarating to investigate jobs in your field, beneficial to try the latest over-the-counter headache remedy, entertaining to talk with an expert on a subject that interests you, and enlightening to listen to a candidate whose campaign you are considering supporting.

Formal Research

Research is more difficult when the topic or methods are imposed on you from without. Obviously, students are sometimes compelled to study subjects that do not fascinate them or to investigate source material that is inconclusive or confusing. It seems that the courses students most dread are those that require a longer research paper than they believe they are capable of producing. But even our everyday lives impose unwelcome research assignments on us. Determining how best to unclog your kitchen sink, for example, might lead to all kinds of revelations about chemicals, mechanical processes, the intricacies of plumbing systems, and the myriad ways in which a typical residence can be connected to water supply and waste removal systems. Or, faced with a choice between replacing your car's fuel pump yourself or postponing your vacation plans for another year, you might be surprised at how much you can learn on a Saturday morning. Ardently you would pursue the differences in price and quality between a new and a reconditioned part, rudimentary lessons about fuel injection, and mechanics' tips about everything from loosening rusted bolts to cleaning electrical contacts, discovering along the way that undesired research projects can become quite fascinating once you become engrossed in the subject matter.

The professional researchers profiled in this book find their work thoroughly rewarding—even those who were not particularly interested in the subjects they deal with before they accepted their jobs. Often we overlook the fact that most of the desirable employment in our culture depends heavily on research skills. Where would an attorney be without access to previous cases and precedents? What helps television writers make their scripts accurate and interesting? From which sources does your physician learn the methods he or she uses to treat your illnesses and injuries? How do architects learn about new building products, appropriately direct historical restorations, or design buildings that fit the local climate or style? The researcher profiles included in this text explore the investigational processes necessary for diverse professional undertakings, from the once-in-a-lifetime venture of starting a new business to the daily race to bring television news footage to a national audience. They demonstrate how the research skills you are learning in college may be useful to you after graduation, and they offer suggestions about how you can start using, right now, some of the hands-on research methods frequently employed by professionals.

The end result of successful research is reliable information and pride in having produced complete, comprehensive work. There are few shortcuts to that outcome. A thorough, dynamic research process is necessary to producing a valid, informative, persuasive end product. Learning to enjoy the process really is part of conducting successful research. This book suggests ways to incorporate the kinds of research you like to do into your investigations of any topic or assignment. It will help you build on the considerable skills you have already amassed in the lifetime of research that has brought you to this sentence on this page.

■ *Kinds of Research*

When you move to a new community, enroll in a different school, or begin a new job, how do you assimilate yourself into that new culture? How do you discover the amenities of your new surroundings, find a group of like-minded friends, search out places to eat lunch, and learn what is expected of you—and what will happen if you fail to meet those expectations? Whenever you are in a new situation, you probably use a combination of hands-on experimentation and reliance on the advice of others. For example, it is not a good idea to intentionally perform poorly at a new job to discover what happens if you fail to meet a sales quota, turn in paperwork on time, or report to your desk at the appointed hour. Most anyone knows it is better to take the word of your boss or coworkers than it is to test such outcomes yourself.

Similarly, it is probably not a good idea to introduce yourself to new neighbors with an exhaustive description of your own personality, interests, and qualifications and then wait for them to suggest the perfect pals for you. Most likely, you would prefer to choose your own friends through the slow process of meeting and getting to know people on an individual basis. No one else could really know just what you are looking for.

Successful research depends on using first-hand exploration (primary research) where necessary to answer specific questions and trusting second-hand information (secondary research) when personal investigation is inconvenient, impractical, or impossible. Nearly all of the professional researchers profiled in this book rely on a combination of primary and secondary research in their work.

Primary Research

When you go directly to the source of information, you are conducting primary research. Archaeologists digging at the site of an ancient civilization—carefully mapping out the placement of dwellings, public buildings, gathering places, houses of worship, and burial grounds—are conducting primary research into the patterns of ancient life (see Figure 1.2). Metallurgists who heat-test various alloys to determine the stability and melting point of those combinations of minerals are likewise engaging in primary research. Biochemists systematically comparing the DNA strands of thousands of rats with and without symptoms of dementia are engaged in the labor-intensive primary research necessary to discover the genetic markers of Alzheimer's disease. These are the kinds of pursuits usually associated with the concept of primary research.

Primary research is useful in all fields of study, however, not just in scientific investigations. An artist visiting a museum to closely examine the brush strokes and shading techniques used on a particular canvas is engaging in primary research into that painter's methods. A student reading a novel and highlighting the author's historical allusions or references to colors is beginning primary research into meaningful patterns in that text. A group of historians might conduct primary research on an historic battle by visiting the place where it was fought, pacing out distances between ridges, viewing the site from a nearby hill, touching the scars on the trunks of trees, and noticing the change in temperature at nightfall.

Figure 1.2   Excavation at Dashar, 1894. © Stock Montage Inc.

Primary research lends your investigation something no other source of information can: your own personal experiences. It engages you in your work in a personal, invigorating way, often resulting in information that you will be eager to report to your readers. People write best when they are excited about their subject matter and truly believe they have something important to say. Engaging in primary exploration of a subject often gives writers a personal "handle" on the topic.

Conducting primary research should be exciting, not intimidating. If you decide to interview an expert as part of your research, for example, tell yourself that you might be initiating a lifelong acquaintanceship or a useful contact for future projects.

Nearly every research topic can benefit from hands-on information gathering. Of course, no one expects you to cure cancer or eliminate the national debt with your college research papers. Indeed, much of the primary research our society needs is beyond the scope of a student's resources, schedule, and knowledge base. It is usually not possible for students to conduct complex scientific studies, since they often require intricate research designs, controlled laboratory environments, sophisticated data-gathering techniques that ensure respondents' anonymity, extremely precise measurements, or complex cross-referencing. There are only a handful of research organizations in the country, for instance, that are qualified to produce valid opinion poll results. Respected research laboratories are few because of the exacting processes and expertise required to reach sound conclusions. The names of such respected organizations are household words in the United States: the Centers for Disease Control and Prevention (CDC) in Atlanta, the National Aeronautics and Space Administration (NASA) in Houston, the American Cancer Society, and J. D. Powers and Associates, among others. We have come to trust Gallup polls, Nielsen ratings, and the U.S. census. The resources commanded by the organizations that produce these measures are far beyond what most researchers have at their disposal. Their phone bills alone are staggering. The amount of computer memory used to process the data they collect is immense. If you are a student at a research university where important primary research is conducted right down the hall from your classrooms, you may know firsthand the extensive resources required to conduct most research. You may have been a participant in someone else's study, or maybe you work as a lab assistant, carrying out instructions from a chief researcher. Whether you are a consumer of large-scale research or a participant in its making, you realize that the limitations of your own situation exceed those of your imagination. Although you can probably conceive of some long-term or large-scale research that would be fascinating to conduct, writing a college paper doesn't provide the opportunity to discover what life forms exist outside our galaxy or whether the majority of world citizens prefer butter over margarine. Neither this book nor your instructor expects earth-shaking data from you during this semester. However, you can certainly rock a little corner of your research topic by employing some simple forms of primary research.

Plenty of primary research projects can be completed on a student's budget and within the time frame of the average research paper assignment. Consider visiting a location that is important to your research. You might even arrange to tour a research laboratory where relevant inquiries are being made. You can interview key persons intimately involved with your topic. You will likely be pleasantly surprised by the number of famous and renowned individuals who will take the time to answer a student's carefully composed request for information. Also, don't overlook your own experiences and contacts. You probably know something about your research topic that led you to choose it in the first place. Consider the knowledge and contacts within the field that you have already cultivated. Think about conducting small-scale research, seeking deep insights rather than broad conclusions. You might choose to observe only a handful of subjects and then suggest some preliminary conclusions. (Be advised, however, that research that involves human beings, even informal surveys and questionnaires, may be strictly regulated by the university where you are enrolled. Find out whether you will have to submit your research plan to a review board before you proceed.)

Secondary Research

You probably have lots of experience with secondary research. In elementary school you might have "written" reports by simply paraphrasing a secondary source such as an encyclopedia or other reference book. If you memorized baseball statistics or eagerly anticipated forthcoming movies featuring your favorite stars, you relied on secondary sources for your information. When you make conversation about events featured in the newspaper, presented on television documentaries, or picked up from an Internet mailing list, you are quoting secondary sources. The best storytellers, more fascinating conversationalists, and most persuasive debaters in your circle of friends are probably very good at incorporating secondary-source material into their fund of knowledge.

Writers engage in secondary research when they consult published data from someone else's primary research and then incorporate it into their own work. A newspaper reporter who includes census data about the number of automobiles per household in a particular community is making use of secondary research. So is a teacher who reads and synthesizes several published reports of the Battle of Appomattox and tells its story to students. Secondary research is vital in determining which vacation site to visit, which employee insurance package to adopt, or what route to drive to a distant city (see Figure 1.3).

Secondary sources may be put to a variety of uses in a research paper. You might simply report that authorities on the subject you are investigating

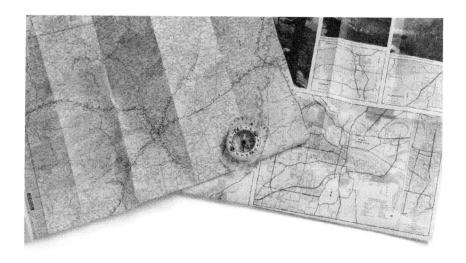

Figure 1.3 Sample roadmap

agree with your point of view. For instance, revealing that a critic published in a respected literary journal shares your belief that *The Adventures of Huckleberry Finn* is a racist novel strengthens your critical stance. Or you might challenge secondary sources, by proving that the authorities on your topic have proffered faulty theories about it. For example, you might argue, on the basis of your own experience, that those who favor a ratings system for popular music overestimate the level of parental involvement in children's entertainment choices. Secondary sources abound in this information age, and you can often combine them or pit them against one another to achieve startling, original conclusions. For example, you could take on critics of the U.S. Postal Service by citing authoritative secondary sources that prove it is the most efficient, least costly government-run mail delivery system in the world. Or you might combine the best of two flawed proposals for national welfare reform to achieve a more workable model. You can use secondary research to strengthen existing arguments and to develop content and strategies for constructing new ones.

Finding good secondary sources can be as challenging and exciting as conducting primary research. Newspapers, magazines, journals, television news shows, and World Wide Web pages are obvious and important sources for any research paper. After all, you can hardly conduct serious research without looking at the most common sources of information in our culture. However, as the researcher profiles in this book demonstrate, there is a huge variety of printed and recorded documents readily available to researchers— emanating from government agencies, businesses, lobbying organizations, consumer groups, private foundations, and individuals—and these can provide new and provocative perspectives on most topics. Although your opportunities for primary research may be limited, your own enthusiasm, tenacity, and creativity may yield surprising data from the pursuit of unusual secondary-source material.

■ Research as a Natural Activity

Whether you have consciously noticed it or not, conducting research is second nature to you. The fundamental human question, after all, is *Why*? All of our attempts to order and control our lives and our universe depend on research. We watch the Weather Channel or learn how to read cloud types and track the movement of storm fronts to determine which activities we can reasonably pursue on a given day. Listen to the conversations around you. Most of what people say is an attempt to gather and disseminate primary and secondary research. Human intellect is the product of information and experience gathering. Stop researching, and you stop thinking. Consciously engage in research, and a whole world of information that you could not have expected to find will reveal itself to you.

■ Summing Up

Research is already second nature to you. You have survived this long and gotten this far in life because you are already good at completing research tasks. You gather information through your senses and from your conversations with friends and strangers, the many public and private publications you read, and the television shows and Internet sites you intently watch or casually notice. Most of the time, the research you conduct in your day-to-day life is so engaging and enjoyable that you don't think of it as research at all; nevertheless, much of the information you have informally gathered and most of the skills you have developed are useful in academic research.

Primary research involves making original discoveries from evidence you encounter, measure, or create yourself. Secondary research consists of studying evidence collected by others and considering their conclusions. For instance, if you watch a movie to determine whether it would be suitable to show to children you plan to baby-sit, you are conducting primary research; if you look up a synopsis of that movie in a critical guide to discover whether you should take it along on a baby-sitting job, you are consulting a critic's opinion and using secondary research to help you make up your mind.

Researching is unavoidable. Research is not merely an academic subject or a requirement for certain papers and presentations—it is one of the most exciting and interesting of human activities. If you think of research as a common and enjoyable activity, it will make accomplishing research assignments in school more fun and successful.

Exercises: Sources and Strategies

1. Make a list of significant research projects from daily life that you have recently completed (for example, selecting a college, buying a car or computer, finding a place to live, choosing a college major). Outline the steps involved in at least one of those processes.

2. Make a list of topics about which you would like to learn more. Be as specific as possible (for example, "digital imaging in advertising" rather than just "photography").

3. Make a list of people or places you would like to visit. Explain what you would hope to learn from each one (for example, "talk to Buddy Lazier to learn why a severely injured race car driver would return to the sport" or "visit Machu Picchu to learn how the ancient Incas differed from the ancient Greeks").

Writing to Know

Write an informational essay about a topic you have researched in your day-to-day life, such as how to shop for a stereo, used car, or house or apartment. Be sure to tell your readers what their options are—where to look, what to look for. Include common mistakes made by buyers of these items, and tell how to avoid problems.

RESEARCHER PROFILE

Matt Roberts indicated during the interview for this profile that he did not wish to be directly quoted heavily. Because he works as one member of a team that is in turn an integral part of a creative staff, he did not want to appear to take credit personally for work or research procedures that the group has performed or developed.

Since readers of this profile are likely to be familiar with *The Late Show with David Letterman* and might be more interested in what Roberts reveals about how the show is put together than in Roberts's personal observations and perspective, paraphrasing works well throughout the piece. Roberts is quoted directly in the last sentence, however, to provide a strong image of him, the profile's subject, in its closing.

Matt Roberts

Talent Researcher for *The Late Show with David Letterman*

Like many of us, Matt Roberts knows what he would like to ask Madonna, Tom Hanks, or the vice president of the United States. But unlike most of us, in his job as talent researcher for *The Late Show with David Letterman* Roberts gets to have some of those questions answered. At age twenty-four, he has worked for the late-night variety show for two years. Admittedly, he has a dream job. He gets to meet many of the celebrities featured on the show, and he occasionally appears on camera in comedy sketches, including stints as a T-shirt model, a policeman dancing in the spray from an opened fire hydrant, and a Broadway lunatic wearing a skimpy bathing suit and a false beard. Most of his work is behind the scenes, however. An intern with *The Late Show* while a Boudoin College student, Roberts wanted to work with Letterman upon graduation. He says he despised research projects in school and even avoided some courses because they required research papers; only a job this good could have enticed him to be a researcher. Now he actually enjoys research, and he realizes that it is part of what makes *The Late Show with David Letterman* original. The show takes its own position on the films, books, personalities, and so on that it promotes, and its host's acerbic candor is based on the independent research conducted by the show's staff.

"The newly renovated Ed Sullivan Theater," as Letterman refers to it almost nightly, includes two buildings. The structure that faces New York's famed Broadway Avenue houses the studio where the show is filmed and a labyrinth of hallways and stairwells connecting staff offices and ancillary spaces such as the show's "tiny green room," and a tall thin towerlike structure attached to the theater holds guest dressing rooms, with each dressing room occupying its own small floor. The staff research office is equally divided into three cubicles, each containing a desk buried under scraps of paper, magazines, and photographs. Matt's own space is decorated with a bulletin board covered with family snapshots and a full wall of neatly shelved popular magazines. These, he explains, are kept close at hand for quick reference, but most of the periodicals used by the research department come from the CBS library at network headquarters, a few blocks away. Interns are dispatched to retrieve materials from there. Along one side of the research office is an enormous bank of filing cabinets containing information on previous guests of the show—the product of the researchers' labors, including notes concerning past appearances and articles photocopied in preparation for interviews. The tabs on the file folders read like a *Who's Who* of popular culture. The file labeled "Madonna" is very thick. The NEXIS terminal, which is connected to an on-line news service, dominates one corner of the room.

Although the chief responsibility of *The Late Show*'s research team is to uncover information about prospective guests, the three-man staff also serves as the show's general research office. If the writers need to know the names of all the characters on *Bonanza*, for instance, the research team responds. Sometimes Letterman wants more information about a current event, or perhaps he will ask for the immediate, street-level temperature reading as part of a joke. The challenge to the research staff is not only to find things, but to find them fast. Sometimes, while the show is taping, Letterman will raise a question that must be answered during that hour. While the show is being filmed, at least one researcher inhabits a minuscule office situated behind the bookcase that appears on the right of the show's set. It is barely large enough to contain a desk and telephone, but it is from there—just a few feet from Letterman's left hand—that on-air questions are answered. There is fun in trying to beat the clock; the researcher tries to get the answer to Letterman during the next commercial break.

In preparation for planned guest appearances on the show, *The Late Show* research staff usually spends about three days compiling information, suggesting questions, and obtaining film clips. Guests are booked through a combination of searching for interesting personages and choosing among those who seek to be included on the show. Some guests are booked well in advance, but there are often cancellations, substitutions, and last-minute arrangements. One wall of the Ed Sullivan Theater's conference room is covered in dry-erase boards apportioned as calendars. The names of upcoming guests are penned in for the next three months, with the first month appearing reasonably complete but long-range plans looking far more sketchy. Of course, talk and variety shows are constantly seeking famous people to appear as guests, but *The Late Show* also contacts people who are surprised to receive invitations to appear on network TV, such as a three-year-old geography whiz and a seventy-year-old surfer. The research team finds unusual guests by reading local news features. The variety of sources available at CBS is huge, and researchers are always looking for new methods of discovering potentially interesting, amusing, or unusual guests.

After a guest booking is confirmed, the research team really earns its title. They use three on-line services—NEXIS, Dialogue, and Baseline—for their initial search for information. NEXIS provides the full text of articles on an almost endless array of subjects. Dialogue is an indexing service, providing bibliographic citations that must be pursued in a library, and Baseline caters specifically to the entertainment industry, offering celebrity biographies, information on stars' current and future projects, and entire credits for finished movies and for movies still in production. Film credits prove to be invaluable in finding contacts who may provide information about industry colleagues.

Subscription news services such as NEXIS, Dialogue, and Baseline are paid to be accurate. Generally, researchers can trust the information they receive from such companies, although NEXIS includes such sources as England's *Daily Mirror*, a tabloid newspaper that is better known for sensationalism than for accuracy. When Roberts finds something provocative in a questionable source, he makes a point of identifying the origins of the information in his work, so that the producer in charge of the segment can judge the quality of the information he supplies. Obviously, photographs and film footage can be aired only with permission from the copyright holders, and credits for those must always be included in Roberts's work.

One of the more difficult things for the research team to find is old advertising clips. However, if the ad was produced for an existing corporation, they usually have a copy in their archives and are happy to help. The most rewarding part of Roberts's job, he says, is coming up with obscure data and materials.

Often, a researcher's best work turns out to be a surprise, even to the researcher. In looking back on completed shows, Roberts can see where elements of research contributed to their success. When he had been on the job only two months and had very few contacts in the business, Roberts was assigned to prepare information for an appearance by actor Tom Hanks. He lucked into footage of Hanks's guest appearance on three old TV shows, *Love Boat, Taxi,* and *Happy Days,* and obtained permission to air those. Letterman and one of the show's producers came up with an idea for incorporating the clips into the show, along with letting Hanks bring a scene from the 1970s television series *Mork and Mindy* in which Letterman had made a guest appearance. Audience reaction to the old footage was terrific.

Most of Roberts's written work takes the form of memos to the show's segment producers. Segment producers act as liaisons between Letterman and prospective guests, with the host determining the final content of the show. Interviews on television are never as spontaneous as they appear, but nothing is etched in granite, either. A lot of spontaneous conversation and behavior occurs during the taping of shows. Sometimes guests say surprising things that researchers and producers could never anticipate, and Letterman occasionally pulls the conversation off into a completely different direction than his staffers have suggested. Solid research, however, provides insurance that Letterman and his guests will have something to discuss.

Because he rarely has to leave his desk, Roberts records all of his research directly into his computer's word processor, omitting the need for note cards or intermediate writing stages. He condenses articles and information-service files, most of the time focusing on funny stories or unusual information that will lead to a funny anecdote on the show. He tries to include everything that might influence a guest's demeanor on the show, even information that he knows will never be talked about on network television. For instance, if a prospective guest is embroiled in a divorce, the researchers will mention that to the producer to keep everyone informed and to ensure that the guest is not unintentionally offended. Researchers' memos might also include possible interview questions. For instance, if a chef who is about to appear on the show was recently quoted on the subject of smoking in restaurants, Roberts might suggest that Letterman ask him about the New York City ordinance against smoking in eating establishments.

When Roberts's information is as complete as he can make it, he forwards it to the producer in charge of organizing that guest's segment of the show. Segment producers use researchers' memos as a basis for conducting primary research. They contact prospective guests and conduct "preinterviews," trying out the subjects the research team has suggested and looking for entertaining anecdotes or funny angles for the show. Guests are usually prepared to tell four or five stories well.

The greatest challenge in Roberts's job is to gather a wide range of current, accurate information quickly. There is never enough time to research guests as fully as he would like. The lead time between bookings and guest appearances does not usually allow for reading full biographies, for instance. Research on current events involving guests is usually reduced to reading news summaries. Researchers for *The Late Show* work ahead whenever it is feasible, but they always seem to be scrambling for footage or getting permission to air something right up to the last minute. Roberts is constantly working on the edge of disaster, always running out of time. He usually feels that he curtails, rather than completes, his work, but he doesn't have much time to reflect on that because there is always another show to be produced, another hour's worth of guests to be researched.

The frantic pace of *The Late Show* staffers' jobs is eased by the atmosphere and camaraderie on the job. The irreverent, ad-libbing spirit that pervades the show itself is very much in evidence among its employees. During one typical day, as a segment producer ensconced in an office decorated with props and *Late Show* memorabilia (including a cell from a *Beavis and Butthead* cartoon in which a likeness of Letterman appeared) met with a CBS executive, another show employee stood in the hallway, holding up bogus cue cards hastily printed with lines such as "Is this your first blind date?" As soon as the show was taped, staffers in the control room below the set flooded its several rows of monitors with a clip from a *Laverne and Shirley* episode, the one in which the characters fold themselves into a Murphy bed. Upstairs, on the red stage floor of *The Late Show* set, where it really is as cold as guests and audience members complain it is (probably about 50 degrees Fahrenheit), cameramen kept warm playing with a Frisbee. Roberts acknowledges that the comedic nature of the show keeps the attitudes of the staff upbeat. "We work very hard to be factually accurate," he explains, "but it's an entertainment show. The main point is to play around."

Suggested Writing Assignments

1. Go behind the scenes of a situation your readers are likely to know well from the public side only. For instance, you might obtain permission to stay behind the food service lines in a residence hall cafeteria during rush hour to observe the processes employees follow to ensure smooth service during that hectic time.

2. Using the Internet and popular magazines, compile possible questions for a *Late Night with David Letterman* appearance by one of your favorite sports or entertainment stars. Compose a memo to one of the show's segment producers, suggesting content for that spot on the show.

3. Write an essay describing your own research process as you generally organize it. How do you find topics? How much time do you spend on a typical research paper? Which sources do you consult first? What are the hardest and most rewarding parts of the process? Include specific examples from past research projects whenever you can think of them.

Chapter Two

Exploring Libraries

Suppose that you are on your way to an important meeting—a job interview, for example, or something else that could positively affect your future—in a strange city. When you scheduled the meeting over the telephone, the person you are meeting told you simply to take a cab from the airport to a well-known square in the middle of the city, from which the meeting site is a five-minute walk. Although you have carefully written down the address and telephone number of the office where you are going, the person you are to meet was unable to fax you a map of the area, showing your exact destination. So, you left for the airport with only a sketchy idea of how to find the street and building where your meeting will take place.

Naturally, your plane is late taking off. As you sit in the closed aircraft above the hot tarmac, you remember that amazing mapping program you came across while browsing the World Wide Web; using it, you could have printed out a map of the exact area you need to know—had you thought of it in time. As the plane begins its ascent, you compare the flight time printed on your ticket with the time on your watch. There is still time to get to your meeting, but you'll have to hit the ground running, with an efficient plan.

As you feared, although the cab driver who brings you into the city knows the midtown square from which you are to walk to your destination, he is unfamiliar with the specific street and building you need to find. You pay him hastily and collect your things from the cab, with the possibilities for your next course of action running through your mind. What should you do? You could find a police officer and ask for directions, but there are none in sight. You could stop the next passerby and take this stranger's advice about finding what could be the most important meeting of your life. You could hail another cab and hope for better luck. You could find a telephone and call home to see if the promised fax ever arrived, or you could call your destination and get more specific directions. Probably the last choice is the most reasonable and efficient option, assuming you can find a pay phone or are carrying a cellular phone in your pocket. Presumably the people you are to meet want as pleasant and productive a meeting as you do, and so they will be helpful and friendly when you call and ask for more help in finding them.

A new library is like a strange city. You can wander aimlessly through the stacks in search of the "address" where the materials you need are located, or you can depend on the people and devices that stand ready to help you navigate this unfamiliar terrain. There are different kinds of libraries, each with its own system for organizing and categorizing its contents. Although learning to use one library will provide you with general skills that will be useful in many similar environments, no one expects you to know your way around any library the minute you set foot inside its doors.

■ School Libraries

Depending on the size of your high school, the library you used there might have occupied most of a building or only a single room. The chief purpose of your school library might have been to catalog and store a range of research materials, to encourage students to read more, or simply to provide a quiet place for students to read and write. It most likely subscribed to some magazines and journals selected by your teachers and the school librarian and received local and state newspapers. And, of course, there were books of all sorts. If you read much for pleasure, you could probably still walk right to the section of your school library that displayed new fiction, or mystery novels, or science fiction stories.

In fact, you were probably fairly familiar with the entire library and so never thought that much about establishing a system for searching through it. The same librarian was there most of the time; you knew his or her name, and you knew how much help you could expect in locating materials for a research paper, finding interesting new reading matter, or getting a specific question answered quickly. You probably also were aware that your school library was limited—by size, by budget, maybe even by censorship—and that there were some topics for which your school library just couldn't furnish up-to-date information.

A school library's purpose is to provide basic materials within the school building or campus and to teach students rudimentary procedures for information retrieval and usage. Chances are that your school library did that and more, but it is still much smaller and more simply organized than the libraries you will be expected to use in college.

■ Public Libraries

The municipal library in your home town may be the source of many pleasant memories for you. Perhaps you attended "story time" readings there as a child or got your first real library card there. Maybe you still have a favorite chair or corner there where you like to go to read and think. In many towns and cities the public library also functions as a museum or cultural center, offering exhibits and visiting lecturers to the community. You may have entered a reading or writing contest or participated in a literary activity at your local library. Your home town's public library could be very small, taking up only a single room in the town hall, or it could be very large, offering materials and services at locations all over your city.

Because public libraries are largely supported by taxpayers, they offer basic reading and research materials selected to satisfy the needs of the populace. Take a look at your local library's "how to" section: you will find everything from cookbooks to home-building plans to books on popular hobbies such as stamp collecting, shopping for antiques, and hiking and camping. Your local library probably carries newspapers from surrounding communities, travel and entertainment books and brochures, and magazines devoted to current events, housekeeping, woodworking, humor, and numerous other topics. It probably lends videos of popular films and audio recordings of a wide range of materials, from readings of Shakespeare's plays to World War I–era love songs to the latest live recording from Carnegie Hall. Some public libraries even own art objects that patrons can sign out for extended periods of time. Local government agencies may donate outdated materials to the public library, including such interesting items as old aerial photographs of the city, plot registrations for area cemeteries, or old campaign literature. All of these sources and types of information are readily available at local public libraries.

Not surprisingly, books are the primary resource available in public libraries. A few patrons will stop by regularly to read a favorite magazine or newspaper, and schoolchildren might gather information for school projects at their local public library, but most users visit the library for the latest novel by their favorite author or for a few books about a hobby or about planning a vacation, which they check out and take home with them. Public library books are usually loaned out for a period of about two weeks to ensure that everyone in the community has reasonable access to these publicly owned materials.

The same librarian who stamps your card and reminds you of each item's due date will direct you to the section of the library where the materials you seek are stored, suggest further reading, or help you make a thorough search of the library's resources on the topic of your choice. Most public libraries subscribe to the *Readers' Guide to Periodical Literature*, an index of articles in popular magazines (see Figure 2.1). The *Reader's Guide*, as it is often called, is useful for locating information about current events and issues in the kinds of magazines to which most public libraries subscribe.

Although public libraries subscribe to a large number of popular magazines and newspapers, they probably don't keep them for many years. Most public libraries dispose of back issues of periodicals after three to five years, depending on the storage and display methods they use. Your local library is a great place to seek useful information and advice, but it may not offer the in-depth reference materials and specialized resources that a college writing assignment requires.

As you know, some music stores are great places to stop by and pick up CDs from the current *Billboard* charts at excellent prices. They display the latest offerings from your favorite artists and groups attractively and efficiently, in a manner designed to encourage impulse buying. Such stores are

READER'S GUIDE TO PERIODICAL LITERATURE 1993

AUTOMOBILES—cont.

Oldsmobile Eighty Eight Royale [owners report] M. Lamm. il *Popular Mechanics* v170 p51–3. F '93
Preview guide: domestic cars to come, 1994-1998. J. McCraw. il *Popular Science* v243 p87-91+ S'93
Road & track sneak preview 1994 [cover story] il *Road & Track* v 45 p 46-53+ S'93

Accessories
See Automobiles—Equipment

Accidents
See Traffic accidents

Advertising
See Automobile Industry—Advertising

Air bags
Blink of an eye. D. Sherman. il por *Motor Trend* v 45 p 81-3 My '93
Motorist injuries caused by air bags [National Highway Traffic Safety Administration research] il *Consumers' Research Magazine* v 76 p 22-5 D'93
When Allen met Johnnie [A. and J. Breed] S. Zausner. il pors *Forbes* v 152 Special Issue p 80-1+ O 18 '93
Which cars are safest in a crash. Il *Consumer Reports* v58 p199-202 Ap '93

Air cleaners
Do auto-interior air cleaners work? il *Consumer Reports* v58 p192 Ap '93

Air conditioning
Air conditioning D. Chaikin. il *Popular Mechanics* v170 p93 F '93
Environmental aspects
A/C replacement kits. P. Weissler. il *Home Mechanix* v89 p84-8+ My '93
Auto A/C update. P. L. Spencer. il *Consumers' Research Magazine* v76 p38 Ag'93
Is there air conditioning after CFCs? R. Paul. il *Motor Trend* v45 p98+ F '93
Keeping your cool in '94 [converting cars from freon to HFC-134a] M. K. Flynn. *U.S. News & World Report* v115 p77 O 18 '93
The long hot summer. K. Zino. il *Road & Track* v44 p37 Ag '93
New A/C refrigerant. P. Weissler. il *Popular Mechanics* v170 p91-2 Je '93

Air fresheners
The freshest car fresheners. H. D. Stanton. il *Interview* v23 p26 Je '93

Airplane combinations
See Aerocars

Alarms
Installing alarm systems. B. Phillips. il *Home Mechanix* v89 p42+ S '93

Alternators
See Automobiles—Electric generators

Anecdotes, facetiae, etc.
Sins [automotive sins] P. Egan. il *Road & Track* v44 p27-9 Mr'93
Uncle Toby's temper. J. Taylor. il *The Mother Earth News* v136 p96 F/Mr '93

Audio systems
See also
Automobiles—Radio equipment
Hot rods—Audio systems
1994 autosound. B. Ankosko. il *Stereo Review* v58 p94-8+ N '93
Build the AFGII [Acoustic Field Generator] T. T. Templin. il *Electronics Now* v64 p37-44+ Ap '93
Car stereo. See occasional issues of Stereo Review
CD for the road. D. Kumin. il *Stereo Review* v58 p54-9 My '93
Digital volume control [Dynamic Sound Optimization system for automobiles] C. Murray. il *Popular Science* v242 p27 Mr '93
Drivers ed [car speakers] D. Kumin. il *Stereo Review* v58 p62-7 Ag '93
Drop in, turn on, tune out [replacing factory-installed car speakers] D. Newcomb. il *Rolling Stone* p61 My 27 '93
Eclipse ECD-412 CD receiver. K. C. Pohlmann. il *Stereo Review* v58 p32-3 My '93
Kenwood KDC-C800 CD changer. K. C. Pohlmann. il *Stereo Review* v58 p66+ N '93
A little travelin' music. I. Masters. il *Stereo Review* v58 p46+ Je '93
Pioneer KEH-M680 cassette receiver. K. C. Pohlmann. il *Stereo Review* v58 p48+ S '93
These heads are meant to roll. B. Wolfe. il *Rolling Stone* p121 My 13 '93
Thirty-five years of autosound. K. C. Pohlmann. il *Stereo Review* v58 p60-5 My '93
What do cars sound like? P. Bedard. il *Car and Driver* v39 p95-7 Ag '93
Security measures
Stealth stereo upgrades. I. Berger. il *Home Mechanix* v89 p42+ Je '93

Awards
See also
Home Mechanix Easy-Maintenance Car of the Year Awards

Ancedotes, facetiae, satire, etc.
Motor Trends Awards
Ten best winners and losers, 1992. il *Car and Driver* v38 p51-2+ Ja '93

Batteries
See Storage batteries

Bibliography
Reviews. See issues of Road & Track

Bodies, Remodeled
See Automobiles, Remodeled

Brakes
See Brakes, Automobile

Braking
See Automobiles—Stopping

Bumpers
See also
Hot rods—Bumpers
It's hard to find good bumpers. il *Consumers' Research Magazine* v76 p32-3 My '93

Business use
See Automobiles in business

Camping equipment
See also
Automobile trailers
Going mobile. T. E. Huggler. il *Outdoor Life* v192 p34+ S '93

Care
See Automobiles—Maintenance and repair

Chassis
Tune up your chassis. il *Popular Mechanics* v170 p90-2 My '93

Child safety seats
See Automobile safety seats

Cleaning
Car care. See issues of Motor Trend beginning March 1989
Deep clean [detailing] E. Zuckerman. il *Harper's* v287 p74-7 S '93
Tune up your exterior. il *Popular Mechanics* v170 p86-9 My '93
Tune up your interior. il *Popular Mechanics* v170 p94-7 My '93
Waxes & polishes. M. Ferrara. *Consumers Digest* v32 p40-2 S/O '93

Clutches
See also
Hot rods—Clutches
Pseudo-manual shifting [Valco electronic clutch control system] R. Grable. il *Motor Trend* v45 p92 Ap '93
Replacing your clutch. D. Chaikin. il *Popular Mechanics* v170 p89-92 Mr '93

Collectibles
A.J. and the wily Coyote [auction and sale of collectibles] M. Padgett. il *Car and Driver* v38 p169 Ja '93
Keeping time [car-related items indigenous to yesteryear] D. Freiburger. il *Hot Rod* v45 p44+ D '92

Collectors and collecting
See also
Hot rods—Collectors and collecting
Affordable collectibles. R. J. Gottlieb. *Motor Trend* v45 p104 Mr '93
Collateral damage [California law on unused automobiles] *Motor Trend* v45 p106-7 F '93
David Koresh, car nut. S. C. Smith. il *Car and Driver* v39 p36 O'93
Hunting for vintage cars? Step on it. C. Roush. il *Business Week* p144-5 N 29 '93
Invest on a budget. R. J. Gottlieb. il *Motor Trend* v45 p114-15 Ag '93
Numbers match [collector car prices] P. Egan. il *Road & Track* v44 p24+ My '93
Retrospect. T. C. Browne. See issues of Motor Trend beginning January 1988
Tax consequences. R. J. Gottlieb. *Motor Trend* v45 p122-3 Ja '93
Top 10 investments. R. J. Gottlieb. il *Motor Trend* v44 p102 D '92

Collision avoidance systems
Automobility: cars that drive themselves. J. Zygmont. il *Omni (New York, N.Y.)* v15 p38-40+ Ap '93
The extrasensory car. D. McCosh. il *Popular Science* v243 p76-9+ Jl '93
Mini-radar is coming. L. Brooke. il *Popular Science* v242 p36+ F '93

Control
Computing on wheels. D. Pountain. il *Byte* v18 p213-15+ My '93

Corrosion and anticorrosives
See also
Hot rods— Corrosion and anticorrosives
Acid-rain repairs for finishes. J. Kirk. il *Home Mechanix* v89 p38+ Jl/Ag '93
Salt cars. P. Egan. il *Road & Track* v44 p22-3 F '93

Cost of operation
The declining (!) cost of owning a new car [AAA survey] E. Henry. il *Kiplinger's Personal Finance Magazine* v47 p99 Je '93

Crash testing
It's hard to find good bumpers. il *Consumers' Research Magazine* v76 p32-3 My '93

Figure 2.1   A page from *The Readers' Guide to Periodical Literature*

like public libraries that meet popular demand extraordinarily well. You are probably also acquainted with a type of store that provides a much broader selection, however—a really great music emporium that deals in used CDs and vinyl albums, maintains a huge inventory of back-list titles and imports, carries promotional items from record companies, and serves as a ticket outlet for performance venues in the vicinity. There are libraries that provide this kind of comprehensive service in the research world, too.

As you may remember from a history course, Benjamin Franklin started the first public lending library in America as a way to share the few books people had brought with them from England and the Continent. Franklin's goal was to increase the amount of reading done by the few Americans who were literate. Today most Americans can read, so public libraries cater to the interests of a diverse group of general readers. Local libraries are often active in the literacy movement as well, helping children and adults become better readers and writers. In addition, many people without direct access to expensive or complex hardware gain their first experience with computers, including the Internet and the World Wide Web, at their public library. As methods for disseminating information proliferate in our society, we will depend more and more on public libraries to provide access for people of all social and economic circumstances. In many places, the word *library* is being replaced by the term *media center,* with residents being encouraged to see this vital community resource as more than just a repository of printed material.

■ College, University, or Research Libraries

If you've been on campus for a while, or if you toured your college's facilities before you registered, you've probably been inside the main library. Think about the first time you walked into the campus library. What did you notice about it—an overt theft-detection system, a sea of on-line terminals, the hum of photocopiers, a plethora of signs offering directions, elevators or escalators in constant motion, more employees at the counters than at a fast food restaurant during the lunch rush?

The next time you visit your campus library, look around for maps or brochures that will help you orient yourself to its facilities. Besides showing you how to find the materials you will need for future course work, such guides and maps will demonstrate the extent of your library's holdings and services. For example, you can learn whether your library is a repository for government publications (such as U.S. census documents), whether it has a rare book and manuscript department, and whether it contains a music-listening center, a map or photography archive, a computer lab, a printing or photocopying shop, an eating area, and so on. A large research library, more so than other libraries you may be accustomed to, can be thought of as being something like a shopping mall. Research libraries are often organized into various departments, or "shops," each with its own hours, staff, and materials or services. Consult your library's map or self-guided-tour brochures to determine not only how to find the specific materials you have come for but also to see what "stores" might interest you and where you might want to "shop" in the future.

A good way to get to know your campus library is to search for something you have found in the past in your hometown or high school library. For instance, you might try to find your hometown newspaper. Is it kept in the library's current periodicals section, stored on microforms or available on a Web site? Find out where the books pertaining to your field of study are shelved by searching key words in the card catalog or on-line catalog; take note of any common locations shared by several pertinent materials. Walk to that section of the library and browse its contents. You will probably find some books that you have read or used before, as well as many new and interesting ones. Ask a reference librarian to show you the CD-ROM and print indexes commonly used by students and faculty studying a particular subject (such as any subject you might be considering for your major). The more you learn about your campus library system, the quicker and better you will be able to complete assignments throughout your college career.

A college research library is probably a busier place than wherever you're used to studying. In fact, in many research libraries studying is virtually impossible. There is so much activity in some college libraries that finding a quiet table or corner to read and complete routine homework is nearly out of the question. In such facilities, people who absolutely must study or write inside the library are issued private offices or closed study carrels where they can reasonably expect to work. It won't take long for you to discern the character of your campus library; an hour or two on a weeknight after dinner should give you some idea of the activity level in the library and whether it is a place where you can prepare for classes and study for exams.

Regardless of the amount of reading and writing you'll be able to do in your campus library, you should be prepared to spend extended blocks of time there. Visiting a research library is like attending an extravagant holiday brunch at a five-star restaurant, where the menu starts with eggs Benedict and omelets made to order and progresses to hand-carved prime rib and an array of desserts. You could breeze through such a setting as if it were a fast-food emporium, but you would not get your money's worth. In other words, you can rush into a university library and quickly gather up the most basic pieces of information necessary to complete an assignment, but you will not enjoy the experience or gain the sophistication that it can provide. Don't miss out on the banquet. Find out about the resources your campus library makes available to you.

Types of Holdings
Books in the Stacks What sorts of "entrees" are available in a research library? Of course, you already know about books. The part of a research library that contains books for general circulation is called the "stacks." This section usually comprises most of the library's floor space that is open to the

public. Its shelves literally *stack* books for storage and display. When books are kept in open stacks, patrons may freely browse through them, removing them from the shelves at their leisure to examine them or check them out. Closed stacks refer to areas that are accessible only to library employees. A few libraries (the Library of Congress, for instance) have only closed stacks, and patrons must use catalogs and bibliographies to determine which books to request. Your library probably has a generous section of open stacks, where you can wander among materials arranged by subject; it probably has several closed stacks, too, where reserve materials, rare books and artifacts, theses and dissertations, audiovisual recordings, and other fragile or irreplaceable things are protected.

Books are neat packages of information, easy to order up from a card catalog or electronic index. They may contain more information than you need or not exactly the material you desire, and they may not be as up-to-date as you would like, but they are easy to locate and take with you, which makes them readily available, portable research tools. Up to this point in your academic life, books have probably been the main staple of your research diet. They may have been the most prestigious and credible sources of information in the libraries you used in the past. In fact, you may still think of libraries simply as collections of books.

The content of your campus libraries is dictated by the areas of academic inquiry emphasized by your college or university. Thus, a campus with a prestigious medical college will strive to keep its library up-to-date with reports on the latest biological, pharmaceutical, and genetic research and government regulations of medicine. Similarly, if your college is renowned for agricultural research or teacher preparation, its libraries will reflect those interests. In the same way that you can guess the academic majors, specific interests, and hobbies of friends and professors by looking over the books they surround themselves with, if you could quickly survey the titles in all of your campus library system's branches and storage centers, you could discern the areas in which your institution specializes, has concentrated its resources in the past, or hopes to gain expertise in the future.

Periodicals Quests for specialized information cannot stop at books. The very latest theories and findings are reported most rapidly by periodicals, publications such as newspapers, magazines, or electronic data services that are prepared and disseminated at regular intervals to keep their readers constantly up-to-date. Think about how you use periodicals in your day-to-day life. An almanac can forecast long-term meteorological trends in your region, but your daily newspaper will give you a better indication of the temperature to expect this afternoon or the chances of rain this evening. Or if you want to find out about the latest haircuts or fashions, you'll find that a book on trends in American fashion (even a recent one) will not provide the up-to-date pictures and shopping tips that a recent issue of a fashion or entertainment magazine will provide.

In many cases, people cannot afford to wait for information to be published in books. How often have you learned about new medical research from a television report summarizing an article in the *Journal of the American Medical Association*? As a researcher, you can obtain very recent information because professionals working in the field you are investigating demand current statistics and results. This type of information is provided by specialized news bureaus and expensive database subscriptions, which are usually available only in research libraries (see Figure 2.2).

College research libraries also archive material that public libraries cannot afford to store. As you know if you receive a lot of catalogs and magazines in the mail, organizing, storing, and even recycling volumes of printed material is a difficult task to manage. If you have ever tried to implement a system for classifying and retaining potentially useful pieces of mail, you know how quickly a home magazine rack or recycling bin can begin to overflow. Even the most humorous or useful magazine article or catalog is eventually sacrificed to efficiency and to the need to reduce clutter. In a library, where a mail bag filled with periodicals arrives daily, the volume of stored paper is mind-boggling. Even with a library's efficient cataloging systems, keeping a lot of periodicals on file threatens order and safety.

Nonprint Materials   Many libraries subscribe to numerous periodicals on microfilm or microfiche. Indeed, a research library may receive periodicals in a variety of formats, including print editions and copies made available on film, on CD-ROM, or through on-line archives. Your local public library probably keeps back issues of newspapers and magazines on hand for three to five years before recycling them. A research library often tries to keep every issue of many periodicals in its holdings forever. Today's timely information becomes tomorrow's fascinating historical record, sometimes revealing with hindsight just where research or official policy went wrong or preserving important discoveries that were overlooked or unappreciated originally; thus a backlog of periodicals and original documents is often a great resource for researchers.

It is easy to surmise that a research library's holdings will include many materials besides books. Indeed, books make up only a fraction of the contents of most college or university libraries. Many research libraries number their holdings in the millions, all cataloged or indexed and retrievable in some reasonably efficient way. Increasingly, library holdings encompass information originally presented via a variety of media, including newsreels, television programs, satellite teleconferences, e-mail, motion pictures, and even amateur videos. Yet, it isn't hard to find a needle in a haystack if you use a powerful magnet, and electronic search tools, databases on CD-ROM, print indexes, and card catalogs are like electron magnets in that regard. But with so many holdings in large libraries, the task is more like finding a few specialized sewing machine needles in a haystack embedded with pins and needles of all sorts. Only a fairly specialized searching process, such as the

LEASING (AUTOMOBILE)
General
"Fraudbusters: Automobile Leasing Scams: 'Pockets of Profit.'" O'Loughlin, Terrence J./Desjardins, Garry. Asserts automobile leasing is one of the most complex financial transactions consumers can enter. Explains leasers have to be cautious at the inception of the contract, regarding the conditions during the contract, and when the vehicle is returned. Considers the scams that have evolved since the inception of the lease, including the flip, trade–

Discusses lease term scams and lease end scams.
Consumers' Research v81 n4, Apr 1998. p19–22.

SAFETY RESTRAINT DEVICES (AUTOMOBILE)
General
"Airbag Switch Seekers Cite Distance and Need to Carry Kids in Front as Reasons for Requests." Presents statistics for people who have requested airbag on/off switches for both driver and passenger airbags. States 20,408 authorizations have been okayed for on/off switches by NHTSA. Points out the main reason for driver-side switches was distance and for passenger-side was transporting children. Two charts illustrate reasons cited for airbag on/off switch requests.
Status Report v33 n3, 4 Apr 1998. p6.
"Car Seats—For Bigger Kids." Gustin, Georgina. States when children outgrow car-safety seats, most parents believe it's safe for them to ride with only a standard seat belt. Asserts this is a dangerous assumption, reporting 95 percent of children who should be riding in booster seats don't. Explains a seat belt should fit snugly across the pelvic region and the shoulder, but for most kids, the belt may fit across the stomach and cut high on the neck, potentially causing serious harm in an accident. Describes three booster-seat style seat belt systems that are safe for children.
Good Housekeeping v226 n2, Feb 1998. p143.

TIRE REPAIR KITS (AUTOMOBILE)
Individual Products
Prestone\\Tire Jack
- Consumer Reports v63 n2, Feb 1998. p10.
  "We...wanted to know how 'Tire Jack' would fare if a tire's tread and sidewall became slashed; if the tire bead...leaked; and if we drove for 20 miles on tires reinflated with 'Tire Jack.' This product passed those tests."

TIRES (AUTOMOBILE)
General
"Automotive Consumer: Tire Terminology." Peters, Eric. Discusses what the letters and numbers on a tire size indicate. Explains most new passenger cars will have a "P," which indicates they are all-season, general purpose radial tires. Considers what different tire sizes mean for performance and durability in various conditions. Mentions such aspects as ride, insulation from road noise, traction, handling, treadwear, and intended purpose/quality of tires.

Consumers' Research v81 n2, Feb 1998. p33,35.
"Technologue: Tire Tester's Dictionary." DeMere, Mac. Provides definitions to several terms used by tire testers. Includes the following terms: breakaway progressivity, buru-buru, delay, enveloping power, front/rear balance, gain, gotsu-gotsu, lateral firmness, linearity, impact boom, initial-impact harshness, initial response, on-center feel, rolling boom, sizzle, slip angle, straight-line stability, tire slap, vertical damping (rebound), and whine or moan.
Motor Trend v50 n1, Jan 1998. p120.

Surveys and Comparisons
"Touring-Performance Tires: Test: Get a Grip." Tests and evaluates several touring-performance tires on the following criteria: cost, braking, cornering, emergency handling, hydroplaning, ride comfort, noise, and rolling resistance. Outlines shopping strategies, such as know the choices and where to shop. Discusses other types of tires briefly. Sidebars address how to care for tires and the environmental concerns regarding disposing of tires.
Consumer Reports v63 n3, Mar 1998. p19–23.

Individual Products
BF Goodrich\\Touring T/A HR4
- Consumer Reports v63 n3, Mar 1998. p19–23.
  <http://www.bfgoodrichtires.com>

Bridgestone\\Turanza H
- Consumer Reports v63 n3, Mar 1998. p19–23.

Cooper\\Cobra GTH
- Consumer Reports v63 n3, Mar 1998. p19–23.
  <http://www.coopertire.com>

Dunlop\\D60 A2 with JLP
- Consumer Reports v63 n3, Mar 1998. p19–23.
  <http://www.dunloptire.com>

Firestone\\Firehawk Touring LH
- Consumer Reports v63 n3, Mar 1998. p19–23.

General\\XP 2000 H4
- Consumer Reports v63 n3, Mar 1998. p19–23.
  <http://www.generaltire.com>

Goodyear\\Eagle GT+4
- Consumer Reports v63 n3, Mar 1998. p19–23.
  <http://www.goodyear.com>

Goodyear\\Eagle LS
- Consumer Reports v63 n3, Mar 1998. p19–23.
  <http://www.goodyear.com>

Michelin\\Energy MXV4
- Consumer Reports v63 n3, Mar 1998. p19–23.
  <http://www.michelin.com>

Pirelli\\P6000 Sport Veloce
- Consumer Reports v63 n3, Mar 1998. p19–23.
  <http://www.pirelli.com>

Yokohama\\Avid H4
- Consumer Reports v63 n3, Mar 1998. p19–23.
  <http://www.yokohamatire.com>

Consult Table of Contents for Indexes Included in this volume.

Figure 2.2 A page from a specialized index.

one outlined in Chapter Eight, will locate exactly the materials you need to complete your research project as effectively as possible.

Special Collections Most research libraries also hold special collections of unusual or rare materials, ranging from the private library of a generous benefactor to exhaustive national census or other government files, the private papers of a famous researcher or author, or reams of unstudied data from large-scale scientific studies. Don't ignore these specialized collections in your library. These materials have been placed in a public setting so that people like you can access them and use them in your own research. Oftentimes, people doing genealogical research will find valuable information in local government, church, or employment records that have been donated to libraries. Occasionally, someone looking through cartons of old documents in a library will find a handwritten draft of an unpublished book by a well-known novelist, a copy of a letter revealing an unknown liaison of historical importance, or the doodles of a famous artist. If you are the sort of person who would like to know what others write in their diaries or who must discipline yourself to avoid reading private correspondence on other people's desks, searching through historical archives may prove exciting to you. Most of life's tedious and monumental details are recorded for posterity, and the special or rare-manuscripts collections of research libraries make much of that detail available for study. Business letters and ledgers, deeds to cemetery plots, church school records, local court decrees, and gifts presented to universities by visiting dignitaries often wind up in research libraries and offer uncensored glimpses of the values and practices of local cultures during times past.

Libraries' special collections often grow out of the interests of a generous benefactor. For example, a philanthropist with an interest in cubist art might bequeath a collection of paintings and rare publications on the subject to a research library. Or a special collection might result from the obsession of a particular librarian. Your library might house an exquisite photography collection, or a trove of political campaign literature and memorabilia, or a video of every film directed by Woody Allen as well as every motion picture parodied or alluded to in one of those—all because a librarian valued that subject or medium and made a concerted effort to amass as complete a collection in that area as possible.

You don't have to consciously tailor your research projects to make use of your library's special collections, but do try visiting them once your research is under way. The one-of-a-kind items found in a special collection might suggest a unique angle or perspective for your research. Obviously, a search of your library's collection of government publications would be relevant to a study of U.S. contributions to the United Nations, but ask yourself what other specialized collections might contribute to your understanding of that topic. For instance, does your library house the private papers or correspondence of a former diplomat or UN delegate? Perhaps you could be the first writer to reprint a striking quotation or anecdote contained therein. Even a maps collection could add a new perspective to the topic. By looking at a current map of Manhattan, you would see that the UN occupies seventeen acres along the East River between Forty-second and Forty-eighth Streets. A map of New York City from 1945 would show that the UN was once housed on the former world's fair grounds in Flushing Meadow Park. A map showing current real estate values in Manhattan could help you calculate the billions of dollars in real estate controlled by the UN. A large collection of any specialized media will demonstrate its applicability to many subjects. There are maps that show political, economic, topographic, demographic, geologic, linguistic, architectural, and religious distinctions between regions—to name just a few of the subjects that can be illuminated by contemporary and historical map collections.

You may not be able to incorporate information from every collection in your campus library into the research you do as a student, but make the effort to check out your library's unique holdings. All of these things have been preserved for some reason, and many of them will fascinate you, too.

Cataloging Systems

Depending on the facilities and financing of your local library, it may rely on a time-worn card catalog or on a streamlined computer system to list its holdings. Physical card catalogs, which contain drawers of cards listing books and articles by subject heading, title, and author's name, are fast becoming collectible antiques in this country. If your library is still using a traditional card catalog, at least it will be familiar to you, following the same system you have used most of your life. Using an old-fashioned card catalog takes time and patience, but it will work during power outages, and many people can use it at once. In many instances, computerized systems contain exactly the same information as the familiar sets of drawers and cards that have served library patrons for centuries.

Most libraries have converted to an electronic cataloging system. The contents of the old card catalog are loaded into an electronic database, which can be searched quickly by title, author, or subject. Some systems cover a limited number of magazine and journal articles as well, and many are linked to the databases of cooperating libraries, to help users locate items that they can then request from a subscription service or an interlibrary loan program.

The Internet, specifically the World Wide Web, holds much promise for the future of library cataloging. Some libraries have already placed catalogs of their holdings on the Web, so that patrons can search them from virtually any computer—at home, at work, at school, or in the library itself. In addition, many libraries now subscribe to on-line electronic resources that provide users not only with bibliographic citations but also with full texts of newspaper and magazine articles. As traditional library holdings are converted to digitized bytes, the massive card catalogs of the past, as well as some of the content of the library itself, are becoming as portable as the latest laptop computer.

Remote Searches

For a long time now, patrons at research libraries have had the opportunity to borrow materials from remote libraries through interlibrary loan programs. Today, the widespread use of electronic catalogs and the relative ease of uploading listings to the Internet makes it possible for researchers to browse the contents of major libraries all over the world.

The ability to Telnet to regional libraries is probably built right into your campus library's electronic indexing system. Searching another library's holdings may be as simple as choosing its database from an on-screen list, using your library's computer system. In addition, many major public libraries have Web sites that allow you to view selected special holdings on-line or to search the catalog of circulating materials. Although you can't borrow library materials directly over the Internet in most cases, you might be able to request them through the interlibrary loan office at your campus library. If you suspect another library has an extensive collection of materials on your topic, it is worth your time to look at its catalog on-line. Everyone who goes to Paris seems to find at least one great restaurant that all of the guidebooks have missed; similarly, "visiting" a library on the Internet may yield a reference that no other index has listed.

Librarians

We call everyone who works on board a ship a "sailor," although we realize that there are many different jobs under that generic title: mechanics, cooks, navigators, communications specialists, and so on. "Librarian" is a similarly generic term. Actually, it takes people with a wide array of specialized training and job skills to keep a large academic library afloat.

Support Staff   The front line of service in most libraries is the support staff. These workers help patrons check out books, find and use basic reference materials, and negotiate the card catalog or computerized index. They also schedule study rooms and equipment requests, process interlibrary loan orders, reshelve materials, look for misplaced or incorrectly shelved items, and clear paper jams from the photocopiers. Indeed, most of the people you come into contact with in a library and think of as "librarians" are not technically trained as such. In fact, in a university library many members of the support staff are student assistants in the college's work study program. Although everyone you interact with in the library should be competent and friendly, you can't expect every library employee to answer all of your questions about library holdings, policies, and services.

Subject Matter Specialists   Every academic department in a university depends on the library to support the learning of its faculty and staff, and this requires that some librarians specialize in the research methods and essential resources required for each subject taught at the institution. Thus many university libraries employ specialists in architecture, art, humanities, law, medicine, science, telecommunications, and so on. But there are many kinds of librarians in most libraries. The job of "librarian" ranges from accountant-like cataloging positions to jobs that resemble a museum curator's. For example, collections development librarians choose the materials that the library purchases and accepts. Acquisitions librarians locate, order, and purchase library holdings. Archivists specialize in the care, maintenance, and repair of library materials, which includes everything from book binding and replacement of stolen or damaged pages to custodial care of ancient Egyptian manuscripts on papyrus and medieval European documents hand-copied onto sheepskin.

Reference Librarians Reference specialists are the librarians you are likely to have the most contact with while a student. If you've ever lost track of something after you've carefully and deliberately put it in a safe place, you know that the problems of storage and retrieval in a library are enormous. Reference librarians help patrons search for materials logically and comprehensively. They know something about all of the library's holdings, and they stay well informed about reference tools such as bibliographies, indexes, encyclopedias, almanacs, and databases. When you are just starting out on a research project, a reference librarian can help you use the library's resources to narrow and focus your topic, generate a working bibliography or list of possible secondary sources to examine, and discover which library holdings will be most applicable to your research. As your research process continues, reference librarians serve as friendly guides to using specialized reference materials. For example, they are usually familiar with the cross-referencing methods employed by popular print indexes and the operation of various CD-ROM programs, and they can usually show you some shortcuts and hints for using on-line services in their area of the library. As your research on a project nears completion, you will often want to consult with reference librarians to help you track down one last vital statistic or a famous quotation that you partly remember, or you might require their assistance in learning how to document an obscure library source that you are planning to cite in your work.

The difference between using only some library materials, haphazardly, and using the library wisely often depends on whether you consult librarians in your research process. Remember that the library employs these specialists to develop and maintain its collections and to serve its patrons. They are the experts in library holdings and usage. Although you should learn to perform basic research functions on your own, such as searching familiar indexes and databases or determining which periodicals the library carries, librarians stand ready to help you conduct your work efficiently or to uncover a truly extraordinary source that will make your research efforts most rewarding. An important part of learning how to use an academic library is gaining confidence in your own research skills and knowing when, who, and how to ask for assistance. Librarians are some of the most important resources your library provides.

■ The Library of Congress

The Library of Congress, in Washington, D.C., is the largest library in the world. But contrary to popular belief, it does not have every book ever published in the United States, it does not copy every law or bill into its records, and it is not necessarily a better resource for your research than is the public library in your home town. The Library of Congress was created in 1800 when the nation's capital was moved to the District of Columbia. It was created for Congress because lawmakers needed books, maps, and other printed materials to research their legislative decisions. In 1814, the original Library of Congress burned, and most of its holdings were destroyed. The library was restarted with Thomas Jefferson's books (partly because the former president possessed the best personal library in the country and partly because he needed money to maintain his home at Monticello). His personal library was purchased by the government for about $23,000, a significant sum of money in the early nineteenth century. Jefferson believed that lawmakers should be informed about every subject, because laws deal with every aspect of life. Therefore, the base holdings of the Library of Congress were eclectic, and its holdings have remained that way to this day.

The card catalog of the Library of Congress is available on the Internet. Most of its general collection is duplicated by libraries of all sizes throughout the United States, however, so in most cases it is not an efficient use of time to request a book or reprint of an article from the Library of Congress. Smaller libraries will respond to such requests more quickly, and the Library of Congress will often redirect your request to a local library in any case. Unlike the National Archives, the Library of Congress will not copy photographs from its collections for patrons. Photocopies of maps are available, however, to inquirers with specific requests.

People often think that federal legislation or reports issued by government agencies must be obtained from the Library of Congress, but many public libraries receive the same materials. The Federal Depository Library Program ensures that such materials are disseminated all over the country. Although the Library of Congress is a great national treasure, it is no more prestigious to use its holdings than it is to use those of your local library.

Visiting and Using the Library of Congress

Government agencies can borrow materials from the Library of Congress, and a few organizations, such as the National Geographic Society, have accounts there, but generally a private researcher must go to Washington, D.C., and use the library's holdings on site. Novelist Herman Wouk is said to have moved to Washington, D.C., so that he could research his books in the Library of Congress, and Neil Sheehan wrote most of his book about the Vietnam War, *A Bright Shining Lie*, in a reading room there. For most citizens it is not practical to visit the Library of Congress personally, however, and so it is used mainly as it was intended: by members of Congress and their staffs.

Tourists and casual visitors will find the Library of Congress rather forbidding. Security is tight in both of its buildings because of the many rare and uncopyrighted items stored there. Materials in the Library of Congress are not kept in open stacks, so visitors cannot browse among the holdings. The genealogy rooms are frequently used by visitors to the library, but appointments are required, and visitors with limited time are rarely able to find what they came for.

Special Collections and Archives in the Library of Congress

The Library of Congress does have special collections and archives that house rare and one-of-a-kind materials. Thomas Jefferson's original library composes one special collection within the Library. The Library of Congress holds the most comprehensive collection of early published newspapers in the country, and these are available for inspection to persons who make an appointment to come and search through them. It is also the home of a huge collection of Sanborn Fire Insurance maps, in which nearly every town and neighborhood in the United States is presented in detail, including notes regarding the building materials used in every structure. The Library of Congress also holds precious materials from other countries, obtained through exchange agreements. The government records of some developing countries are housed there to protect them. And the library occasionally purchases antiquated materials of global interest, such as the Gutenberg Bible. In general, the Library of Congress aims to preserve its rare materials, however, not to disseminate them.

■ Summing Up

You probably think of a library as a place where books are collected and made available for patrons to borrow. Most libraries are that and much more. There are many sizes and kinds of libraries, from the shelf full of picture books in the corner of a kindergarten classroom to multibuilding libraries such as the Library of Congress and large campus library systems. Generally, the information a person seeks will dictate the type of library he or she should seek out. For most college research projects, a campus library will be necessary. Your school's research library has probably developed extensive collections of the kinds of materials you will be expected to read and cite in your assignments. More indexes, periodicals, microfilms, audiovisual materials, electronic resources, and curious objects are available to you now than ever before.

If your campus library offers an orientation program or a self-guided tour, be sure to take advantage of it. Learning to use the campus library efficiently will make your study time much more productive. If your library does not offer such a program, explore it on your own by seeking familiar and unfamiliar materials. Ask reference librarians to help you. Remember that no one expects you to arrive on campus with full knowledge of reference libraries and their holdings. Typically, campus libraries contain many more departments and materials than do the types of libraries you are accustomed to using. You must learn new methods of library exploration to take full advantage of the resources they offer.

Exercises: Sources and Strategies

1. Complete a tour of your campus library system. (Many academic libraries offer a self-guided tour brochure at their circulation or reference desks.) As you tour the library, make a list of the subjects in which it seems to specialize. List some of the things, besides books, that your library collects.

2. Using the microfilm department in your library, read a newspaper from the day you were born, from the day that one of your parents was born, or from the day a momentous historical event occurred (such as the day the Erie Canal opened, the day Robert E. Lee surrendered to Ulysses S. Grant, the day Charles Lindbergh completed the first transatlantic flight, the day President Kennedy was assassinated in Dallas, or the day Neil Armstrong walked on the moon). Write a summary of the other current events of the date you examined.

3. Go to a special collections area of your campus library and ask how the holdings are cataloged there. Browse through a list of the holdings and request an interesting object or document, or ask a librarian or staff member there to recommend an intriguing artifact (for example, a first edition of a book; a handwritten manuscript; an old photograph; a journal or other possession of a locally or internationally famous person). Or, learn about a rare document held at the National Archives or Library of Congress through its Web site. Write a page explaining the history of the object and describing it. Tell why it is important for the library or archive to preserve that object.

Writing to Know

Write a letter to students who will be enrolling at your college for the first time next fall, telling them about the resources available in your campus library. Provide examples from your own experience, instead of citing the library's published pamphlets and guides. Be frank about the kind and quality of library services and materials you have used (and the ones you later realized you *should* have used). Be sure to include (or make up) "lore" about the library (for example, a lucky study carrel, a photocopier that operates for free if you hit it just right, the purported oldest object in the library, and so on).

This profile is presented in the first person, consisting entirely of an extended quotation by the interviewee, Elizabeth McIntosh. It was written this way because McIntosh is much more familiar with the topic than is either the writer or the audience. By choosing this method of presentation, the writer lets the subject explain a complex subject in her own words. Because the interview yielded a lot of text (the transcript of the interview was twice as long as the finished profile), it was easy to select only salient points from the discussion for the finished piece. The interview was also very coherent, so it was not difficult to make the quotations flow logically and to develop each point adequately. This format works best when the subject is readily forthcoming with information and addresses an audience that is compatible with that for the finished essay.

Elizabeth McIntosh

Former Project Director for the Barbara Bush Foundation for Family Literacy

Elizabeth "Ruthie" McIntosh is twenty-nine years old, blonde, and energetic. She exudes the kind of self-confident ease that makes others feel at home. Former project director for the Barbara Bush Foundation for Family Literacy, Ruthie has learned that the work of high-profile Washington agencies only seems to be done with a quick vote or the stroke of a pen. She and her husband, David, are just coming off his first, successful campaign for a seat in the U.S. House of Representatives. It is a cold December evening, and Ruthie is sitting on the kitchen floor in their new house, as she and David have had the opportunity to unpack only partially. Her eight-week-old puppy, Madison, is untying her shoelaces, naughtiness that Ruthie enthusiastically encourages.

The Barbara Bush Foundation for Family Literacy is a granting agency that gives money to literacy projects nationwide. So far it has raised $13 million, and it grants away about one-half million annually. Its target endowment is $35 million, so it is now in its middle stages of development—still soliciting donations, but also operating at full swing. It is designed to be an ongoing foundation, one that will last in perpetuity.

It was my job to run the day-to-day operations, everything from phone referrals answering requests for regional family literacy help to managing volunteers and distributing all of our written materials. One of the first things we did in starting the foundation was publish a book called *First Teachers* about ten family literacy programs already in action and successful. This was to encourage others with good ideas to apply to the foundation and to provide models for effective programs in the field. That part of the project didn't end when the book was published; we still had to market our work, make sure it got to the audience we wanted. We initiated a big mailing to pioneers in the field of literacy, distributed complimentary copies along with information about how to order more. We went to trade shows and tried to sell the book.

At the same time, we started compiling and writing an informational brochure about the foundation and a brochure filled with writing and reading tips. These were high-quality brochures, designed to raise awareness of family literacy issues. We produced brochures on a three- to six-month turnaround time, depending on how in-depth each pamphlet was. We had to keep ourselves to six months on everything because information gets old so quickly.

Highly skilled people drafted the brochures, so we didn't spend a lot of time rewriting, but our boss was a scrupulous editor. During my third year of working for her, I finally got a text past her without changes. She was very precise, insightful. I learned a lot about literacy myself, from writing for her! If you want someone to edit your work, choose a person you respect, someone with a thorough grasp of the content, not just a good knowledge of grammar.

There were eight of us on the foundation board, each overseeing different projects. A variety of work went on concurrently all the time, but we were also working together. One volunteer was nearly one hundred years old. She covered Department of Education research, especially Head Start studies, and had the job of keeping us up-to-date on that work. We had this "hit by a bus" theory—that is, if you were hit by a bus, how could someone else go on with your work? It was important to make sure everything was written down. The hit-by-a-bus concept disciplined me to write things down in an orderly way.

Getting information efficiently is always a problem with investigations. Referral is the key to successful research. It may take five phone calls to get the answer you want. We used the Library of Congress a lot because they have great cataloging. They have practically everything, and you can borrow from other places through them, too. They were especially good for supplying us with good photographs. You can get copies made there; you just have to credit the Library of Congress and acknowledge the photographers to use them.

Deciding to fund a proposed literacy project is a complex process. We required a very thorough grant application, including letters of recommendation. I got very good at reading into letters of recommendation. A lot of our decisions were based on the quality of the referrals submitted, and we also checked out other activities already offered in each area. We eventually found that state agencies were nearly hopeless in following through with our requests, and we learned to go to some expert in the area, such as a researcher we had worked with previously or the head of a local library. We networked a lot, and we learned to depend on the personal accountability of concerned individuals.

After grants were awarded, we conducted site visits with the literacy programs we sponsored. We sent board members to visit projects to learn what was working. As it turned out, the board members didn't always know how to do discriminating observations. Later, though, we got people who could help steer the grantees. We hired a grant consultant who was well versed in family literacy issues to help implement the benefits of research in the local programs.

Site visitation was very organized. We made a file for each grantee, divided into six aspects of evaluation. Each file was identical. It is important to be consistent, even repetitive in firsthand research. We developed a questionnaire to gather statistics to publish about the effectiveness of our grants. It was very heavy on statistics, such as retention figures. We tried to document the goals each program achieved, for example, helping people find jobs or get a G.E.D. We filled out the questionnaires at each site, hoping to compile statistics establishing our success, but the results were not very cohesive, sort of divergent and boring. It ended up not making a very good story, and we found that our results were very unpredictable. Sometimes research does that to you; you dedicate a lot of time and then find out it's not such a good idea to go ahead with your original plan.

The best part of working for the Barbara Bush Foundation for Family Literacy was awarding the grants. That is a culmination of research. A foundation is a venture capitalist bank; it bets on ideas that it believes in. You have to do a lot of research to be sure the grant you're awarding will be well used. It made all the research worthwhile to know you could give the grants with confidence.

Sometimes we followed up on grants that were good ideas, but we just couldn't fund them. We passed those applications on to other granters. Grant makers are always hungry for good programs, so we helped find sponsors for those we couldn't fund. We used our influence to get things we really believed in funded. We had such a high-visibility person in Barbara Bush, with her reputation on the line, so our recommendations were usually well received.

People identified with Barbara Bush herself. Once a woman called our office from the steps of a courthouse because she was about to be evicted from her home. She had two small children, and she wanted Mrs. Bush to help her. We called her governor's office and asked for a caseworker. We were able to refer her to some help. We responded to a huge amount of correspondence every day, answering Mrs. Bush's letters regarding literacy issues. She had high standards; she insisted on a five-day turnaround on personal letters. The incoming mail was sorted into barrels. Because the person at the top wanted personal correspondence, we had to make it work. Mrs. Bush loves personal letters.

Barbara Bush has incredibly high credibility. You can be very creative if your product is seen positively. Essentially, we looked at Barbara Bush as our product in a lot of ways. We were promoting her ideals. Many people are out there peddling worthless things. You must believe in your product. You will have to push it from a lot of angles, so love learning more about it, learn to love researching your product. I really believe in family literacy. Before you commit to working on a project, talk to as many people as possible about it in advance. Seek the advice of specialists. If you gather enough opinions and facts, the truth will win out.

Suggested Writing Assignments

1. Transcribe a conversation. Either make it a point to overhear an exchange in a restaurant, on a bus, or in some other public place and record it (changing the names of those involved), or ask friends to let you tape-

record a conversation among them and type it out. Edit your transcription to make it fast-paced and coherent. Add stage directions and description to it, as if it were a scene from a movie script.

2. Analyze a job you have held or a group project on which you have worked. What assumptions did you make before you started? What mistakes did you make at first? What did you learn in the process? How has that experience shaped your goals or beliefs?

3. Dream up a great grant opportunity for yourself—a grant from an agency that gives money to students wishing to study abroad, for example, or free snowboarding equipment from an outfitter who provides its products to qualified competitors. Write a narrative paragraph explaining how much money or materials you would need, what you would do with what you received, and how your use of grant money or materials might benefit the organization sponsoring you.

Chapter Three

Using the Internet as a Research Tool

Research sources and methods are constantly evolving. Indeed, ever since the "information age" began, they have been changing so fast that whatever one writes about an individual source or tool, such as an informational Web site or a new electronic index, may be inaccurate by the time it is read. It is a cliché and an exaggeration to say that by the time information is printed on paper it is already out of date, but as more and more periodicals go on-line and frequently updated Web sites proliferate, waiting for a magazine, newspaper, or book to arrive in your mailbox or local library is like waiting for the evening news to show you footage of an earthquake that happened in your own backyard. Not long ago, many teachers considered electronic sources untrustworthy or invalid, and some suspected that students who relied on them were merely being lazy, avoiding necessary library work by depending on others to "send them" information via computers instead. Currently, however, most college-level instructors would deem incomplete any research project that did not utilize the searching and information-delivery systems available on-line. Computer-based communications have changed the process of gathering information, both inside academia and outside it, forever.

The amount of information delivered by computers to libraries, offices, homes, and businesses increases exponentially every day. The world's citizens have quickly adapted to the convenience and speed of on-line information gathering, for everything from monitoring stock prices to planning a vacation. The virtual world is almost as wide as the actual one, and it is growing every hour. As computer-delivered information gains credibility and an ever-increasing number of people gain access to it, more and more traditional print and broadcast media outlets are going on-line, supplementing or replacing their usual services with information delivered electronically. As a result, the Internet has begun to surpass conventional sources of information, especially when up-to-the-minute data is needed. It now takes a newspaper only seconds to land on computer screens all over the world, which is considerably faster than even the most enterprising young entrepreneur on a bicycle can manage, and that gets information to consumers days earlier than do papers that arrive by conventional mail.

The process of researching has changed dramatically as well. In most libraries, card catalogs made of wooden drawers have been moved out to make way for computer terminals. But computer technology didn't arise one day and revolutionize research the next. Rather, the researching process has been constantly evolving, sparked by advances in electronic information storage and retrieval systems. If you are about to embark on your first research project requiring computer assistance, you don't have to learn a whole new system of searching, reviewing, and note taking. Computers were invented to expedite and enlarge the scope of human activity. Fortunately, computer programs are constantly changing so as to simplify the technology most people need. The term "user friendly," which described computer programs with helpful prompts and easy-to-learn procedures, is fading from the language as ease of use becomes the standard, with most computer software and on-line procedures now incorporating on-screen help. Computer literacy is becoming easier to acquire than literacy itself.

■ E-mail

The Internet, as its name suggests, is an *inter*connected *net*work of computers, linked together for the purpose of sharing information. The Internet was developed by the military and was originally used by scientists and computer programmers to share technical information quickly. However, once e-mail (short for "electronic mail") had been refined, the endless possibilities it presented—for conveying information, disseminating literary texts, distributing important notices, engaging in interactive "chat," sending personal greetings, and even sharing office humor worldwide—made it phenomenally popular. The widespread availability of e-mail has revolutionized communication. It is now routine to send and receive written information across great distances in seconds. This development has had a profound impact on research.

"Netiquette"

Unlike a telephone call, e-mail is never intrusive. It interrupts no one. Instead, it waits in a directory on a computer somewhere until it is called up and read, at the recipient's discretion. It gives people a chance to compose responses more artfully and often more articulately than telephone conversation affords. Also, the easy, efficient nature of e-mail makes it less of an imposition than is a telephone call. E-mailing a stranger with a brief comment or question, as long as it is respectfully worded and appropriately directed, is perfectly acceptable and, in most cases, preferred over placing a phone call. Many people encourage strangers to send them e-mail: notice how many personal and professional Web pages contain direct links to their creator's e-mail address.

The text of an e-mail message is a hybrid between written correspondence and verbal conversation (see Figure 3.1). Its tone may vary from the curtly formal to the ridiculous or profane. You will probably find it much easier to dash off a quick comment on e-mail than to write someone a letter or even call him or her on the telephone. Remember that once you press the powerful button or combination of keys that sends your message out over the network for reassembly on your intended recipient's screen, it is irretrievable. Unless you or your e-mail program saved a copy of it, its contents will be lost to you, although it can easily be copied and redistributed by its recipient. Thus you may want to take some time to compose your messages and reread them before you rashly or overenthusiastically scatter your thoughts around the globe, your university, or your classroom.

In general, be brief and formal in an e-mail note to someone you have not met in person. There is no business stationery for e-mail, no laser-printed letter on heavyweight, cotton bond paper. Until you have corresponded with someone a few times, use an unornamented screen and plain typeface to substitute for such conventional formalities. Refrain from using colloquial e-mail conventions, such as the "smiley face" sign that indicates a humorous passage. (As you probably know, it is composed of a colon and right parenthesis: :)). If your e-mail account routinely appends any colloquial or offbeat personal signatures or artwork, you might want to suppress those by turning them off before writing to someone you have not corresponded with before. Ultimately e-mail is a relaxed and open forum for friendly communication, so if you eventually feel you can be yourself with an e-mail correspondent, add those personal touches into your messages. Remember that such things are the electronic equivalent of personal stationery, however, and may best be reserved for correspondence with friends.

E-mail Text Editors

Most e-mail text editors are not as sophisticated as word processing programs. They cannot reformat text extensively after alterations are made. Few of them "wrap" lines after additions are inserted, and few (as of this writing) offer spell checking. You may want to get into the habit of composing letters intended for e-mailing in your word processing program, where you can double-check and fine-tune them readily. Read your e-mail software manual, call a campus computer help line, or ask someone with experience to teach you how to save word processed documents as text files and transfer them to your e-mail account for sending them. In older programs this process requires a complex series of special log-in commands and steps for uploading files from your hard drive, but in newer programs this can be accomplished by simply dragging and dropping file icons into the appropriate spot on your computer screen. In almost any case, and especially if you are sending a long or technical message, the process of transferring files from a word processing program to an e-mail text editor is fairly convenient and takes less time than manually inserting hard returns in altered text and using

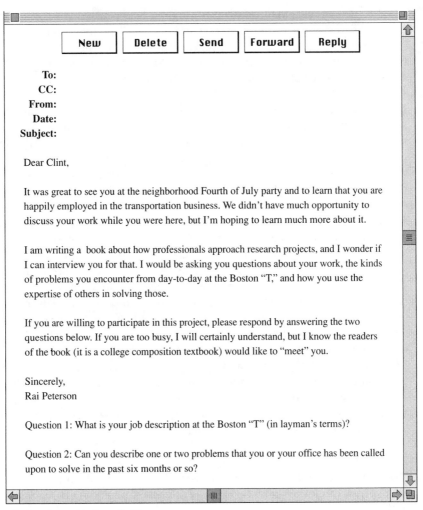

New | Delete | Send | Forward | Reply

To:
CC:
From:
Date:
Subject:

Dear Clint,

It was great to see you at the neighborhood Fourth of July party and to learn that you are happily employed in the transportation business. We didn't have much opportunity to discuss your work while you were here, but I'm hoping to learn much more about it.

I am writing a book about how professionals approach research projects, and I wonder if I can interview you for that. I would be asking you questions about your work, the kinds of problems you encounter from day-to-day at the Boston "T," and how you use the expertise of others in solving those.

If you are willing to participate in this project, please respond by answering the two questions below. If you are too busy, I will certainly understand, but I know the readers of the book (it is a college composition textbook) would like to "meet" you.

Sincerely,
Rai Peterson

Question 1: What is your job description at the Boston "T" (in layman's terms)?

Question 2: Can you describe one or two problems that you or your office has been called upon to solve in the past six months or so?

Figure 3.1 An E-mail Message

a dictionary to look up all questionable spellings, and there will be no need to apologize for shoddily prepared work.

Specific possibilities for using e-mail in your college research projects have probably already begun to occur to you. Sometimes you will know the name of a person you want to contact (occasionally you will already know that person's e-mail address), but often you will only know the subject you are interested in discussing with some qualified person you hope to find on-line. E-mail will probably "net" you some exciting results. Electronic communication is enjoying its halcyon days; nearly everyone who tries it likes it and believes it borders on the miraculous. People have not grown weary of it, and it hasn't been overrun by commercial interests and marketers, as have other means of communication (such as the telephone). Usually, when someone spots an unfamiliar address in his or her e-mail "in box," the corresponding message contains a pleasant surprise, such as a note from a long-lost friend, a new acquaintance with a similar interest, or a researcher with an intriguing question.

If you know the e-mail address of an expert you would like to contact via the Internet, you already have part of what it takes to make yourself either a pest or a protégé to that person. No one likes to be asked questions with obvious answers or to divulge personal information about themselves or others. Phrase your e-mail messages as thoughtfully and tactfully as you would any letter. Do as much reading and searching of secondary sources as possible before deciding to e-mail someone about your topic. E-mailed research correspondence is essentially an interview conducted over time and often across distance. (It might be a good idea to read Chapter Five, about interviewing, before you send out e-mail requests for information on your topic. If you know who you want to contact but do not have his or her e-mail address, see the discussion later in this chapter about searching for addresses on the World Wide Web.)

■ Mailing Lists and Newsgroups

If you want to find information about a particular subject or get the opinions of individuals who are interested in a specific topic, you may want to subscribe to some Internet mailing lists or browse through some "newsgroup" postings. A mailing list on the Internet is a lot like its corollary in the tangible world; it is a list of e-mail recipients who share an interest in a topic and have asked to receive the e-mail equivalent of mass mailings on that subject. A "letter" on an Internet mailing list is addressed to the whole group of subscribers and is usually referred to as a "posting." Subscribers post messages to the list by sending e-mail to the list server, a central computer that compiles messages from list members and then redirects them to everyone who subscribes to the list. Thus a single message sent to the appropriate list server is actually delivered to the e-mail accounts of a number (perhaps thousands) of people who are knowledgeable or interested about the subject to which the list is dedicated.

Subscribing and Unsubscribing to a Mailing List
Subscribing to a mailing list costs nothing, is very simple, and takes only a few seconds. A few lists are private, established to conduct the business of a committee or work group that does not welcome outsiders, but these are rare, and the list server will politely inform you of their exclusive membership if you try to join. There are thousands of lists established on the Internet. Larger lists will send you a generic welcome message, and participants on some smaller lists may take the time to welcome you personally. Some lists are more active than others, with more members and frequent postings;

usually you will start getting messages from a new list subscription anywhere from within a few minutes to a week. Be patient. List discussions, like conversations held in person, have lulls and heated exchanges. Usually a flurry of postings will follow one member's provocative question or intriguing idea.

Lurking and Listening on Mailing Lists

It is a good idea to "lurk" for a while after joining a list. Lurkers are list members who read postings but don't contribute messages of their own. On some lists, long-term lurking is accepted, but on more intimate lists there will occasionally be pleas to lurkers to make themselves heard. Every list has its own culture. Each is like a group of people engaged in conversation at a huge party. You might walk up to one group, listen for a while, and determine that you don't like or understand the topic of their conversation. As you drift around the room, you stand at the fringes of several conversations, trying to determine whether you will fit in with each group. Eventually, you find some people talking about a subject that interests you on a level at which you can contribute thoughts of your own. You politely listen for a while, and then you begin speaking. If you disagree with a participant, you are careful to watch how others in the group react. By watching them, you can assess how much you should say, if a joke would be considered appropriate, whether there are fellow supporters for your position in the group, and so on. On an e-mail list, you cannot observe the reactions of group members as they read your postings, so you should spend a longer time just listening than you would when you enter a conversation in person.

Save several of the e-mail messages you receive from a mailing list and read through them again before you post your first contribution. Notice how list members address one another. Are they all on a first-name basis? Also note how they disagree among themselves. Are they polite and cautious or forthright? Is "flaming" allowed? (*Flaming* ranges from verbal horseplay, such as joking or punning, intended to lure others into joining humorous or ridiculous exchanges to verbal attacks designed to provoke a heated response; essentially, it is the kind of disruptive behavior that often erupts during meetings in which participants are physically gathered together.) Are off-topic distractions permitted? (How do they handle humor or other unrelated material?) Is it a long-established group? (Do they refer to postings made months or even years before?) Long-time list members may be impatient with those who raise questions addressed repeatedly in the past. In general, the rules for joining an Internet mailing list are the same as those for entering any existing social or professional discussion. Be a bit reserved at first. Also, do some research before you post questions to a mailing list. Serious professionals engaged in focused debate don't want to be bothered with obvious questions, and they might suspect that you want them to do your research for you. A query like "I am writing a paper about William Faulkner for my English class and wonder if you can tell me anything about his work" is likely to elicit some rude responses. Instead, ask questions that show you've done your homework. A question like "I've been reading about the reliability of Faulkner's narrators in his novel *As I Lay Dying,* and I'm wondering which of the characters in that novel you believe is most trustworthy?" Don't try too hard to establish your own authority or to win acceptance from the group, You must give the other list members time to get to know you as well. And when you get a response to your posts, remember that e-mail does not convey affect or tone of voice.

Finding Relevant Mailing Lists

There are e-mail lists devoted to most any topic you can think of, and if you think of your topic in broad enough terms, you will probably find several that will give you access to experts or practitioners in fields related to your research project. For example, a quick search of Internet mailing lists on the topic "Genetics" revealed six lists, four concerned specifically with human genetics and two that discuss the topic more broadly. At the time of this writing, there were six lists registered on the subject "Poetry," with one focusing directly on contemporary American poetry, a constantly changing field that is probably best monitored through electronic media. Three mailing lists were devoted to discussing in-line skating. A search on the topic "Marketing" yielded impressively varied results. Of thirty-five marketing-related lists, seven were concerned with international aspects of the topic, and one concentrated on gender-related marketing issues. There were marketing forums for college faculty, students, and alumni, a list just for health care marketing professionals, and a list sponsored by a motorcycle marketing firm that was directed at "Thunderlizards." (Presumably, if you are one of those, you know it.)

You can conduct a very fast, comprehensive search of Internet mailing lists on any topic by sending a message to the following address: listserv@vm1.nodak.edu. Include only the following as the text of your message: list global/your topic. Send the message, and usually within minutes you will receive the results of your search, including directions for subscribing to the lists suggested. With a few searches, you can discover dozens of communities of on-line correspondents who are concerned with the same issues as you. A word of caution: don't oversubscribe yourself. Very active lists can fill up the average student account e-mail box in a matter of hours.

Accessing Newsgroups

Newsgroups are similar to mailing lists, but their postings are held in one remote location, like an electronic bulletin board, instead of being distributed to members via e-mail. You must check in with a newsgroup periodically to see what information has been posted recently. Newsgroups are accessible through some Web browsers. You can access UseNet newsgroups through the following URL: http://sunsite.unc.edu/usenet-i/home.html. On-screen commands will help direct and focus your search. There may be a reference book in your library that lists Internet newsgroups and mailing lists. UseNet newsgroups encompass a wide variety of topics, including forestry, boat repair, cellular thermodynamics, graduate schools, military science, Shakespeare, and others. If your computer is connected to the Internet but you don't have access to the World Wide Web, there are still many professionals and groups you can access on-line.

■ The World Wide Web

The World Wide Web (WWW, or simply "the Web") is the famous offspring of the Internet. Although the Web has received more attention than the Internet has recently and seems to have eclipsed it in the public eye, the Web is actually part of the Internet and could not exist independently of its parent. The great invention of the Swiss particle physicists who made the Web what it is today is Hypertext Mark-up Language (HTML). Web site builders insert HTML codes into their pages to tell Web browsers, the software programs that read HTML and display Web pages on your computer screen, how the pages should look. The browser filters out those codes, like sunglasses eliminate ultraviolet rays but admit visible light, so that the pages users pull up display the pictures, links, text, animations, and sounds that make Web pages attractive and easy to use, without showing the apparatus that make them work.

Gophers, FTP, and IRC

As the parent of the Web, the Internet has had to add on to its "house" to accommodate the rapid expansion of its genius child's experiments. But the Web cannot move out on her own yet, because she is still dependent on her parent. Besides, the Internet is her link to her siblings, Gopher, FTP, and IRC. Gophers are sort of like the older brother of the Web. Born at the University of Minnesota, Gophers are another incredibly useful byproduct of the union of computers that produced the Internet. Gophers are servers that store huge data banks of text not written in HTML, such as the job listings from each issue of *The Chronicle of Higher Education* and the full text of classic books that have been made available on the Internet as part of Project Gutenberg. Many Gophers are linked to the Web and accessible using popular browsers like Netscape or Explorer. In fact, with newer browsers (developed within the past seven years or so), you can access most Gophers with a couple of clicks of your mouse button. FTP, or File Transfer Protocol, is a computer program that allows files that have not been written for Gopher or Web display to be downloaded (copied long distance) from one computer on the Internet to another, where they can be opened and viewed.

The IRC, or Internet Relay Chat, feature of the Internet facilitates real-time discussion groups. IRC discussions are like chat rooms on America On-line; they allow two or more people who are logged in and at their terminals to "converse" on-line, receiving responses from one another almost as quickly as they are sent. Participants in IRC discussions may log on using aliases (much like customers of America Online and Prodigy do). IRC is useful for disseminating civilian reports during military crises, such as the Gulf War or the repatriation of aggressors in Rwanda. The immediacy of IRC, coupled with the anonymity it offers, makes it a good forum for unofficial reporting. However, most of the chatting conducted on the IRC from day to day ranges from the mundane to the risqué. Generally speaking, anonymous texts are not very reputable sources to cite in a college research paper.

MOOs and MUDs

A more reputable real-time forum, available on the World Wide Web, is a MOO. MOO is short for something that is actually short for something else: MUD Object Oriented, with MUD being short for Multi-User Dimension. MOOs provide "virtual" discussion rooms where participants can "meet" and converse in real time. Verbal or graphic representations of physical space are presented on-screen to make participants feel more "at home." Originally created for game playing, MOOs provide imaginary settings where on-line conversations can take place. For instance, Diversity University (Telnet: moo.du.org 8888, or Web URL: http://www.academic.marist.edu/duwww.htm) is a virtual campus with a conference center, faculty offices, classrooms, and other representations of typical physical spaces on a university campus, where on-line "students" can "meet" one another and "talk." Generally, when you log on to a MOO, either through the Web or by Telnet (telephone network), you will be assigned a guest name and given the opportunity to visit an orientation site that will explain common commands used in the program. From there, you can wander around the site and listen in on conversations in progress or obtain a list of people currently logged in to the site and go to the same location as an existing group. The same rules of decorum apply as when joining any live conversation. "Listen" for a while to determine the topic and tone of the conversation. Be polite and respectful of others. You may stumble on a provocative or useful conversation by randomly touring MOOs, but their best potential for research is to use them as virtual meeting spaces for real-time interviews on the Internet. Once you have discovered a favorite MOO site, you can suggest it to others when you are searching for a forum in which to conduct conversations or live interviews.

MOOS and MUDS provide research opportunities similar to those provided by Internet mailing lists. Once you enter a MOO site dedicated to discussing propulsion physics, for example, you will find others gathered in the same "room" who have come to talk about that topic. It can be a sort of virtual club meeting for propulsion physics students and scientists. You can ask questions, and, if you're lucky, get them answered immediately. Because MOOS are synchronous forums, your audience is limited to those who are on-line with you at the same time and in the same "place." Chances are that you won't enter a MOO when a famous physicist like Stephen Hawking is on-line; it is more likely that you will "stand around" the virtual site with one or two other curious students like yourself, wondering when MOO and MUD technology will live up to its potential.

The best use of MOO technology for research is when there is a virtual conference at a MOO site. These are often publicized on related mailing lists. Occasionally, an organization will sponsor an opportunity to communicate with someone such as an eminent physicist or political official. Interested persons are invited to visit a designated MOO site and "attend" the conference, which usually includes a discussion among principle participants and an opportunity for others to ask questions of them. MOO and MUD technology can provide students with a chance to "hear" and interact with experts in their field without having to travel to professional meetings.

The World Wide Web's Vast Holdings

It might help you to imagine the World Wide Web as a physical place, something like a giant bazaar or a library with holdings all donated by its patrons. The materials it contains include advertisements, airline and train schedules, celebrity fan club information, film clips, magazines, current newspapers, photographs, transcripts of television shows, weather reports, unpublished essays, and letters. You can shop for most any product, from sunglasses to dog sleds. You can read an amazing assortment of information about nearly every topic, including personal opinions and published reports from conferences, scientific journals, consumer services, government offices, and regional newspapers from all around the world. It is important to remember, however, that every item in the World Wide Web's library has been donated, and you must ask yourself why the donor placed each piece of material on the Web. There may be many reasons for disseminating information, whether it is poems or propaganda. A site on the Web may feature education, products, information, services, entertainment, software, or communication with others. The really magical thing about this bazaar is that you don't have to walk between vendors' booths or search the whole bazaar yourself for the things that you want to examine or buy. You can ride a magic carpet; many sites contain links to similar or related sites, and you can "go" there immediately simply by clicking on the link.

HTML and Links

Hyperlinks are probably the greatest benefit that HTML provides to the Web. Each link (either a graphic or a highlighted word or words on a page), when clicked with a mouse, invokes a hidden, embedded command that makes a Web browser jump to a different URL (Uniform Resource Locator), or Web address. Glide your cursor around the screen when you are visiting a Web site. When the cursor changes, you have "touched" a link. With a simple click of your mouse button, you will initiate the series of commands necessary to contact and display the site the link represents. For example, a Web page advertising summer jobs abroad might contain links to specific vacancy notices, classified by country, or a Web article on astronomy might contain

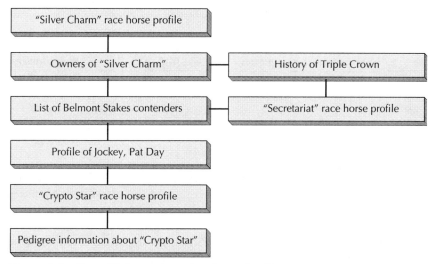

Figure 3.2 Tree of Information—Racehorse Profile

links to pictures taken through the Hubble telescope. It is easy to spend hours just "surfing" the Web, going from site to site pursuing interesting topics, using links and the "Back" button on your browser (which allows you to page back through the sites you've left and explore promising links you noticed earlier).

Navigating the Web with links can be time-consuming and misleading, however. Many sites consist of several pages all linked to one another but not to other sites. If you stumble onto such a site, you may find that its various pages look physically different from one another—and thus you might think you're traveling all over the Web when instead you are caught in the labyrinth of a single information source. For example, a student hoping to learn information about the humane treatment of racehorses chose to start with a site about "Silver Charm," a specific racehorse. By clicking on a link on that page, she accessed eight different articles about racehorse-related issues, included the "tree of information" in Figure 3.2.

By the time she pulled up the third racehorse profile page and noted its similarity to the others, she realized she had been wandering around in a single Web site, reading eight works by the same author. However, a quick search using the key words "thoroughbred," "veterinary," and "racehorse" on the search engine AltaVista yielded eighteen promising articles, in different Web sites, focused on the treatment (and mistreatment) of various common health problems in thoroughbred racehorses.

Web Search Tools and Techniques

Simply surfing the Web in search of information for a research project is like wandering around in a specific area of a library and looking at items at

Table 3.1 Number of Sites Returned in a Search for Four Broad Topics on Three Popular Web Search Engines

	Search Engine		
	100 Hot Sites	*Yahoo!*	*WebCrawler*
genetics	516	327	5,344
poetry	1,299	2,463	16,380
marketing	4,802	6,624	81,830
skating	316	469	4,247

random or channel surfing on a TV that is not programmed to display all of the channels it receives. To make effective use of the World Wide Web, start with a systematic approach, using a Web search tool (or search "engine," as they are often called).

When you click the "Search" button on the Netscape or Explorer tool bar, for instance, you are automatically connected to a search engine Web site. These services, including AltaVista, AOL NetFind, Electric Library, Excite, HotBot, InfoSeek, LookSmart, Lycos, Snap!, WebCrawler, and Yahoo! consists of organized databases containing thousands or millions of URLs. By entering key words or phrases on the site, you can search through these databases to find the information you are looking for amazingly quickly. Try several until you find one whose format and search results you like. You may want to use a handful of search tools every time you initiate a hunt for a new topic. There will be some repetition or overlap between them, but each will also turn up some materials that the others have missed or omitted. Some search engines catalog only topic headings for Web sites, whereas others scan the entire text of Web pages to identify and catalog their contents. A few search engines limit the field by listing only relatively new Web sites, and a few concentrate on very popular sites, by listing only those that have already received a huge number of "hits." For example, asking three different search engines to identify sources relevant to four broad topics resulted in an overwhelming number of Web sites returned, as Table 3.1 illustrates.

Obviously, eighty-one thousand sites are too many to read for a college research project, as would be six thousand or even three hundred. The best Web search is not the one that yields the *most* sites but the one that identifies the most relevant ones—sources that researchers are likely to find useful to learn more about specific topics. Professional researchers often advise that "good" search results produce a list of twenty or fewer applicable sources.

To narrow the results of a Web search down to a manageable number of URLs, learn to use some search-customizing techniques. The system devised by English mathematician George Boole to delineate sets using the words *or, and,* and *not,* or Boolean operators, helps users focus their search requests. A researcher seeking information might link key terms with Boolean operators in the following ways:

- Use *or* between two terms to broaden a search. For example, instead of requesting information on *hemp flax,* you could enter *hemp or flax* to get a list of all sources or headings in which the word *hemp* is used as well as all those in which the word *flax* is used. When you are just beginning your research, you might get some useful background information by casting such a big net.

- Search for synonyms, using *or* between them, to make sure you find as many sources on the topic as possible. For example, asking for information on *hemp or marijuana* would generate a list of all sources and headings that mention the word *hemp* as well as all that mention *marijuana.* Using *or* between terms tends to result in greater numbers of returns.

- Use *and* between terms when you want to find sources that name both terms. For example, entering *hemp and marijuana* will produce a list of articles or headings that contain both words. You might search in this way if you were writing a paper about the differences between hemp and marijuana and hoped to find materials comparing the two.

- Use *not* to eliminate sources connected to a topic but not relevant to your specific interests. For example, searching for *hemp not drugs* or *hemp not smoking* would eliminate articles that referred to both *hemp* and *drugs* or to both *hemp* and *smoking,* helping to narrow the results to materials concerned only with the industrial uses of hemp.

Even more efficient results can be obtained by using *truncation,* the shortening of words with many possible endings so that all forms of the word are included. For instance, entering the topic *hemp not smoking* as *hemp not smok* would eliminate items that mentioned the word *smoke* as well as items that mentioned the word *smoking.*

The designers of Web search tools are aware of the enormous proliferation of information on the World Wide Web, and they continue to refine their software so that users can define their searches with greater and greater precision. Explore the hints and search strategies offered on-screen. AltaVista, one very powerful search engine, gives its users the option of defining their search using a category tree. To begin, the user selects a broad category, and a drop-down menu of more specific subtopics branches off from the main category. The user then selects one of these subtopics to reveal a second, even more precise list of topics. When the user gets to the end of the series of "branches," a list of URLs is displayed. The result is a far more precise search result than most of us could generate on our own. Using the search assistance programs built into most web search engines greatly reduces the number of suggested sources resulting from a search. Used patiently, searching program trees can quickly reduce a bibliography of over one million Web sites down to a manageable number of sources. Most Web search engines and directories make suggestions to help users focus their searches. Do not ignore prompts and help screens that appear after an unsuccessful search. Search engines are constantly being refined to make them more efficient; the future of the medium depends on its organization and accurate information retrieval systems.

Even if you haven't spent hours surfing the Web, you probably realize that it is *enormous*. Just the WWW addresses included on billboards and in magazine and television ads provide ample evidence of the plethora of information out there. But despite this abundance, the Web does not replace the information available in libraries, archives, and other physical sites. It is best used as a first line of investigation of a topic or a place to discover and narrow ideas for research projects. Before heading for the library or making contacts for interviews, do some preliminary reading by searching cyberspace from your desk or a workstation in a campus computer lab. Visiting sites on the Web is kind of a cross between watching television and reading magazines. It is both an educational activity *and* a leisure activity.

Evaluating the Reliability of Web Sources

Because information can be posted to the World Wide Web by virtually anyone with access to a computer and a modem, the reliability of the data on the Web is inconsistent. Searching a topic such as airline safety, for example, can turn up a range of sources, from an in-depth series of reports by the *New York Times* to a prankster's list of practical jokes that will scare fellow air travelers during takeoffs. The various kinds of materials available on the Web have different audiences and purposes. If you need demographic information about Americans' discretionary spending, a government source would provide the most comprehensive and authoritative data. However, if you want recommendations about which Colorado ski resorts offer the most challenging runs, an individual's home page filled with such personal opinions may be all the advice you require. Always look for the name of the person or organization that posted the pages you are reading, and judge the reliability of the information they have provided by even more stringent criteria than you would apply to books in a library.

Sometimes it may be difficult to determine who posted a particular Web page. Just as printed pages are bound together into books or periodicals, Web pages are "bound" or bundled together into Web "sites," identifiable by their URLs. If you are looking at a Web page that contains information you might want to report in a research paper but can't tell where the information is coming from, try eliminating the last parts of the URL and reentering the address in your browser until you find a home page. For instance, a search for "chemistry and gold particles" may lead you to a page with a very long URL, like http://www.jmu.edu/acad/sci/chem/classes/braithw/560/labs/pearce/sem.1.html. By eliminating all except the root address (http://www.jmu.edu), you can get back to the home page for James Madison University. Following links from there, you can relocate the page you accessed via the search engine—the one with the extensive URL listed above—and discover that it is seminar paper number 1, submitted by a James Madison student named Pearce, enrolled in a lab for Chemistry 560, taught by a professor named Braithwaite. Although the page you originally pulled up may not be signed, various pages that link to it will indicate its author and his or her purpose in posting the information.

In general, large news-gathering organizations (such as major newspapers and television networks) and reputable agencies and institutions (such as universities, the American Cancer Society, and the World Wildlife Foundation) recognize that their reputation is at stake on the Web, just as it is in printed or televised media. Such distinctive sources of information are as reliable in computerized formats as they are in print or microforms in the library, although on-line versions of publications may not be as complete as their printed counterparts. One reliable search strategy is to start on the home page of a recognized national newspaper. For instance, a recent edition of the *Washington Post* Web site contained a front-page story about pending litigation against tobacco companies. That story featured a sidebar column with links to related stories on several other Web sites, including those of the American Medical Association, the Centers for Disease Control, and the Wilmington Institute. Organizations with a reputation for accuracy try diligently to include links to other authoritative sources. So if you start your search with a qualified news agency, you can be reasonably well assured that the information and sources you find will be reliable and accurate. You might even find it convenient to make the Web site of a major national newspaper or network (such as the *New York Times,* the *Washington Post,* the *Wall Street Journal, USA Today,* ABC, CBS, NBC, or CNN) your browser's default opening page.

Using the World Wide Web to conduct some of your research can be incredibly convenient. You can download entire Web pages onto your hard drive or copy highlighted text into other applications, such as a word processor—in effect, taking notes without pen or paper. Many Web sites also contain e-mail links to persons closely affiliated with your topic, and you can easily send queries to those people from the same page that you are reading. (Just remember to follow the rules of "Netiquette" described earlier in the chapter.) At its very beginning, the Internet was conceived of as a research tool, and advancements in the World Wide Web have concentrated on putting a wider variety of information at more people's fingertips with less effort than ever before. Undoubtedly, the future of research includes electronic information delivery, and the more familiar with it you can become now, the more readily you will adapt to its changing applications over the course of your career.

Easy access to great amounts of information, such as the World Wide Web provides, can be problematic for students compiling research under pressure. The need to meet deadlines and achieve good grades, coupled with the near effortlessness of downloading or printing out information from the Web, from a good paragraph to a finished research paper, can lead to unintentional (or blatant) acts of plagiarism. Remember, however, that anything you take off the Web can be just as easily accessed by others using the same key words you used to search. If the Internet makes cheating on research assignments twice as easy to attempt, it also makes plagiarism ten times easier to detect.

■ Summing Up

The World Wide Web and its parent technology, the Internet, have revolutionized research. Most public libraries and an increasing number of homes and residence hall rooms are "wired" for Internet access, which places a whole universe of information within keystrokes of most people. These new information and communications tools are the most revolutionary in history, even more so than the telephone, the fax machine, and the photocopier. However, communication in cyberspace adheres to the same fundamental rules as face-to-face discussion or traditional written correspondence. Users must be polite and respectful of others on-line, and they should consider the source of all information they read there.

In general, the Internet is a great place to begin taking in information for a research project. Students can "surf" the Web for information on topics they might wish to pursue in their assignments. They can subscribe to Internet mailing lists or read UseNet newsgroups to discover what aficionados and experts in any given field are saying about it, and they can visit MOO sites to attend virtual meetings or engage in one-on-one conversations with fellow researchers. Students without Web access often make good use of the Internet through such tools as e-mail, Gophers, FTP, and IRC.

Although Internet communication is useful throughout the research process, it supplements, rather than supplants, primary inquiry and more traditional secondary investigations. Reliable data, as well as a good deal of propaganda, personal opinion, and undifferentiated dreck, abounds in cyberspace. As their research progresses and their knowledge of a topic increases, students can use e-mail to conduct interviews on-line, they can post questions on electronic bulletin boards, and they can learn about and attend on-line conferences that give them access to authoritative, firsthand information. Electronic communication is a permanent addition to the world's information-dissemination infrastructure. We all must learn to use it fully and responsibly.

Exercises: Sources and Strategies

1. Using the search engine of your choice, locate several pages about any specific topic that interests you (a sport, an opera or theatrical production, a piece of scientific research, and so on). Discover the home pages of the sites that contain each of these pages, and determine if these sites are reputable sources you could cite in a college research paper.

2. Search the Internet for a mailing list that discusses a topic of interest to you. Subscribe to the list, and keep a log of the kinds of topics discussed over a week's time. (Be sure to save information about how to unsubscribe.)

3. Choose a consumer item that you are considering purchasing (a new bicycle, in-line skates, a stereo, a computer, a car, and so on). Using the World Wide Web, try to collect advice from each of the following: competing manufacturers, a retail sales outlet, a club or organization devoted to aficionados of that item, and satisfied (or unsatisfied) users of the item. *Or*, compile an itinerary for a "dream trip," using information available on the World Wide Web. List your flight times and ticket costs, choose a series of interesting hotels to stay in and restaurants where you would like to eat, and provide pictures of some of the sites you would visit.

Writing to Know

Study the World Wide Web sites of at least six businesses or organizations in the same general category (for example, colleges and universities, clothing retailers, antiques dealers, charitable foundations, magazines, and so on). Compile a chart analyzing the features of each site. (For example, is it easy to navigate within the site from any page? Are the graphics and animations attractive? What categories or services and information are included?) Write an essay expressing the qualities that make an excellent Web site for that category of organization. Include URLs of relevant examples throughout your essay.

RESEARCHER PROFILE

An integrated paraphrase-and-direct-quotation format seems to work best for this interview because it contains an intimidating amount of specific information, yet Aaron's own voice is casual and conversational, even encouraging. The profile describes Aaron's research process, gives a walk-through of her average workday, and offers her advice to aspiring television news producers. Such a wide-ranging outline requires some authorial intervention to make it all flow together logically, so two voices make up this text: the writer's and the subject's (Aaron's). The writer's voice makes it possible to conclude the profile with a striking observation instead of a quotation from the interview, thereby providing an unexpected ending.

Suzanna Aaron
Segment Producer for *The NBC Nightly News with Tom Brokaw*

"Being able to say, 'I called and left a message' is not making progress," cautions Suzanna Aaron, segment producer for *The NBC Nightly News with Tom Brokaw*. "The biggest mistake researchers make is waiting for people who aren't forthcoming with information. Don't wait around. Think of different ways to get the same information." Aaron and her colleagues apparently live this advice; her office at 30 Rockefeller Center, or the G.E. Building, is cluttered with mail and internal NBC memos, but the telephone, which occupies a cleared space in the center of her desk, dominates. Her officemate, a man in his early thirties, is establishing connections for a conference call. Next door, in an identically small, cluttered office, a man is shouting in another language into his telephone in order to be heard halfway around the world over a poor connection. The nearby conference room contains few permanent fixtures: a long table that seats about sixteen people is topped by a single object—a large speakerphone.

Aaron's first research source is NEXUS, an on-line service whose terminals are a staple in news-gathering agencies all over the world. "Mere mortals cannot access NEXUS," she laments. Most students don't have the chance to use NEXUS, which Aaron explains is "a very expensive computer system." NBC's data central pays the hourly fees for NEXUS connections. It saves the news staff thousands of hours, because "it's an amazing service with hundreds of publications. You can do word searches, pull up profiles on people; it will even search for stories under or over a specified length." Most of the secondary sources that news producers rely on are on-line. Electronic data services are not just convenient; they are crucial to the fast-paced research behind a daily news broadcast.

News producers find the majority of their ideas or assignments in secondary sources. "Most story ideas come from the printed press or wire service," Aaron admits. "Actually, most come out of the printed press. Occasionally we have a source; for example, we might get calls from people involved in a situation they want us to cover, or we just hear of something that starts an idea or raises a question, but we usually get ideas from reading news stories." Because television is a different medium than printed news sources, it must delve into and present topics according to its own strengths. The television news cannot simply recap or summarize print journalism.

Aaron and her fellow producers rely heavily on the telephone when conducting research for broadcast news. "A story may take place in five different cities, and we don't leave New York to write it," she explains. "We don't do a lot of scouting, but we research a lot before we go out and film things." Stories are usually written before camera crews are dispatched. Aaron explains, "We have crews all over the world, and we issue assignments to our camera crews. We sometimes use local affiliates for stuff they've already shot."

A surprising amount of information is available just for the asking, Aaron has learned, but she concedes that her position as Brokaw's producer opens doors for her. "When I say I'm from NBC News, basically everyone in the world talks to me." Her problem with the plethora of information that crosses her cranium is the same as that of any researcher: determining who and what to trust. "It's important to get a sense of how reliable a source is." Most organizations, she warns, have a bias. Researchers should not discard biased information but should simply be aware of the potential for bias and be wary of it. For example, Aaron notes that "the National Association on Anorexia and Eating Disorders inflates the number of anorectic people." Although physicians and scientists say there are no clear data indicating the number of people with anorexia, the association has a number. "Be skeptical of quick answers," Aaron cautions. "If it is an organization's business to inform the press, don't always believe the information they want to get out to the public. For example, lobbying organizations have a definite bias." By contrast, trade organizations can be quite helpful, she notes. "Ask yourself what the source's motivation is in providing this information." While doing research on the possible correlation between pollution and socioeconomic status of specific geographical areas, Aaron discovered that a United Council of Churches study found that inordinate numbers of people of color reside in or near polluted areas. The study was well designed and reliably conducted, and the council had nothing to gain by publishing this information. It was a surprising source for compelling, valid information.

Aaron advises researchers to "try to get a feel for your sources, and always talk to the opposite side and see what their arguments and statistics are." It is necessary, she says, to "always hear what the other side has to say." Be an intelligent consumer of conflicting data. "Ask where numbers come from, how they are tabulated. Question the origin and method of compiling statistics." She remembers getting very specific data about automobile tire wear from the National Tire Dealers and Retreaders Association. That group polled its members to get statistics, and accuracy was very important to them. "You never really know that your sources are accurate," Aaron concedes, "but you eventually learn who to trust."

The *Encyclopedia of Associations* is a source Aaron depends on nearly every day. "You can't believe the associations that are out there, and they know a lot of stuff." Aaron is most enthusiastic when talking about her primary research. "There's a whole world of information, and a lot of associations don't get that many calls. They are often happy to talk, send literature, make referrals." The best part of original research, she says, is getting to know people. "It's always wonderful to meet people and make personal contacts." People in public affairs offices are among her most useful, knowledgeable contacts. When talking to others, she advises, "listen for names that keep coming up. Those are the next people you need to call. Keep narrowing your research down to individuals. When you get to someone directly involved with your topic, then you know you're getting somewhere."

Knowing your audience is crucial in determining which information will be useful in the finished product. A lot of researchers think very complex information will be the most impressive, but, Aaron warns, if it is too detailed or specialized, it may just confuse the audience. "Once you get into statistics," she explains, "they're either incredibly easy or very difficult." For example, once she needed to know how popular assisted reproduction is in this country. She called an agency that faxed elementary statistics on in-vitro fertilization in the United States to her immediately. Another time, when she was researching a story on body image, Aaron tried to "get a grip on the numbers of images of women in the media and their effect on female psyches." She telephoned "a bunch of doctors" who said the media were "a significant influence," but she wanted statistics to back that up. She hoped to find someone who had measured the effect of fashion magazines on teenage girls, but "there was no easy statistic on that." Instead she found that scientific studies tend to be too elaborate for quick reporting. The "complex measures of response among studied groups of girls who read fashion magazines weekly, and so forth, got too complicated to report in a broadcast news segment." So, Aaron tried another angle. She had heard that *Playboy* centerfold models had gotten thinner over the decades. She wanted to find a concrete number to report, like "'the average weight of centerfolds has dropped seven pounds in the last decade,'" but the statistics she was able to obtain were "too precise for the audience. A lot of scientific research is just too detailed for viewers." There is no time on a news show to teach the audience how to interpret the results of complex data.

Producing segments for a daily news show means taking on new assignments nearly every day. "Every morning, we come up with ideas for that day's show," Aaron explains. "The long-form stories, the ones I often work on, run as many as three minutes of air time" (the average television news story is one and a half minutes long), "so my assignments are often for as much as a week hence." The longest features take three weeks to produce; the shortest are done in one day; and the average long-form news story merits about two weeks of preparation time from inception to air time. "I once did a story on environmental racism that took a month," Aaron recalls. "The more subtle it is, the longer it takes. If you have a thesis to prove, you need a lot more research. If the point of the story is self-evident, such as 'There has been an earthquake in Kobi,' that is just facts. You go right out and cover it."

The maximum number of researchers working on a single story is usually three. Aaron always begins with "a review of what has already been written on the topic." Every story has a reference librarian, but that person comes in and goes out; he or she does not stay involved with the whole research process. Aaron is sometimes assisted by another researcher, but that depends on the amount of time she has to pull the story together. "The faster the turnaround time, the more of us are put to work on the story," she explains. "At the top of the pole is the correspondent," the person who will actually report the story on television. "In theory, the correspondents are supposed to do research, but they actually do very little. On magazine-type shows, they don't do their own research. On a breaking, live news story, such as street battles in Rwanda, the correspondent is doing research because it's all primary information, and the correspondent is at the source."

Although citing specific sources is infrequently done in television news broadcasts, Aaron is careful to keep track of the sources she uses in her work. "When I do research," she explains, "I turn over the page and write down the phone number, person, title, extension number." There is no "Works Cited" list at the end of the news, but occasionally researchers need to "retrace their steps." Aaron is ever-mindful that she "may need that contact again someday."

When Aaron has finished her work, including researching the topic and filming it, the correspondent writes a story, and she and the correspondent "hash it out." Their work is submitted to Aaron's immediate supervisor, who is responsible for editing all long-form stories. After he has approved the piece, it goes to the executive producer. "The executive producer," she explains, "is responsible for pulling the whole news show together; that person is the chief." At NBC, he is just under the anchor and the president of the news division. The anchor always has the final say about the contents of the show, however. Brokaw rarely looks at scripts in progress, but he often sits in on run-down meetings and helps to guide each show as it shapes up every day.

At 2:30 each weekday afternoon, the news staff conducts its run-down meeting. Aaron summarizes that as "a lot of tinkering going on." The lead story is chosen during the run-down, but it may be changed several times throughout the afternoon. "If an earthquake happens at 5:00, we're going to lead with that," she explains. "Any story can die, be killed in the last minutes. It's difficult logistically to change the show after 4:00, but we do it all the time. It's not fun. It's always a shame to write stories and decide at 6:00 that we won't need them, and that happens very frequently." News is extremely current or topical, and stories that are stricken from the lineup may never get air time. Each show is exactly twenty-eight minutes and twenty-five seconds long.

A colleague barges into Aaron's office to ask whether she will produce a story for the next day's broadcast. She says she is already working on the

"America Up Close" segment, due in two days. Her counterpart suggests moving that to another date so that she will be free to produce the story he's proposing. She runs down her progress on the "America Up Close" project: Brokaw has already interviewed its subject, and a camera person and correspondent are shadowing the subject in a foreign country today. She concludes, however, by conceding that if she is reassigned, she will get to work immediately on the story due tomorrow.

As her colleague retreats, Aaron offers some advice to students interested in entering her profession. "Study politics, history, or literature. You'll need that information when you're thirty, and it's hard to make up for that kind of knowledge gap. I studied film, and I watched many, many movies. I know what's visual, what works, what is good storytelling. Be willing to move around. There are television stations all over the country. Sarah James is one of our best correspondents, and she started out as a reporter in Tupelo, Mississippi." Aaron advises becoming well-grounded in the liberal arts, and she is not the first in her profession to suggest that. Above the Fifth Avenue entrance to 30 Rockefeller Plaza, the door through which Aaron must pass every day, there is an art-deco inscription that reads *Wisdom and knowledge shall be the stability of thy times.*

Suggested Writing Assignments

1. Write an essay describing a typical day in your life as a college student. What plans or promises do you make for yourself at the start of each day? How do you decide what is absolutely necessary to accomplish? How do you accomplish all of the tasks necessary to complete each day? How do you revise your plans as the day progresses? What happens to the things you must forgo each day?

2. Go to a library and examine *The Encyclopedia of Associations,* which Aaron recommends, or find a similar source in the reference section. Look up an association that is concerned with a topic about which you know something (a hobby, a subject related to your college major, and so on), and write to that organization, requesting general information.

3. Write a piece of investigative journalism yourself. For example, you might discover whether the cafeteria where you eat lunch donates surplus foodstuffs to a local soup kitchen or whether there are charitable organizations that could make use of food it routinely discards. Or, you might follow your tuition dollars through the system, noting what percentage goes to each department and program. Write your findings up as an article for the campus newspaper.

Chapter Four

Gathering Information from Government Offices, Museums and Other Archives, and Corporations and Associations

You might not think of the textbooks you own as a personal "library," but your own system of buying and selling back or choosing to retain college textbooks amounts to a personal acquisitions plan. You might also collect audio CDs or cassette tapes. Whether you simply buy the music you like or try to get every recording ever issued by a select group of bands, you are amassing a collection that adheres to specific selection criteria. When you start thinking about it, you will realize that you collect several things almost accidentally: T-shirts, pencils, old letters, photographs of friends, ticket stubs, concert or theater programs, magazines, coffee mugs, and so on. Perhaps you also make a concerted effort to accrue items that are highly regarded as "collectible," such as antiques, art objects, coins, stamps, obsolete computer or stereo equipment, or more specialized artifacts related to a hobby or career goal.

Ask yourself why you collect the things you do. Undoubtedly, some of the stuff you collect is practical. You collect books and pencils and a whole variety of other student-related paraphernalia because they are useful and even necessary to your work. Some of it provides a personal historical record. You can't use a torn ticket stub again, but you want it to remind yourself of a special event. You know essentially what old letters say, but if you ever reread them, you will remember how you felt at the time you first received them. Sometimes a treasured letter or snapshot is the only thing we have by which to remember someone special. Some collections represent continuity, such as a series of objects received as birthday or anniversary gifts. Maybe you like the challenge of gathering a complete set of something, such as a press pass from every venue on a Grateful Dead tour. You might collect things simply to show the differences between them:

chess sets from around the world, radios before and after the invention of transistors, and so on.

You might also collect some things because they are useful to your friends. Perhaps you've kept maps and guidebooks to loan to friends taking trips to places you've visited. Maybe you enjoy letting others borrow CDs and tapes that are hard to find. Perhaps you keep a couple of spare tennis racquets, a stockpile of Frisbees, some old hockey sticks, or an extra baseball glove around in case someone wants to borrow it.

Some collections may be worth keeping around because they may prove to be valuable some day. We've all heard stories of rookie baseball cards that sell for thousands of dollars when the player they feature is elected to the Hall of Fame. As hard as it is for those of us who remember scratching and warping to believe it, vinyl records have begun to appreciate in value again, after being rendered worthless by the widespread preference for CDs.

The same needs and purposes that guide the collecting you do also influence the creation of museums and archives. Human beings have a compulsion to hoard things for functional, aesthetic, and instructional reasons. The range of collections open to the public is mind-boggling. Archives in the United States range from the various presidential libraries to the many Christian Science reading rooms scattered across the country. Museums commemorate specific periods or practitioners in art or national or international movements over the course of history. They re-create the private lives of people at all levels of society and during all periods of history. They showcase technological achievements in aerospace, agriculture, building trades, business, mining, radio, warfare, and whaling, to name just a few. You probably think of museums as vacation destinations or tourist attractions, so it might surprise you to learn that the official mission of most museums and archives is educational. Everything from the original, signed copy of the Declaration of Independence to the Smithsonian Institution's display of a script and costumes from the set of *The Wizard of Oz* is put before the public as a learning experience.

As you add your thoughts about museums and archives to what you know about libraries and even the World Wide Web, it may seem to you that there is a fine line distinguishing these cultural institutions from one another. Consider, too, that there are "hands-on" museums that allow visitors to interact with exhibits, as well as "closed-stack" and noncirculating libraries that do not allow patrons to physically browse through their collections or remove materials from their premises, and that there are commercial Web sites that actively seek "hits," as well as password-protected sites that bar examination by unapproved visitors. Begin thinking about publicly held collections of all sorts that are located in your area or that you can travel to, either actually or in cyberspace. How might those holdings be incorporated into your college research projects?

■ Government Publications

Many American libraries have a government publications archive, or collection of documents published by various government agencies. Most government publications are printed by the U.S. Government Printing Office and consist of individual papers, books, or pamphlets. They usually offer more in-depth information than the typical magazine article, and they are almost always more up-to-date and easy to skim than books. You may think that government publications are filled with "fine print" and "legalese," but actually they represent some of the most readable technical information available.

Every government branch and office publishes reports. Agencies whose documents can be found in your library's government publications archives include the Census Bureau, the Defense Department, the Department of Labor, the Federal Bureau of Investigation (FBI), and the Office of the Surgeon General. A government publications archive can supply you with information on the latest inventions or products registered at the Patent and Trademark Office. The National Science Foundation publishes everything from advice on surviving in Antarctica to zoological cloning. Virtually every issue that becomes a current event in the United States is a topic of concern for the U.S. Congress. The same statistics and testimony that inform government policymaking on current issues is available to you through the *Congressional Record* for use in your college research projects. The most reliable and easy-to-use compilation of statistics in print is the *Statistical Abstract of the United States*, published annually by the U.S. Government Printing Office (see Figure 4.1). It contains statistics gleaned from the reports of virtually every federal and federally sponsored agency in the United States. If you want to know the population of a specific city or region according to the latest census, the rate of food consumption worldwide, the average rate of seat-belt law compliance across the nation, or the teenage pregnancy rate by region, race, and educational level, the *Statistical Abstract* can furnish those numbers. Government agencies deal with practically every aspect of life in the modern world.

Evaluating the Information in Government Publications

Think of it this way: the U.S. government is composed of elected representatives and the many officials they appoint. These officeholders have to tell their constituents, the people, what they've been doing with their tax money and in their name. However, like everyone else with access to a printing press, they only have to tell you what they want you to know, from their point of view. Government publications are notorious for their one-sidedness. For instance, if you are writing a paper supporting the legalization of marijuana, government publications may provide an exhaustive list of arguments against your thesis but little or no supporting evidence for your position, because the government is currently against relaxing the marijuana laws. If you are writing a paper in support of speed limits on the U.S. interstate highway system,

No. 729. Children under 6 Years Old Below Poverty Level, by Family Type

and Race: 1992

[Excludes unrelated individuals and foster children. Based on Current Population Survey; see text, sections 1 and 14, and Appendix III. Numbers and percentages may not add due to rounding]

RACE AND FAMILY TYPE	ALL CHILDREN		CHILDREN BELOW POVERTY LEVEL		
	Number (mil.)	Percent distri- bution	Number (mil.)	Percent	Percent distri- bution
All races:					
All family types	23.2	100.0	5.6	24.0	100.0
Married-couple	17.0	73.4	2.2	12.7	38.7
Single-parent \1	6.2	26.6	3.4	55.2	61.3
Mother-only	5.4	23.3	3.2	58.9	57.1
White, non-Hispanic:					
All family types	15.7	100.0	2.3	14.4	100.0
Married-couple	12.9	82.3	1.1	8.4	48.3
Single-parent	2.8	17.6	1.2	42.2	51.7
Mother-only	2.3	14.6	1.1	46.2	47.0
Black, non-Hispanic:					
All family types	3.6	100.0	1.8	50.7	100.0
Married-couple	1.3	34.7	0.2	19.3	13.2
Single-parent	2.3	65.3	1.6	67.5	86.8
Mother-only	2.2	61.3	1.5	69.2	83.6
Hispanic \2:					
All family types	2.9	100.0	1.3	44.0	100.0
Married-couple	2.0	69.1	0.7	34.3	53.9
Single-parent	0.9	30.9	0.6	65.5	46.1
Mother-only	0.8	26.9	0.5	68.6	42.1

\1 Includes father-only, relative-only, and nonrelative-only families.
\2 Persons of Hispanic origin may be of any race.

Source: Susan Einbinder, National Center for Children in Poverty, Columbia University, School of Public Health, New York, NY, unpublished data.

Back | Subject | Next

Figure 4.1 *Statistical Abstract* of the United States 1994.

government publications can provide excellent evidence to back up your assertions, since the government officially favors limiting and monitoring speeds on national highways. U.S. government publications rarely, if ever, comment on or survey religious practices. In general, government publications are highly reliable, prestigious sources to quote in college research projects. However, as with any secondary source, it is wise to remember who is furnishing the information and what their motives might be.

Local and State Government Offices

Public records that are no longer active are usually made available through archives, but current records are available for inspection, too. You just have to go to the government office or agency where they are used and request information or copies of documents. In most cases, you will not be allowed to look at private case files, but general statistics are kept by most government agencies, and they are a matter of public record. City and county records are kept separately in different offices, usually located at city hall and in county buildings. State agencies are usually headquartered in the state capital. You can request information from government offices over the telephone or by mail or fax, but you may want a clerk to help you locate and decipher the records that will be most useful to you, so a visit to the office is preferable.

If your research concerns an issue of local concern, you don't have to settle only for the information reported by major news-gathering organizations; in most cases, pertinent information and statistics are collected by local governments and organizations and are available to you for the asking. If you read your local newspaper, you know that your area's officials are embroiled in controversies and decision-making processes that are not reported in the national or statewide media. You may be interested in a local issue and want to know more about it but have not considered writing a research paper about it because your library does not have much to contribute beyond back issues of the local newspaper. However, issues involving tax dollars, public safety, or public policy must be debated and decided in the open, which means that you can attend city council meetings, county commissioners' meetings, and local forums and hearings to gain information. Check your newspaper or call the county courthouse for a schedule of public meetings. If your community has a public-access television channel or public radio station, it may carry those meetings on the air. The best way to make contacts and to learn who the major players are in local decision-making processes is to attend public meetings, take notes, and talk to people on both sides of issues. If you wait for the newspaper to cover local government action, you will miss out on a lot of the details and most of the fun.

County Clerks   Visiting local government offices for information can be intriguing. For instance, the county clerk's office keeps records from court cases, as well as marriage licenses and some last-will-and-testament documents. Many files from criminal court cases are a matter of public record and are open for your inspection. You may go to the clerk of the court's office and request to see the complete files of any criminal case in the jurisdiction. Such files contain dockets, or complete summaries of the proceedings of the court in each case, including motions filed, witnesses summoned or subpoenaed, and results and verdicts imposed by the courts. Court cases involving juveniles, adoptions, divorce proceedings, and some parts of wills and estates are closed and can be requisitioned only by attorneys for interested parties. Actual transcripts from trials must be obtained from the courts themselves and usually require a judge's permission and a processing fee, but many materials in the clerk of the court's office are available for immediate inspection free of charge.

City or County Recorders   The city or county recorder's office houses abstracts that list a chronological history of ownership for individual parcels of land within its domain. The assessor's office records features of every developed property in the county for tax purposes. It maintains a file containing a detailed description of every building, including the year it was built, the total square footage of the structure, and its plumbing and other amenities, along with a floor plan drawing. One of the most fascinating things available in most assessor's offices is an aerial plat of the vicinity. These large, accurate-to-scale maps or aerial photographs of a region really make zoning come to life. By paging through plats, you can clearly see the boundaries of various neighborhoods, districts, and parks as well as the impact of major highways and industrial regions on the surrounding landscape. Looking at an aerial photograph, in particular, enables you to "tour" huge tracts of land and judge for yourself whether a proposed development would rob the area of woodlands or whether the mayor's proposed enterprise zones adequately encompass an old warehouse district.

The city or county building or planning department keeps statistics on "building starts," or new structures initiated in the district. This information is often used as a local economic indicator, because a high incidence of new building suggests a rise in the local population or new businesses. Planning departments also compile environmental impact statements, which may include measurements of chemical concentrations in soil samples or air pollution statistics.

Assistance Agencies   As you know, many government agencies exist to offer assistance to the people they serve. The county welfare or trustee's office keeps track of living assistance payments, food stamp issuance, and other government financial assistance. Child Protection Services can provide statistics on reports of child abuse or describe the mandated procedures for removing children from abusive homes. State departments of health maintain accurate counts of persons infected with HIV and tuberculosis, compile statistics on teen pregnancy, and can provide information about virtually any other health-related issues pertaining to the citizens of the states they serve. State police track the incidence of arrests for driving under the influence, rates of seat-belt use, trucking violations, and automobile accidents and highway fatalities. This is some of the same information sought by news-gathering agencies, but you don't have to wait for the six o'clock news to get around to airing it.

Many states have numerous agencies that monitor and regulate very specific government-sponsored activities. By simply opening the phone book to its business pages and looking up the name of your state, you may discover an agency such as the Emergency Medical Services Department, which catalogs all of the ambulance runs in the state and classifies them according to type of mishap or illness, severity of injury, incidence of fatality, and so on. Don't overlook the phone book as a valuable research tool. Check your topic against your phone book's list of local and state government agencies for sources of up-to-date regional information relevant to your subject.

■ *Museums*

According to Ann Bay, education director at the Smithsonian Institute, many people think of art history when they ponder museum research, but the Smithsonian and other museums actually offer learning and research opportunities for an infinite variety of subjects. The Smithsonian is the world's largest museum complex, and although it houses such attractions as the Hope Diamond, several complete dinosaur skeletons, Benjamin Franklin's printing press, Eli Whitney's cotton gin, and the Enola Gay (the airplane that dropped the bomb on Hiroshima during World War II), it offers essentially the same services to the public as do smaller museums around the world: exhibits, lectures, demonstrations, films, talks by curators, and classes on special topics. If the Smithsonian is the nation's attic, as it is sometimes called, the nation has drawers, closets, trunks, and armoires absolutely crammed with treasures, with revealing artifacts spread out all over the rest of the country.

A visit to the right museum can enhance almost any research project; re-orient yourself to think of museums as research tools rather than as entertainment. Think about what you can learn from an object, what it reveals about the life and times from which it comes. Who made it? Why was it used? Whose hands would have welded it? Think of yourself as a detective, searching for minute clues about the origin and purpose of objects. To learn from objects, you have to be imaginative and inquisitive. It is harder to guess what sounds the various surfaces on a tribal drum will make than it is to listen to a recording of them, more disturbing to imagine stuffing yourself into the false bottom of a hay wagon or lying motionless between the floor joists in a reconstructed attic than to read about it in a slave narrative, but the discoveries you make from such imaginative processes are your own, a new contribution to your topic.

Imagine examining a tool in a museum. Perhaps it is a hunting weapon made of sticks and flint, a harvesting tool of hammered metal with a hand-carved handle, a pestle and mortar crafted of smooth stones, or maybe even a wooden baseball bat from the nineteenth century. What does it tell you about its user? How tall was he or she? (How long is it?) How strong? (How heavy is it?) How ingenious was its user? (Is it homemade or modified in some way?) Was the owner proud of it? (Does it seem to have been maintained or polished or branded by its owner?) Might it have been handed down through generations? (How worn is it?) What other tools might be used with it?

Consider the Burgess Shale fossil collection at the Smithsonian. During the summer of 1901, a paleontologist named Charles D. Walcott discovered some unusual fossils. He collected thirty-seven thousand slabs of shale during four summers of blasting and chiseling and sent them to the Smithsonian's Museum of Natural History. These date back to the middle of the Cambrian period, which makes them about twice as old as the first dinosaur fossils. Most fossils, as you know, are imprints of the hard parts of organisms, the bones and teeth of fish and animals and the woody parts of plants. It is unusual for fossils to contain imprints of fleshy material, but the fossils in the Burgess Shale collection do, providing the most complete picture available of very early prehistoric life. Would examining such signs of ancient life inform your thoughts about geology, evolution, or protecting the environment? Scientific writer Stephen J. Gould wrote a whole book based on his examination of the Burgess Shale fossil collection, and he compiled most of his research at the museum.

Visiting Local and On-line Museums

Maybe you live a long way from Washington, D.C., or any major population center where grand museums are located, and you don't have the time or the budget to visit one in the course of preparing your English composition research paper. Consider the museums that are located in your area. Might they offer something rare and revealing? You can also "visit" many of the world's major museums on-line on the World Wide Web. Many people who have never been to Paris and cannot speak French have studied exhibits at the Louvre through its Web site. Many museum Web sites allow you to download photographs and text from major exhibits, permitting you to include excellent visual materials in your finished research project.

Corresponding with Museum Guides and Curators

You can also correspond with docents (guides) and curators at many world-class museums. If possible, visit the museum on-line first, or find a magazine article about the museum department you want to access. The more precisely you can direct your correspondence to a person who can answer your questions, the more likely you will be to get a prompt response. If a recent publication mentions a curator by name whom you think could help you, try writing directly to that person, in care of the museum. Many museum Web sites provide links that allow you to post questions on-line. Don't write to a curator just to get a prestigious reference for your Works Cited list, however, and don't give the person receiving your letter the impression that you expect him or her to do your research for you. Ask specific questions that you cannot answer using the secondary sources available in your local library. For example, you don't have to ask a museum curator how much cotton a gin could process in a day; such general information is on file elsewhere. When or where a specific model of cotton gin was manufactured or how portable the devices were are more appropriate questions for a curator, who may have an actual cotton gin on hand. Research the topic as thoroughly as possible before requesting additional information from a museum curator. If you can demonstrate enthusiasm and interest in a topic, curators will be more willing to correspond with you. Research contacts at museums can be invaluable. Orville and Wilbur Wright corresponded with experts at the Smithsonian about aerodynamics while they were building the airplane they would fly at Kitty Hawk.

■ *Archives*

Archives, as you have probably surmised, are repositories for outdated or inactive public documents. The largest collection of this type in the country is at the National Archives, headquartered in Washington, D.C. The National Archives complex houses government documents created from 1774 up to the present day. These include written discourse, photographs, maps, architectural drawings, motion pictures, audiotapes—essentially, anything ever used to document government activities. Some things you wouldn't normally associate with government work are included in the National Archives, such as artwork commissioned by government agencies for placement on posters to advertise war bonds, promote patriotism, or encourage people to recycle. Many of these are the work of famous artists. (Incidentally, the Bureau of Engraving, which is responsible for the printing of stamps and currency, retains its own files, separate from the National Archives.) The most requested item from the National Archives is the often-published photograph of President Richard M. Nixon welcoming Elvis Presley to the White House (see Figure 4.2).

The main building of the National Archives contains twenty-three floors of materials stored in boxes and file cabinets. It is a specially built building, with stack floors (where things are stored) only seven feet high (lower than most ceilings) to facilitate retrieval of objects. The National Archives house some materials in the nine presidential libraries around the country and include regional branches in Boston, New York, Philadelphia, Chicago, Atlanta, Kansas City, Fort Worth, Denver, San Francisco, Los Angeles, and Seattle. Even so, the National Archives do not receive the records of *every* government agency.

Figure 4.2   Nixon and Elvis, December 20, 1970. *Source:* Corbis.

Government records do not come to be housed at the National Archives until they are considered inactive. The archives are a storage and research facility containing the billions of documents deemed "permanently valuable" by the U.S. government. The records of most confidential government proceedings are not opened until they are at least fifty years old, and privileged census documents must remain sealed for seventy years. In general, Senate records may be examined after thirty years, and House documents are available after fifty years. However, some congressional committees release their work immediately after they are finished with it.

Differences Between Library and Archival Research
Wynell Schamel and Paula Poulos, archivists with the National Archives, advise students that there is a big difference between library research and archival research. They explain that whereas the aim of much library research is to narrow one's topic in search of the most applicable sources, a researcher must think more and more broadly, casting wider and wider nets, to find relevant materials in an archive. Archival materials are almost always cataloged by the principle of *provenance*, meaning that they are grouped according to the person or agency from which they originated, instead of by subject. Provenance also dictates that records be kept in the original order in which they were filed. Archivists do not reorganize materials, because the chronology of their filing often demonstrates how a series of events evolved.

To research a topic in the National Archives, you must first ask yourself whether the government might have been involved in whatever you're researching. Next, ask how the government might have contributed to or studied the topic. You must be willing to chase down many references and allusions and follow many dead-end streets. Archival research is not about pinning down information that you know you can find; it involves making original discoveries through ingenuity and intuition.

Genealogical Research in Archives

The largest category of archives users is genealogists. Since archives at all levels may contain birth and death records; military induction and discharge papers; immigration files; titles and deeds to land and other property; church, club, and school membership rosters; or records of financial and business transactions, they often provide proof of the existence and activities of specific ancestors. Alex Haley depended heavily on documents in the National Archives while he was writing *Roots,* and Ken Burns used many archival materials in the production of his PBS series on baseball. The National Archives are used, as you might guess, by government officials who need to check historical records and by lawyers seeking original copies of statutes and exhibits for trials. Journalists visit the main building in Washington, D.C., every day. Media producers depend on the National Archives for historic film footage and photographs. Anyone can take cameras and tape recorders to the National Archives and copy materials housed there.

Requesting Materials from the National Archives

Every U.S. citizen who is sixteen years old or older is welcome to request materials from the National Archives. Actual archived materials do not circulate, but you can obtain copies of most documents and photographs in the collection. You do not have to visit the archives to obtain materials; many requests are handled by mail every day. Remember, however, that much of the contents stored in the archives are unbound pages in boxes that have not been minutely inventoried. Archivists will retrieve the materials you request, but they will not conduct your research for you.

Be as specific as possible when requesting archival material by mail. To learn what items are available and how to request them, look at *The Guide to Federal Records in the National Archives of the United States,* which is probably available at your campus library and is also posted on-line at the National Archives' World Wide Web site (http://www.nara.gov/). For example, if you request military discharge papers, supply the name of the service person whose records you want, the branch of service in which that person served, and the date of his or her discharge. Military records are often sealed because of privacy laws, and you may be asked to prove a familial relationship to the person whose records you request. If you wish to see proceedings from a Supreme Court case housed at the archives, you should supply the record group number of the file, the specific U.S. court where the case was originally heard, the case number and case name, the year the case was heard at the Court, and a brief description of the issue and list of participants involved. Pay close attention to footnotes and Works Cited entries in secondary sources. Many times other writers will have done detective work in the archives that is useful to you. It is usually a good idea, however, to phone the archives to check the completeness and accuracy of your request and to find out if the materials you seek are available.

If you are conducting research on a historical event or issue, whether related to agriculture, diplomacy, immigration, Indian affairs, the law, the military, navigation, trade, transportation, or some other topic, an archive probably has relevant material. As Paula Poulos of the National Archives tells researchers, "Sooner or later, every topic is connected with history." Be resourceful in your quest for archival material locally. Generally, students should exhaust research possibilities in local holdings before contacting the National Archives. The oldest, most fragile items preserved in the National Archives are likely to be available on microfilm at your local library, and copies of frequently requested materials are often accessible through interlibrary loans. You can conduct archival research through local historical museums, courthouse records, minutes of councils and organizations, hospital records, military legions, or cemetery records. You don't have to leave town to accomplish really significant firsthand research.

■ Publicly Held Corporations

By now you have probably realized that the many information repositories and research facilities throughout the country support the ongoing work of academics, writers, journalists, scientists, advertisers, politicians, students, and people in most every occupation. Research is necessary or useful in most human endeavors. The abbreviation by which corporate research and development departments are known, R&D, has become a familiar term. Although most of the news to emerge from R&D laboratories around the world is eventually reported in business periodicals and newspapers, it is possible to get information about the activities of corporations from the businesses themselves.

Corporate Annual Reports
Annual financial-disclosure statements are required of companies whose stock is traded publicly. Usually this information is disseminated among stockholders in the form of annual reports. A corporate annual report may be as simple as a letter to stockholders, detailing the financial status of the company, including its debts, assets, dividends, and losses over the past year. Within large corporations, the annual report is usually a professionally prepared brochure that represents the premiere project of its public relations department. You can request an annual report from any company whose business or products interest you. Companies are not required to provide persons who are not shareholders with this information, but most are pleased to encourage potential stock buyers and will favor your request. A short, polite letter will usually work. Many not-for-profit corporations and

other agencies that depend on grants and gifts for support also publish annual reports, which they will send to persons expressing an interest in receiving them.

Financial disclosures in an annual report must be honest and straightforward, but remember that the accompanying text will still be designed to put the best possible "spin" on those numbers. A company with an enviable success record will project healthy earnings for the future, and those with losses to report usually will promise to reverse that trend through prudent business strategies. A wary reader can nonetheless discern significant information about a company or its products by examining the company's annual report. For instance, most annual reports either explicitly state or subtly embody a corporate philosophy. Notice whether a report mentions environmental issues and politically conscious investment strategies or whether workers' pictures and contributions to the company are prominently featured.

In addition, annual reports often carry stories about successful product lines or new developments or outputs from the previous year. Comparing the annual reports of several product-packaging companies, for example, could help you determine whether glass, metal, cardboard, or plastic is currently in greatest demand and why. Changes in corporate structure and leadership, as well as plant closings and expansions, are often described in annual reports. You can learn a great deal about trends in specific industries by studying the publications of companies directly involved in them. Annual reports often outline a corporation's proposed direction for the future, forecasting continued growth in an area or projected changes in the market. Usually printed on the best paper and featuring the most alluring graphics a company can afford to print, annual reports reveal how a business sees itself and how it wants to be seen by the public.

Advertising and Public Relations Documents

Most corporations are sensitive about their public image. Corporate advertising and public relations departments consciously address this issue every day and welcome the opportunity to provide positive information about their company's products or services. A telephone call to a corporate consumer information hotline or a brief letter to a corporate public relations office will often elicit a packet of informative materials by return mail. In addition, many large corporations maintain a visitor's center at corporate headquarters, and tours of local factories and laboratories can often be arranged by calling the local office or information number published in the phone directory.

Experts of all kinds are employed by businesses, and some will be willing to help students with engaging research projects. For example, companies that import or export goods or parts may employ people who are knowledgeable about other cultures and languages. A corporation's attorneys might be willing to help you interpret an intricate document from the U.S. Patent Office. Local business leaders can be important contacts and resources for research projects. As it is when contacting any expert, it is important that you exhaust secondary sources and determine that your question really requires the attention of a busy businessperson before you ask it. The primary goal of most businesses is to make a profit, but many working people will temporarily put that aside for the few minutes necessary to encourage a student or increase the public's understanding of the issues that concern them.

■ Professional Societies and Trade Associations

You probably have a few groups of acquaintances that spontaneously formed around a common interest: your usual pickup basketball group; fellow Web page writers who share Java applets among themselves; a study group that meets to prepare for exams; car pool members who travel together on vacations; fellow chess players, skateboarders, mystery readers, or ornithologists. You can usually count on such groups to keep you apprised of interesting developments in your common areas of interest. Banding together with people who share your interests gives you someone to talk to, practice skills with, or match wits against. It helps ensure that you will hear the latest news and acquire the latest software, notes from a class session you missed, a book that is out of print, or tickets for performances. You may even pool your money to buy a piece of community equipment or a block of season tickets.

For many of the same reasons, persons with related careers or proponents of a single cause will form a group to advance their beliefs. Professional societies and trade organizations collect information and statistics about a subject so that they can share it among their members or use it to lobby the government to act in favor of their causes. These associations range from professional groups seeking to maintain high standards in the manufacture of specific goods to film and rock star fan clubs. They are an assemblage of experts united around a common cause.

Many popular associations are well known to you already. You have probably read or heard information provided by the National Heart Association, the National Cancer Society, the Planned Parenthood Federation of America, or the Sierra Club. In fact, you have learned to recognize a number of professional societies and trade organizations by abbreviations. See if you can provide the full names of the following nine associations: AAA, AARP, AMA, AMS, CDC, NAACP, NIH, NWF, and SPCA.

If you named the American Automobile Association, the Association of American Retired Persons, the American Medical Association, the American Meteorological Society, the Centers for Disease Control, the National Association for the Advancement of Colored People, the National Institute of Health, the National Wildlife Foundation, and the Society for the Prevention of Cruelty to Animals, you are probably aware of more formal associations than you initially suspected. See how many more you can name.

Your library may have a copy of the *Encyclopedia of Associations*, published by Gale Research and available on CD-ROM and on the Web at http://www.lib.duke.edu/databases/descriptions/encasso.html. This source can help you get in touch with proponents of almost every cause imaginable.

Professional societies and trade organizations have a great deal of credibility. They are frequently quoted by news agencies, and they are the authors of many pamphlets and information sheets distributed by professionals to their patients and clients. The reputations of associations are at stake every time they go public with announcements and statistics; however, they may be biased by their commitment to their cause. Always consider who is providing the information you receive from secondary sources. Ask yourself what their motive is in getting these facts before the public, and try to balance the information they provide with information from competing organizations. It may be true that numbers don't lie, but they can be reported in ways that are intentionally misleading.

The final judgment about what to include in your own work is always yours to make. Read and listen judiciously, even skeptically, and refuse information that does not ring true to you.

■ Summing Up

Useful research documents and objects can be found in any town, city, county, or state. Libraries are a readily apparent source of secondary research materials, but when you start thinking about it, you will realize that many local museums, government agencies, and businesses preserve important materials and provide access to them. Research projects with a regional focus, such as a paper on whether or not mandatory recycling would work in the town where you live, depend heavily on sleuthing beyond the library. Any project, however, can be enhanced with information from sources other than libraries, and imaginative use of such information can help you generate primary research and original examples. By going directly to the organizations where statistics and reports are compiled and used, you can include more up-to-date facts and cite more authoritative sources in your work.

Most of the articles, essays, books, and newspaper columns on file in libraries were written by people with the same access to primary data that you have. You do not have to settle for what writers before you have deemed noteworthy. Materials from local government offices, archives, corporate headquarters, professional societies, and trade associations can provide ready answers to many of your research questions. Maps, planning documents, pictures, minutes from meetings, court records, accident reports, and birth, marriage, and death certificates are just some of the things available for your inspection locally. If you seek out such documents, you will have more original information in your own reports, and you will probably learn the answers to some questions you had not even thought to ask.

Local and national organizations can also provide advice and expert opinions on issues related to the subject you are researching. A trip to a local business or municipal office can yield helpful interviews, consultation with legal and medical experts, and assistance in deciphering complex documents. Government, trade, and civic associations exist to serve the public and advance the causes they represent. Find out how you can incorporate the holdings of such resources in your work.

Exercises: Sources and Strategies

1. Go to a local museum, antique store, or city park containing historic objects. Carefully describe one item displayed there. What questions can you ask about it that will help you understand its purpose or the people or culture that created or used it?

2. Attend a local government or association meeting (for example, a city council, zoning commission, or student association meeting), and keep your own informal minutes of the proceedings. (Minutes are really just an outline of the activities, motions, and votes that occur at the meeting.) Which of the board members impresses you most favorably? Why? Which of the issues addressed at the meeting do you find most interesting?

3. Borrow a corporate annual report from a library or shareholder, request one directly from a corporate public relations office, or visit the World Wide Web site posted by a large corporation. Carefully read the information you find, and determine what goods or services the corporation produces, whether the business showed a profit in the last year, and whether you would like to invest in or work for that company.

Writing to Know

Take a stand on a public issue. Consult your newspaper or go to a coffee shop and ask some patrons there what controversies divide local citizens. Issues such as proposed annexations of neighborhoods by the city, construction of new municipal facilities, tax abatements, expenditures for street repairs, new government regulations, or propositions for the next election ballot are likely to dominate many communities' local agendas. Visit the sites concerned (neighborhoods, schools, urban enterprise zones, or government offices) and learn as much as you can about the issue. Read newspaper articles and editorials (especially letters to the editor) expressing differing opinions about the issue. Write a letter to the editor expressing your opinion about the problem or suggesting a compromise that could resolve the issue. Support your suggestions with references to your own experiences.

A narrative approach seemed the best choice for this profile, to involve readers and to get them thinking about museum exhibitions they have seen. Telling stories made it easy to work in the observations of the schoolchildren and the father and son that the interviewer glimpsed before Mr. Melder appeared. It also provided a good vehicle for making personal observations about Mr. Melder, his office, and the museum in general. Finally, it provided a way to tell the story of the director's interruption and his disagreement with Mr. Melder from purely an observer's point of view.

Notice, though, that this is almost as much a piece about the narrator as it is about the subject of the profile. Interview questions are sometimes reported in this text, so that both sides of the conversation are included.

Keith Melder

Curator of Presidential Memorabilia, *Smithsonian Institution*

Maybe you are the kind of museum goer who sees everything, the sort of person who lingers over each exhibit, who reads all the information displayed for each piece. Maybe you rent a tour on audiocassette and follow its directions, pausing in front of every object and observing the details discussed by the voice in your ear. Perhaps you are even the sort of person who pays attention to museum schedules, who stands at the information desk and waits to be part of a guided tour narrated by a knowledgeable docent who answers your thought-provoking questions about the exhibition. If you are like that, I wish I was more like you.

I have a short attention span when it comes to displayed objects. Assemble a museum full of precious artifacts, and I will walk briskly past them, focusing on large, bright-colored, famous, or personally relevant bits. I am forever wandering away from friends in museums, and I have the irritating habit of circling back to tell them what intrigues lie ahead. My patient fellows are always describing later, over dinner or during the cab ride home, the marvelous things my cursory observance missed.

Because I reduce the contents of museums to a choice few exceptional objects, I often want to return to visit my favorite icons. At the National Museum of Space and Aeronautics, I keep a fairly regular visitation schedule with Charles Lindbergh's plane, *The Spirit of St. Louis*. At the Art Institute in Chicago, I go directly to the reconstructed stock exchange trading floor. For the same reasons, I always seek out the Japanese tea house ensconced inside the Metropolitan Museum of Art. At the San Diego Zoo, I beat a quick trail to the polar bears' habitat. These exhibits are like friends. If I visit an acquaintance living in an apartment, what business have I with the other residents of the same building? That is how I feel about most of the contents of most of the museums I have visited—that I am glad they are home when their friends come to call, but my brief sojourn must be spent ministering to and learning from the objects of my own affections.

The Smithsonian Institution's National Museum of American History is home to many cherished friends of mine. I have been visiting them regularly for about twenty years, as often as business, lobbying, or vacations take me to Washington, D.C. One day last spring, I decided to pay a visit to a human being who works at the Smithsonian. Mr. Keith Melder is the curator of presidential memorabilia at the National Museum of American History. Stored adjacent to his office are Abraham Lincoln's signature top hat and Thomas Jefferson's desk. He is the man who requested and received the saxophone President Bill Clinton played while he was a member of the high school band in Little Rock, Arkansas. Mr. Melder is as interesting as the stuff he collects, authenticates, catalogs, and exhibits.

Keith Melder is a portly man, probably in his late fifties. His pure white hair and medium-length white beard make him look exactly as a mutual acquaintance described him to me, "like Santa Claus." He is shy, but not reticent; he likes to talk about his work. When we meet for the first time near the visitor's desk in the museum, I tell him about the Alabama schoolchildren I have just encountered outside. Their teacher, attempting to corral her charges, kept asking, "Children, what do you remember about the Hope Diamond?" Finally one boy, perhaps a fourth grader, raised his hand exuberantly. "What do your remember, Charles?" the teacher asked.

"Since when did cops start riding Harleys?" young Charles asked incredulously, pointing to a traffic policeman dismounting from his Harley-Davidson motorcycle.

Melder laughed. "I suppose that's what he'll remember about the Hope Diamond, too," he added with a sigh. Encouraged, I tell Mr. Melder about another overheard comment. Minutes earlier I had run upstairs to visit the ruby slippers worn by Judy Garland in the movie *The Wizard of Oz*. While I stood transfixed in front of the glass case where they are kept, a man and his very small son crowded in front of me. "Look," said the proud father, "that scarecrow costume was worn by Ray Bolger, and he was born in Dorchester, Massachusetts, same as you! That could be you someday!" Melder and I both shake our heads. It's hard to predict what people will take from a museum exhibit. He says, "all information is received subjectively." We have little control over what others perceive. I think of my own museum-galloping tendencies and have to agree.

Melder explains that exhibits always start with a theme, an idea that someone wants to communicate. He chooses words carefully, like a person who spends a lot of time alone, not so much with his own *thoughts*, in a dreamy reverie, but with his own *ideas*. He appears to be constantly processing millions of clues from history. I remind him that for most museumgoers, it is the objects displayed that form the nucleus of an exhibit. "Exhibits are often organized around three-dimensional things," he concedes, "but themes are of primary importance. Covering the subject adequately is our main objective.

Each exhibit makes an argument to the visitors; objects are simply illustrative of those arguments."

When I asked Mr. Melder to describe a typical day at work, he dismissed my question. "No such thing," he chuckled. However, he did agree to describe the process by which a museum exhibition is conceived and eventually presented. Creating an exhibit involves conceptualizing the subject, finding a specific idea to explore, developing themes, choosing artifacts and visual evidence, and writing a script. An exhibit script usually includes labels, notations describing visual objects, captions for graphics and photographs, sources for cited information, and a complete plan for the exhibit.

Because museums are educational institutions, it is important that their information be comprehensive and up-to-date. A curator working on an exhibit must review a wide range of sources to know the latest thinking about a given subject. He says it is important to "read other critics"—and not just those who agree with you. Melder also relies on newspapers and rare documents. "Personal papers, diaries, and government records contain valuable information. . . . Don't be averse to dealing with artifacts which are not conventionally treated as evidence by historians," he advises. "You get a lot of ideas from asking questions of objects." (For example, What was the function of this? Why was this made in this way? Who would have used a thing like this?) Campaign materials, for instance, reveal a lot about the politics of their time, just in the way party symbols are incorporated. "There is repetition of archetypal ideals; our national mythology contains the idea that everyone has a chance to do anything, even become president. That is reflected in the symbols used in printed campaign literature, log cabins and that sort of thing." Everyday objects related to a research topic may yield a great deal of speculation, leading to some original discoveries.

Melder writes all of his notes in longhand, using separate sheets of paper for each idea. Sometimes he photocopies documents and highlights pertinent information. Keeping track of sources is important in his work. "Documentation is important to me as a curator," he reasons. "I need to know where I got information so I can include that in the exhibit. It is important to tell people what your facts are based upon, so they can weigh their value. It is part of creating the whole argument of an exhibition; reputable sources lend credence to your interpretation."

Although a curator is ultimately responsible for the content of an exhibition, more than half a dozen personnel might contribute their efforts to a single presentation. Because the Smithsonian is "an organization of great complexity," it retains "many specialists who do parts of the project." Melder explains that his work often involves collaborating with editors, exhibit planners, production crews who construct exhibits, and film and audiovisual staff who prepare an introductory movie or film clip display. A finished exhibition script is first reviewed internally by Melder's supervisors; then scripts are often sent out to consultants for review. They will be revised until the experts are satisfied with it.

Mounting an exhibition is a slow process. It may take from three to five years to write and revise a script. It usually takes an additional year to physically construct the exhibit. If a museum takes on a particularly controversial topic, getting that exhibit to the public can take much longer, especially if the experts argue over matters of interpretation or it is difficult to obtain funding. Melder advises researchers to take the time necessary to do the job right. "Don't jump to conclusions," he grumbles; "try not to be caught with your pants down." He cautions that "mistakes are embarrassing" and confesses that he's made errors, ranging from getting a date wrong or spelling a name wrong all the way up to presenting a skewed interpretation of history. "When you are caught in a mistake," he laments, "it challenges your credibility as a scholar, a critic, and a writer."

Suddenly one of the museum's directors bursts through the closed door. He needs an immediate answer: will Melder release Lincoln's top hat or Jefferson's desk for a traveling exhibition? Slowly, Melder responds: "both are priceless and irreplaceable; those are two big problems." The director counters that they are important American symbols. Melder argues that they could be destroyed: "The environmental conditions of display would be detrimental to either." The director waits anxiously. We all look around the office. It is a long, narrow, windowless configuration. Maybe that is why a tourist-trap plate imploring "God Bless our Trailer Home" and emblazoned with the likeness of an Airstream has been nailed to one of the short walls. I imagine Melder wearing the Burberry coat that hangs from a peg on the wall. It is easier to picture him in the Black Watch plaid cap hanging above it. Melder's eyes glance around the office, too. There are two desks, a round table about four feet in diameter, and bookshelves stretched all along the enormous back wall. Occasional typing tables and vertical surfaces catch documents (most of them in Melder's firm handwriting), resource materials, and mail. Mail seems to be overflowing everywhere in the room. On the desk beside me is a letter with Oliver North's return address neatly lettered in the upper corner. At length, Melder agrees to let Jefferson's writing table go, but only if no substitute can be made.

When the director leaves, Melder is visibly deflated. So, I ask him to tell me about his best work to date. He beams. "The most satisfying exhibition I've done was for the Essex Institute in Salem, Massachusetts. It was called *Life and Times in Shoe City*. It depicted the experience and community of people who worked in the shoe industry." Melder is fond of that project because he "played a key role in researching it" and because "the final project was well done." Melder explains that "the project was small enough to really grapple with it. Yet it was well defined and very manageable. We didn't leave stones unturned in that one," he remembers.

Before leaving this hidden den on the third floor of the National Museum of American History—a space I'd never guessed existed during previous visits to the museum—I asked Melder what advice he would give to students who hope to work as historians or curators. "Read," he said simply. "Do lots of reading, and find something that you're really interested in. Make your life fascinating to you." Sitting at his nearly buried desk, Melder appeared to be a man steeped in work that he loves.

I realized as I walked briskly through the three floors of the museum to make my exit that I had closely examined everything available to me in Melder's office, and I thought ruefully that perhaps I'd learned amid that plethora of interesting stuff to give more attention to things. But as I hurried past Edith and Archie's chairs from the set of *All in the Family*, a steam engine, and the museum's famous collection of dresses owned by first ladies, I laughed at myself. "Nope," I said out loud to no one in particular, unless it was the Virginia schoolchildren collected on the steps, their teacher trying to focus their attention on the colorful banners overhead.

Suggested Writing Assignments

1. Put yourself in a position to overhear a brief (not confidential) conversation, and write a brief anecdote around that dialogue. Where were you? What did the speakers look like? What were they doing? Was something they said particularly ironic, incongruous, or surprising?

2. Tell the story of an experience you've had. Write about taking a lesson (flying, skydiving, playing the piano, ballroom dancing) or about visiting an impressive site (a power plant, a waterfall, a grand government building). What happened? What did you learn about yourself as a result of this experience?

3. Visit a museum or a museum Web site and write a review of an exhibit you see there. What kinds of sources were used to compile the information presented? What sorts of objects are displayed? What is the theme of the exhibition? What arguments is it making? Do you agree with them?

May 18

Review

Literature Revi
March 12

Chapter Five

Conducting Interviews

Think about any person from history whom you wish you could talk to. Maybe you want to show George Washington a dollar bill or chauffeur Henry Ford around in your car. Perhaps you'd like to listen to Socrates or Buddha teach or go into battle with Attila the Hun, Constantine, Napoleon, or Custer. Would you stand in waiting for Charlemagne, carry the pack of Marco Polo, or raise sails for Columbus? What if you could ask Sappho, Virginia Woolf, and Sojourner Truth about politics and the women's movement? Does one of your own ancestors fascinate you? Are there people whose lives intersected with yours that you did not question when you could have? When you think about all the great topics you could discuss with those you cannot contact, it makes every living person seem relatively easy to approach.

As a student, you have a tremendous advantage in terms of getting people to talk to you. Most everyone feels good about helping students with their homework, and many people want to be regarded as mentors, as people willing to share the benefit of their experience with others. People who would not take a call from a newspaper reporter or a freelance writer will talk to you. When you want to interview someone for a research project, always start with big dreams. Ordinary students at average universities have interviewed authorities and celebrities alike. The assignment to incorporate an interview into your research may result in a once-in-a-lifetime opportunity to talk with a sports or entertainment star, a powerful politician or businessperson, or someone you have long admired. Take stock of the interests and contacts you have. Who do you really want to talk with? You may be brushed off or ignored or flatly turned down by your first choice, but you never know until you try. Researchers who conduct interviews for a living know that every day the riches of the information world are handed out to those who show up to collect them. Ask, and you may be surprised at the generosity of the response you receive.

■ Finding People to Interview

If you want to write a profile of a person or learn about a specific topic, think about those who are renowned in the fields you know best. Who is an important figure in a field you are considering majoring in at college? Who do you admire because of a personal interest or hobby? Often people who are "famous" in small circles make the best subjects for interviewing. For example, a local performer or businessperson may be willing to spend more time and reveal more "inside" information than will someone who does not share a hometown connection with you. A politician from the state or town where you are a registered voter is more likely to make a friendly response to your request for an interview than is an officeholder in another region, where you are not a constituent. If you can demonstrate an earnest interest and a reasonable amount of background knowledge about a subject that a recognized authority is passionate about, you can often convince that person to grant you an interview.

Consider the "connections" you have. Maybe someone you met briefly told you to call if he or she could help you. Maybe someone you know is acquainted with an authority you would like to speak with and would be willing to make the contact for you or let you use his or her name in attempting to reach that person yourself. Students have used such tenuous connections as having a cousin who cleans someone's pool or a friend who cuts someone's lawn as a method of getting in touch with people they hope to interview. Don't use just any contact simply because you have it, but if you have a sincere interest in talking to a particular person and a legitimate research project to which that conversation would contribute, try to arrange for an interview. You don't necessarily have to have an inside contact to get an interview with a heavy hitter. If you have the business phone number or e-mail address of a person you want to interview, you can make a request yourself. Don't forget that your final project won't be graded based on the notoriety of your sources but on the quality of the information you ascertain and the style with which you present it.

Although many professionals will be happy to help a student in need, people whose living depends on their public persona or on the image they project in professional interviews might not be eager to talk to a student writing a research paper. For example, movie stars, sports heroes, national news makers, recording artists, television personalities, and CEOs of huge corporations are probably not going to spend their time or risk their image on a college English essay. They and their public relations staff very carefully release information about them through recognized channels; they don't want to be caught off guard by a disarmingly naive or friendly student interviewer. They also don't want to risk giving their well-honed messages to an inexperienced reporter. When celebrities speak to the press, it is usually a carefully coached and orchestrated event, designed to enhance the subject's image through the broadest media available. If you think that superstars won't talk to you because you are not important, that is only half the story. They also won't talk to you because every interview is important.

An interview is not merely a conversation held at an agreed-upon time and place. It involves an understanding between two individuals: one may ask any manner of questions (within reason), and the other is expected to answer them unless they are unethical or biased or incriminating. For example, if you were to bump into a baseball player on the street outside a stadium, you might ask for an autograph or ask him to describe a great moment from his career, but it would almost certainly seem rude to demand that he tell you his salary. If you were interviewing that player about salaries in the National League, however, you would expect to ask such a question, and he would expect to answer it. Similarly, you would not expect a doctor to tell you during an office visit for a sore throat whether he or she knows anyone who has committed insurance fraud, but if you were interviewing that physician and had made it clear that you were researching problems with the current health care situation in the United States, both of you would expect that topic to be brought up. Interviews are investigations.

Most of the interviews you see on television, hear on the radio, or read in magazines and newspapers are heavily edited versions of the actual meeting that took place between the researcher and the subject. This can make interviewing look deceptively simple or unduly adversarial. In reality, interviews are usually a bit awkward at first and often contain tangents and irrelevant comments and information, but by the time the public hears or reads them, they appear to consist wholly of cogent exchanges and repartee. Few interviews take on the character of "investigative reporting" as portrayed by the media. Student research projects are usually friendly and nonconfrontational. Most research has more to gain from an amicable exchange of information, anyway, than it does from ambushing the interviewee. Try to discover information honestly, and don't attempt to elicit incriminating confessions from a research subject. Don't expect to turn into Barbara Walters when you start interviewing. If you can simply hold up your end of a conversation, even by just nodding and looking interested, you can conduct a successful interview.

■ Requesting Interviews

It is usually difficult to introduce oneself to strangers. During the nineteenth century, young people or newcomers to a city were introduced to influential citizens through letters from family and friends. Right now, that probably sounds like a pretty good idea to you. Wouldn't it be nice to have a wealthy uncle or famous second cousin present you to whomever you would like to meet and interview? Fortunately, the telephone has become popular since then, and although that means you may halt and stutter a bit in the process, it is perfectly acceptable for you to make yourself and your request known to your subject with a phone call. You probably don't have time to exchange the number of letters necessary to schedule an interview in such an old-fashioned manner, anyway. With a quick exchange of phone calls or e-mail, you can often schedule an interview in a matter of minutes or hours.

Try to contact the person you hope to interview at his or her office or business address. If you telephone, you should expect that a receptionist or administrative assistant will take your call. Whether you phone or e-mail, be direct. Tell who you are—that you are a student conducting research for a college course and would like to make an appointment to interview the subject in person. Usually, the person you want to interview will decide whether to talk to you. So if you telephone, you might ask for a time when you could call back and make your request personally. It is a good idea to ask the name of the person with whom you have spoken initially, so that you can ask for him or her again when you call back. That saves you from having to start over and reestablish your identity and purpose with each call, and it also begins to form a relationship between yourself and the person who may ultimately make your request heard. Remember that many people who answer the telephone for others are charged with the duty of screening calls to preserve uninterrupted work time for their supervisors. You may have to convince the person who answers the phone that you are sincere and prepared and that your request is worthwhile. Be polite. You may be asking for a considerable amount of that person's time, which, depending on the position he or she holds, may equal a substantial amount of money.

Be sure to explain the purpose of the interview. Outline your research assignment for your potential subject, and quickly describe the focus of your inquiry. If you give the person an idea of what you want to talk about, he or she can begin thinking about the subject before your appointment. Sometimes, interviewees will request a copy of your questions beforehand. Don't hesitate to agree to send four or five core questions. Similarly, ask if there is any reading material or other secondary sources he or she would suggest you examine before your meeting. Experts in most fields have been asked this question before, and they frequently can make excellent recommendations that will save you a lot of time in the library.

Briefly explain your time constraints with the assignment. You should plan to complete your interviews a few days before your paper is due, at least. Before making contact with your subject, figure out a few dates and times when you will be free, to offer as possible meeting times. Remember to include plenty of travel time for yourself, and if possible, some time immediately following the interview to collect your thoughts and observations in private. The length of time you request depends on your needs. If you just want your subject to clarify something you have read, fifteen minutes may be adequate; however, it is advisable to request thirty minutes or an hour, especially if you are writing a profile of the person you will be meeting. In fact, if you plan to write an in-depth profile of your subject, you might want to ask if you can "shadow" him or her on the job for several hours before or after the interview. Determine how much time you need, but try to let the interviewee choose the time and place for the meeting, if possible. You want him or her to be relaxed and well prepared for your questions. Also, you will learn more about the person if he or she selects the site for your meeting. You may be invited to visit the person's office or be asked to meet at a favorite lunch spot. Anything you can observe about your subject may be useful to your research, and being invited into his or her "territory" might provide some valuable insights about your subject's character or interests.

Although it is preferable to meet with your interviewee face to face, distance or time constraints may make that impossible or impractical. Be prepared to suggest a telephone interview or e-mail exchange if necessary, but if you plan on asking more than two questions or expect detailed or specific answers, avoid proceeding with the interview during your initial contact. Both you and your subject could use time to prepare for a formal interview, even if it must be conducted over the phone or the Internet.

■ Preparing Yourself

Try to do as much reading and preliminary research as possible in advance of your interview so that you can maximize the value of your contact with your primary source. You don't want to waste your or your subject's time establishing basic facts that you could have gleaned from an encyclopedia article. Don't ask an expert to provide elementary data. Although it is wise to start scheduling interviews early in your research process, don't plan to conduct them until you have had time to examine secondary sources on the topic. One reason to interview a person is that he or she can respond to the questions left unanswered by the written materials you've reviewed. Researching your topic in advance of the interview will also make you a better listener, as well as a more capable questioner. If, for instance, you are interviewing someone from another part of the world, spend some time with a map or a globe, familiarizing yourself with the terrain and political boundaries of that region. Preparing yourself will make you a more enthusiastic and active listener, and it may inform some follow-up questions or comments that will enhance your credibility. Consider taking a relevant map with you to the interview, so that your interviewee can show you the location of events he or she narrates. If you are there to ask questions about a confusing or difficult secondary source, be sure to take a copy of it with you to the interview. The more you demonstrate that you have been educating yourself about the subject you plan to discuss, the more cooperative your interviewee will be about spending time talking with you.

Whether the focus of your interview will be on the interviewee himself or herself (on his or her life story or personality, for example) or on some subject about which he or she is an expert, you should find out some basic facts beforehand about the person you will be meeting. You should definitely get the correct spelling of his or her name and a current job title. Be aware, for instance, that various government posts carry with them specific forms of address. A U.S. senator is referred to with the title Senator before the name, as in Senator Kennedy, whereas a member of the House of Representatives is called simply Mr. or Ms. A state governor or city mayor may be addressed either as "Your Honor" or with the title Governor or Mayor before the name.

Military personnel use their rank (Lieutenant, Colonel, Sergeant, and so on) as a title.

Depending on the stature and influence of your interviewee, a number of different sources may yield information about him or her. People who have appeared in articles in the *New York Times*, for instance, are indexed in the *New York Times Personal Names Index* (see Figure 5.1), which can be a valuable source for turning up information about people from many walks of life. A business executive may have been profiled in his company's annual report (which you will want to request well in advance of conducting your interview, if possible). Oftentimes, a Web search for a person's name will produce a relevant newspaper or magazine article or even a personal Web page for that person. If you gained access to your interviewee through a mutual friend or other contact, you may want to ask that person what he or she knows about the person you are planning to question.

Obviously, if you are writing a profile of the person you are planning to interview, you will want to discover all you can about that person, including where he or she was reared and educated, some of his or her interests and chief accomplishments, and the kinds of details he or she has told to interviewers in the past. If you are talking with your interviewee to mine his or her expertise in a particular subject, you will want to locate anything he or she has published on that topic and read it thoroughly to avoid asking uninformed questions. Even if your subject's personal history or information never comes up in your conversation, it never hurts to know all you can about the person you will be interviewing. At the least, it can make you less apprehensive as you contemplate the approaching meeting.

■ Compiling Questions

The questions you write for an interview determine the quality of the answers you will get, and the answers you get determine the content of your finished research project. So, although you will be anxiously anticipating the interview as you begin to formulate and develop questions, you must focus on the product you expect to produce as well as the process of information gathering.

Construct Your Questions Around a Core Thesis or Focus

The first thing you must determine is the thesis you hope to explore. At the very least, you must determine the focus of your intended research paper or presentation (see pages 177–120 for an in-depth discussion about determining and developing your thesis). For instance, if you are interviewing a veteran of the Vietnam War but know very few specifics about that period of U.S. history, you should focus on an aspect of that experience that you do understand. It is too much to hope that you can educate yourself completely about such a broad and controversial topic between the time you schedule and conduct the interview, and you cannot reasonably expect your interviewee to

Jordan, June 248

Jordan, June - 1977, 165; 1977, 683; 1979, 679; 1981, 147; (Prof) 1981, 567; 1982, 132; 1983, 662; 1987, 677; 1988, 680
Jordan, Kathy - 1979, 679; 1983, 662; 1984, 663; 1985, 649; 1986, 698
Jordan, Krassimira - 1989, 695; 1989, 859
Jordan, Len B - d 1983, 368; 1983, 662
Jordan, Leonard E - 1982, 502
Jordan, Lewis - 1976, 776; d 1983, 368; 1983, 662
Jordan, Lewis H - 1980, 710; 1984, 663; 1986, 698
Jordan, Linda - 1977, 683
Jordan, Louis - d 1975, 578; d 1975, 1166; 1978, 526
Jordan, Luther - 1983, 662
Jordan, Lynn B (Mrs.) - 1976, 776
Jordan, Mabel L - 1983, 662
Jordan, Marc - 1979, 679
Jordan, Margaret - 1975, 1166; 1977, 683
Jordan, Mark - 1989, 695
Jordan, Martin - (Police Officer) 1987, 677; 1987, 1063
Jordan, Mary - 1976, 1166
Jordan, Maurice -1982, 502; 1982, 643
Jordan, Michael - 1983, 662; 1984, 663; 1985, 649; (Basketball Player) 1986, 698; 1987, 677; 1988, 680; 1989, 695
Jordan, Michael H - 1984, 663; 1986, 698
Jordan, Michael J (Dr) - d 1982, 260
Jordan, Michael L - 1981, 567
Jordan, Millicent Dobbs (Prof) - 1976, 776
Jordan, Milton - 1977, 683
Jordan, Monte - 1978, 526
Jordan, Ned - 1976, 776
Jordan, Neil - 1981, 147
Jordan, Oscar - 1984, 663
Jordan, Pat - 1975, 254; 1975, 1166; 1977, 165; 1977, 683; 1984, 181; 1985, 649; 1986, 698; 1989, 695
Jordan, Paul - 1975, 1166; 1983, 662
Jordan, Paul T (Mayor) - 975, 1166; (Mayor) 1976, 776; (Mayor) 1977, 683; 1980, 710; 1981, 567
Jordan, Philip - (Dr) 1977, 683; 1980, 710
Jordan, Philip Harding Jr (Dr) - 1975, 1166
Jordan, Phillip - 1979, 679
Jordan, Ralph - (Shug) d 1980, 372; 1982, 502
Jordan, Ray - 1975, 1166; 1979, 679
Jordan, Raymond - 1977, 683; 1977, 873
Jordan, Richard - 1976, 776; 1978, 526
Jordan, Richard A - 1975, 1166
Jordan, Richard C - 1975, 1166
Jordan, Richard D - 1976, 996
Jordan, Richard G - 1976, 776
Jordan, Richard J - 1983, 662
Jordan, Richard L - d 1978, 288
Jordan, Ritchie - 1980, 710
Jordan, Ritchie (Mrs) - 1980, 710
Jordan, Robert - 1977, 84; 1977, 683; (Atty) 1977, 683; (Judge) 1977, 683; (Maj) 1983, 662
Jordan, Robert A - 1979, 679
Jordan, Robert B 3d (Sen) - 1978, 526
Jordan, Robert D - d 1979, 363
Jordan, Robert O - 1978, 526; 1979, 679; 1981, 567; 1983, 662
Jordan, Robert P (First Selectman) - 1986, 699
Jordan, Robert W (Justice) 1- 1978, 526
Jordan, Rodney W - 1975, 1166
Jordan, Sally - 1980, 710
Jordan, Sam - 1982, 502
Jordan, Sheila - 1978, 678; 1979, 860; 1980, 899; 1981, 567; 1983, 662; 1983, 850; 1984, 663; 1984, 841; 1985, 649; 1985, 818; 1986, 699; 1986, 885
Jordan, Shelby - 1975, 1166; 1976, 776
Jordan, Shirley - 1977, 683
Jordan, Shirley Yarbrough - d 1985, 361
Jordan, Shug - 1975, 1166
Jordan, Stanley - 1984, 663; 1984, 837; 1987, 677
Jordan, Stanley Marvin - d 1979, 363
Jordan, Susan - 1976, 776; 1977, 683; 1977, 694; 1978, 526
Jordan, Suzanne Britt - 1977, 683; 1979, 679
Jordan, T D - 1892, 600
Jordan, Taft - 1976, 1014
Jordan, Ted - 1977, 683; 1989, 695
Jordan, Terrence - 1982, 502
Jordan, Theresa J (Dr) - 1985, 649
Jordan, Thomas - 1976, 776; (Winery Exec) 1980, 710
Jordan, Thomas F - 1976, 776
Jordan, Thomas J - 1984, 663
Jordan, Tom - 1979, 679; 1980, 710
Jordan, Trehnolm D - 1976, 776
Jordan, Valerie - 1976, 776
Jordan, Vernon E - 1976, 776; 1981, 711; 1984, 817
Jordan, Vernon E Jr - 1975; 1166; 1976, 776; 1977, 220; 1977, 683; 1978, 526; 1979, 679; 1980, 710; 1980, 711; 1980, 872, 1980, 1279; 1981, 567; 1982, 502; 1983, 662; 1984, 663; 1987, 677; 1989, 695
Jordan, W L - 1984, 663
Jordan, Walter H (Dr) - 1977, 683
Jordan, Warren - 1980, 711
Jordan, Wayne - 1975, 1166; d 1979, 363
Jordan, Wilbur K (Dr) - d 1980, 372
Jordan, Wilford W - 1985, 649
Jordan, William A (Dr) - 1975, 1166
Jordan, William B - 1984, 663
Jordan, William B Jr - 1986, 699
Jordan, William H - 1979, 679
Jordan, Wilma - 1982, 502
Jordanova, L J - 1986, 214; 1986, 699
Jorden, William J - 1975, 1166; (Amb) 1976, 776; (Amb) 1978, 526; 1984, 181
Jordheim, Steven - 1984, 663; 1984, 833
Jordon, Daniel B - 1975, 1166
Jordon, Don D - 1988, 680
Jordon, Gerald - 1978, 526
Jordon, William (Dr) - 1975, 1166
Jorge (Singer) - 1976, 1014
Jorge, Blanco, Salvador - (Pres) 1982, 502; (Pres) 1984, 663; 1987, 677; 1988, 680
Jorge, Alberto - 1981, 567
Jorge, Jesus - 1978, 526
Jorge, Paulo (Min) - 1978, 526; 1981, 567; 1982, 502; 1984, 663
Jorgen, Hans - 1986, 878
Jorgen, Robert - (Dir) 1977, 683; 1983, 662; 1984, 663; 1986, 603; 1986, 699
Jorgensen, Albert N (Dr) - 1978, 526
Jorgensen, Albert Nels - d 1978, 288
Jorgensen, Alfred H - 1982, 502
Jorgensen, Anker - 1983, 662
Jorgensen, Anker H - (Premier) 1975, 1166; (Prime Min) 1976, 776; (Prime Min) 1977, 683; (Prime Min) 1978, 526; (Prime Min) 1979, 679; (Prime Min) 1980, 711; (Prime Min) 1981, 567; (Prime Min) 1982, 503
Jorgensen, Anker H (Mrs) - 1979, 679
Jorgensen, Barbara - 1979, 679
Jorgensen, Bill - 1979, 679
Jorgensen, Christine - 1977, 683; d 1989, 375; 1989, 695
Jorgensen, Dan - 1986, 699
Jorgensen, David G - 1982, 503
Jorgensen, Dee (Sheriff) - 1980, 711
Jorgensen, Dick - 1983, 662
Jorgensen, Earle - 1988, 680
Jorgensen, Earle M - 1980, 711
Jorgensen, Eigil (Amb) - 1986, 677
Jorgensen, Glen - d 1979, 363
Jorgensen, Glen E - 1976, 776
Jorgensen, Henryk - 1988, 183
Jorgensen, Herman (Police Inspector) - 1980, 711
Jorgensen, James - 1980, 680
Jorgensen, Janel - 1988, 680
Jorgensen, Jason - 1977, 872

Figure 5.1 *New York Times Personal Names Index*

bring you up to speed on all the issues involved in the war. Choose an aspect of your subject with which you can empathize. You might ask a war veteran about being drafted or about his or her decision to enter the military. Put yourself in his or her place. What do you want to know about that situation? Construct questions that approach the information you want to know from different angles. You might ask, for example, whether your interviewee enlisted or was drafted, what he or she originally thought wartime service would be like, and how the actual experience differed from those expectations. Don't ask questions for which you already know the answers, but do try to make queries that will prompt comments you will understand and be able to assimilate into your final research project.

If you construct your questions around a core thesis or topic, it will be easier to organize your subject's responses into a coherent paper. Don't let your original idea or hypothesis control the interview, however. Be ready to change your focus if the interview starts to move into a more fascinating direction. You can't decide what the final project will include before you conduct the interview, because you haven't discovered everything about your topic yet. For example, if a Vietnam veteran you are interviewing says in response to your question about his preconceptions concerning military service that he didn't have any—that he simply didn't know what to expect at the time—but he would like to show you some objects he collected in Southeast Asia, you should be ready to invent questions about those artifacts instead of pursuing your prepared line of questioning. Sometimes an interview will veer off course this way, and the questions you have constructed will get left by the wayside. If you have no trouble inventing new questions as you go and find that the conversation has gone in a more fascinating direction than what you had planned, you have probably stumbled on a better focus for your research project.

Interview questions usually move from general to specific and from generic to personal. You've already learned that comfortable conversations begin with a few pleasantries or "ice-breaking" questions, and it's best to let those arise naturally from the situation rather than plan them in advance. This gives you a chance to interact as yourself at the outset of the encounter and to test the rapport between yourself and your subject. If you interview a person in his or her own terrain, look around the space and ask about the origin of an intriguing object or express interest in the building or the neighborhood. In a telephone interview, you might start by commenting on a time zone or climatic difference between your location and your subject's. Of course, you can always start simply by thanking the person for agreeing to talk with you.

Know Your Questions

When compiling a list of potential interview questions, it is better to have too many than too few. You can conduct a successful hour-long interview with six or eight basic questions. Remember that the goal of an interview is usually to get in-depth information, so choose two or three fairly constricted topics and write two or three questions about each. The object is to let the person being interviewed do most of the talking, and too many questions will confound that goal. After you have written out a tentative list of questions, read back through them and make sure that none invites a simple yes-or-no answer. Instead of asking, for instance, whether a person likes his or her job, ask what that person's favorite aspect of the job is. When you think you like the questions you have written, use them to interview yourself. How would *you* answer each? Which is most complicated and difficult to answer? Which is most personal? Rank your topics and questions from easiest to hardest to answer and from most general to most personal.

Keep your questions short and direct. Memorize them, so you will have an outline firmly fixed in your head of the material you hope to cover. Imagine the interview as you prepare for it, and try asking your questions out loud, for practice. Then, when you say them in the actual interview setting, you will already know how they sound, and it will be almost like practice again.

■ Conducting the Interview

This is easier said than done; but try not be nervous during the interview. This is your meeting. You have called the assembled parties together, you have set the agenda, and you will control the outcome. You must be in charge. If you are not confident and in control during the interview, the person you are interviewing will probably try to "rescue" you by providing short answers and getting things over as quickly and "painlessly" as possible. That is exactly the opposite of what you really want. A poised but relaxed tone will elicit the best conversation in most cases.

Although the mere thought of questioning some of the people you will interview might make you nervous, there are several things you can do to control your overt response to the situation. Dress comfortably but pleasantly. If you have represented yourself as a student, you don't have to show up in a business suit, if that makes you uncomfortable. Try to convey respect for the situation and the person with whom you will be meeting. Be early. Don't stress yourself out by scrambling to make it to the interview on time. If it is too early to go inside when you arrive (more than ten minutes ahead of schedule), walk around and familiarize yourself with the neighborhood, or find a quiet corner and study your questions one last time. Remind yourself that the outcome of this situation is largely in your control. The interview will last only about an hour. Focus on what you want to accomplish in that time. If you are nervous, you will probably make your subject uncomfortable. Your interviewee has agreed to help you with this project and wants the best possible outcome for you. You are qualified and prepared to ask a few questions of this willing subject. Smile occasionally. Make eye contact whenever possible. As a student interviewer, no one expects you to be flawlessly glib and accom-

**Proposed Core Questions for *Real World Research* Interview
Suzanna Aaron, Producer, *NBC Nightly News with Tom Brokaw***

1. How do you find topics, get assignments, etc? How do you decide what the news will be?

2. Which resources are most useful to your library research staff? What sort of library does NBC maintain?

3. How many people comprise your research team?

4. What original research is involved? (Please give examples for a story currently in progress.)

5. How do you assess the reliability of your sources (particularly print sources)?

6. What editing process does a script go through?

7. Do you document or somehow keep track of sources as you go?

8. What mistakes have you learned to avoid?

9. How long is the process of scripting a story from start to finish?

10. What is your favorite work so far? Why do you like it best?

11. What advice would you offer a college student interested in entering your profession?

12. What other important information do you want to add?

Figure 5.2 Proposed Core Questions for Interview with Suzanna Aaron, Segment Producer, *The NBC Nightly News with Tom Brokaw.*

plished, but you can impress everyone (including yourself!) by being poised and prepared. You will see that interviews are among the most straightforward and enjoyable conversations you have ever experienced.

As much as possible, try to conduct your interview so that it resembles a pleasant conversation. Carry your list of questions along, but don't read from it. If you constantly remind your subject that he or she is being interviewed, you are stressing to that person that he or she is going to be quoted, which can be an intimidating proposition for anyone. Instead of saying things like, "Let's see . . . My next question was . . . ," just ask the question, or preface it with something less mechanical, like, "I wonder if . . ." Don't rush your interviewee or cut off an answer too early. Oftentimes the first thing a person says in response to a question is not his or her best answer, and if you wait patiently for a few more seconds, the speaker will elaborate. If waiting for words makes you nervous, pretend to take notes a bit more slowly than the person speaks.

The most useful follow-up question is the one you have used ever since you learned to speak: Why? Frequently speakers think they have exhausted a topic when they have only revealed the basic facts of the matter. Instead of going on to your next question when your interviewee stops talking, ask "Why?" (as long as it is appropriate and you think the response will be relevant to your final project). You'll be amazed at how often such a simple question elicits the information you are really seeking.

Conversely, you cannot afford to let your subject go on and on in response to your first question, usurping the interview time with the answer to a background query. To ensure that you collect enough information to complete your research project, you must control the interview and steer the conversation along the lines you have planned. If necessary, you might have to "get a word in edgewise" when the person pauses, or interrupt him or her as politely as possible to ask your other questions. Some people talk almost endlessly when they are nervous or feel put on the spot, and your interviewee may be grateful for the interruption. Responding positively to the things your subject says—by giving nonverbal clues like nodding, smiling, making eye contact, or writing things down—will help reassure the interviewee that he or she is giving you the information you seek. Sometimes subjects who ramble on and on do so because they are afraid their responses aren't meeting the interviewer's expectations. If you have to interrupt the person you are interviewing, you will learn after the first time you do it whether or not it is acceptable to that person.

Interpreting Nonverbal Cues

Remember that an interview is more than just the words exchanged during it. An interview is an encounter with a person as well as an exchange of information; don't focus entirely on the verbal dimension of the exchange. It is preferable to meet your subject in person so that you can observe his or her dress, mannerisms, facial expressions, interactions with others, physical surroundings, and personal objects. However, even if you converse with your interviewee over the telephone or by e-mail, there are nuances that you should remember to record.

It is often interesting to note how people greet callers when they answer the phone and how they converse on the phone in general. Do they respond to questions immediately, or do they take a few seconds to compose themselves? Do they sigh at difficult questions (or laugh nervously)? Do they chuckle to themselves as they remember things? What do the tone and timbre of a person's voice seem to indicate about their manner or personality?

With e-mail, you may want to note the time of day that messages are posted; for instance, does this person work late at night or early in the morning? Does the person's e-mail automatically append a revealing quotation, or "signature"? How formal (or informal) is the person's diction and grammar in e-mail? Are the messages impeccably typed, or does an occasional typographical error suggest that the messages are sent without being reread?

Tape-Recording Interviews

A lot of interviewers use tape recorders during meetings with subjects so they can devote their note-taking efforts to recording visual and emotional impressions of the encounter. Although audiotapes do provide incontrovertible evidence of what was said, making it possible to include verifiably accurate direct quotations in your final paper, relying on tape recorders during interviews does present some potential liabilities. The most obvious risk is that of mechanical failure. Although tape recorders are available in shockproof, waterproof, rechargeable models that seldom fail, the cassette tapes themselves are less reliable. You could blithely trust the reassuring purr of a tape recorder's motor beneath your conversation, only to discover later that the tape got stuck at some early point and did not advance during the hour or that a dragging tape produced a sound like earthworm communications. Horror stories abound among writers who used a tape recorder during an interview, only to be left to depend entirely on their memory due to mechanical failure. But such failures are rare; don't squander time worrying about problems that are statistically unlikely. If you feel most comfortable using a tape recorder, and your interviewee assents to being recorded, it is probably safe to depend on one.

Realize, however, that a tape recording makes a rather unwieldy set of notes. You can review it only one syllable at a time, unlike written transcripts, which can be spread out and rapidly scanned. Many writers have discovered that it is difficult to locate statements they wish to quote directly when they are buried somewhere in an hour's worth of audiotape. If you tape-record your interview, you may well end up taking written notes when you play it back later.

The greatest dangers in using a tape recorder are psychological. Some people will not speak as freely if they are being recorded, and you usually cannot conduct an interview again, without the recorder, to know for certain if the presence of the electronic equipment hampered your conversation. You must ask for the interviewee's consent to tape-record your exchange (especially for interviews over the telephone), and that may cause some awkwardness at the outset. Tape recorders are great interviewing aids because they take down the words said during the meeting, freeing you up to write your observations about details in your notes. However, that convenience can have a detrimental effect on your interviewing style. If you leave it to the tape recorder to pay attention to the conversation for you, you may discover that you are not as involved in the conversation as you need to be.

Maintaining Your Interest Level

Undoubtedly, the most important variable in a good interview is the interest level of the interviewer. You must remain absolutely fascinated with the person and subject you are researching, throughout the interview, to get the full benefit of it. You know what happens if a listener stops paying attention to a speaker during a routine conversation; as soon as the person talking discerns that his or her partner is not listening, that person becomes embarrassed and winds down the discussion quickly. The listener is similarly ashamed and anxious to end the unpleasant interchange. Imagine what happens in a formal interview if the person who requested the meeting stops listening. The interview is effectively over at that point, and the memory of it can be quite unpleasant for both parties. Constantly remind yourself that your spoken and nonverbal cues provide important feedback to your interviewee. It is easy in interesting new surroundings or in the presence of someone you admire to drift off into thoughts about an object in the room or your imagined scenario of that person's life, but you must resist all urges to lapse into daydreams. Almost everyone appreciates a rapt audience, and you can provide that for your interviewee. Even if you discover that your background preparation was inadequate and your prepared questions are useless, you can still conduct a relatively productive, positive interview with enthusiasm and a demonstrated willingness to learn. If you are really "plugged in" to the conversation, you will take many more details and ideas away from it than you would if you were to let your attention wander.

As your allotted interview time nears its end, you might want to ask your subject simply if there is anything he or she would like to add to what you have discussed. Often, if the interviewee has thought much about the subject matter or the interview beforehand (and he or she probably has), that person will have some pithy or witty final thought to impart. Give your interviewee the chance to introduce a topic that interests him or her or to say something that sums up the subject. Often an open-ended last question will yield a stunning quotation that you'll want to include in your finished paper.

■ Ending the Interview

Always end an interview by thanking the interviewee for his or her time and expertise. You might want to assure the person that the meeting has been helpful to you in your research. Ask if you may call back with further questions that arise while you are writing your paper. If the person you interviewed asks you to show him or her a copy of your finished project, politely defer that request. The subject and the audience of your research should not be the same. You will write much more confidently and candidly about what you have learned if you are not envisioning your interviewee as the first reader of your work. If the question arises, simply explain that it is your policy to keep your work to yourself. The conversation you have arranged and orchestrated is your property to use as you said you would when you negotiated the interview. If you want to publish information you gathered under the pretext of writing a college paper, you will need to ask your interviewee to consent to that; but you do not have to show him or her your work in progress or the finished paper you submit to your teacher. You should, however, send a written note thanking your interviewee for participating in your project, and you may want to tell him or her some of the highlights of what you learned from your meeting. In most cases, that will satisfy the interviewee's curiosity about what you have taken away from the conversation.

■ Writing Up Notes

Emerging from an interview is like waking from a detailed, fascinating dream: at first you remember the whole conversation with astounding clarity, but as the minutes pass you begin to forget details, and eventually you may find it hard to remember much of anything that was said. Like dreams, interview conversations are often only superficially inscribed on your thoughts, and your nervousness and the accompanying adrenaline rush prevent you from committing the details to memory.

Thus just as it is necessary to write down, immediately upon waking, the details of a dream you would like to remember, it is a good idea to record as many details of your conversation as possible, either during the interview or immediately following it. As soon as you leave the interview setting, find a quiet place to collect and record your thoughts. That may be in your car, on the bus or train, in the corner booth of a diner, on a bench in the afternoon sunshine, or anywhere that is convenient. The key is to start putting details down before they fade. Read back over your notes and fill in any blanks you left while writing hurriedly. If you tape-recorded the interview, bring along headphones and play back the conversation. Review anything you wrote about sights, sounds, or your subjects' reactions, and try to associate these things with specific words or passages on the tape. If your notes are handwritten, make sure you can read all of them; if you typed them into a laptop computer, fix any typos. Add additional details in the margins, or write a paragraph recalling observations that did not find their way into your notes during the interview, such as your impressions of the subject's personality or the setting.

Record physical and sensory aspects of the meeting, even if you don't think you'll use them in your project. Just as a smell, taste, color, or mention of a person's name can trigger memories of forgotten dreams, evocative details recorded during or immediately after an interview will help you remember the tone of certain phrases or the general character of the interviewee after specific memories of the interview have left the frontal lobes. Before moving on with your day, make as clear as possible a record of the interview. It is the raw material that you will use—in unforeseen ways, perhaps—in your finished research project. Figure 5.3 shows the notes from the interview with Suzanna Aaron that became the researcher profile following Chapter Three.

■ Choosing the Best Rhetorical Strategy for Your Paper

The researcher profiles in Part One are each written in a different format, or using a different rhetorical strategy, to demonstrate some of the options writers have for presenting information collected during an interview. The

Notes from interview with Suzanna Aaron, Producer
NBC Nightly News with Tom Brokaw

The Fifth Ave. Entrance to 30 Rockefeller Place is the view we often see on television. Flags of the United Nations ring the gilded statue of Prometheus which dominates the outdoor cafe (in the winter time it is the famed Rockefeller Center skating rink). Above the door there is an art-deco relief of a Greek God and the inscription, "WISDOM AND KNOWLEDGE SHALL BE THE STABILITY OF THY TIMES."

Interviewed 29 June 1995, 10:15 a.m. at 30 Rockefeller Center (the G.E. Building). Inter-view started in Suzanna Aaron's office over breakfast cereal with milk. Her desk is cluttered with papers, memos from NBC. A bulletin board above her desk is filled with photographs of Aaron with cameramen, anchor personnel. A photograph of staff with Tom Brokaw, taken on the set of the show is framed and hangs on the wall to her right. The telephone dominates the clear space at the center of her desk.

Aaron is opening her morning mail when I arrive. She stops, but I encourage her to finish eating breakfast and perusing parcels while we get settled. Among her mail is a personal letter from the famous family member of the victim of an internationally-publicized murder case. The writer thanks Aaron for a sensitively-produced news segment that aired the previous week.

We move to the office next door when her office mate comes in and announces that he has a conference call coming within minutes. Minutes later, we relocate again when the owner of the office arrives and begins making phone calls. Most of the face-to-face interview is conducted in a conference room with a long table which seats 16 people. The only thing on the table is a large speaker phone.

A colleague of Aaron's interrupts to see if she can produce a story for Thursday (tomorrow) night's broadcast. She says she is already doing the "America Up Close" segment for Friday night. The colleague (male) suggests moving that to a later date so that she is free to produce Thursday's story. She runs down a list of tasks completed for Friday's show: Brokaw has interviewed the subject; a camera person and correspondent are shadowing the subject in a foreign country today. But she ends by saying that if she is reassigned, she will get to work immediately on the Thursday story.

Most of the people I come in contact with during the day at NBC News are young—late 20s and early 30s, not the audience I would imagine for network news, let alone its producers and reporters. Aaron is attractive, simply but elegantly dressed in a shift and flat shoes. Her co-workers are similarly attired in skirts or slacks with little or no jewelry (except wrist watches). They seem to expect long hours and act at home in the office, working with feet on the desk, food in hand, or shoes under a table.

Figure 5.3 Interview Notes

profile of Matt Roberts, the researcher for *The Late Show with David Letterman,* consists almost entirely of material paraphrased from the interview. By contrast, the profile of Elizabeth McIntosh consists entirely of the subject's own words, directly quoted (though edited), except for a brief introduction. The Suzanna Aaron piece uses a blend of direct quotations, paraphrases, and narration to describe Aaron's work as a producer for *The NBC Nightly News with*

Tom Brokaw. The writer's voice is clearly evident in the profile of Keith Melder, curator of presidential collections for the Smithsonian Institution, because it follows a narrative format A conversation with Myles Ogea, entrepreneur owner of the MT Cup coffeehouse, is presented in the question-and-answer style often associated with interview reporting. The profiles illustrate the strengths of each rhetorical strategy for transforming interview notes and transcripts into essays. You should decide which method of presentation you will use before you begin drafting your paper.

Some professional interviewers advocate writing a draft of your piece as quickly as possible following an interview. That may not be feasible, especially if your work requires further research, but you can at least write a quick synopsis recounting the event. Some writers find it helpful to pen a letter about their experience to a friend who is interested in the same subject but knows little about it. Doing that will help you recap the highlights of your interview experience and begin putting the information you gathered into terms a general audience can understand. If you do write a letter to a friend, don't forget to make a copy before you mail it, or you might have to interview your friend to get your details back.

Many students think that writing up an interview will be easy. They believe they will not be held responsible for an interviewee's grammar or for development of specific topics and that if they just present a transcript of the meeting as it occurred, they will have completed an acceptable Q&A-format piece with very little effort. Good writers do not surrender control of their texts that way, however, and the best results for an interview project require more planning than that. The need to standardize usage and grammar in an interviewee's quoted speech is a matter of personal opinion. Some writers believe that preserving a subject's distinctive dialect lends their piece authenticity. It would sound artificial, they might argue, to have a gang member or a ranch hand speak like an evening news reporter. Others believe it is courteous to standardize the reported speech of interview participants. It is belittling, they would say, to put into print subject-verb disagreements or other nonstandard usage in the spoken discourse of someone who would write much more carefully. Before you submit a paper that reproduces ungrammatical speech, ask your instructor whether you are expected to edit the quotations you use.

Q&A Format

Frequently when we think of interviews reported in magazines or newspapers, we envision the question-and-answer, or Q&A, format, because it retains the structure of an interview or conversation. Q&A texts usually begin with an opening paragraph explaining who is being interviewed, where the meeting took place, and the main idea or purpose of the piece. Highlights from the interview may also be given in this introduction, as well as physical details about the subject, the setting, or the interviewer. The main body of the text is composed of the interviewer's questions, followed by the subject's responses. (See the interview with Myles Ogea, entrepreneur and co-owner of the MT Cup coffeehouse, pages 101–104, for an example of a Q&A organizational strategy.)

The chief strength of the Q&A format is its illusion of immediacy. The structure of the piece invites readers to imagine they are present during the interview. They have the feeling that they are looking over the interviewer's shoulder, that nothing has been left out, that they have been privy to the whole conversation between writer and subject. That is a magic trick, though.

In reality, plenty has usually been left in the writer's notebook or wastebasket. Writing a Q&A piece is not as effortless as it may at first appear. A literal transcript of most interviews reveals that they tend to wander in an unruly pattern. Parts of answers to a single question may be strewn all over the transcript. Some questions fall flat, eliciting little or no response, and others provoke torrents of tangential monologue. In constructing a coherent essay from a transcript of an interview, writers usually want to rearrange some information, edit some answers, and totally excise others. Writing a good Q&A piece is a bit like writing a play. One must establish motivation for each question, keep the plot moving mainly with dialogue, and reinforce certain themes and issues without repetition.

Unless the actual interview was amazingly coherent and fast-paced, turning your record of it into a polished end product may be trying. Emphasizing key points in the discussion is difficult when the answers to all of the questions are given equal weight in the presentation. Readers of Q&A pieces often find them boring or hard to stay with. They frequently end up skimming the piece or skipping over large parts of it, since they can tell at a glance whose words and what topics they are avoiding reading. Although Q&A writing looks simple, a truly captivating question-and-answer text is very arduous to engineer.

First-Person Quotation

A format that was popularized by New Journalist Studs Terkel in *Working*, his chronicle of the quest for the American Dream, is the first-person quotation form. Like the Q&A format, this all-quotation style opens with an introduction that explains who is being interviewed, where, and why. The rest of the text, however, is presented as an uninterrupted monologue spoken by the person who was interviewed. (See the profile of Elizabeth McIntosh, former project director for the Barbara Bush Foundation for Family Literacy, at the end of Chapter Two, pages 33–35.)

The first-person quotation format is like a close-up photographic portrait of the person interviewed. Seemingly, nothing comes between the interviewee and the audience, since the speaker appears to address the audience directly throughout the essay in his or her own words. Readers enjoy the illusion of getting to examine the speaker at very close range without his or her being aware of the intrusion. The writer becomes a completely transparent medium, seemingly conveying the speaker's message to the audience word for word. But the writer of a first-person quotation piece is more like a photographer, who sets the lighting, determines the composition of the portrait, and so on. The writer must cut and edit the interviewee's answers to questions so that they flow together like an unprompted lecture on the topics covered. Generally this is possible only if most of the questions followed a single theme, the speaker was very forthcoming and prolific in supplying quotable text, and the writer is willing to leave a good bit of the actual transcript out because it doesn't seem to belong logically in the monologue.

However, if the writer knows little about the topic or the interviewee leaves essentially nothing unsaid, this may be the most effective way to present information gathered in an interview. Writers who believe they have little to add to what the person interviewed has said about the topic may feel most comfortable presenting information this way. It helps, of course, if the subject is a captivating speaker who uses interesting expressions and great turns of phrase. Writers of first-person quotation pieces are also like photographers in that the quality of their finished work depends a great deal on their subjects. First-person quotation writers must rely on the natural beauty of the speaker's diction and style.

Paraphrase

An essay that reports information learned during an interview but uses no direct quotations from that conversation is an example of paraphrased discourse. (See the profile of Matt Roberts, talent researcher for *The Late Show with David Letterman*, at the end of Chapter One, pages 12–15.) At first, it may seem pointless to interview someone and rarely or never quote his or her exact words, but there are some circumstances in which this approach is preferable. For instance, if the person interviewed speaks for a group of people and does not want to take individual credit for the ideas he or she presents, the writer may want to distance the speaker from specific statements by putting them into the writer's own words. Occasionally, persons who agree to be interviewed will ask that they not be quoted directly in the finished project. You can oblige such skittish subjects by summarizing the contents of the interview. If the information disclosed in the interview should take precedence over who said it and how, paraphrased reporting of the discussion will emphasize the facts.

A profile without any direct quotations may cause readers to arch their eyebrows, however. Some will wonder whether you ever actually spoke or corresponded with the person. Including very specific information available only from someone in the interviewee's position will allay such suspicions.

First-Person Narrative

You probably already know that narrating is simply telling a story. If you are new at interviewing, or if you feel it will benefit your piece to include your subjective thoughts and reactions, you might decide to tell a story about the meeting, from your own point of view. This is known as a first-person narrative strategy. (See the piece on Keith Melder, curator of presidential memorabilia at the Smithsonian Institution, at the end of Chapter Four.)

Narrative forms work best if things besides just discussion happen during the interview. If the writer encounters something relevant and interesting on the way to the interview or the interviewee is engaged in an activity or conversation with others during the meeting, a narrative approach may help the writer relate those stories to the audience. If the gist of the piece is that the writer learned something profound or was somehow transformed by meeting the interview subject, then a first-person narrative format, which focuses attention on the narrator, might be most appropriate.

The chief criticism directed against first-person narrative profiles is that they do tend to emphasize the writer over the subject, and seemingly holding oneself up as more fascinating than the interviewee can appear egotistical. Thus many writers choose a humble, almost self-denigrating voice for first-person pieces to avoid the appearance of narcissism. Some instructors or writing programs value expository prose over first-person narrative, so you should ask whether a narrative form is acceptable before you decide to use this strategy.

Integrated Paraphrase, Quotation, and Narrative Form

Reporting on the information gathered during an interview is usually best accomplished by drawing on more than one of the rhetorical or organizational strategies just discussed. For example, narration might be used to establish the setting or circumstances of the interview. Forceful, brief, epigrammatic, or otherwise memorable statements could be included as direct quotations, for maximum effect, and information-intensive statements could be paraphrased. (See the interview with Suzanna Aaron, segment product for *The NBC Nightly News with Tom Brokaw*, at the end of Chapter Three, pages 54–58.)

An essay or paper that draws the best from each organizational strategy will be able to incorporate more of the information gathered during an interview than will any of the forms used exclusively. Narration helps create transitions between topics, allowing diverse subjects to be smoothly integrated into one paper. Direct quotations provide a vivid picture of the speech and personality of the person being interviewed, and paraphrasing some material allows writers to include a lot of information compactly.

Integrating various rhetorical strategies results in a complex writing task that may be difficult to organize and plan, but it creates a very polished, striking discourse. Using two or three voices (the thoughts and speech of the writer and the spoken words of the interviewee) gives variety and depth to the finished product. It also gives the writer plenty of latitude in determining how to introduce, develop, and conclude the piece.

■ Summing Up

You will probably like interviewing as a form of research. It is amazingly exciting to meet new people and ask them questions about things you are genuinely interested in. Many networking contacts are formed through interviews, and you may find a new friend or mentor in the process of gathering information in this way. You may be pleasantly surprised as well to discover what fun writing is when you are conveying someone else's ideas and stories to an audience that has not heard them before. If interviewing is a developing skill for you, expect to enjoy it more as you practice it. Most students report that it gets easier over time, but their first attempts convinced them that it is a highly gratifying research method.

Consider an interview assignment as an opportunity to meet someone you admire or have long been curious about. It may surprise you to discover that many people are willing to talk with students to help them prepare assignments. Start by contacting an interview subject you are truly impressed with, such as a professional athlete, an aspiring young star, a highly visible politician, an expert in your field of study, a favorite author, or someone with access to information you and your audience really want to know. Generate a list of three or four possible interview subjects, and immediately begin contacting people associated with them. Then, if your first choice falls through, you will have alternate plans in progress.

Schedule interviews by telephone or e-mail for efficiency and convenience. Recognize that it may take several attempts to reach the person you want to interview. Don't give up easily or spend days waiting for someone to return your calls. Use any contacts or leads you can find. Whenever possible, arrange face-to-face interviews, and let the interviewee choose the time and location (within reason) for the encounter.

Use advance research to prepare yourself for the interview. Learn as much as you can about the person you will be meeting and the subject you will be discussing so as not to waste valuable interview time going over widely available information. Talk to mutual acquaintances, read newspaper and magazine articles, and carefully study anything your interviewee has recommended so that you can write apt questions and arrive well prepared to conduct your interview. Think about potential areas of focus or theses for your finished research project as you write your interview questions, so the interview will concentrate on specific topics that can be developed into a coherent final product.

Conduct the interview smoothly, so it resembles a pleasant conversation. Concentrate on appearing calm and interested in what your interviewee is saying. Recognize that, in granting an interview, your subject has tacitly agreed to answer some mildly probing questions, and work your way up to those through "ice-breaking" and general background questions. As the interviewer, you must control the pace and direction of the interview. Observe the time limits established when you scheduled the interview, and steer the conversation subtly so that most of your intended questions are covered. Always thank the person at the end of an interview, ask whether you can call him or her later if questions arise as you are writing up your article or essay, and politely refuse to show the interviewee work in progress. Follow up with a written thank-you note expressing gratitude for the time and information your intervie-wee has given you.

Decide which of the many available rhetorical formats you will use to trans-form your interview transcript or notes into a product intended for readers. You might begin drafting your final project as a paraphrased, fully quoted, narrative, or question-and-answer text, or you might choose to use all of those organiza-tional formats in your final piece. Whichever format you choose, extensive edit-ing of your interview transcript or notes will be necessary.

Interviewing is a fun and exciting way to gather information for research papers. You can use it to meet fascinating people, learn information firsthand, and make valuable contacts. Interviews may provide the primary subject matter for an essay or serve as one of many sources for an extensive research project.

Exercises: Sources and Strategies

1. Interview someone from your class and try to discover something about him or her that the other students in the class do not know (a hobby, past travel experience, future plans, and so on). You and the other stu-dents in your class can then take turns introducing the people you have interviewed to the rest of the class.

2. Identify a famous person whom you would like to interview. Conduct background research on that person, and write six to eight questions that you would use if you had the chance to meet with him or her. If your cam-pus subscribes to Nexus, West Law, or a similar private research tool, use it or another on-line research database accessible through the Internet to dis-cover recent information about the person you would like to interview. In-clude at least one question about that person's very recent activities.

3. Analyze an interview published in a magazine, aired on television, or conducted live during an on-line celebrity appearance on an Internet subscriber service. What is the focal point of the interview? Where and when was the interviewee during the conversation? Why do you think the subject agreed to participate? What questions did the interviewer ask? What did the interviewer most want to know, and was he or she successful in learning that information?

Writing to Know

Conduct a formal interview with a person you have not met previously. Write an article profiling that person, using one of the rhetorical strategies demonstrated by the interview profiles following each chapter in Part One.

This is an information-gathering interview. Its purpose is to get advice for students who hope to start a business after graduation. The questions are to the point, crafted to establish Ogea's background as a non–business major, discover the research process that led him and his business partner to choose to start a coffeehouse, learn the general process they followed in starting up their business, and get some idea of what they have learned from this experience. Since conveying information is this profile's primary purpose, the Q&A format is ideal, as it makes content accessible, in an easy-to-skim style.

Myles Ogea
Entrepreneur Co-owner of the MT Cup Coffeehouse

It is 9:00 A.M. on a Tuesday. Myles Ogea rounds the counter of the coffeehouse he co-owns with a business partner, cheerfully greeting employees and customers as he moves. Unconsciously he surveys the sandwiches and cheesecakes displayed in the refrigerated case against the counter, takes in the steam tables where soup will soon be kept, and looks to see that the customers in line appear patient and happy. He is trim and energetic, a bicycle racer as well as the lead singer in a band. His countenance and affect smile at what he sees. Seven customers are lingering over breakfast in the shop's dining room. Morning newspapers and arts magazines are haphazardly stacked beside the cash register. The whole building smells of coffee; the air is so dense and rich you can taste it.

Ogea has just returned from a 5:30 A.M. emergency run for parts for his cappuccino machine, bringing to an end a five-day loss of revenues because of broken equipment. The part, which was supposed to be next-day express mailed, was mistakenly shipped via regular surface mail. His good cheer is undaunted, however. At age twenty-seven, Ogea is exactly where he wants to be, doing precisely what he has always dreamed about.

Q: *Both your background and your future are in music. Is that right?*
A: My undergraduate degree is in voice performance. I am a soloist with the symphony, and I also sing popular music, opening for headlining performers. I do a lot of traveling to perform in other places. I meet a lot of people through music. It's not just being a performer; it's learning about different cultures, meeting people. A lot of different fields offer those opportunities, but music is an international language. Ultimately, I want to go to Los Angeles and try to make it big as a singer.

Q: *How did you determine that a coffeehouse would be a viable business?*
A: I guess you could say we did our research. My business partner, Todd, and I looked at what this community didn't have. I enjoy small cafés in cities. I like to interact with people in quaint cafés; I like the free, inviting atmosphere. Everything here was fast food; the employees and cus-

tomers are too distant. Todd suggested a coffeeshop—a specialty shop and a small restaurant combined. A lot of people—my friends, my girlfriend—thought a small restaurant was a good idea.

We read different magazines, like *Inc., Entrepreneur, Indianapolis Monthly.* We traveled and looked at coffeeshops from Arizona to Ohio. We studied a lot of existing businesses. Our business is constantly evolving. We continue to read those magazines. The field is moving very quickly. We don't want to be trendy, but we want to offer the best for our customers. It's a fast-growing business. Everyone is secretive about where they get coffee beans, etc.

We each kept notebooks. Todd and I each took notes, writing what we liked, what we would do differently. We copied the menus of stores we visited and wrote down things we wanted to do in our own store. We ordered a lot of samples of coffees and organized them in our refrigerators. A lot of it was just in our heads, ideas we'd been thinking about for a long time.

Q: How many people helped you reach this decision?
A: Really just two. Because of the newness of it, my partner, Todd, and my girlfriend were the only people with input into the decision. People have stolen my ideas before, so we kept it quiet. We couldn't let the word out until we had the business under way. We wanted foot traffic, so we decided locating near a college campus would be good. We found a building for sale near campus, so we knew the time was right.

Q. How did you learn about the restaurant business?
A: I still don't know much. I worked as a captain at an upscale restaurant uptown. I managed the main dining side of the restaurant. I had ten or twelve employees underneath me. I was a singing captain, and I did a lot of entertaining.

I didn't learn about managing books, or ordering, but I did learn how to interact with customers. I always asked questions. I asked the cooks, the chefs, the waiters, the wine steward. I got a lot of information by expressing an interest in other people's jobs.

We also go to food shows and talk to purveyors. Salespeople can give you advice.

At first, we just went on guesswork and luck.

Q: How did you learn about the coffee trade?
A: Working in a fancy restaurant, I learned what cappuccino was. I had never heard of it before then. Todd spends a lot of time in coffeehouses; his history is deeper.

I sought out coffeehouses in different communities. I learned about two years ago that there were all of these great drinks out there. When I go to coffeehouses in other cities, I ask about how drinks are made there.

Some of the salespeople selling the coffee machines gave us advice about products, drink preparation. We plan to go to the West Coast to learn about some of the drinks referred to in magazines. There are new machines being made; we want to see those in use.

Q: *How did you decide which sources or people to trust in your decision-making process?*

A: With banks and things like that, you expect your banker or realtor or product supplier to say certain things—if you don't trust them, you can't get anything done. You ask the bankers to keep things between you, and if they let your secrets out, you don't go to that bank for your next deal.

We bought the building on contract, so we wouldn't have to disclose our plans to any bank until the business was under way. We will have to make a balloon payment on the building eventually, and we will have to approach a bank before then.

Q: *How do you continue to keep tabs on the market, your competition, and changes in the specific coffee-restaurant business?*

A: We consult specialty magazines, such as *Gourmet News*. The Specialty Coffee Association puts out literature in a magazine form, and restaurant associations have journals as well. A lot of our regular customers try other coffeehouses in other areas; they come in and tell us about their experiences.

A customer approaches our table and hands Myles an article called "Java Jive" from Architecture Minnesota. *Myles accepts it graciously, promising to read it later.*

Q: *What kinds of things did you have to put into writing?*

A: We had to write three-month and twelve-month business plans for the banks and for ourselves. It was important to get down some concept of what we wanted to do here. We constantly revise that: Where can we cut down? Where can we expand? The plan is like our Bible; we stick to it. It helps us predict all of our costs, our taxes, mortgage payments, losses, etc.

Q: *What mistakes must one learn to avoid in initiating a business venture?*

A: Let others who can do things much better than you do those things for you. For me, that's building construction. We wasted a lot of time trying to get this building ready. We lost a lot of money trying to do things ourselves. Have a professional do what he or she does best, even if it means going further in debt.

Q: *How much time passed between when you definitely decided to go into business and the day the MT Cup opened?*

A: It took about six months from the time we decided to go into business until the door opened at the MT Cup, and that was much longer than I imagined. We had to wait three months to acquire the building. Once we got the building, it took about two months to open.

Q: How much money does a person need to make a legitimate start at his own business?

A: For a coffeeshop, you should have enough money to carry yourself for three years. I've heard that McDonald's charges $750,00 to $1 million to start a new franchise. Todd and I were very fortunate. We got credit; we got the building on contract. We slowly but surely pay our bills. It's like an "infomercial" scenario: we bought everything with no money down, and we didn't take the hundred-dollar course. After eight months, I still don't take any profit out of the business. I live on a college student's budget.

Q: What advice would you give to a college student with entrepreneurial aspirations?

A: Business can be very rewarding and a lot of fun, but be prepared to work. It takes eighty to one hundred hours per week. In order for a small business to be a success, you have to be there. Don't plan on making money at first. It's not a get-rich quick scheme: it has to evolve slowly. Don't be easily discouraged. But you have to get out of bed after five hours of sleep and go to work, even when you need to sleep for about nine days.

Be realistic. Owning a business changes your life. I don't know what it's like to give birth to a child, but the changes in your life a business brings have to be comparable. It's like nurturing a child, you know, teaching it to be independent. There are no good rule books for establishing a business. We are writing our own book as we go. Everyone has to. That's the real formula for success.

This is one business. There are other things I will do. I'm sure of it.

Suggested Writing Assignments

1. Interview the proprietor of a business like one you sometimes dream of owning to discover how that person got started. Try to discover what it would take for you to start a similar venture today.

2. Write a preliminary business plan as described by Ogea: include the kind of business you would like to start, and make some rough estimates of major expenses involved (for example, site remodeling, inventory purchases, advertising costs, hiring expenses). Explain why your hypothetical business would be unique or successful enough to recoup these expenses.

3. Write a proposal for a bank loan officer, explaining an idea you have for starting a small business. Be persuasive and thorough. Why is this product or service needed in your community? Approximately what start-up costs would be involved? Why would the bank want to support your project?

PART TWO

Strategies

Chapter Six

Selecting and Narrowing a Research Topic

Some people call the type of project described in Part Two of this book a "term paper," but that puts undue emphasis on this assignment. You will probably write many papers—short and long—for your classes this term, and a number of factors will determine your success and demonstrate all that you have learned during this semester or quarter of the school year. One paper cold not show everything you've learned in this or any other class. Indeed, if you tried to use every research method you will study this term in a single project, the final result would resemble a messy scrapbook more than a coherent paper. So don't be intimidated. A research paper is but a single assignment.

■ Terminology and Process

The term *research paper* is flawed as well, because it overemphasizes the contribution research makes to your final product. Although research is certainly important, as the means by which you collect information for your project, it is not by itself the purpose of the assignment. So instead of a "term" or "research" paper, try to think of this type of project as a "researched" paper. Although you will be required to incorporate ideas from a number of different sources in your final project, the research involved does not take precedence over your own thoughts and conclusions about your topic.

The process of writing a research paper is essentially the same as that for most other writing assignments. In fact, writing a research paper *is* just another writing assignment. Although you may not have submitted an exhaustively researched or comprehensively documented essay before, you have plenty of experience with the fundamentals required. First, you must decide what subject to write about. Then you have to think up and look up some content: ideas, arguments, and examples to illustrate and support your ideas. Finally, you need to assimilate all of your ideas into a coherent, logical, persuasive final product.

Even though you will be incorporating the findings and ideas of other writers and authorities in your research paper, it will still be primarily *your* essay, written by you and presenting your ideas about the topic. Therefore, the most important advice anyone can give you about writing a researched paper is this:

- Be yourself.

- Choose to write about a topic you care about.

- Include your own ideas and opinions.

- Maintain your own voice throughout.

- Include other sources because they interest you.

- Say what you really think about the topic.

Remember that your final paper will have *your* name on the cover sheet and that the names of the experts you consulted will be listed at the back, on the Works Cited page. Keep your contribution and theirs in perspective as you work on this project. You will get "top billing" in this production—earn it.

■ Meet Kyle Parker

Kyle Parker is a first-year college student who has agreed to let us look over his shoulder as he completes a researched writing assignment for his English composition class. He grew up in Versailles, Indiana, a small community of about 2,500 people in the southeastern corner of the state. He says it is "the kind of town where everyone knows everyone else, and people usually know what you are doing before you do it." During the summer months in Versailles, he worked as a clerk and stock person at a local grocery store. As a high school student, he managed the varsity basketball and baseball teams, but volleyball is his favorite sport. His parents let him dig a seventy- by forty-foot pit in their yard and fill it with sand to create his own volleyball court at home.

Kyle sees college as a series of opportunities to have fun and learn. "Once I made it to college," he says, "I told myself from day one that I was not going to just sit back and watch life go by without enjoying it and making something out of what was offered to me." He started college as an architecture major, but after about two days he realized that "my dream since the sixth grade was not to be." He has recently changed his plans and will major in computer science. Since he has been "working with computers since the fourth grade," he feels pretty comfortable and confident about his decision to change career goals.

Kyle insists that he is not "a stereotypical computer science major who is glued to the computer and plays Doom for twenty-four hours each day." He says that "in a heartbeat" he will choose to be "outside or hanging around with friends" instead. He describes himself as "an outgoing person who likes to have fun," but adds that when he has to, he "buckles down and gets a job done." As you will see, this is just how he approaches the researched writing assignment we'll be observing. He says, "I am not a geek who loves to write researched papers, but I know that writing can be a creative outlet for me." We will check in with Kyle periodically throughout Part Two to find out how the advice given here works for a real student.

■ Choosing a Topic

If you want to, you can sit at your desk and concentrate on finding a topic for a research project, but the small amount of the world illuminated by your desk lamp will not suggest many ideas to you. The best way to find a subject for a researched paper is to go about your daily life with the question of what you want to write about in the back of your mind. What do you see that interests you? What topics do you and your friends debate around the dinner table? What catches your attention in the newspaper or on television news shows? How would you like to change the world now or in your coming professional career? What strong opinions do you hold? Which issues make you angry or prompt you to donate time or money? Which are you afraid to discuss because others disagree with you? Do you have experiences that have made you more aware of certain social problems, inadequate legislation, or needed safety measures? What are the chief controversies associated with your job or hobbies? What would you talk about if you were the host of an hour-long talk show?

If you simply sit at your desk and ask yourself "What's a good topic for a research paper?" you're likely to come up with a string of clichés. Lots of papers have been written about the "big" social issues and problems: euthanasia, handgun control, national welfare reform, cloning, the legalization of marijuana, the raising or lowering of the legal drinking age, and so on. Many very good papers have been written on such topics, but if you ask yourself what you would really like to study in depth for two weeks or a month, you can probably be more specific and original in your topic selection. Don't just choose a topic that will satisfy the requirements of the assignment; choose a subject that will satisfy your own curiosity as well.

Topics to Avoid

There are some topics you should simply avoid. Some issues have been so overdebated in the mass media that it is difficult to discuss them without just rehashing familiar arguments and offering well-known examples. Abortion and the death penalty, for instance, are topics that are at a saturation point. So much research and money and emotion has gone into creating and disseminating propaganda on such issues that it is unlikely you will discover anything new or even be able to summarize all the existing points of view. Since most adults have had extensive exposure to the various positions on such topics, you might feel somewhat defeated before you even begin writing your paper, knowing that the majority of your readers will have already made up their minds about the topic.

Similarly, avoid one-sided issues, or theses that don't suggest a reasonable contrasting point of view. Such issues include some very important social problems, such as teen suicide and drunk driving, but they are difficult paper topics, because virtually everyone knows what the "right" position is in relation to them. No one advocates committing suicide or driving while under the influence, for example, so how would you write about these issues without feeling that you are telling the audience what they already know? It's hard to build a strong argument when there's nothing to contrast it with. You might find yourself repeatedly making the same points because there is nothing much to argue against.

Finally, don't pick a topic you've researched before. If you have already done extensive research on a certain topic and written a successful paper or speech about it, you should probably move on to a subject that is relatively new to you. It may be difficult to muster much enthusiasm for such a topic the second time around, and you will be tempted to fall back on your prior research, to use sources you have already found instead of conducting a full-fledged, fresh inquiry into the topic.

Try to look at the research process as an opportunity to interact with experts and to make some new and exciting discoveries. If you rely too much on past experience in completing your research project, you will not get the full benefit of studying the subject in the class you are currently enrolled in. Similarly, you should not select a topic simply because good sources are available for it. If, for example, you have the opportunity to interview an expert in a field that does not really interest you, don't be tempted to choose that subject just because the expert is available. Choose a topic you *want* to study; if you are truly interested in the subject, you'll be able to find materials to support your research. Open yourself up to new learning experiences and research techniques—you can start by choosing a research topic that is new and exciting to you.

Taking a Stand

Generally, the most successful research questions are those that the writer feels comfortable eventually answering. If you simply present all sides of an issue and in effect say to your audience, "now *you* decide," your paper will be less satisfying than it will be if you take a strong stand and defend it. For example, don't simply report on the pros and cons of privatizing social security; do some reading on the subject, decide if you would vote for or against such a proposal, and then try to persuade your audience to vote with you. It is easier to plan the content and structure of a paper with a clear purpose than it is to pull together disparate points of view of equal weight. A decisive point of view will produce a stronger tone, a more personal voice, and a more compelling thesis than a simple "report the facts" approach can. Also, if you have strong convictions about your thesis, you will probably enjoy the research process more and produce a more spirited, imaginative, and complete final product.

Choosing a Workable Subject

Be realistic about your assignment. You will have to complete your library research, visit related archives, conduct any original studies or interviews that you hope to include, and draft and polish your final presentation or paper in the time allotted. Successful time management is vital in completing a research project. In most classes, research papers and presentations are absolutely due on the specified date. It simply isn't fair to other students to ask the instructor for an extension. If your final product is a presentation, class time scheduled for that purpose often cannot be postponed. Also, evaluating research projects is a time-consuming process, and your instructor must have sufficient time to assess your work carefully and return it to you by the end of the term.

Build in time for misdirected interlibrary loan materials, rescheduled interviews, holiday office closings, computer malfunctions, bad weather, and other human, natural, and supernatural obstacles. Part of being a successful researcher is learning to take dead ends and setbacks in stride, to persevere when the evidence you seek does not fall easily into your open notebook. You really can't leave any aspect of a large-scale research project until the night before your paper or presentation is due. Computer disks get scratched, printers run out of ink, and information gets lost—and the more frenetic your schedule, the more likely, it seems, that such complications will occur. Don't expect others (classmates, computer lab supervisors, instructors) to compensate for your disappointments and disasters.

Do You Already Know Something About the Topic?   You may be tempted to take the opportunity presented by a research project assignment to learn more about a subject you have always wished to pursue; however, it is best to choose a topic you already know something about or have some prior experience with. Promising to resolve the problem of Scottish independence, for instance, because your ancestors are from Scotland is probably a mistake. If you have to take in a lot of historical information, examine analogous examples (Irish independence, for example), make contacts, focus your topic, determine your position in the matter, and synthesize a great deal of learning into a relatively short presentation or paper, your task will become overwhelming. Great new areas of interest are best investigated gradually in an entire course about that topic or during an intensive summer reading program. Although you should see a research assignment as an opportunity to concentrate on a topic that fascinates you, learning everything about a subject that is completely new to you is most likely more than what you or the assignment can deliver. It is okay to select a topic even if you haven't yet made up your mind about it—a reasonable amount of study will help you decide where you stand on the issue—but do not plan to become an expert on a complex topic *and* complete a focused research project at the same time.

Remember that any research project ultimately culminates in the lonely process of sorting out what you have learned and putting your findings and ideas into words for an audience. Choose a topic that you will enjoy investigating *and* telling fellow students about. Don't choose a topic because you think it will impress someone else. For example, even if other students in your class elicit a positive reaction from your professor with proposals to study politics, don't promise to write about foreign policy or economic embargoes or trade agreements or anything else you don't already know or care about just because you think your instructor or classmates will like the idea. A good final product is what's important, not an impressive proposal.

Conversely, don't worry that your favorite subject is too idiosyncratic or erudite for others to comprehend. Nearly any subject can be presented from a basic or human-interest angle without "dumbing down" the content. A real expert, no matter what his or her field of expertise, can make material engaging for general readers.

Is Information Available?   Make certain that you can research the topic you choose. A student once came across a short piece in her local newspaper indicating that the laws of her home state did not prohibit the sentencing of juveniles to death for premeditated capital crimes. She was outraged and immediately set out to change that situation. However, her research revealed that no juvenile in her state ever had been sentenced to death because other laws on the books prevented citizens under age twenty-one from being tried in cases with such dire potential consequences. No one in the justice system was willing to comment on the issue, since it was a moot point anyway. The student had hoped to discover dramatic anecdotes about abused children who had been driven to commit capital offenses and were again victimized by "the system." Instead, she found nothing to help develop her thesis except the inch-long article in her local paper that originated her inquiry. In general, others must be willing to talk and write about a subject before it becomes a viable topic for a research project.

Is Your Thesis Too Subjective?   You also cannot prove a thesis that is too subjective to derive from empirical evidence. For example, you may believe that Richie Sambora is the greatest guitar player who ever lived, but you could never demonstrate that conclusively in a research paper or presentation—even if Sambora came to your class and laid down some amazing licks, blindfolded, on a broken Stratocaster. You could demonstrate, however, that many rock and roll stars are talented musicians, not merely outrageous performers as is commonly believed. A lot of information on virtually any topic is on record and available for the asking. Examine your ideas from various angles, and you will probably find a way to present the information you want to explore in a credible college research project.

Is Your Topic Compelling?   Finally, choose a topic you can take a stand on and prove something about. Try to say something new about your topic; don't merely compile a report on it. Writing a report involves simply gathering and organizing existing knowledge about your subject, but conducting bona fide research means attempting to bring new ideas and understanding to the issue. Bring a fresh perspective to an old problem by combining the ideas of earlier researchers or interviewing someone with unpublished ideas about a topic. Reinterpreting existing data in light of newer findings yields discoveries in all fields of study, every day.

Consider the many research options available to you. Could you visit a site that will add a new dimension to discussion of a topic, or can you bring other personal experience to bear on your subject? Could you talk to a person who has been overlooked in previous coverage of a subject? Can you supply a local example that suggests a way to solve a national problem or demonstrates why a particular approach to such a problem is or is not working? You are surrounded by experts in virtually every field who are dedicating their lives to helping learners answer such questions. Take advantage of the resources available to you. Think big. Why would you choose to simply write a report when you can make a genuine discovery?

■ Kyle's Subject Selection Process

In thinking about a topic for his research project, Kyle determined that he wanted to write about his college major: computer science. Specifically, he wanted to write about some aspect of this highly technical field that his classmates, whose fields of study include everything from food service management to environmental preservation, would like to read about and for which they could provide useful feedback. Since telecommunications deregulation has implications for persons in virtually every profession, he decided to think about that for a few days. He read several articles in print journals and on the Web about proposed changes in cable television franchises, satellite television services, and telephone networks. Lacking the proper business and economics background, Kyle found the information he discovered about telecommunications deregulation specialized and confusing. In fact, the more he searched for information on the topic, the less interested in it he became. He couldn't imagine finding a "corner" of such a complex topic that he could master and present confidently to his readers.

One evening he logged on to the World Wide Web and navigated to the search engine Yahoo! He entered a key word that he predicted would bring ridiculously copious results: *cyberspace*. His plan was to read the first source Yahoo! suggested and, by following hyperlinks, surf until he found a topic that really captured his interest. Not long into this browsing experiment he came upon an article about Internet security. He read with interest about breaches of e-mail security and court cases in which deleted e-mail files had been recovered from routine mainframe backups and subpoenaed. Although he was fascinated by a couple of such cases, he decided he did not want to focus on a negative aspect of the Internet, since he had already perceived that paranoia about the electronic gathering and dissemination of information was high among the general public. He began to wonder what he could do to reassure the public about Internet security and its usefulness.

Kyle remembered hearing something about people's reluctance to give their credit card numbers over the Internet, so he entered a search string that included *on-line shopping* and *credit cards* and *security*. Yahoo! returned a substantial list of sources, and many of these suggested questions Kyle could answer with a research project. In fact, he found many Web pages that were directly related to the question of securing credit card information transmitted over the Internet. He briefly considered covering other privacy issues related to on-line shopping, such as how computers can be used to track consumer purchases and create personality profiles of shoppers, but again, he did not like the idea of adding to the negative publicity already out there about the computer industry, in which he hopes to work someday. He tentatively decided to argue the thesis that it is generally safe to provide credit card account numbers to merchants who deal directly with customers over the Internet.

Recognizing that the Internet is not the most objective source for information on economic issues crucial to the development of the World Wide Web, Kyle visited the library and found that many newspapers, magazines, and other print sources also covered the issue of credit card security and electronic shopping on the Internet. He checked with one of his computer science professors, who agreed to be interviewed on the topic once Kyle knew more about it, and he made a list of other primary research he could conduct, including calling mail order companies to see if they would divulge the ratio of telephone orders to Internet orders they currently receive. He also hoped to interview consumers who had purchased items on-line. Kyle surveyed the opportunities to purchase goods and services on-line and found that he could make airline and hotel reservations and buy computer equipment, clothing, bicycles, used cars, books, and computer software from the convenience of his own keyboard. He could even compare the prices offered by different Internet service providers in his area. He wondered whether consumers were more willing to buy certain types of goods on-line and whether he might need to further restrict his topic to address a single type of product or service, but he determined that he would have to read and explore further before making that decision. He created a diagram illustrating the evolution of his research topic (see Figure 6.1), which he could consult later if he wanted to expand or narrow his search for information.

■ Summing Up

Choosing a topic for a researched paper is not that much different from finding a subject for any other writing assignment. Think about what interests

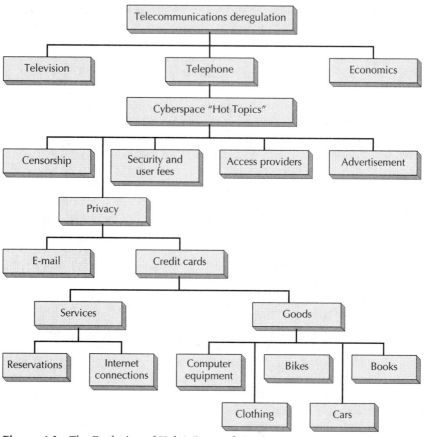

Figure 6.1 The Evolution of Kyle's Research Topic

you and what you already know. As with any writing process, you will have to figure out what you want to say about your topic, organize the information you come up with, and present it to your readers clearly. Although a researched paper incorporates ideas and information from other writers and speakers, it must essentially be your own essay. It should present your opinions and thoughts about the subject, reinforced by observations and proof from verifiable outside sources.

Choose a topic as Kyle has done it, by exploring the contents of his own memory as well as the World Wide Web and the library. Don't automatically settle for the first idea you get. Notice that Kyle decided, before he conducted any research, that two of his ideas would lead to theses he did not wish to defend. Try the process that Kyle used to discover his research paper topic. Think of a very general area of interest that you would like to pursue, and conduct a search of the World Wide Web that will yield thousands of sources. Look through the titles of those, and notice subtopics you'd like to learn more about.

When you have found one or two topics you might wish to pursue, make a quick check of your library to be certain that print materials on the topic are available as well. You might ask a professor or other expert you know if he or she is willing to be interviewed about the topic after you have completed some of your research, as Kyle did. Finally, think about your own experiences and interests and how what you already know and believe about the topic will provide content for your finished project.

Make sure that you can research your topic adequately with the resources available to you and that you can find a variety of sources to support your thesis. Select a topic that will interest you for the duration of the project, one about which you have something to say and are willing to learn more. A good choice at this point may prevent your deciding to change topics later in the process. Choosing the right topic will minimize your researching time and focus your energies from the outset.

Exercises: Sources and Strategies

1. Brainstorm a list of your hobbies and other interests, and list any controversies or problems common to some or all of them.

2. Log on to the World Wide Web and type in a very generic description of a topic you might like to research. Follow hyperlinks through a chain of related sites until you find a specific issue that would make a good research topic. Draw a diagram tracing the evolution of your topic, like the one Kyle made to show how he found the subject of Internet credit card security.

3. Make a preliminary list of possibilities for active research for one of the topics you are considering. Who might you interview? What experience do you already have with the subject? What sites could you visit to learn more about it? What information could you gather from government offices or other archives to support your research?

Writing to Know

Grab a pencil or keyboard and blow off some steam! What really irks you? What subject do you think the general public is completely wrong about? How has the government (or other bureaucratic entity) made life seriously inconvenient? What is the most unfair thing about life? What is the *obvious* thing that news media accounts of a current event are leaving out? What topic could you go on about loudly for several minutes? Grab a soap box and start recording your thoughts. Write fast and furiously until you have at least two full pages of text. Then, take a breather and figure out if there is a topic for a researched paper in there.

Chapter Seven

Determining What You Already Know

O nce you have tentatively settled on a topic for your research project, you might begin to wonder whether you'll be able to find enough to say about it. The number of pages your instructor has asked you to write may seem like too many to fill without repeating yourself or digressing from your thesis. You will most likely be hoping to find lots of secondary-source material to clarify your thoughts about your topic or to just plain fill up the number of pages you have been asked to write. You don't need a great quantity of secondary-source material to stimulate your thinking, however. Although it is true that reputable outside sources and relevant information are essential elements of a good research paper, it will be *your* thoughts and ideas, not those of others, that will make the real difference between an adequate project and an excellent one. Researching and writing are active, *thinking* activities, not passive exercises in collecting information and reporting it.

Preparing a research paper is like cooking a gourmet meal. Just as a discriminating cook learns to select only the best ingredients, you must learn to identify reliable, pertinent sources. Freshness is vital, so you should seek up-to-date information. Variety is important, too, so be sure to include multiple points of view. Likewise, color and texture matter, so you should try to gather information from different kinds of sources, such as magazines, journals, interviews, government documents, and primary sources. But the difference between raw sources and a finished research paper is as great as the difference between a bag of groceries and a seven-course feast. The essential variable is what you do with the information you collect. Although quality ingredients or sources are vital to producing a palatable end product, the skill of the chef is the most important factor in the outcome.

You will not gain all or even most of the information you will eventually include in your research paper directly from the library, from interviews, or from other documents. Instead, much of your paper's content will be *suggested* to you as you actively read and analyze the information you access during the researching phase of your project. Your own responses to the things you hear, see, and read will constitute a great portion of your finished project. Although it may not seem like it right now, you already know a good deal of the content of your eventual paper or presentation. You will have to remember some of it, and you will need to use your skills of concentration and analysis to deduce the rest, but the most persuasive parts of your argument will come out of the very unique archive that you carry around inside your own head.

■ Exploring Your Memory to Develop Your Thesis

One of the best sources available to writers is their own experience. You have often heard teachers advise students to write about what they know; the same holds true for research assignments. Start your research process by searching your own memory. How did you first learn about the topic? Maybe a personal experience or a television or magazine feature you saw long ago introduced you to the subject. Think about that experience, and ask yourself these questions:

- When was it?

- Where were you?

- What do you remember about it?

- What contact have you had with the subject since then?

- What was your response to the topic when you first learned about it?

- How have the events of your lifetime and your thinking over time influenced your position on the topic?

Recording your thoughts and experiences related to the topic you intend to research will aid your memory and help you guess how readers who have not thought much about the subject will respond to it. The evolution of your own thinking on the topic will suggest ways to develop your argument to make it more persuasive. For instance, someone who first became aware of the gun control issue after seeing TV news reports on the shooting of President Reagan might have initially thought that outlawing guns would solve the problem. As he matured, however, that person might have reasoned that making guns illegal does not eliminate them. He may have pondered the arsenal of toy weapons he owned as a child and remembered the disapproval he encountered from pacifist parents who did not allow their children to play with such toys. Perhaps as an adult he even considered purchasing a gun himself, for protection. Remembering the evolution of his own position on the issue of guns—from toy gun owner to gun control advocate to potential gun owner—would help that writer craft arguments that would reach readers on both sides of the issue. He could use his memories of the Reagan shooting as an anecdote to enliven his discussion of the topic. What he learned about guns and about himself in the process of deciding whether to purchase a gun could serve as primary research for his project. Although this writer would not consider himself an expert on gun control, by any means, his own experience, however limited, would provide depth and immediacy to his work.

■ Freewriting

You've probably had the discouraging experience of spending a beautiful Saturday or Sunday afternoon brooding over something you were supposed to write for Monday morning. As the crumpled pieces of paper mounted up and the minutes ticked away, you paced the room or stared into space, wishing you could just get some words, *any* words, down on paper. Maybe you eventually produced the required text on that sacrificed afternoon, or perhaps you still resent the day you lost to fruitless frustration. Whatever your experience was, you could have made it less painful by starting off with a freewriting exercise. Freewriting is a strategy designed to help you get words down on paper quickly. Often, having *something* in writing can help you push on with an assignment that seems overwhelming. At the very least, it gives you something to show to a friend, peer editor, tutor, or teacher as you seek help with the task.

Freewriting about your research topic will help you discover what you already know about it. It is a high-energy method of generating text and stimulating your own thinking about a topic. Start by naming your topic in a single word or phrase at the top of a piece of paper or the beginning of a new document in your word processor. Allow yourself just twenty minutes to complete a freewriting exercise. You might want to set an alarm clock, or check your wristwatch at the outset. Begin by writing anything that comes into your mind about the topic you have identified at the top of your document. Keep your fingers or pen moving constantly. Don't censor or edit any of your thoughts; just write them down as they occur to you. Try to stay focused on the topic you've named at the top of the page. If you can't think of anything to write, write "I can't think of anything, I can't think of anything" until you do think of something. Write as fast as you can without regard for penmanship, spelling, grammar, punctuation, or anything else you would work at if others were going to read your text. Freewriting is for yourself; if fellow students or teachers read your freewriting as part of an assignment, they should not comment on superficial elements unless you ask them to. Do not quit until twenty minutes of continuous writing have passed. If you run out of time before you've exhausted all of your ideas, however, you should keep writing for a few more minutes.

Freewriting is a very simple concept, and you may have invented such an exercise for yourself already. It is useful to writers not only because it produces raw text (which can then be edited, elaborated on, reorganized, and amended) but also because writing ideas down quickly frees up one's mind. Think back to the last time you spent hours trying to get started writing a paper. You may have spent several minutes thinking up a mundane first sentence like "In this paper, I am going to discuss something important to people everywhere." Because the sentence was not a provocative opener, you didn't write it down. Yet, as you tried to think of better first lines, that boring opening just kept reasserting itself. Freewriting allows you to get such nonstarters out of your head, freeing your mind to produce better material.

You may have discovered that talking about your writing assignments with friends or classmates is a good way to come up with content. Similarly, freewriting provides a way to talk to *yourself* about your ideas before you air them in public. Just as a stimulating conversation with others helps you think of ideas and see connections that you might not otherwise have perceived, the act of quickly and freely writing down your ideas may produce revelations.

Freewriting also tends to produce more integrated text than simply sketching an outline for your paper does. The ideas generated during a freewriting exercise may flow together more logically than do ideas generated to conform to an outline. A few minutes spent in high-energy concentration and determined writing may lead to content and organization that whole afternoons of procrastination and frustration would never yield. Like a conversation about your topic, however, the output from freewriting is not a finished discourse. Although a single freewriting session may produce pages of text, it is essentially raw material; do not expect to freewrite coherent drafts of your research paper.

■ *Inventing and Shaping Your Arguments*

If you make a concerted effort to think about your topic before you begin reading or interviewing other sources, you will find that you can imagine much of what you will eventually encounter in the course of your research. With just a few minutes of concentration, you can probably list many of the arguments on all sides of your topic.

Understanding the Pros and Cons of an Argument

At the top of a blank sheet of paper or at the beginning of a new document in your word processor, state your topic as a proposition or motion. For example, if the subject of your research paper will be rain forests, take a general position on the topic, such as "Rain forests should be preserved" or "Rain forests belong to the people of the countries where they are located and should be left in their hands." For ten minutes or so, list as many arguments in favor of that statement as you can, as quickly as you can. Write every argument that comes into your head, without censoring it. If it occurs to you to write "Rain forests are pretty" or "I haven't been to a rain forest yet," go ahead and put those thoughts down. With some refinement, even the simplest observations can be shaped into reasonable arguments. Maybe you will decide that rain forests' beauty is reason enough for preserving them—many people agree that natural resources must be preserved for future generations to enjoy. For the time being, don't worry about *how* you will use the arguments you are inventing; just write down as many reasons for agreeing with your main proposition or thesis as you can. Don't quit listing reasons until the ten minutes or more that you have allotted for the exercise have elapsed. After you have remembered that rain forests harbor many plants and animals that will probably become extinct if their habitat is destroyed, that many of the plants in rain forests have medicinal value that is yet to be discovered, that rain forests are vital to the ecosystem of the entire earth, that once lost they cannot be replenished or renewed, and that they hold long-range economic value for the regions where they exist, keep going. Think beyond what you have read or heard about rain forests before. Why do *you* want rain forests to persist? No reason is too trivial or silly at this point. Perhaps you think they provide a nice contrast with deserts, which the earth has in abundance. Or maybe you appreciate the general environmental awareness and fund-raising efforts rain forests have inspired. When your time is up, draw a line across the page or start a new page with the same heading and, with equal enthusiasm, generate a list of arguments *against* your stated proposition.

Why the Pros and Cons Matter

Listing all of the arguments you can think of for and against your thesis will help you appreciate how much you really do know about your topic. It will make researching the subject more interesting, as you seek arguments you did not think of yourself or find specific information to reinforce those you have suggested. It will also provide you with a list of ideas that were familiar to you *before* you encountered them in the words and ideas of others. That is, it will help you establish which ideas you must document as the property of other writers and which are part of your own prior knowledge.

Finally, this exercise is likely to demonstrate to you that you need to further refine your thesis before you even start hunting for secondary material. If, for example, one argument against preserving rain forests is that the United States should stay out of other countries' domestic affairs, then you might wonder which other countries should take action to preserve rain forests—and which rain forests, specifically, they should preserve. Maybe you would decide to argue that the United States should encourage Brazil to protect its rain forests with a loan or debt forgiveness plan. Even if you decide that you do not yet know enough about your subject to sharpen your focus in this way, your list will still get you thinking about possible ways to narrow and shape your topic, and you can hunt for the specifics as you begin looking for secondary sources to consult.

■ Writing Your Provisional Draft

Once you have some ideas about the kinds of information and arguments your final paper might include, it is time to write a provisional draft. A *provisional* draft is one that stands as accurate *for the time being*. You are free to refine or even reverse your thesis later in your research process. The provisional draft is a document that records what you knew and thought about your topic before you began formally studying the ideas and writings of others.

At first, it sounds silly: write your paper before you conduct your research. But when you actually try it, you will discover that it is a very helpful exercise. If you write a provisional draft of your paper now, you will get a sense of the kinds of information you hope to discover and eventually include in the finished paper. Start by writing an introduction. What aspect of this topic first drew your attention? If you had to write a paper or give a presentation about it today, how would you begin? Make your opening as provocative or informative as you can. State your thesis by making the main assertion that you hope to support in your finished paper or presentation. You can be completely blunt about it in your provisional draft; indeed, you should be certain that you've stated your thesis perfectly clearly. Anyone reading this draft (including yourself) should know exactly where you stand on the issue at this minute.

Present the best arguments you have thought of so far, one by one. If you don't have information or statistics to back up a point you are making, indicate what you hope to find to support your argument and where and how you hope to find it. For example, if it would strengthen one of your arguments to cite how many traffic fatalities in your state occur among persons not wearing seat belts, but you don't know that number offhand, write right into your provisional draft your intention to include that information and your plans for discovering it (perhaps by calling the state highway patrol, say, if the library cannot supply that statistic readily). Besides providing a record of what you already know, your provisional draft can serve as an indicator of the things you will need to learn during your researching process.

Try to write a provisional draft of at least two double-spaced typed pages. That should be sufficient for you to determine whether the topic you've chosen has the potential to really interest you and whether you will want to pursue detailed research on it. Your provisional draft can serve as a topic proposal, too. You can show it to a classmate or friend and ask whether he or she thinks you've chosen a good subject for research. Your teacher might ask to read your provisional draft and then might offer advice about how to further restrict your topic, what kinds of sources to examine in libraries and archives, or persons you might want to interview as part of your research.

■ Kyle's Provisional Draft

Following is Kyle's provisional draft. As you read it, look for examples of how he is shaping his argument. Ask yourself whether he seems to understand the pros and cons of his argument. If you were Kyle's classmate, what advice or comments would you give him about this draft?

Over the past couple of years, a new and dynamic source of information has swept the world, enticing and luring people into an exciting, yet unknown frontier. The Internet and the World Wide Web (or the Net and the Web for short) have become woven into almost every facet of life; from the business environment to educational institutions to households everywhere, the presence of the Internet is evident. With a couple clicks of the mouse button, a person can find the current value of his or her stock portfolio, check out the latest sports highlights, e-mail a friend halfway around the world, or even write an entire research paper with sources from the Web, while never leaving the comfort of his or her chair.

Information is not the only inexhaustible resource that cybersurfers can stumble across while on the Web. As with everything else in our culture, businesses and entrepreneurs alike see the Web as the perfect medium to buy, sell, and trade various goods and services. The World Wide Web is a 24-hour-per-day, 7-day-per-week, 365-day-per-year nonstop commercial, where businesses and corporations can reach anyone who is on-line. Wal-Mart, Nike, Sony, and an endless number of other corporations have jumped at the opportunity to embed their names even deeper into the consciousness of consumers. If a person wants to find a site on the Web, there is an excellent chance that if he or she types in www.store-name.com, the corporate logo will appear in a matter of seconds on that person's computer screen.

For a short time, on-line commercials and advertising were enough to keep corporations content, but it did not last long. Soon the Web sites transformed into virtual shopping malls and storefronts, where a consumer could browse through page after page of products and merchandise, enter a few lines of information, and expect a shipment in five to seven business days. Everything from clothing to electronics to food was, and still is (with more being added every day) available with a couple of clicks of a mouse and a few keystrokes. All the consumer has to do is enter his or her credit card information (a sequence of the most important numbers in a person's life) and send it off to some computer thousands of miles away. Whoa, what did I just say? Send credit card information over the Internet—the same Internet that is accessed by millions of computers all over the globe?

To many people, fear is a real and present hindrance to using the Internet for anything but a one-way transfer of information. The Internet is simply too new and unknown for people to trust it with such crucial and vital information as their credit card numbers. People see it as a dark and dangerous place where hackers and thieves spend every waking minute breaking into so-called secure Web sites and stealing or destroying valuable data. Unfortunately, this view has caused many smaller businesses to settle for a static, brochure-like on-line presence. They simply do not have the financial or technical resources to implement security precautions that would alleviate the apprehension of many consumers. Even those companies that can afford the security measures still have not been able to significantly increase on-line purchasing, according to the articles I have read in computing magazines.

Whenever a story dealing with a company suffering an attack from hackers breaks, the media publicizes and emphasizes the mistakes of the company or institution, and this image has been ingrained into the minds of many people. The Internet is a new medium to many people, and when they hear that it is not safe, it scares them away from sending any information at all from their computers, even though it may be as simple as their name and address.

In essence, sending credit card information from computer to computer is not different from calling up an 800 number and giving your card number to an operator at the other end of the phone. What if that person copies down every card number given to him, or someone has bugged that phone? People do not worry much about those possible security leaks, because the phone is an integral part of our lives, and we ignore its dangers. At some point in the evolution of the Internet, people will laugh at those who were afraid to type in their credit card numbers. Once people become more educated about the security of the Internet and find they cannot live without it and the things it makes available to them, on-line shopping will be widespread and acceptable.

■ Summing Up

You probably know more about your research topic than you realize, right from the moment it first occurs to you. If you consider the time you first learned of the subject, what you have read or heard about it since then, and why you have maintained an interest in it, you will probably find that you have a plausible thesis for your research project right now and can already list some arguments for and against it. Start by freewriting about your topic to determine what aspects of it interest you the most and which of your own personal experiences relate to it and could shed some light on it. Next, in two brief, high-energy brainstorming sessions, list all of the arguments you can think of to support your proposed thesis and all of the arguments you can think of to counter it. When you have completed these steps, you will have generated most of the outline for your research project entirely on your own. Then, it is time for you to write a provisional draft—a version of your research paper without sources—to demonstrate for yourself what you already know and want to say about your topic.

Kyle's provisional draft proves that he knows a lot about his subject, even though he didn't think he knew much about it when he first proposed it. The draft draws on Kyle's own experience with surfing the Web and on reading he's already done about electronic marketing and sales on the Internet. Kyle has witnessed firsthand much of the history he will need to recount in his paper. He blames media coverage of crimes committed by hackers for the widespread apprehension among consumers about participating in online business transactions. He surmises that many people are still afraid to submit their credit card numbers over the Internet but offers assurance that it is really the same thing as providing an account number over the telephone. Kyle predicts that someday "people will laugh at those who were afraid to type in their credit card numbers." By the end of his provisional draft, Kyle has discovered that he wants to argue that Internet shopping is the wave of the future, and those who resist it are overly cautious.

Exercises: Sources and Strategies

1. Freewrite about your history with the topic you have chosen to research. When and how did you first hear about it? What have you learned about it since then? Have your thoughts about the topic changed over that time?

2. Working with one, two, or three of your classmates, take turns thinking up arguments for and against a topic proposed by each person. For each topic, have one person keep a written list of the ideas generated while the others state as many ideas as they can think of in ten minutes.

3. Write a short (two- or three-minute) speech or paper about your topic that you can read aloud to your class. Following your presentation, ask your classmates to discuss your thesis for three to five minutes. Take notes but do not participate in the discussion. Then listen to your classmates' presentations and discuss their topics as they take notes.

Writing to Know

Write a provisional draft describing the paper you intend to write, and ask a peer to read it and suggest arguments on either side of the issue that you have omitted or possible sources that you might want to consult in your researching process.

Chapter Eight

Researching the Topic

Sitting around home, you can think of lots of perfect solutions to specific problems—a scarf or necktie in exactly the right colors to coordinate your best slacks and blazer, inexpensive concert tickets for the weekend when you have a special date, a scholarship created especially for students just like yourself—but when you go out into the real world, you'll find that compromising is often the key to meeting your needs. The same is true of researching. You can imagine all kinds of data that would be perfect for your project, but you have to be realistic about what you are likely (and willing) to read and consider as part of your researching process. You can't know that the ideal information you wish for exists and is available until you actually see it, hear it, or have it under your fingertips.

An exhausting search culminating in a mammoth bibliography used to be the method used by the best students as they embarked on the researching phase of a big project, but the widespread availability of information and efficiency of electronic searching today has fostered a new model for search strategies—"smart searching." Smart searching is better than dogged exploration. Anyone with an Internet connection and a Web browser can download lists of thousands, maybe even millions, of print and electronic sources applicable, at least generally, to nearly any topic. In fact, finding information has become too easy for most topics. A quick electronic search can offer up more source material than a full-time researcher could comb through in a year; obviously, a college student with other classes to study for and a deadline looming could not even hope to review every item on such a list. However, the same inventions that produce such overabundance—Web search engines—also provide tools to streamline and customize your search requests, resulting in very specific and applicable results. (Chapter Three describes methods for electronic searching in detail.)

■ Getting Started

Referring to Encyclopedias

Your goal at this point in the researching process is to create a *working bibliography,* or a list of potential sources from which to draw evidence in support of your arguments in your final researched presentation. When you were a child, you probably wrote reports for school that relied completely on a single information source, such as an encyclopedia. Do you remember painstakingly copying information from the *Encyclopaedia Britannica* or *World Book* and later holding up the huge, heavy, unwieldy books in class to show the illustrations that accompanied your presentation? When I was a child, the encyclopedia introduced me to all kinds of wonders: oceans, whales, bears, tigers, dinosaurs, the Hope diamond, the Grand Canyon, the solar system. You may be surprised to learn that the encyclopedia is still a good place to start your library research. The information in an encyclopedia article is usually succinct, general, and reliable, making it a good first source to consult because it will summarize your topic efficiently for you, help you identify the kinds of information you need to find, and suggest other sources where you might find it. At the end of most encyclopedia articles is a list of related terms. Make note of these—they may come in handy later when you need to widen or restrict a computer search on your topic. You will be pleased to discover that it takes only minutes to read an encyclopedia entry when you are not copying it using a tightly gripped, oversized pencil.

Most encyclopedia articles are written by leading experts in their fields. It would seem, then, that encyclopedia articles would be outstanding sources to quote in a college research project; but as you probably know, they are not usually considered prestigious additions to a Works Cited list. One reason they are not esteemed in university research circles is their sheer availability. Nearly every library on campus, including residence hall study rooms, has an old set of encyclopedias on hand. Anyone seeking the information collected there has only to peruse the alphabetized listings. Almost anyone who can read can locate an encyclopedia and study a specific entry in less time than it would take you to compile a simple working bibliography for a college research project. A college student is expected to collect and synthesize both a wider range of information and more specialized information than a common set of encyclopedia offers.

Thus neither encyclopedias nor dictionaries are acceptable secondary sources for most college research assignments. These sources may oversimplify information so as to present it succinctly in a volume or series covering everything from Aardvarks to Zurich. A research project must take into account the complexity of its subject. Consequently, a source that provides a quick gloss on your topic may not add much to your final product. Don't mistake a source that should not be quoted with one that should not be consulted, however. Encyclopedias and dictionaries can help you quickly crystallize your ideas and condense complex topics into manageable units. If, for instance, you are arguing in favor of the theory of continental drift, the scientific assertion that the land masses on Earth have gradually shifted over time to create the continents as we recognize them today, it would be useful to review that topic in a general encyclopedia, refreshing your memory before surveying articles in specialized scientific and geologic journals. At the end of the encyclopedia article, you would find a list of related topics, such as plate tectonics, geography, and paleogeography. Since plate tectonics is closely related to the topic of continental drift, you might want to read that article as well and keep that subject heading in mind as you search various indexes for further information.

Checking Indexes

An *index* in the reference section of your library is generally an organized bibliography. It does not contain actual articles or other documents; rather, it is a directory of material in print, organized by subject. An index provides you with the "names and addresses" of information on your topic. It lists books, articles, and archival items by title and name of author, and it tells briefly (usually using abbreviations, explained at the front or back of each volume) how to find the material you want, whether it is a book, a magazine or newspaper, or the published proceedings of a conference or meeting. An index is a list of items from which you will choose the entries in your working bibliography.

Checking Specialized Encyclopedias   After you have read general encyclopedia entries on your topic, search the reference section of your library for specialized encyclopedias that may be useful to you. A librarian can show you how to limit your search to the reference section of the particular library you are using. Specialized encyclopedias may consist of full sets of volumes that provide comprehensive coverage of a general topic, such as the *Grove Encyclopedia of Music*, but they are often single-volume references that concentrate on a narrow academic discipline or subject. They are useful to your researching process in the same way that general encyclopedias are, but they offer slightly more in-depth coverage, and because they are smaller and more economical to edit and reissue, they may offer more current information than general encyclopedias present. For instance, if you do a key word search of your library's electronic card catalog for "geology and encycloped(?)" and confine the search to that library's reference section call letters, you may find that the library has one or more intermediary, or specialized, encyclopedias on your topic, such as *The Encyclopedia of Structural Geology and Plate Tectonics*, edited by Carl K. Seyfert. These highly portable authorities provide another good introduction to your subject, and they usually provide a list of related and alternate subject headings that you can use in future searches.

■ Finding Descriptors

The first step in compiling a working bibliography is to create a list of *descriptors*, or words that describe the topic or information you hope to find. Your library will have a set of reference books called *The Library of Congress Subject Headings Index*, which names the descriptors under which the materials on various topics are filed in a typical research library. Add to your list of possible subject headings gathered from the end of encyclopedia articles the official and alternate descriptors given by the Library of Congress cataloging system. If you use subject searches in your library's electronic card catalog, you will need to use the standard Library of Congress headings.

Because the Library of Congress cataloging system has been in use for a long time, some of its terminology is archaic. For instance, if you search in most libraries for "movies" or "films," you will not have much luck, because the descriptor used by the Library of Congress system is "moving pictures." The contemporary term "African-American" is included in the printed listing of *The Library of Congress Subject Headings Index*, but it is cross-referenced to the descriptor used by the electronic system ("Negroid Race"), which is the one that will access the sources you want. Searching a card catalog without first consulting the index can be marginally successful, but it is like guessing at an address instead of looking it up. You may be narrowly or vastly misdirecting your search.

A music student once observed that parents who would not give their children violins and expect them to learn to play them on their own will give their offspring traps sets and assume that children can teach themselves to play percussion instruments. He wanted to argue in a research paper that it takes training to play any musical instrument, and parents should provide lessons with drum sets so that children will be successful in their experimentation with them. He searched the subject "drum(?)," anticipating that he would find information on drums, drumming, drum lessons, and the like. Instead the computerized card catalog in his college library offered him several dozen sources about oil production, embargoes, and price predictions for petroleum products. By using *The Library of Congress Subject Headings Index*, he determined that searching for materials on "percussion instruments" would yield the information he wanted.

In a comprehensive research library, information about nearly every topic imaginable is available. Therefore, if you discover that your library has "nothing" on your topic, chances are that you are not using the appropriate descriptors to access what is there. If you are searching by subject, it is well worth the extra few minutes it will take to verify that your descriptors are included in the catalog. Once you've entered an accepted subject heading, the electronic search program in use at your library may suggest related subject headings when it provides results. The subjects shown in a topic tree on a World Wide Web search engine or directory page may prove useful as well.

Using reference sources to establish a list of descriptors, a student searching for information on plate tectonics could compile a list of terms including the following:

Earth	Atlantic Ocean
continental drift	Cenozoic era
geologic history	Arthur Holmes

paleogeography	Permian period
oceans	F. J. Vine
Alfred Lothar Wegener	fossils
ice age	Devonian period
paleoclimatology	dinosaurs
Carboniferous period	geophysics
continental shield	Jurassic period
geology	Mesozoic era
Asia	Triassic period

Obviously, some of the related subjects suggested by preliminary sources will be off your topic. *Dinosaurs*, for example, although tangentially related to plate tectonics, probably would not lead to much useful information. Given the enormous variety of material about dinosaurs in print, one would be wise to avoid including that descriptor in a search for information on plate tectonics. The various geologic periods and eras that turn up as related subjects may indicate potential ways to focus this topic, by restricting the discussion to just one of the alleged shifts in Earth's land masses (arguing, for example, that North America and Europe were connected during the Triassic period). Notice, too, that personal names often surface in lists of descriptors. These often make possible the use of biographical sources and anecdotes to enliven expository prose. After you have amassed a sizeable list of potential descriptors, you will want to eliminate those that are too broad or tangential and concentrate on just three or four that you believe are most closely applicable to your subject and thesis.

■ Defining Search Parameters

Now you have to ask yourself some questions about the kinds of sources you hope to find. How current must your sources be? If you chose your topic because of a sensational news story, you may find that most of what was said about the topic before the media took hold of it is outdated. It is highly likely that for any "current events" topic you choose there will have been a watershed in the media coverage of the subject following some high-profile event, such as a revolutionary medical discovery, a Supreme Court ruling, or, at the very least, a celebrity endorsement. If, for example, you are arguing in favor of euthanasia, anything printed prior to the first trial of Dr. Jack Kervorkian might be dated and supply insufficient data.

Ask yourself when you first became aware of the issue you plan to research. Your own awakening about the topic was, more than likely, stimulated by media attention to it. Identify major newsworthy events related to your topic and define a period of not more than ten years when information about the topic would have been reported in the media. For very current events, you may find that only the last three or four months of coverage will be relevant. For some topics—for example, a reexamination of an enduring piece of literature that has been deemed a classic for fifty years or more—it will be harder to limit the time period to ten years. A piece of literature may be heavily reviewed shortly after it is first published and again when its author produces another masterpiece or when another writer releases a comparable text. However, when you begin compiling a list of articles and books on your topic, periods of high activity around your issue will begin to reveal themselves if you pay close attention to publication dates of the sources you locate.

At this point, you may be tempted to limit the kinds of sources you want to cite in your research paper. For example, you may want to avoid articles in general interest periodicals and news magazines, deferring instead to the authority of specialized journals. Although most college-level researchers will avoid tabloid publications such as the *National Enquirer* or *People*, you should not rule out other, reputable sources. General news publications such as *USA Today*, *Time*, *U.S. News and World Report*, *Science*, and *Psychology Today* may prove as valuable to you as the *Journal of the American Medical Association* or the *Journal of Physics of the Earth*. Wait to see what individual writers have said, and then weigh the evidence each presents. You are conducting research to find good information, not impressive sources.

As you discover what your library and the Internet have to offer, do not think in snobbish or restrictive terms. Your working bibliography should serve as a catalog of what is available and what you might read or consult; it implies no promise that you will study each item on the list, so be inclusive. Restrict your topic and descriptors so that you find information that is directly applicable to the research project you are proposing, but do not limit the kinds of sources you will consider at this point.

Now is the time, however, when you may want to decide how far you are willing to go for information. Will your local or campus library supply you with all of the materials you need? Or should you consider making a trip to a regional library? Such libraries offer, for example, comprehensive collections of government publications, important archived artifacts, and specialized collections on specific topics. If your college or university does not offer an academic major related to your subject, but one nearby does, you may want to consider traveling to that school's library for a day to use some advanced materials. Maybe you could combine your trip to the library with an interview of a faculty member or student in a specialized academic discipline there. A less adventuresome but equally useful course of action is to request materials through your interlibrary loan program, so long as you have enough time to wait for them and still complete your research project. Calculate whether you will have time to travel to out-of-town interviews, wait for e-mail responses to your questions, or have lengthy telephone conversations with distant experts. Budgeting your time now will help you decide how much reading you can realistically do and thus how far you should fling your net in searching for working bibliography items.

While you are at it, decide how much, if any, money you are willing to spend on your project. You can complete a comprehensive, exciting research project with equipment and materials borrowed at no cost from your school's facilities. You can conduct first-rate interviews over the Internet, thereby avoiding long-distance phone charges, and you can download video clips and transcripts of network news and entertainment shows from the World Wide Web, possibly onto university computers in student labs. You may even be able to sign out video and audio recording equipment or digital cameras and use college-owned editing and computer graphics equipment to get professional-looking results. Or you may want to budget money for travel, purchased or rented video footage, television transcripts, postage, books bought in stores, video or audio tape, camera film, and long-distance phone calls as part of your project. Decide in advance how much money you are willing to commit to your assignment so you don't end up feeling resentful of your project later on. Remember, too, that your teacher is not going to give "extra credit" for your spending money on your project. The only extra return you will realize from financial commitments to your project will be personal satisfaction.

■ Determining Whether a Topic Is Too Broad or Narrow

As soon as you begin looking for possible materials to read for your research project, you will know if you have defined your topic too broadly or narrowly. The number of sources your preliminary bibliographic searches turn up will help you decide which of your descriptors produces the most information. For example, the following descriptors were used in a single bibliographic index, which listed the indicated number of articles for each one:

continental drift	166
paleogeography	276
Wegener, Alfred Lothar	57
Vine, F. J.	2
geophysics	69
continental shield	0

Clearly, "continental shield," although it was suggested by an encyclopedia, was not a useful descriptor for this index. However, don't be too quick to decide that "continental drift" and "paleogeography" were too broad. If you combine two such terms in a key word search in an electronic index, you may find as few as twenty matches. (Indeed, in a quick test search, combining "continental drift" and "geophysics" yielded only a dozen articles, all squarely debating the theory of continental drift.) Although you will eliminate some descriptors as you search through indexes (a couple more results like the one above for articles and books on the subject of "continental shield," and you would soon tire of looking under that heading), you will be most satisfied with your working bibliography if you continue to search using the majority of the descriptors you have discovered.

It is also likely that you will continue to add to your list of descriptors as your preliminary searching continues. Words in the title of books and articles that you discover will suggest themselves as possible descriptors, and cross-referencing advice in indexes may contain additional words to add to your list. Don't be afraid to add words to your collection of descriptors or to go back through the sources you have checked already, looking up words you have recently added to your list. Your goal at this point in the process is to determine exactly what information exists to support your projected thesis.

■ Compiling a Working Bibliography

As you have probably gathered from the preceding discussion, a working bibliography is simply a list of sources that may be available for consultation in your research process. The working bibliography you compile now will be much longer than the Works Cited list that will accompany your final research project. The working bibliography is like the wish list many children write to Santa Claus each winter. It contains everything you would use if you had world enough and time to truly become an expert on the topic you are researching. Just as kids often ask for things they know they cannot have in their letters to Santa (ponies and spaceships, to name a couple), it is okay to include obscure or rare materials on your working bibliography. If you ever wrote a letter to Santa, you may remember asking for gifts that you knew were redundant or extravagant, such as "every electric train in the hobby shop." You can do that again when you compile your working bibliography. Although you know you will probably not read every article on your list, even if you could locate them all, you are merely assembling a list of your options, to be sorted out later. You also know, if you have any experience at compiling wish lists, that you should not waste your time requesting things you do not really want. Don't forgo that shiny new bike for a dishwasher unless you really would rather unload sparkling warm glassware while your friends are out peddling around in the park. Similarly, don't include items on your working bibliography just because it would be nice to know more about an ancillary topic in addition to or instead of the information you will need to complete your research assignment. For example, a researcher attempting to validate the theory of continental drift should by-pass sources about animal evolution, a closely related subject, even if the researcher finds that topic interesting and it surfaces frequently in his or her searches. Carefully differentiate between the information you want and the information you need, both now and on future wish lists.

■ Generating a List of Print Sources

It doesn't matter where you start looking for potential sources to include on your working bibliography since you're really in a scavenger phase of the project. Collect every possible lead you can find, any source you may be able to use to inform yourself, and ultimately your audience, about your topic. You may want to begin by generating a list of print sources, however, because what you don't find in the library will dictate what you must learn elsewhere. Start with the search tools that are easiest to use, such as your library's computerized card catalog or a CD-ROM index. Try entering your descriptors as subject searches and key word searches, singly and in combinations. It won't take long to discover which words or combinations yield the most applicable results. Remember, the goal in looking for sources is not to find a huge number of articles and books that you will eventually have to sort through and read but to lead yourself to the information that your provisional draft and your vision for the final project indicate you will need. Of course, you will discover that there is information out there that you haven't yet imagined, and you will want to check some of that out, too. For example, a researcher who advocates probation and public service for white-collar criminals rather than burdening our overcrowded prisons with such offenders may discover that alternative, residential supervisory facilities for white-collar criminals are already in use around the country.

Although it's true that you cannot judge a book by its cover, you will be surprised how much the titles of the articles and books you find about your topic will reveal concerning what kind of information is available on that subject. Don't be surprised if you are tempted to alter your topic or change the focus of your research project once you begin to discover the kinds of information that already exist on your topic. Just make sure that if you decide to deviate from your original proposal, you are doing so because the information you've found warrants changes in your ideas, not because it makes changing your topic more convenient in the short run. A student looking for information about alternatives to prison for white-collar criminals, for example, might stumble on a trove of fascinating stories about prison violence and so decide to change her topic to tightening prison security. Eventually, she may feel that she sold out an intriguing topic for a dull one, simply because provocative information fell into her path. Changing topics in the middle of a research project usually results in disappointment or disinterest later on in the process.

Keep a clear notion of the kinds of information you need in mind while you are searching for items to include on your working bibliography. It might help to reread your provisional draft periodically throughout your searching process. A good definition of your topic will help you focus your search for relevant materials. If you start with an electronic search of library materials on your subject, keep refining your search by adding descriptors until you generate a workable list, usually twenty to fifty potential sources, that seem to be directly applicable to the project you intend to produce. Don't print out the results of your search until it looks like about 90 percent of it is potentially useful to you.

Expect an exhaustive search of your library's on-line indexes to take at least a couple of hours. Computers work fast, but they don't make logical generalizations, so you may have to enter dozens of searches and combinations of searches for subjects, authors, titles, and key words before you can be certain that you've thoroughly searched the database for items related to your topic. When you have finished using your library's on-line indexes, you may have quite an impressive list of possible sources in hand, but you will be cheating yourself and your audience if you stop there. Recognize that indexes are not customized to reflect everything in any individual library. They are generic guides intended for use in all kinds of libraries all over the nation or world. That is why you will frequently find references to materials your library does not possess, and why the corollary is also true—that your library contains much more information than any single index will predict. Your library's card catalog is an accurate list of the cover titles in your library's actual holdings, but when you use an index that tells you what is *inside* books and periodicals, it almost definitely will not have come from your library and will not attempt to accurately describe the contents of the unique facility you are using. That is why you must consult a variety of indexes covering a wide range of periodicals and collections of material to access most of the relevant information in any single library. No library will have everything in any given index, and no index will list every object in any specific library.

■ Specialized On-line Databases

Some specialized on-line databases already exist, and more are sure to be developed soon. One of the most popular ones is the Education Resources Information Center (ERIC) database. ERIC catalogs journal articles and documents of interest to the teaching profession. You will probably want a librarian to help orient you to the on-line databases you use, because each has its own format. In ERIC, for example, items are cataloged according to "accession numbers," which indicate whether the data is printed in a journal or on microfilm. ERIC also has its own dictionary of subject headings, called the *Thesaurus of ERIC Descriptors*, against which you should check the descriptors you are using to make sure they are recognized by the ERIC search software. Individual indexes, whether on-line, on CD-ROM, or in print, each have their own organization and referencing systems. Don't be daunted by these, and don't give up easily. Vital information that you seek may be encoded in these documents. Always ask a librarian to help you when an index does not produce the kind of results you expect from it.

CD-ROM Indexes

Another type of index you will probably want to check out, with the help of a reference librarian, is a CD-ROM index. Searching a bibliography on CD-ROM is a lot like searching an electronic database: using a computer, you type in subjects and key words from your list of descriptors and get back nearly instant results. A CD-ROM index is basically an extensive bibliography that can be read by a computer. The information is recorded on CDs, which are periodically sent to your library and can be read using the appropriate software. CD-ROMs tend to be used for specialized indexes, so it is a good idea to ask a librarian which, if any, CD-ROM indexes your library subscribes to that might pertain to your search. Because very sophisticated information from technical and professional journals is not included in general on-line indexes, you need to consult CD-ROM indexes to find highly specialized recent information.

Consulting Print Indexes

There is one serious limitation to many electronic indexes: they don't go back far enough. Johann Gutenberg printed his first book, a Latin Bible, about 550 years ago, and copies of it are still housed in rare book libraries today. Computers, by contrast, have only been in widespread use since the 1980s. Even with optical scanners and other inventions that speed the work, it's going to be a long time before everything printed in the last half millennium is cataloged electronically. Most electronic indexes only include material published after 1991. Even if your topic is a very current event, chances are your understanding of it could benefit from at least a sampling of sources from before 1991. For a listing of items published more than a decade ago, you will need to consult print indexes.

The most widely recognized periodical index in most libraries is *The Reader's Guide to Periodical Literature*. Intended as an inclusive, basic bibliography, the *Reader's Guide* lists articles in popular magazines and journals by subject. You may want to start your search of print indexes with the *Reader's Guide* because it is familiar, is easy to use, and contains references to information on almost every imaginable subject. It will lead you to articles in such popular magazines as *Time* and *Look* and to subject-orientated periodicals aimed at a general reading audience, such as *Psychology Today* and *Business Week*. A good research library will still have on hand many of the articles listed in back issues of the *Reader's Guide*, so it is a good place to begin combing through pages of small print and abbreviations to find source material for your research project.

It may be difficult to persuade yourself to use print indexes when electronic searching seems so easy in comparison. When you use a print index, you have to skim through lists of article titles in search of ones that look potentially useful. Key word searching is impossible with most print indexes, and those that publish abstracts of articles take longer to skim. Then, once you find a title that sounds promising, you actually have to use a pen and paper and create your own "printout" of the relevant bibliographic information. Sound arduous? Don't complain to your teachers about the tediousness of the process. For most of us, electronic searching was not common when we were students. Most of your college teachers wrote huge research papers and dissertations hundreds of pages long, compiling enormous bibliographies, using this crude method.

Print indexes are going to introduce you to some magazines and journals you've never seen in your dentist's waiting room. Journals like *Publications of the Modern Language Association* and the *Journal of Psychosocial Nursing and Mental Health Services* have a relatively small readership (just in the thousands of subscribers), and the information they report is very specialized, even esoteric, so their contents are not surveyed for most of the general indexes to which libraries subscribe. Instead, their articles are listed in specialized print indexes such as the *Bibliography of the Modern Language Association* and the *Nursing and Allied Health Sciences Index.* Journals exist for most every profession. Doctors, for example, can subscribe to the *Journal of Endocrinology*, the *Journal of Otolaryngology*, the *Journal of the History of Medicine and Allied Sciences,* the *Journal of Adolescent Health Care,* the *Journal of Psychosomatic Research, Tropical Medicine and International Health, Holistic Nursing Practice,* and *Death Studies*—to name just a few, and these and hundreds more like them are included in a print index called *Index Medicus.* There are journals that deal solely with a single disease, such as leprosy. Thus you don't have to wait for the *Journal of the American Medical Association* or the *New England Journal of Medicine* to publish a study on a particular topic; if you locate the right specialized index, you will find that articles are published on almost every topic almost every month.

Before you leave the library for the time being, stop by the special archives or government publications area and run a check of your most useful descriptors through the cataloging systems there. Both of these are potential sites for key evidence that other researchers have overlooked.

■ Keeping a Research Process Journal

You might want to start keeping a research process journal. Set aside some space in your notebook or start a file in your computer's word processing program where you can record what you've attempted and accomplished each day toward completing your research project. Because an assignment such as this is daunting, and many of the steps involved in the process are time-consuming, you may think that you won't have an opportunity to work on your research project every day. However, if you start listing the things you do for it each day, you will find that you will want to do *something* every day, just so that you can record it as proof that you are thinking about and working on your assignment. A research process journal will also remind you which phone calls and e-mail messages you need to follow up on, which questions you need a librarian to answer, and with whom you have spoken in your quest to gain an interview with an expert on your topic. You might choose to write a short narrative at the end of each day, telling of your triumphs and frustrations with the researching process. Or, you might prefer to simply list the things you have done and include reminders to yourself about what you must accomplish in the coming days. Whatever you make of it, use the journal to motivate yourself, *not* merely as a substitute for really accomplishing the work you must do.

Most research libraries are mammoth. You can't wander the stacks until the information you need falls down on you. You want to spend the least amount of time possible "shopping" for materials and the most amount of time you can actually reading and taking notes on them. But you want the very best data that your time and ingenuity can buy. Making thorough use of the indexes your library offers will pay off not only in the depth and detail of your working bibliography but also in the sources you cite in your research project and, ultimately, in the quality and reliability of your paper or presentation.

A working bibliography should not begin and end in a library, although library materials may account for the majority of sources on your wish list. Using the same descriptors you generated for library searching, try finding information about your topic on the World Wide Web. As you know, the Web is different from an index because it supplies actual documents on your screen, not merely addresses for them. Searching the Web may take longer than browsing through library indexes, because you might as well take down notes on Web items when you have them on screen.

As you probably know, the Web is a great source for consumer information and for tracking fast-breaking news stories. The date listed for journal articles posted on the Internet can be misleading, however. Often, material is not uploaded to the Web until after it has been released in a print version, and most Web sites are dated with the day the material was posted on-line, not the day it was written or originally pulished. People are still posting to the Web articles and documents that were published in print form long before the rise of cyberspace, so beware of very recently dated information on the Internet. Furthermore, some documentation models suggest listing Web materials on Works Cited list by the date they were accessed, which makes dating information on the Web even more confusing. Because the Web is still considered unreliable in some academic circles, it is a good idea to corroborate or balance information gathered on the Web with print data whenever possible. (See Chapter Three for a more detailed discussion of World Wide Web searching.)

Once you have compiled your working bibliography, although it may still be a bit early to decide who you'd like to interview, you can make a list of the kinds of people you might want to consult during your researching process. Which professionals are involved with the problem you are examining? Are ordinary people affected by it? Is there someone closely involved with this issue who is well respected by his or her peers, if not exactly famous? Using the library and the World Wide Web, can you locate e-mail addresses or telephone numbers for these people? Are there businesses or large corporations with an interest in your issue? Which professional societies or trade unions are involved with it? Try to collect the information you need to contact important individuals and groups, so that you will have a list of potential contacts who might be able to answer your questions later on.

Consider whether there are relevant geographical sites nearby or in places you can feasibly visit. Be creative. It may be impossible for you to take a hike in an actual rain forest, but perhaps you could journey to a simulated rain forest at a zoo or spend an afternoon in a local wetland, observing the variety of plant and animal life that proliferate there. What would make your topic come to life for you? Meeting people or visiting places that have some relevance to your research will probably enhance your enthusiasm for the subject, and that, in turn, will pay off in a more exciting, engaging final product.

At this point, you should have a real mess surrounding you:

- Printouts from library catalogs and CD-ROM programs

- Notes and photocopies from print indexes and government publications catalogs

- Call numbers from archival collections

- Printouts of pages from the World Wide Web

- Phone numbers and Web addresses on scraps of paper

- Business cards or names of people your friends have suggested

- The occasional neatly lettered note card containing a full bibliographic citation for a library book (maybe)

Don't attempt to over organize your working bibliography, and don't even think of typing or alphabetizing it. Your working bibliography is no more than an evolving set of "leads," a pile of possible sources. It will grow and diminish throughout your researching process; it is never "done." As you begin accessing some of the sources you have there, they will lead you to others. Your working bibliography is always an open case, an active file. Stuff all of its contents into an envelope or folder with room for additions. Even though you have probably collected references to more source material than you can possibly read this semester, you will soon be glad that you have it all. A thorough working bibliography reduces the world of information to a set of navigable maps.

■ Kyle's Working Bibliography

Because his computer is running almost twenty-four hours a day, seven days a week, Kyle started by looking for information on his topic on the World Wide Web. As you might guess, his topic, credit card security in electronic commerce, was hotly debated. He printed out a large number of the on-line sources that he found and immediately realized that "finding the necessary sources would not be a problem." In the library, he tried entering a key word search for "Internet and credit card(?)" and found that most of the "matches" produced by his library's on-line periodical searching program were not as relevant as he'd hoped they would be. Most of the articles suggested by that database dealt with charges for Internet connections by commercial Internet service providers. However, certain that the library had more to offer (based on his overwhelmingly successful Web search), he tried an on-line business periodicals index. The same key word search yielded nearly four hundred "hits," and among those he found several promising titles, such as the following:

Author:	Rupley, Sebastian
Title:	Virtual plastic: banks to issue digital Visas. (VeriSign to provide authentication services for Visa on the Web.)
Journal:	PC Magazine Sept 24 1996, v15, n16, p34(1)
ISSN:	0888-8507

Author:	Lewis, Peter H.
Title:	A technology for the cyber-marketing age. (First Virtual Holdings; electronic commerce scheme.)
Journal:	The New York Times Sept 18 1996, v145, pC1(N) pD1(L), col 2
ISSN:	0362-4331

Author:	Shein, Esther
Title:	The virtual storefronts. (The Web sites of Wal-Mart, Sam's Club, and other retailers support electronic commerce.)
Journal:	PC Week Sept 23 1996, v13, n38, pE1(3)

Author:	Kutler, Jeffrey
Title:	Infrastructure ready, but the waiting has just begun (Merchant Processing: Cards and Electronic Commerce)
Description:	(graph)
Journal:	American Banker Sept 30 1996, v161, n187, p14(2)
ISSN:	0002-7561

Author:	Stipe, Suzanne E.
Title:	High-tech cure is at hand for Internet insecurities.
Journal:	Best's Review—Life-Health Insurance Edition Sept 1996, v97, n5, p106(2)
ISSN:	0005-9706

Author:	Field, Christopher
Title:	A web of misconception. (Improvement of Internet commerce security continues despite evidence that risk is minimal.)
Description:	(photograph, table)
Journal:	Computer Weekly Sept 26 1996, p46(1)
ISSN:	0010-4787

Title:	Commercial transactions on the Internet
Journal:	International Journal of Retail and Distribution Management Sept 1996, v24, n9, pS8(1)
ISSN:	0959-0552

Author:	Emert, Carol
Title:	Online shops linger in future.
Description:	(photograph)
Journal:	HFN The Weekly Newspaper for the Home Furnishing Network August 5 1996, v70, n32 p12(1)

Author:	Hisey, Pete
Title:	Wal-Mart seeks shoppers with on-line service.
Description:	(other)
Journal:	Discount Store News August 19 1996, v35, n16, p1(2)

Title:	Worry-free Web shopping: save your customers from security scares
Description:	(photograph)
Journal:	Success July-August 1996, v43, n6, p56(1)
ISSN:	0745-2489

Author:	Tebbe, Mark
Title:	Credit card fraud hype hurts Web.
Journal:	PC Week July 15 1996, v13, n28, pN17(1)

Title:	Sign here: electronic commerce.
Description:	(Other)
Journal:	The Economist July 27 1996, v340, n7976 p54(1)

Author:	Kutler, Jeffrey
Title:	After truce on on-line security, card groups come out fighting.
Description:	(Table, chart)
Journal:	American Banker July 26 1996, v161, n142, p1(2)
ISSN:	0002-7561

Author:	West, Diane
Title:	Virtual cash called secure for net transactions.
Journal:	National Underwriter, Life & Health-Financial Services Edition June 10 1996, n24, p62(1)
ISSN:	0893-8282

Author:	MacConnol, Martin
Title:	Forgers surf the Internet.
Description:	(graph)
Journal:	The Financial Times June 29 1996, n33022, pWFT8(1)

The range of periodical titles provided by the business index, from a home furnishings marketers trade journal to financial newspapers, looked promising to Kyle. He could get many different perspectives on his topic from these sources and possibly bring together ideas that he had not connected before. He asked a librarian for help, and she suggested he try a CD-ROM index called *Computer Select* that gave him another diverse list of possible sources (with only some repetition from the business index). Several corporations' names began to appear frequently in the titles of magazine and journal articles, so Kyle used on-line directories to find e-mail addresses and phone numbers for marketing executives at Wal-Mart, L. L. Bean, Pizza Hut, Gateway, and Microsoft. He asked one of his computer science professors to suggest local people he could interview about Internet credit card security, and she suggested two possibilities: a purchasing agent at the university and a marketing professor with a keen interest in the Internet. When Kyle called, the purchasing agent said she knew very little about the topic and was unwilling to be interviewed for Kyle's paper, but the marketing professor set an appointment for a meeting a week in advance, to give Kyle time to read more about the subject before the interview.

In the following week, Kyle continued to gather information from the World Wide Web and the library. Suddenly, he found himself caught up in his research. His research process journal for three days during that time shows the number of leads he was pursuing simultaneously:

September 10

I e-mailed Dr. Buis today. I hope he responds.

September 11

Today I did a little bit more Web surfing. I found a few new things, including a proposal between Wal-Mart and Microsoft on creating an Internet economy, some other general topics related to e-mail rights,; and credit card security issues. I also went back to the library and looked in the *Computer Select* database and found a few more articles from magazines.

September 12

Today I followed up on ideas:

- Talked to someone at Gateway on the phone, and they are going to send me some information by overnight mail.

- Talked to a representative at L. L. Bean on the phone, and he said they are waiting for some security issues to be resolved before going on-line with sales, although they have advertising on-line now.

- Looked on the Web for other big-name companies with product sales over the Web now—no luck, though.

September 13

Today I received the package of information from Gateway. The information was mainly financial reports for 1995, along with some press releases—not much help.

September 14

An area that I need to look into is finding an article concerning the joint cooperation of VISA and MasterCard in solving security problems. *The New York Times* or a larger paper like that may have that information in it, but I've got to go looking for it.

I talked to a friend, and she gave me a name to contact: D_____ T_____. My friend thinks he may have bought something on-line from Gateway. She gave me his e-mail address, and I need to send him a letter to see if he has any knowledge or opinions about the subject.

A couple of other things I need to do:

- Call Gateway and see if I can talk to a real person, get an interview to include in the paper, talk to someone associated with direct sales and on-line sales (someone important)
- Call a professor who once mentioned buying airline tickets on his computer
- Track down some smaller companies doing business on the Web
- Put out a question on the SEI data list
- Find a consumer protection agency or firm that advises on credit card use

■ *Summing Up*

Before you can start researching your topic, you must start "researching your research," or discovering what information is available to you. Reading general and specialized encyclopedias is a good way to get an overview of your topic and start a list of terms, or descriptors, under which information about your subject might be filed in electronic and print indexes. You should also look in the *Library of Congress Subject Headings Index* to discover the key words used to describe your topic in most research libraries.

As you begin examining indexes in search of materials on your topic, notice when most of the information about your subject was published. From the titles of the sources you encounter, try to infer some of the specific controversies and related subtopics surrounding your topic. For instance, if you are looking for information about choosing host cities for the Olympic Games and articles and books about security keep cropping up, you might want to focus your research on that angle. Also, notice which of your descriptors consistently yields relevant results, and modify your list of searching terms as you work. Combine one or more of your most successful descriptors in key word searches, and expect to add and delete descriptors as you experiment with them.

Your objective at this point in the researching process is to compile a working bibliography, or a wish list of the articles, books, government publications, archival matter, World Wide Web sites, interviews, and experiences you hope to learn from. To gain access to all of the materials in your library, you will need to use some print and CD-ROM indexes, which a librarian can help you locate and learn to use. Your working bibliography will be an organized chaos of computer printouts (like Kyle's, reproduced in this chapter), hand-copied citations from print indexes, library call numbers, phone numbers, URLs, and personal names.

Start a research journal, like Kyle's, so that you will have a place to record all of these "leads" and your progress in following up on them. Notice that Kyle's journal tracks his pursuit of printed, electronic, and interview sources. Like Kyle, you should try to discover as many relevant sources as you can.

Exercises: Sources and Strategies

1. Using encyclopedia entries, the *Library of Congress Subject Headings Index*, and the cross-referencing and indexing headings in several on-line or CD-ROM indexes, compile a list of descriptors that might lead you to information about your topic.

2. Start a researching-process journal like Kyle's, and use it to record what you have attempted and accomplished and to motivate yourself to make some progress on your research assignment every day.

3. Compile a working bibliography on your topic. Be as thorough as possible. Try to find bibliographic citations for as many sources as possible that are perfectly suited to your research needs.

Writing to Know

Write and design a trifold pamphlet (made from a regular 8½ x 11" page, folded into thirds) about researching a topic in a specific subject (such as history, chemistry, Caribbean literature, advertising, vintage vehicle restoration, historic preservation, and so on). List useful words and phrases to use in Internet and library searches, the titles of magazines and journals that are pertinent, special library collections of interest, even names of experts in the field who are widely published on the subject. Plan to leave a few copies of your pamphlet with your instructor so that he or she can pass them on to future students writing on similar topics.

Chapter Nine

Collecting Information

*M*ost writers dread the start of this phase of a research project. They know it will involve setbacks and frustrations, confusing articles that must be carefully deciphered, unreturned phone calls and lost e-mail, crashed servers and jammed photocopiers, materials that aren't where the indexes say they are, books that don't deliver on the promises their titles make, and work days that turn into long work nights. Especially if your working bibliography is filled with references to promising sources, the task of beginning to read, listen, look, and take notes can seem overwhelming. Worst of all, you probably feel that you need to be an expert on the topic before you begin so that you can understand the assumptions, assertions, and allusions in every source you read. The good news is that the worst part about collecting information for a research project is the dread everyone feels at the outset of the task. Once you start finding the information you want and delving into opposing opinions about your topic, you will probably find yourself engrossed and fascinated by the researching process. It is a common phenomenon, after literally dragging yourself off to the library to conduct research, to eventually find yourself still there at closing time, wishing they would just keep the lights on so you could stay and read for a few more hours.

Anyone with a working bibliography holds a map to some promising, if untested, fishing holes. It is best to get right to work scoping out the sources you have found reference to in your library. Seasoned researchers can tell you about "the ones that got away," such as the perfectly relevant title affixed to an article that turned out to be about another topic entirely, or the heaven-sent special issue of a journal that was lost heaven knows where. One of the most discouraging experiences a library researcher can have is to locate the proper bound volume of a periodical, find the correct issue inside, discover the sought-after article title on its table of contents, and then eagerly page through the yellowed paper only to find that the relevant leaves have been "lifted" or cut away by a thoughtless vandal who would destroy a book rather than just use a photocopier. Fortunately, technologies such as microfilm and digital scanning are making the effects of such selfish crimes less and less common. Nevertheless, the range and number of things that can go wrong at this seemingly simple stage of the game may surprise or dismay you. Remember that setbacks and dead ends can occur at any stage in the researching process, and they are neither omens of defeat nor signs that you should change your topic.

■ *Organizing Your Search*

Researching is not a linear process. As you read articles and books, review relevant data, visit places and people connected to your topic, and discuss with your professors and classmates the information you discover, you will find that items you did not list on your working bibliography and angles for examining the topic that you had not considered will be suggested to you. Keep your eyes open for sources cited in other people's research that you did not discover in your own library search. Take a moment here and there to consider what kinds of sources you might consult or how you might approach your topic if you were to start all over, back at square one. Ask the experts you consult if there is anything else you should read or see as part of the preparation of your final project. A good researcher moves back and forth between the different stages of the researching process—reading, writing up findings, interviewing, looking for further information, reconsidering the focus of the investigation, and taking down notes—right up until the time that the completed project must be released or presented to its audience. Once you've compiled a good working bibliography, you still will come across references to articles that you should consider studying for yourself. Don't close the book on any part of your research project until you've finished the whole thing. Always allow yourself to make additions to the list of sources you hope to consult, the growing stack of note cards in your possession, the number of people you want to speak to about your topic, and so on. The goal of research, remember, is discovery, and so you are naturally going to continuously uncover new leads and bits of information. Be receptive to these; even though it may seem at times that a new revelation is nothing more than a stumbling block, it may ultimately turn out to propel your project along.

The Role of Self-Discipline

Curiosity, compulsiveness, and confusion are the occupational hazards of researchers. As your task takes you to exciting new places, through specialized source materials, and across the paths of fascinating human beings, you will be tempted to stay too long and drink too deeply at many of the wellsprings of information you discover. As you scan the table of contents of a magazine, you are almost certain to find articles on topics besides the one you are researching that you would like to read. When you encounter an obscure journal for the first time, you will want to check it out fully, reading its letters to the editor and perusing the advertisements in the back. You are likely to find an amazing synchronicity with at least one person you interview: he or she owns nearly all the same books as you, attended a conference or concert you did, even vacations in the same place where your family does. You are, after all, researching a topic that interests you, so it should come as no surprise that the publications and people who share your interest hold a deep fascination for you.

Sometimes it is imperative to keep your eyes on the horizon and steer a straight course toward meeting your deadline. Especially as your research progresses and you have collected a mind-boggling amount of material, you will be tempted to read and discuss simpler things that won't add to your confusion. You may have to lash yourself to the mast sometimes to resist the Siren calls of irrelevant information.

Categorizing Sources in Your Working Bibliography

As you compiled your working bibliography, you began organizing your search process in a limited way just by restricting what you would pursue. For example, if you decided that sources over ten or twenty years old were not relevant to your research or you narrowed down your topic or eliminated some descriptors, you were, in effect, deciding to not even consider reading some things. But at this point your working bibliography is still just a useful resource, not a coherent plan. It is a map without a route marked on it. It may well be that you do not even attempt to follow all of the leads you have uncovered. But once you have your working bibliography in hand, you must decide what to read or study. You need to begin marking a route on your map.

Look over your working bibliography and categorize or rank-order the sources there to distinguish between those that are most general (for example, articles that summarize the topic for a news magazine or book) and those that are more specific (such as detailed examinations of a single element or facet of the problem reported in journals or professional research reports). Think about the audience for each of the sources on your working bibliography and the audience for your final project. Most likely, your audience will not share your level of expertise on your subject. Therefore, you should begin your research by consulting sources aimed at a general audience; these will help you frame your topic so that it remains accessible to a wide group of learners. Keep your final deadline in mind, and recognize that if you run out of time, general sources will provide more help in achieving a complete, coherent product than several isolated pockets of information can. Although journals, interviews, rare documents, and the like may be more prestigious sources, and you will be eager to get to work on those, appreciate that magazine articles, television news shows, newspaper articles, and books are the solid foundations of the information structure you are erecting.

The following four articles are each about carbon fiber monocoque (one-piece) bicycle frames. They are listed below in order, from the least to the most technical discussion of the topic:

"Superbikes," *Washington Post*, 10 May 1996, p. A26.

Coy, Peter. "Peddling Better Bike Designs," *Business Week* 3482 (1996): 103.

Thisdell, Dan. "For Sale: The World's Fastest Bicycle," *New Scientist* 135, no. 1838 (1992):23–25.

Ashley, Steven. "Software Leads to Gold: Computer Software Used to Optimize Bicycle Design," *Mechanical Engineering* 115, no. 8 (1993): 16–18.

The least technical of these is published in a very general periodical (a newspaper), and the most technical comes from an engineering journal.

Acquiring knowledge and understanding of complex problems and processes is a cumulative process. Every brain surgeon began by learning about the basic anatomy of brains and then moved on to dendrites, neurotransmitters, and the chemical reactions found in the synapses of normal cells versus those that have been damaged. The general sources on your working bibliography will help prepare you for the more erudite sources. As you examine basic materials, you will notice that their authors take time to define specialized jargon, explain the assumptions and history that shape practices and beliefs, and make explicit the causes and effects involved in solving the problems related to their subject. Ironically, paying close attention to fundamental information will prevent you from oversimplifying issues related to your topic, because general sources often tend to be broadly conceived and try to take divergent viewpoints into account. Use the general sources on your working bibliography to educate yourself so you won't need a dictionary and a handful of reference books at your side to make your way through the scholarly sources you will consult later on. Many specialized sources assume their readers are already experts on the topic—and even experts on a subject often must struggle to understand complex information about it.

Study the passive sources on your working bibliography first. That is, start with library materials and work your way up to site visits, requests from offices and organizations, and interviews. Library materials have essentially nothing to do but lie there and wait for someone like you to use them. You cannot waste their time. It would be almost tragic if you went to visit a site and failed to look at an important detail or if you wasted a hard-to-get interview asking questions that can be answered by the most basic textbooks on the subject. You wouldn't want to fly to England to look at the famous Stonehenge and miss seeing the larger stone circle nearby at Avebury, and you wouldn't want to ask the Speaker of the House of Representatives how a bill becomes a law.

Let print sources prepare you for your more dynamic research activities. Study a map of a place you are going to visit so that you'll have the "big picture" in mind when you go. Read biographical information about people before you request interviews with them so that you can make knowledgeable requests of them. Know the contents of some popular articles and books on a subject before you speak to experts in the field so that you can demonstrate your interest in the topic, ask good questions, and understand the answers you receive.

Arrange the items on your working bibliography into a hierarchy before you begin delving into individual sources. You can either cut and paste your bibliographic citations or devise a system of symbols to rank them and to identify which sources you plan to examine at each phase in your process. In addition to producing a research strategy for yourself, arranging the items on your working bibliography will help you cut the big list of sources you have collected down to a more manageable size.

Read your general sources first, then graduate to specialized periodicals and journals. Examine archival materials after you have exhausted the common library holdings. Save interactions with experts for last. Of course, this system is not foolproof. The last person you interview may suggest a basic print source that you have overlooked, and you will want to go back to the library and search for that simple source before you complete your project. Or you might in the first article you read discover the name of an innovator in the field you are studying and suddenly, in your enthusiasm to talk to that person, find yourself in an e-mail exchange or telephone conversation with him or her at the outset of your research process. A rough plan of attack, however, will help you budget your time and use the full range of resources you hope to include in your finished project.

■ Evaluating Sources

The first thing you should do when you have a source in your physical presence is to make a bibliography card about it. That is, once you've located, for example, the proper bound volume of a periodical; found the correct issue inside; discovered the sought-after title and author on the table of contents, exactly where your bibliographic source said it would be; and determined that time and previous researchers have left the article intact for you to use, seize the moment. Routinely take down the following information for each source the first time you take it up:

Books

- Author's name or names of general editors for the volume

- Chapter authors and title if you are interested in a specific chapter

- Title of the book

- City where the book was published

- Name of publishing company

- Year the book was published

Magazine or Journal Articles

- Author's name
- Title of the article
- Title of the periodical
- Volume number
- Issue number
- Cover date of the periodical
- *All* the page numbers upon which the article appears

Newspaper Articles

- Author's name or name of news service providing the article (if it is signed)
- Headline of the article
- Name of the newspaper
- Cover date of the newspaper
- Page numbers where the article appears (including section name or letter)

Web Pages

- Name of the organization or person that posted the page
- Identifying text from the heading or title graphics for the page
- Full URL address for the page
- Date that you accessed the page

Unpublished Documents

- Name of author or corporate or government entity that issued the document
- Title of the document or identifying heading
- Name and address of office or person from whom copies of the document are available
- Date the document was written (if it is dated)

Interviews

- Name (and preferably title) of the person being interviewed
- Medium by which the interview was conducted (that is, in person, by telephone, by e-mail, and so on)
- Dates the interview was conducted

Collecting this information on individual note cards for each source eliminates two potential problems. First, when it comes time later for you to compile your Works Cited list, you will have the necessary information in order. Second, it provides a convenient way for you to review the relevance, timeliness, and scope of the sources you are collecting.

Determining Whether Your Sources Are Reliable

You have heard the old saw about computers: "Garbage in, garbage out." And you know that straight, seasoned lumber is required to build a plumb structure. You can probably guess, then, that strong, reputable sources contribute to the integrity of a research project. It is important for you to consider the reliability of sources as you read them and to periodically review the materials you are using to make certain that you are using information that is up-to-date and credible.

Some things to consider when evaluating source material for your research project are the reputation of the publisher, the credentials of the author, and the contents and conclusions of the material itself. You might spend time running down reviews of books and criticisms of various periodicals and authors to get a published opinion about the authoritative value of some of your sources, but in most cases you are qualified to judge for yourself whether the sources you are using are trustworthy and bear repeating. Does the information you are about to use sound credible to you? Do other sources corroborate it? Is the book or article from a reputable author, publisher, or periodical? Is it cited in other sources you have consulted? What might its author or publisher stand to gain from advancing its thesis? Do other reliable sources directly challenge or contradict it? Does the author present evidence to support the claims he or she is making? Are specific examples included to illustrate the author's assertions? Can you efficiently paraphrase or restate the author's arguments simply and adequately?

As your research on a given topic progresses, you will learn to recognize the names of leading authorities in the field. Often you will find that one person or group of researchers has published several articles on your topic. In addition, you will discover that leading experts in the field are frequently mentioned in publications written by others, and their work shows up regularly on Works Cited lists and in recommendations for further reading. Pay close attention to the names that surface in your research. Most likely they offer clues about whose work you will want cite or refute to cover your topic well.

Many magazines and journals publish brief biographical statements about their contributors, enumerating their professional and academic experience. As you know, you shouldn't believe everything you read. Many published books and articles originate as somebody's academic research project. Ask yourself what each author's qualifications are and what he or she potentially has to gain from publishing the opinions the book or article contains. It doesn't matter where an article is published if it doesn't make sense, is biased, or uses data improperly to mislead readers.

Some publications are obviously unreliable. You know that the tabloids displayed in grocery store checkout lanes, proclaiming that two-headed Martian babies have been born in Nova Scotia, singing Elvis tunes, are not reliable sources of information. Even what little valid information such publications may report is unusable because of these publications' reputations for sensationalism. And anything legitimate within the pages of the *National Enquirer*, the *Globe*, or the *Star* will be reported by more reputable publications.

But other publications not obviously reliable can be less than objective. For example, the U.S. government periodically examines the feasibility of developing high speed rail transportation between highly populated urban areas, or even linking the east and west coasts. Whenever this topic is in the news, you can find congressmen and transportation trade organization spokespeople quoted in the nation's most respected newspapers, dismissing the whole as "economically unfeasible" or "impractical." Someone who represents any facet of the automobile industry, from vehicle manufacture to scrap metal recycling, may oppose the development of an American monorail system because it could reduce the sale and use of personal transportation devices. As a researcher, you must constantly ask yourself what your sources may have to gain or lose in the issue under consideration. Even reasonable assertions are often motivated by hidden agendas, and reputable publications could not possibly exclude all biased opinions.

Distinguishing Between Magazines and Journals

Periodicals are publications that are issued *periodically*, such as daily newspapers, weekly magazines, quarterly journals, and annual reports. A strict (although not always readily evident) division exists among reliable periodicals. They can be classified as either general interest or specialized publications, depending on the audience they are intended for. Those that are written for and marketed to the general public are often referred to as magazines, and those that seek an exclusive audience among specific groups of professionals are usually called journals. The word *journal*, however, simply means a regularly kept record of information, and it can be applied to any periodical and even used as part of its title. For example, *Ladies Home Journal* is a magazine sold at newsstands everywhere, but the *Journal of the Water Pollution Control Federation* and the *Journal of Glass Studies* are intended for practitioners in their respective fields and are distributed through professional societies.

The real difference between magazines and journals is the kind and quality of research reported in each. Magazines describe issues of current interest; their reporters interview experts and compile stories designed to keep the general public informed. Journals report in detail about recent research in a given field; journal articles are usually written by practitioners and researchers themselves, people who have personally conducted the studies reported in the journal.

Many college students begin their research with news magazines, such as *Time, Newsweek,* and *U.S. News and World Report.* These are considered very general sources, reporting on a wide variety of information. Newspapers also cover a wide variety of topics, by their very nature. Most magazines define their audience, to some extent, through the subject matter they cover. Magazines such as *Sports Illustrated, Computer World, Psychology Today, Science,* and *Architectural Digest* may have a more limited audience than do magazines like *Time,* but they are still addressed to members of the general public. *Comparative Physical Education and Sport, Communication Technology Update,* the *Association for Women in Psychology Newsletter, Medical Repository,* and *Living Architecture* report on similar topics as their general interest counterparts, but they are "journals," aimed at practicing professionals. (And notice that none of these examples contains the word *journal* in its title.)

Until you have examined a range of general and specialized periodicals, it may be difficult for you to determine exactly what sort of publication you are using. One quick way to judge the audience for a periodical is to survey the advertisements it contains. If they are for general consumer items available from local and national retailers, you are probably dealing with a magazine. If they are for specialized products such as medicines or lab equipment, or if they consist primarily of notices about conferences and new books available in the field the periodical reports upon, then you are probably looking at a journal. Usually, if you can guess the kind of person who would respond to the advertisements in a publication, then you have profiled the audience for its articles as well.

You should try to incorporate some information from specialized sources in any college-level research project. As an aspiring professional, you need to begin reading and relying on the discourse of practicing professionals. Remember, however, that the main goal of a research project is to prove a thesis, not merely to showcase the work of learned practitioners in the field. Only you and your audience can judge the significance to your work of any particular source. Consider all materials carefully, regardless of their origin (within sensible limits). Notice where the information reported in the article comes from. Did the writer conduct original research on this topic? Is this a compilation of research reported by others? If a hypothesis or opinion is advanced, has the writer thoroughly tested it? If you fully understand the information you read in other sources, you are unlikely to misrepresent it when you pass it on to your readers. A pamphlet by a local chiropractor can be as useful as a study published in the *Journal of the American Medical Association* if it addresses your topic exactly, states its case clearly and logically, and is not made to look like more than it is in your final project.

Another way to gauge the effectiveness of source material is to note whether it addresses both or all sides of an issue. How well does the author refute challenges to his or her thesis? Writers may build good cases for their own positions, but if they fail to answer the best arguments against their theses, you and your readers might find their assertions untenable. The ultimate test of an article's effectiveness is whether you, as you continue to read a variety of facts and opinions about the topic, continue to be persuaded by it. At first, everything you read may sound logical and worth repeating, but as you labor through the items on your working bibliography, you will begin to see that some arguments are stronger than others. It is okay to trust each source until it is trumped by a better one or by your own growing understanding of the subject. You are only taking down notes at this stage, and you already know that you won't use everything you write down now in your final research project.

■ Taking Notes

You have been taking notes throughout your college career in a variety of forms: writing down the most interesting things your professors say, outlining difficult reading assignments, highlighting textbooks as you read them or jotting notes in the margin, keeping lists of expectations for important assignments, and so on. If you have ever borrowed a friend's notes after missing a class meeting or compared notes with other students while studying for an exam, you know that note taking is a highly individual process. Even though you have read or listened to the same discourse, you and your classmates may have taken down radically different information in your notes.

What you write down in your notes depends on what you already know about the subject under discussion, what you think you can remember without a written record, and what you believe you will find useful later on when you review your notes or try to incorporate them into a finished product. *How* you take notes is only a slightly more standard process than deciding what content to include. You have probably already figured out how to take notes, and to some degree, at least, that self-taught process works for you. This book will suggest methods for note taking that you should try at least once. You may find that you want to make short-cuts in the process in the future, and depending on your propensity for procrastination and the amount of reading and writing expected of you in your academic career, you will probably have several opportunities to experiment with these techniques in the future.

Before you start reading the materials on your working bibliography, make a list of questions that you hope your secondary sources will answer. What statistics do you hope to discover? What sort of research do you think has been done on this problem? Who are some of the people you hope to quote about this topic? What solutions do you want to advocate? You are conducting research to discover more about your topic, but you should have some idea what you are looking for as you study. If you don't have some idea what you're looking for, you won't necessarily know when you have found it.

At first, when you begin reading secondary sources, every statement of fact in each article or book might seem like relevant information that you ought to copy down. Remember, however, that *you* are the one completing this research project—you are collecting the observations and opinions of others mainly to corroborate your own arguments. You cannot possibly use every interesting fact or clever quotation that you run across in your reading and interviewing. Read your first several sources carefully. Concentrate on retaining what you read, and take down very few direct quotations as notes. When you have finished reading an article, summarize the position its author takes and briefly sketch his or her main arguments. If you need to glance back through the article later to gather direct quotations, it will not take long.

As you work your way through the sources from your working bibliography, your finished research project will begin to take shape in your head, and your note taking will become more efficient. You will realize that some of the things you wrote down early in the process are common knowledge among authorities on your topic, and you will not want to use them all in your finished product. That is part of the necessary activity of researching a topic. You have not wasted your efforts or made mistakes if you realize that some of your early notes are no longer relevant to the work you are planning. You have decided what your project will *not* include—which tangents and related information it will not cover—as well as what it *will* present.

Deciding exactly what information to include in your notes is part of your own contribution to the project you are completing. It depends partly on some practical considerations as well. For example, you may want to consider the time of day and place where you will likely be writing your final paper or presentation. In spite of their best efforts at careful time management, many students end up finishing their research project at home, in their dorm room or apartment, late into the evening and the very early morning. Because it will be inconvenient or impossible to use the library very late at night, you should take notes carefully. Make sure that you take down all of the information necessary to document the information you will cite in your finished project. If you are in doubt about the significance of something, write it down anyway. Your project will take some surprising turns before it is finished, and careful note taking will forestall the frustration of fruitlessly searching for a half-remembered piece of information you suddenly need but can't locate.

■ Understanding and Avoiding Plagiarism

Researchers take three kinds of notes, basically: direct quotations, paraphrases, and summaries. Good note taking is crucial to the success of your research project. Most students who commit unintentional plagiarism do so because they have not taken notes carefully enough. *Plagiarism* means presenting the ideas or words of another writer or speaker as your own. If you take down someone else's exact words in your notes, be sure to indicate it using quotation marks, ellipses, and brackets. If you paraphrase or summarize the words or ideas of another writer or speaker in your notes, take time to read the original source carefully. Be certain that you understand the text that you are summarizing. Think about it for a few minutes. Generate your own examples to illustrate the idea. Imagine yourself explaining the ideas you are paraphrasing or summarizing to a friend. Then, write those thoughts down *in your own words*. After you have drafted a paraphrased or summarized passage, reread it along with the original source to make sure that you have not unconsciously adopted any of that text's word choices or sentence structures.

Direct Quotations

You will probably want to use all three types of attribution—direct quotations, paraphrases, and summaries—in your final paper, but if you are going to write it without the original sources in hand, you may want to include mostly short, emphatic, memorable direct quotations in your notes. If you are assembling your final project with note cards in the middle of the night, you can easily reduce a direct quotation to a paraphrase, but you can't simply add water to a summary or paraphrase and stir to reconstitute a direct quotation. Direct quotations are the most painstaking notes to collect, because you must be absolutely certain that you have copied every letter and punctuation mark exactly as it appears in the original. Additionally, you want to be certain that you are not lifting remarks out of context, so you should precede direct quotations in your notes with a brief description of the surrounding argument that the author is making. Whenever possible, you should quote and cite the *original* source of any other author's statement that you include in your paper. That means that if you are quoting one article that reprints comments from another, previously published essay, you need to track down that earlier work if at all possible and copy the quotation and citation information from it instead of from the article that quotes it. Although you will want to keep direct quotations in your final product short and to the point, make sure that you take down a long enough section of your source's prose to ensure that what you want will be in your notes when you need it.

A direct quotation from Kyle's notes appears in Figure 9.1. Notice how it can be shortened using ellipses and brackets to show that words have been deleted and altered.

Because this quotation is excerpted from e-mail correspondence (between Kyle and Josh, a fellow student at another university whom Kyle met through an Internet mailing list), it is very informal. Although both Kyle and the other student understood that *it* in the first line referred to on-line credit card purchases, this will not be clear to Kyle's readers unless he alters the original text for use in his paper. The quotation is also wordy and conversational; the two were essentially chatting, not writing formal, academic discourse. In an attempt to clean up the diction and sentence structure somewhat, Kyle deletes some of Josh's words, inserting ellipses to indicate that he

> "No. In fact I feel it is more secure than a phone conversation. To put it simply, on a good system, what you type goes directly to the billing program. Human eyes never see it. When you are talking on the phone, the salesman may write the wrong number down."

Figure 9.1 A Direct Quotation from Kyle's Notes

has abridged the original text. He also substitutes for Josh's colloquial use of the word *feel* the more formal *believe*, in an attempt to represent Josh accurately in the context of a formal research paper. The revised quotation appears in Figure 9.2.

As you can see from Figure 9.2, you are not "stuck with" direct quotations exactly as you discover them in secondary sources, but it takes diligence and commitment to accurately adapt them to your purposes without misrepresenting their originator.

Paraphrasing

Paraphrases are useful when the passage you want to use is simply too long or complicated to copy as a direct quotation. Misconceptions about paraphrasing cause some students to unintentionally plagiarize material. Many people want to believe that if writers just change a few words or leave out part of a direct quotation they have made it their own. That is a little like saying it is okay to borrow your neighbor's car without their permission as long as you add a little of your own gas to the tank. You can't appropriate someone else's words, even if you don't pretend to actually own them yourself. Figure 9.3 contains a direct quotation from Kyle's notes, followed by an unacceptable attempt at paraphrasing it.

This is clearly a miserable paraphrase. Although it does not use exactly the same words as did Kim Nash, the author of the original passage, it copies her sentence structure almost exactly, merely substituting synonyms for nearly all of her word choices. It is built almost entirely on Nash's syntax; therefore, it is neither a direct quotation nor a legitimate paraphrase, because the words are not hers but the sentence structure is. It can't be presented in quotation marks as a direct quotation, because Nash did not write this. And it can't be presented as someone else's sentence, either, because it is not really the work of another author. This paraphrase, as well as others that do not so

> "I [believe on-line credit card purchasing] is more secure than a phone conversation. . . . What you type goes directly to the billing program. Human eyes never see it. When you are talking on the phone, the salesman may write the wrong number down."

Figure 9.2 Kyle's Revised Quotation

> **Direct quotation:**
> "Early this year, on-line managers at First Chicago began studying hacking methods, encryption and other security issues. They soon realized that 'there was a lot more complexity there than meets the eye,' Heuberger said."
>
> —Nash, Kim. "Firms Learn 'Net Security Lessons." <u>Computer World</u> 29 (1995): 70.
>
> **Unacceptable paraphrase:**
> At the beginning of 1995, cyber-management at a Chicago bank started examining computer crime tactics, how to scramble electronic information, and other Internet safety considerations. Quickly they came to understand that this was a much more intricate set of problems than they had first guessed, one of the bankers explained.

Figure 9.3   An Unacceptable Paraphrase

obviously parrot their source, are "neither fish nor foul nor fine red herring," as the saying goes. There is no place for them in academic research.

Figure 9.4, by contrast, presents one of the myriad possibilities for an acceptable paraphrase of the Nash quotation.

You can include a paraphrase such as this in a college research paper, as long as you credit the original author with the idea by appropriately citing the source. You may have to experiment with paraphrasing and write a few versions of each passage until you get material that you know is both accurate and in your own words into your notes. It is worth the effort to struggle with getting paraphrases right while you still have the original material in front of you and fresh in your mind. That way you can be certain that you are remaining faithful to the original, without copying it.

> Chicago bankers were recently surprised to learn how complex issues surrounding Internet crime and safety measures are for businesses that hope to conduct transactions on-line.

Figure 9.4   Acceptable Paraphrase

Summaries

Unlike paraphrases, which usually try to restate a single argument or relatively small passage from a source, summaries tend to describe large passages or completed discourses. A summary restates an article's thesis and, usually, its main points. It may take the form of a short essay, analyzing the rhetoric and contents of a source, or it might look something like a detailed outline of an article. It might even be as simple as a single sentence stating an article's thesis.

Electronic retailing increases revenues and lowers costs.
—allows merchants to reach more customers
Internet never closes
—virtual site is easier to maintain than physical retail facility

Figure 9.5 A Cryptic Summary

Figure 9.5 contains a fairly cryptic summary that Kyle wrote about some pages promoting electronic retailing from Microsoft's Web site (http://www.microsoft.com). Although it is brief, it contains the information Kyle will need to complete his assignment.

Summarizing is not the same thing as creating your own personal archive. Today the temptation is great to simply photocopy piles of information rather than to process it in a way that will help you use it in your final paper or presentation. I think sometimes of the monks who created intricate illuminated manuscripts before Gutenberg invented moveable type, or of the scriveners who copied legal documents in longhand before mechanical printing became widely available. Would they marvel at the availability and efficiency of photocopiers and optical scanners? Or would they feel that the ease with which we copy information today actually causes us to devalue it?

All of us have raced into a library, located a few important articles for a project, duplicated them with a photocopier, and emerged a few minutes later, only a couple of dollars poorer, with a stack of "research" in our hands. What a consolation it seemed at the time, to carry away our own reproduced versions of noncirculating library materials! What a wealth of information we possessed! If you go to your campus library during a semester break when there is no one waiting to use the photocopiers, you could, for about the cost of a good meal, emerge with your own library of the best of what has been published on any given topic, all uniformly printed on crisp white paper and stashed in your book bag.

Today, amid the aftershocks of the information explosion, it is easy to confuse having access to information with having actual knowledge. In the case of photocopies, possession is nine-tenths of procrastination. If you spend a whole day locating books and articles, flagging pages, waiting at the photocopier, and then finally making copies of the information you need for your research project, you have squandered most of that day simply duplicating information that you could have been reading and absorbing in that time. If you carry a stack of photocopies home and put them on your desk, you still have to read them and take notes on them later.

Photocopying may or may not simplify your library research. Too often, photocopies of texts do not contain the information necessary to construct a bibliographic citation of the original, and researchers forget to record that data while they are making copies. Many students photocopy articles, assuming that they will be relevant to their research, and then rest assured that they can pull their final project together hurriedly with the copies they have amassed, only to discover too late that the articles they copied are not as useful as they assumed. Had they read the articles face-up before putting them face-down on the photocopier screen, they would never have wasted their time or money on making the copies. Too often, student researchers discover late at night that the information they really need is still in the library, now closed, and their photocopies provide little aid or comfort in their late-night panic and distress. Remember that the library owns copies of materials so that you don't have to.

Collecting copies is not a substitute for collecting actual data. Photocopies make library materials portable and infinitely accessible, allow researchers to take notes directly on the text, and provide absolutely trustworthy direct quotations, but you should not be mislead into thinking that they are research notes. Many students believe that by highlighting or underlining important text on photocopies, they can greatly simplify the note-taking process. It is true that highlighting photocopies shaves entire minutes off the note-taking process, but it makes drafting a coherent paper or finished project much more difficult later on.

Personally, I find highlighting markers incredibly entertaining to use. They come with firm tips that make sharp-edged lines in great fluorescent colors that practically glow in the dark. When I use them to highlight text, I become more interested in coloring than in reading. Usually, researchers find that they highlight much more text than they would copy by hand onto note cards. Suddenly more of an author's prose seems important. You must ask yourself if this is really what you want when you are reading a thirty-page article in search of information for a fifteen-page research paper.

The most serious drawback to keeping research notes on photocopies is that they remain embedded within the context of the original discourse, following the organization used by the authors of the source documents. Each passage you highlight remains intact and unabridged. That might be useful if all you were doing was compiling a bunch of direct quotations; but since you are trying to create an original paper or presentation using information and excerpts from a variety of sources, you are likely to find that full photocopies of documents provide cumbersome and confusing chunks of data with which to work.

You will read many more pages of secondary materials, watch many more frames of video footage, and listen to many more minutes of interview conversation than you can possibly include in your finished research project. The goal of researching is to assimilate the best of what has already been written and said about your topic with your own ideas. You must condense many pages of information into a few, and you must synthesize all that you read and hear so that you can organize your finished product logically and coherently. To take up all of the information that you take in so that you can reorder and organize it in your head, you must make your sources as portable as possible. The more efficiently you can reduce whole discourses into a few direct quotations, paraphrases, or summaries, the more easily you can integrate that information into the project that is taking shape in your head.

If you sit right down and read through a complete article or book chapter just once carefully in the library, you can take genuinely useful notes from it. The more times you pour over a photocopy of a source, seeking the parts you want to import into your own work, the harder it will be for you to separate out the most useful passages. There is an inverse correlation between the number of pages you carry out of the library and the number of pages of your final paper or presentation you stand ready to complete. Therefore, try to use photocopying sparingly, for pages of information that are just too dense to excerpt onto note cards.

Note Cards

If you have a personal computer or access to one, its word processing or office suite software probably offers you an electronic card file program that allows you to type notes onto virtual cards on your hard drive and move them with the aid of a notepad directly into the draft of your paper without retyping the information. However, such programs do not allow you to lay out an unlimited number of cards and consider them at once or to easily reorganize your notes by physically stacking and restacking them until you're happy with an organizational plan for your finished project. You may spend more time figuring out how to add, delete, and shuffle virtual cards than you save by copying text from them electronically, and even a notebook computer is a lot heavier and more cumbersome to carry around than a pack of 3x5 note cards.

A lot of attempts have been made to improve on the standard index card, but as with cane fishing poles, steel waiter's corkscrews, tortoise-shell fountain pens, shrink-to-fit blue jeans, and standard-transmission sports coupes, the so-called improvements don't have quite the feel, utility, or performance of the genuine article. A pack of one hundred standard ruled note cards will do more to help you organize your research than any other tool you can buy. The standard 3x5 card is just the right size to permit the recording of a lengthy quotation yet discourage excessive copying of secondary sources.

The classic, lined index card provides space for all of the information you need to carry around with you. Record just one passage or idea per card. Start by putting in a corner of the card a code letter, number, or symbol keyed to your bibliography cards or working bibliography that identifies which source the information on the card comes from. Next to that, record the page number of the passage you are quoting or summarizing, if relevant. At the top of the card, indicate in which part of the finished paper or presentation the information recorded on the card will be used. If you have already prepared an outline for your paper or presentation, you can use the headings from it to label your cards. At the very least, give some indication of the kind of material contained on each card, such as "Arguments for legislation," "Conclusions," "Conservative viewpoint," "Accident statistics," and so on. Write the actual note (quotation, paraphrase, or summary) on the lined side of the card. Do not permit yourself to record anything longer than what will fit on one side of an index card;. this will prevent you from collecting too much information in another writer's voice. If you really must collect a very long passage from a secondary source, consider photocopying a page or two only.

As soon as you are satisfied that you have copied a direct quotation exactly or made a faithful paraphrase or summary on the front side of your note card, turn it over and write a reaction to it on the unlined side. Make a note to yourself, explaining why you thought this passage was relevant to your research, how it supports or contradicts another study, whether it fits your own ideas or experience, or simply why you thought it was, literally, noteworthy. The information on the backs of your cards will form a very early draft of your final paper or presentation. You can most clearly state why you recorded certain information, and your responses to it, while you are actively studying and taking notes from that source. Later, if you decide to incorporate the information into your research project, you will find that you have a surprising amount of the first draft of your final text already written if you have filled the backs of all of your note cards with your own ideas.

Taking notes is time-consuming. In fact, gathering information will probably occupy most of the days allotted to the completion of your research project. Don't be anxious to get it over with too soon. While your library research is progressing, post questions to Internet mailing lists and contact potential interviewees to request meetings with them. E-mail conversations provide motivation for finishing library work, and scheduled interviews give you a tentative deadline for completing background reading. Personal contact with other people interested in your subject gives you an opportunity to ask the questions that printed sources have not answered. The success of your final product depends on your patience and thoroughness during this phase. It is like studying for a test or practicing with a team; at times you might think that no one credits you for your hard work, especially for the notes you gather and find you cannot use in your finished project, but like drill, memorization, and rehearsal that no one sees, diligence provides its own evidence and reward.

■ Kyle's Notes

Kyle read print sources in the library and took notes on them for a couple of days, but he found that work difficult compared with studying the things he was finding on the Web and learning from conversations with computer science professors and professionals in the university's computer labs. He front:

20	Use stats
number of households using the Web	
has doubled in the last half of 1995	
to 7.5 million	

back:

Great. That's less than 8% of households. And access doesn't guarantee use as a retail medium. There have to be buyers out there before we can tell if this is going to be popular.

front:

Retailer, example	E-mail 7
Hyperlinks on the Outerwear, Inc. site are	
designed to resemble trail signs similar to	
those found on many of the nation's hiking	
trails.	

back:

Frankly, I'm a little disappointed with this. I finally got someone at Outerwear, Inc. to respond to my e-mail questions about retailing online, but the public affairs people there (who wrote this e-mail) are not very forthcoming about the kinds of things I want to know. I know sales volume is a confidential matter, but I wish they would give me some kind of ballpark figure.

front:

Traditional Security	D6
"Credit card information is given out to	
hundreds of thousands of low-paid clerks	
all over the country every day—it would	
be hard to imagine a less secure approach."	

back:

I'm really glad that someone else said this, and said it so bluntly, so that I don't have to figure out how to say it myself. I would like to show some of the newspaper articles I saw about credit card fraud in retail stores in malls—and something about football players at this university who were caught in a credit card theft ring.

Figure 9.6 Kyle's Favorite Note Cards

decided to concentrate on library sources in the afternoons, when he was usually most awake, and take notes from Internet sources, including e-mail correspondence, in the evenings.

Kyle posted a question to an Internet mailing list for technology professionals, asking whether any of the list members had considered purchasing consumer goods over the Internet and whether they were worried about security issues connected with electronic commerce. He put the same question out to another list whose subscribers are mainly American college students majoring in computer science. He got about twenty responses, which is "pretty good for a bunch of jaded computer hacks," he said. Some people had actually purchased items on-line, such as magazines, CDs, computer equipment, and airline tickets. Most were happy with their experience and believed that on-line shopping is the retail wave of the future. A handful of people wrote opposing the idea, saying that they would never send their credit card numbers over the Internet.

At the end of the week, Kyle counted his index cards. He had over 175 information cards, and about one-fourth as many bibliography cards. Looking back over the evidence of his considerable research, he said, "I'm sure that a lot of them will be dropped due to lack of relevant content." But he agreed that he had learned a lot about Internet security. Before he had begun reading and conversing with others about the topic, he thought he could predict what people would say about it. He was surprised to find that many marketing consultants were advising retailers to jump into Internet business with both feet, and it shocked him that some professionals in the technology industry were leery of making credit card transactions on-line.

His favorite note cards (front and back) appear in Figure 9.6.

Just as he was finishing his note taking, Kyle got a call back from the CEO of the largest regional data processing company in the Midwest. He interviewed the man on the phone, and he felt that it went very well: "I got a lot of useful information out of [the interview]. It will definitely add a lot of support to my research." After that call, he believed he was ready to start writing a rough draft of his research paper.

■ Summing Up

Your working bibliography probably consists of several lists of sources that sounded useful to you when you were trying to discover information pertinent to your topic. The items on these lists may be chronologically or alphabetically organized, depending on how the index you accessed them with was arranged and your need to prioritize the leads you uncovered to create a research agenda for yourself.

First, determine which of the sources on your working bibliography seem most relevant and interesting to you, so you can reserve time to examine each one closely. Try to differentiate between discourse intended for a general audience and that directed at professionals and serious researchers. Distinguish between magazine and journal articles, and plan to read the most general sources first, because they will help you better understand the more scholarly ones. Remember, however, that you might discover general sources later than you had planned, and you might discover highly specialized information in general interest magazines.

Once you have source material in hand, immediately take down all the data necessary to document that source in your final paper. You might want to look ahead at Chapters Thirteen and Fourteen and note the information required for Works Cited entries in the APA, CBE, Chicago Style, and MLA documentation formats.

Evaluate the reliability of each source as you examine it. Is the author a well-known authority on the subject? Was the book or article published by a respected publisher or organization? What biases does the author betray?

Are assertions in the text backed up with specific examples and proof? Is the information reported in the book or article adequately documented? Does the author cite other sources on the same subject to corroborate his or her arguments? In short, do you believe what the source says?

Although taking notes on sources is a highly individualistic process, most writers will benefit from following a fairly standardized procedure, using traditional 3x5 note cards. Put only one passage or idea on each card, and follow up by writing your reaction to that information on the back of the card.

Your goal is to collect the best material available to prove your thesis. Therefore, design your information-gathering process so that you will end up with a manageable amount of information. Throughout the process, you will be reading, listening, writing, corresponding, requesting library materials, setting up interview appointments, and talking with people. The more you learn, the more engrossed in the subject you will become. You are not finished with researching your subject until you have read most of the sources that look promising on your growing working bibliography and answered all of your initial questions. At that point, a draft of your paper or presentation should be taking shape in your imagination.

Exercises: Sources and Strategies

1. Divide the items on your working bibliography into general and specific sources. How many of the first group are from magazines and newspapers? How many of the more specialized items appear in journals and publications for professionals?

2. Practice writing effective paraphrases of some of the direct quotations you have copied from printed sources or interviews. Exchange original quotations and paraphrases with other students in your class and check one another's work for acceptability.

3. Summarize an entire article or World Wide Web page in one page, using only one or two direct quotations. Describe the author's thesis and list all of his or her supporting evidence and arguments. What is particularly persuasive about the source? How, specifically, has its author succeeded in convincing you?

Writing to Know

Write a review comparing two sources on the same topic (for example, a printed magazine and its on-line version, an individual's World Wide Web site and one posted by a national corporation, a local newspaper article and a national or international newspaper article). What is best and most problematic about each source? As a researcher, which do you find most useful? As a reader, which do you find most credible? Why?

Chapter Ten

Planning an Argument

You might still write as I once did: without an outline or plan to guide your creative process. That can work just fine when you have a personal story to tell or a brief paper to complete, but a research paper requires more thorough planning. Writing a research paper without an outline is like driving through unfamiliar territory without a map. Since a research project incorporates the ideas of many sources and involves some complex organizing, it is more like following a mail route than like taking a Sunday afternoon drive. You will want to organize and prioritize your information delivery in advance.

The first thing you should do is ask yourself what you really want to say about your topic. Don't just assume you'll want to try to prove the same thesis you started with. Your research may have prompted some nagging questions about your initial hypothesis. Most researchers discover that their topic is more complex than they initially recognized, or what looked like a perfect solution to a problem has some flaws that can't be ignored. Perhaps you'll want to amend your thesis or temper your recommendations to reflect some worrisome doubts or exceptions you have acknowledged since you first defined your topic. Spend ten minutes or so just writing about what you want to prove in your paper. Or, if you have a friend who is a good listener, call him or her and talk about what you initially hoped to prove versus what you think you've actually discovered as a result of your research. Take notes during your conversation, recording any questions your listener asks.

Don't try to make all of the evidence fall into line, single file, behind your thesis. The mark of a sophisticated researcher is the ability to recognize and accommodate contradictions and gray areas. Experienced readers will be suspicious if you twist every bit of evidence until it supports your thesis, however tenuously. It is better to admit that a few questions remain unanswered or a few details contradict your findings than to try to manipulate facts or hide some of the details from your audience. Every topic worth considering at length contains some mysteries and contradictions, and you will not seem to have looked behind every page and under every stone if you don't acknowledge a few leftover pieces in the elaborate model you are building.

■ Understanding Your Audience

Knowing to whom you are speaking is essential for any kind of discourse. When you are making an appeal in person, you can easily size up your audience. Think about the last time you wheedled a favor out of someone, convinced your friends to participate in an activity you preferred even though they wanted to do something else, or influenced your boyfriend's or girlfriend's viewpoint on an important issue. Most likely, you employed some persuasive devices. You may have argued, threatened, pleaded, begged, cried, or even shouted to get what you wanted. With each salvo in your verbal campaign, you assessed how well the tactic you were using was working and adjusted your strategy accordingly. Depending on the seriousness of the issue, the level of disagreement between you and your audience, and the degree to which you wanted to win, you may have tried every tactic in your argumentative repertoire. Some persuasive methods that work in person just won't work on paper, however.

For a lot of people, the word *argument* connotes confrontation, or an angry or petulant exchange of words. As you have probably already learned, words like *argue* and *criticize* have different meanings in conversational use than they carry in academic discourse. Intellectual opposition may not be heated or angry at all. In research papers, arguments are simply statements of the proofs amassed by authors to defend or counter a thesis or proposal. Tempers are not usually engaged in an intellectual argument. In fact, most academic writers attempt to at least appear patient and respectful of their readers, whether they hold similar or opposing views on a subject.

You already have experience conducting calm, rational arguments. If you have ever been involved in a minor automobile accident, for example, you probably pleaded your case before a full range of audience types. The driver of the other vehicle might have been upset, enraged, or apologetic, depending on whom he or she perceived to be at fault. The investigating police officer was hopefully a neutral observer, and your family and friends likely were supportive and rallied around you. Even if you've never dented a fender, you can imagine what you would say in this situation to each of these "audiences."

Readers of Research Papers

Potential readers of a research paper include those who will strongly agree with your position, those who will be neutral about the issue, and those who will be vehemently opposed to your suggestions. A full range of readers exists for virtually any topic. Pretending to write for an adoring, ideal audience works for some kinds of projects, but usually you need to anticipate the responses of a realistic readership. When you are presenting a piece of research, it is imperative that you prepare for all kinds of reactions.

There have been a few famous cases in history when a rhetorician or writer misjudged the sympathies of his or her audience, and the results were disastrous. Shakespeare's history plays abound with such situations, but the real world affords several as well. One of the most well-remembered examples is Richard Nixon's "Checkers" speech. When Nixon was a vice presidential candidate on the ticket with Dwight Eisenhower, he went on television to explain his acceptance of gifts that many voters believed were inappropriate because they left Nixon potentially indebted to the contributors. Nixon did not believe the antipathy toward him was as great as it actually was. He tried to dismiss his critics' misgivings with simple assurances and a few examples illustrating the relatively small monetary value of the gifts he and his family had accepted. He attempted to tweak his listener's heart strings by focusing on Checkers, a cocker spaniel that a supporter had given to his daughters, Julie and Trisha. But Nixon's audience was skeptical about his integrity to begin with, and the ploy left them even more doubtful of his sincerity. Nixon's sentimental observations concerning his daughters' affection for their donated pet were met with scorn and derision. The populace believed that he had not adequately answered the charges against him. The "Checkers" speech is remembered as a great political faux pas because Nixon did not properly judge his audience in advance.

Although you were probably not part of the original audience for Nixon's speech, you have probably responded in a similar manner to friends or family members who misgauged your anger and tried to win your sympathy with a hard luck story that did not adequately take into account your hurt feelings. In your state of exasperation, you probably mocked your friend's attempts to explain himself or herself, and both of you ended up even more frustrated. That is usually the result when a writer doesn't anticipate the thoughts and feelings of his audience regarding a controversial topic.

You cannot afford to assume that all or even most of your readers will agree with everything you have to say in your research paper. Do not think that just because you can muster an impassioned defense of a topic everyone else will feel the same way about it. There will be others out there who are willing to argue just as zealously for the other side, and still others who are maddeningly apathetic about your cause. You must address all of these readers in one research paper.

Readers Who Agree with Your Argument

Audiences who agree with you before you write your first word may seem like the easiest to write for, but they can be demanding in unanticipated ways. Such readers may have already considered all of your arguments before they ever encounter your text. If they are very interested in the topic, they may be familiar with most of your sources and might even know more about your topic than you do. Such readers will generally be supportive of your attempts if you demonstrate your sincerity by proving that you have researched the topic thoroughly and shown respect for its leading authorities. These readers will be most interested in the things *you* bring to the discussion of the subject, such as your original observations. Information that you have gleaned from interviews, archival and government documents, or site visits will add to their store of knowledge on the topic. Your first-person experience with the issues may become important secondary source material for those readers.

In general, readers who already agree with you will be very supportive of your attempts to champion their cause, and if you convince them that you share their convictions and knowledge base, they will welcome a new writer into their company graciously. Supportive readers especially hope to see their convictions stated with vigor and originality. Ironically, these are the readers for whom it takes the longest to write effectively, because their expectations are higher. You must painstakingly develop and refine the elements that these readers will expect to find in your work. They will expect provocative turns of phrase and apt expressions that can serve as slogans for their cause. Thus the more that you can anticipate the desires of this friendly faction as you draft your research paper, the easier and more effective your writing process will be.

Readers Who Are Neutral About Your Argument

Neutral readers are also an important faction within your reading public. You will have to use persuasion to get the attention of some neutral readers; they may have no opinion on the topic because they consider it unimportant. Others will be interested in the topic but unsure of where they stand on it. These are the audience members for whom you have conducted the bulk of your research. Because they are trying to make a well-reasoned decision about the issue, they will be looking to you for convincing evidence: facts, figures, an authoritative overview of the history of the problem, and a comprehensive assessment of what you and other writers on the topic have proposed. They require clearly presented, unbiased information, and if you provide that for them, your work may be the turning point that makes them decide to support your position. If you leave them with unanswered questions, however, they will turn to other writers for answers and may end up embracing their ideas instead of yours.

Readers Who Are Skeptical About Your Argument

The faction of your reading audience that may intimidate you somewhat is the skeptical readers. These people will challenge your discourse as they read it, because it contradicts what they already believe. Like those who agree with you, this group may be very knowledgeable about the issue and already familiar with the sources you cite. Like Nixon's audience, they will scoff at trite examples, inappropriately emotional passages, and examples or analogies that do not directly apply to the topic at hand. Try to remember, however, that although these readers may be skeptical of your conclusions, they will not necessarily be skeptical of your integrity, unless you give them reason to be.

To convince these readers, you need to make an appeal that is both strong and ethical. This means that you must present yourself as well-informed and qualified to make the recommendations you suggest. Back up your generalizations with evidence and examples. Demonstrate that you have done your homework and know what you're talking about. Don't let insecurity about a skeptical audience lure you into adopting a confrontational tone. Don't be belligerent or haughty; remember that you want to persuade your readers and that this involves teaching them, not winning an argument with them.

■ Rhetorical Strategies You Can Use to Make Your Argument

As you can see, the type of audience you address determines the rhetorical strategies you must use. These include persuasive strategies, rational strategies, and ethical strategies. The terminology used to describe these strategies can be confusing, but they go all the way back to the ancient Greek rhetoricians, so plenty of students before you have survived the confusion they cause. An *argument* may refer to the whole discourse you are writing, one type of rhetoric you are using to win over your audience, or an individual assertion presented in your paper. *Persuasion* is the end result you hope to obtain, with your reader finally agreeing with your thesis; it is also a distinct rhetorical strategy that employs evidence to work on readers' emotions. *Rationality*, which is akin to logic, is something that all research papers strive for throughout, but *rational proofs* are pieces of evidence that cannot be controverted; they are those things that appear to be just plain true. Finally, *ethics*, as you know, usually refers to matters of morality and personal integrity; thus *ethical appeals* in arguments are based on the reliability or expertise of the writer. So the assertion that parents who really love their children will restrain them in car seats belted into the back seat of their cars, away from air bags, is a persuasive ploy; the evidence that seven children have been killed by air bags in the past two years is rational proof; and the revelation that you strap your own child into the rear of your two-door sports car, even though access to the back seat is difficult and you must ignore your child's tearful protestations, is an ethical appeal.

Persuasive Rhetorical Strategies

Persuasive rhetorical strategies include all attempts to sway the emotions of your readers. These might include hypothetical examples, stories, anecdotes, various manipulations of tone, and biased or slanted diction. For example, you could tell the story of a person with a terminal illness, such as intractable cancer or Alzheimer's disease, to argue that assisted suicide should be legal in the case of debilitating illness. A writer who chooses a friendly or an outraged tone is deliberately manipulating his readers by trying to win their approval or incite their anger. Emotional ploys must be carefully constructed, right down to the word level.

Think carefully about the connotations of words. Because English is a rich language, with words assimilated from ancient Anglo-Saxon, Latin, and the Romance languages, there are often three synonyms for basic nouns and verbs. For example, consider the basic article of clothing that every person puts on one leg at a time. Some people prefer the simple Anglo-Saxon term *pants* to describe these. Others use the Latin-influenced term *slacks*, which entered the English language around the time of the Roman invasion of Great Britain in A.D. 43. Still others (my grandparents among them) favor a more fancy, French term, as new to the language as the Norman Conquest of 1066, and call them *trousers*. You will most likely agree that although all three words refer to the same type of clothing, each term has a different connotation. You probably would not, for instance, refer to a pair of jeans as "slacks."

The subtle variations between synonyms in English allow for intricate shades of meaning based on which words are chosen. For instance, whether you say you are going to your *house*, your *home*, or your *domicile*, the physical destination is the same, but each of these words suggests a different image. The *denotative* meaning of a word is its literal meaning, and in practical usage, at least, these words share a common denotative definition. Your listeners would understand that you could be found in the place where you live. However, the *connotative*, or implied, meaning of these words is quite different. Of the three choices, *home* carries the most connotative weight, because there are more emotional associations connected with that word than with either *house* or *domicile*. Consciously choosing words with emotional connotations is a very effective persuasive strategy. Consider the pairs of terms in Figure 10.1. Which terms have the more positive connotation?

If you're thinking that this kind of attention to wording is too detailed, that readers won't notice subtle differences between words, consider this

baby	infant
sibling	sister
nation	homeland
brazen	presumptuous
criminal	perpetrator
servant	slave
cop	police officer
inconsiderate	rude
maternal	motherly
leaders	bureaucrats
Iowa	Hawkeye State
insurer	health maintenance organization

Figure 10.1 Connotations

revision of the best-known verse of Francis Scott Key's "Star Spangled Banner":

> By the way, does the five-pointed emblem-embossed pennant still hang above the country of the autonomous and the nation of the courageous?

Obviously, a lot was lost in the "translation."

Emotional ploys are dangerous, because they can easily be turned against their creators. Remember this: if you are dropping tears on your keyboard in response to what you are writing, you had better be certain that your readers started crying a page or two before you did. It's okay to take some risks and to be yourself in your paper. Reach out to the humanity of your readers. But remember, they probably won't cry about your dog any more than Richard Nixon's television audience did, unless you skillfully make them care about it first.

Rational Rhetorical Strategies

Rational rhetorical strategies are the kinds of arguments most students know they will have to make when they write a research paper. They rely on hard evidence—statistics, court decisions, legal statutes, the testimony of expert witnesses, and so on—to persuade. Remember, however, that statistics can be manipulated to serve various biases, and opinions are not facts. Be careful to report statistics and quotations in context. For instance, if you report the percentage of persons who responded favorably to a survey question, also include the number of people polled, so your audience can judge the significance of the sample for themselves. When you quote an authority on your subject, be sure that you describe that person's experience and expertise.

When you began your researching process, you probably thought you would mainly be seeking rational evidence, but you should not be surprised if you have very little of it to report in your paper. Truly rational proofs are difficult to come by. That is what makes controversy so lively. If you can provide all the answers in black and white and there is absolutely no room for dispute, you don't have a very engaging topic. By contrast, if you leave a lot of unanswered questions, then you are not finished with your research. Readers want writers to back up their assertions with solid facts: statistics indicating the widespread nature of the problem, the exact wording of problematic legislation, the names of states where relevant propositions will be voted on next year, and so on. When readers criticize an author for not backing up his or her theses with evidence, it is these kinds of rational proofs that they are looking for.

Ethical Rhetorical Strategies

Ethical appeals are arguments based on personal experience. You may be thinking that, as a college student, you have little personal ethical weight, but think about how you first became interested in this topic. You have some connection, possibly a long-standing one, with your subject. Perhaps it grew out of a hobby, a job responsibility, or a news story that you followed from beginning to end, either as it unfolded or retrospectively during the course of your research. You don't have to hold a Ph.D. in a topic to qualify as an expert in it. Your interest in and experience with the issue are enough for you to make an ethical appeal related to it, but you must establish that interest and experience clearly so that your audience will appreciate it.

The ethical appeals in your paper need not all come from you personally. Many of the outside sources you cite will lend credibility to your arguments. Articles in professional journals are called "refereed submissions" because they have been selected and edited by accomplished professionals in that field. They are generally very reliable sources, and it will advance your case if you reveal that the information reprinted in your work was first reported in a respected journal.

Authorities are constantly quoted in newspapers, in magazines, and on television news shows. When you cite an expert opinion collected from another source, it's important to take the time to establish the reputation of the person cited. Take a look in Chapters Thirteen and Fourteen at the common formats for listing an interview on a Works Cited page; you will see that very little information is revealed. The name of the person interviewed, the medium used to record the conversation, and the dates when the researcher spoke or corresponded with the interviewee is all that is revealed. So when you use information gathered during an interview with an expert on your topic, establish the ethical appeal of that person in the text as you report the findings from your conversation. Borrow credibility where you can. There are probably only a dozen or so experts at the top of any one field; at least one of those should be directly quoted or paraphrased in your finished research project.

A successful research paper will combine all three strategies—persuasion, rational proofs, and ethical appeals—in its arguments. Rarely is a discourse built around only one element of argumentation. Some advertisements rely solely on a single strategy, and ceremonial discourse is composed mainly of persuasive elements. Ceremonial discourse, is, as it sounds, a routine speech or text delivered as part of a formal occasion. Generally, ceremonial discourse is uplifting and inspiring, embodying the grandest elements of persuasion. Funerals, dedications of civic structures, political marches and rallies, and graduation exercises are events that occasion ceremonial discourse.

Your research paper will be held to different standards of accountability than a ceremonial speech, however. It would be superb if it were as inspiring as Abraham Lincoln's Gettysburg Address or Martin Luther King, Jr.'s, "I Have a Dream" speech, but it will have to be more heavily corroborated and documented than either of those great examples of persuasion. In academic arguments, rational and ethical strategies are the foundation of successful persuasion. As you may have noticed as you read your way through magazines and newspapers and then moved on to journal articles, the more scholarly and erudite a text is, the less it relies on persuasion. Professional research reports occupy the opposite end of the rhetorical spectrum from ceremonial discourse; they tend to be composed entirely of ethical and rational arguments. Medical journals, for instance, report extensive statistics on disease-related mortality without ever mentioning surviving family members, and they discuss the clinical role of prenatal care without ever revealing if the babies born to the study's subjects were male or female or named after favorite uncles. Writers of scientific studies assume that their readers know the ethical qualifications of their sources and can supply humanistic details from their own practice and research if they want to, but that most will be persuaded by the rational data itself.

The preference for persuasion in popular discourse and for rational proofs in professional journals gives persuasive appeals lower status in some academic circles. In scientific writing, as well as in some humanities courses, students are forbidden from using the first-person pronoun, *I*, in their research papers. There is nothing wrong with a writer's occasionally acknowledging that he or she is producing the text the audience is reading. Indeed, readers often like to hear the author's voice come through as an active agent. Nevertheless, your instructors may ask you to avoid using the word *I* in your final paper. If so, you can identify yourself as "this researcher," and you can think of this device as an ethical appeal, because it stresses your status as a dispassionate observer or member of a research team. In English composition classes, however, you will generally be encouraged to write in the first person and to employ persuasive rhetorical strategies to accomplish your goal of convincing your audience to agree with your thesis. Appealing to an audience's emotions may be dismissed as "pure rhetoric" in some elite circles, but almost everyone will admit that more readers will alter their behavior, change their beliefs, or spend their money because of persuasive devices than because of rational arguments.

■ Deduction and Induction

By now you probably realize that writing a research paper is more complex than you thought it was. You have been cautioned to consider not just your thesis and the individual arguments leading up to it but also the very words you will choose, including even how you will identify yourself. A research project is often a major assignment requiring many hours of work and determining a significant portion of your grade. More than likely, you will want it to be favorably reviewed and judged. Moreover, you will nurture a degree of interest in your topic during the course of your research, and you will probably want to do your part to advance the thesis you have worked to support. You will want your readers to agree with you, perhaps even to take the action your paper will recommend. By the time you get to the writing stage you will have already invested a lot of time and thought in your research paper, and to give the final product anything less than your best efforts would undermine all your preparation. As you near completion of your project, a final burst of enthusiasm and exertion will likely pay off handsomely when your grades are reported. Therefore, you would do well to cancel every aspect of your social life until your project is completed; sequester yourself in your room without television, computer, or stereo; have your telephone disconnected and newspaper delivery stopped for the duration of this task; eat pizzas slid under your door for every meal; and put out the word that you have entered the federal witness protection program so that no one will even bother looking for you until this ordeal is over.

But wait! How did your assignment become so unreasonable? You probably agreed that the job ahead was daunting and important, that it would require considerable effort, and that it was worthy of your concerted efforts, but you never intended to sacrifice your social life for it. Still, since you agreed to all of the "evidence" leading to such a demanding "conclusion," maybe you should consider the suggestion. Or should you? You might be wondering how anyone could demand such austere study habits, and then again you might be thinking that a milder form of seclusion would be a good idea, at least until you have a rough draft on paper. After all, it'll only be for a week or so . . .

You have just been the audience for an argument premised on *deduction*. A deductive argument follows the pattern of the syllogism, a logical construct promoted by Aristotle. The most famous example of a syllogism is the following:

All human beings are mortal.

John is a human being.

Therefore John is mortal.

This information comes as no surprise to anyone. But consider the use of the syllogism on a more controversial set of assertions, such as the following:

All crimes are despicable.

Assisting in a suicide is a crime.

Therefore assisting in a suicide is despicable.

You can see how a deductive rhetorical strategy can be used to lead the reader to false conclusions, or at least to prompt readers to consider assertions they would find untenable if stated bluntly, without any preceding arguments.

If you believe that many members of your audience will be skeptical of your thesis, plan to follow a deductive rhetorical strategy when organizing your paper. Begin with the most palatable of your assertions, and slowly build your readers' confidence in your logic and reasonable nature. Introduce assertions that point toward your conclusion, striving all the while to achieve audience agreement. That way, when you arrive at your logically deduced conclusions, readers will have participated in building a stone wall from their own convictions. Then, even if they reject your final conclusions, they will have been sympathetic to the logic that produced them and will be more likely to grant your recommendations some credence. Clever organization will not make a ridiculous deduction acceptable, but it does help ease skeptical readers into accepting a position they otherwise might not have even considered.

Conversely, use *induction* if your conclusions or recommendations are likely to be perceived as laudable but the supporting evidence or assertions make certain, perhaps unpleasant, demands on your readers. An inductive argument begins with the general thesis stated plainly up front and elaborates on it with individual qualifications and assertions. If, for example, you are arguing that we must conserve endangered natural resources, few readers would disagree with that general position. However, many taxpayers are opposed to expensive mandatory recycling programs, retailers and advertisers do not generally favor reducing product packaging, consumers would rather not pay more for recycled products, and virtually no one wants to live next door to a recycling plant. Therefore you would want to organize your paper so that readers embraced the noble idea of conservation before considering the expense, inconvenience, and sacrifice involved.

As you begin planning the rough draft of your research paper, you may be tempted to start by simply revealing your thesis to your audience. Consider withholding some of your argument, however, until your audience has accepted the most innocuous parts of it. Begin with assertions that are likely to be greeted with widespread approbation, so that you can share common ground with your readers initially. If you make unpopular suggestions too quickly, you risk antagonizing your audience. That will put them on the offensive and make them want to hunt for flaws in your assertions. If you can start by gaining your readers' trust, however, you will have the chance to present your case to a crowd that is listening instead of protesting.

Kyle had no difficulty finding rational data to include in his paper about Internet security and on-line credit card use. The economy is one of the most closely studied subjects in American society, and there are plenty of demographic statistics available for economic research. He quickly found the number of households with computers in this country, statistics describing the proliferation of the World Wide Web, and illustrative data about credit card transactions in stores, over the telephone, and via computer. From computer journals he collected technical details about encryption and firewalls. In addition, several companies conducting business on-line offered him authoritative assurances that Internet purchasing was becoming prevalent and protected.

At first Kyle thought there were no possibilities for persuasion in a paper about such a scientific topic as computer security. He quickly realized, however, that since it is an emotional response—fear—that keeps many people from making on-line purchases, persuasion must play a central role in his attempt to promote Internet commerce. He would have to *convince* his readers that engaging in on-line commerce is safe, not just *report* that it is safe. He discovered that many people fear change, technology, or both and that he would have to portray on-line shopping in a positive light to reduce readers' anxieties. Also, he thought he could appeal to merchants' goals of taking advantage of cutting-edge technology and appearing progressive, if he chose his words carefully in describing the virtual marketplace.

As a computer science major and recreational computer user who surfs the Web about as much as most people his age watch television, Kyle has considerable ethical appeal. The range of examples he can call up to illustrate his points demonstrates his considerable familiarity with the World Wide Web and its offerings, and his programming knowledge helps him understand Internet security systems and evaluate them with more than average competence. Still, his knowledge of this minute corner of computer science was not enough for him to ask readers to simply take his word about it, so he sought to expand his credibility by interviewing experts in the field.

■ *Writing a Working Outline*

You now know that a working bibliography is a list of sources for your own private use during the researching process and that it contains sources that you ultimately will not use in your final project or include on your Works Cited List. A working outline is similar. It serves as a private guideline for your draft-writing process, and it may contain options and tangents that your final paper will not pursue and more information than your final outline will include. The working outline is a tool for organizing, remembering, and making sense of all of the data you have collected and all of your thoughts on your subject. It can be typed and orderly, but it might be better to let it be sloppy, with lots of room for changes and additions. You will probably want to alter this plan as you write, so put it in a format that encourages you to be flexible and open to new ideas as you write. If you create your working outline on a computer, print it out so that you can keep the whole thing in front of you as you write and pencil in changes and new details as necessary.

Start with a blank sheet of paper or a new document in your word processor. Ask yourself the first question you began with when you started inquiry into your topic. For instance, although Kyle eventually decided to focus on credit card security, he started by wondering how the Internet has changed daily life for people—how e-mail has affected correspondence, for example, or how computerized transactions of all sorts could threaten personal privacy. Although neither his final paper nor his working outline will include the "dead ends" or other possible specific subjects he considered but rejected, he will probably want to turn back to his first, very broad question in writing his working outline, to provide a context for the specific topic he finally chose to write about. His first question—how the Internet has changed and will change daily life—appeals to a wide audience, so it provides one reasonable starting place for the introduction of his paper. Begin writing your working outline by jotting down the first questions you asked yourself about your topic and listing the answers or additional questions those queries produced.

Next, define your topic as you will cover it in your final paper or presentation. What arguments will you use to advance your position? List the examples and facts you will use to reinforce each argument. Include your refutations of the opposition's best reasoning. Be brief and specific, citing information you remember learning during your researching process as well as data you still must discover.

Try to think in terms of what it will take to convince your audience; don't be constrained by the limitations of the evidence you have gathered. It is not uncommon to find that you are lacking some necessary evidence at this point. As you begin organizing your presentation or paper, you will probably discover new research questions. Most likely, you will find that you need relevant facts that are relatively easy to discover. For instance, as Kyle constructed a working outline for the first draft of his paper, he determined that he needed to discover the percentage of American families with access to the World Wide Web and the incidence of credit card fraud in face-to-face and telephone transactions. Don't be discouraged at the prospect of going back to the library or picking up your telephone to do more research now. It is much easier to answer a few specific questions than to learn about a whole subject in general. You are not going all the way back to square one, by any means. In fact, you will be surprised at how quickly you can find the answers to the questions your working outline prompts. You may simply have to call back someone you've interviewed and ask a couple of follow-up questions or flip back through the pages of a reference book you've already reviewed. Your previous research and the specificity of your remaining questions will simplify these remaining tasks.

When you are satisfied that the notes you have made are adequate to construct a complete and persuasive treatment of your topic, get out your note cards and determine which pieces of information you have collected will fit into your paper or presentation. If you wrote headings on your note cards as you made them to suggest where they might be useful for your final product, find out how those headings correspond to your working outline. If you did not remember to label your note cards or if they don't seem to correspond to the outline you have started, read through them and attempt to place them alongside related parts of your outline.

As you read back over the notes you have taken, you may discover pockets of information that you have omitted while imagining your working outline. Consider each carefully before you decide to insert it into your proposed draft. Remember that excess material is an almost unavoidable part of the researching process, and your final paper or presentation will not accommodate all of the information you have uncovered. Finishing a research project is like assembling furniture from a kit that provides for some optional customization; there will be parts left over. Some of the notes you have taken will look totally foreign and unreasonable to you after you have begun to compile the final product. Others will seem fascinating but just not relevant to your thesis as you have defined it. Don't include any information just because you have it. That would be like wedging too many shelves into a bookcase or putting eight legs on a chair just to use up all the parts you have lying around. The result would be a clumsy, confusing product that is ruined by its excesses.

Match your note cards up to your proposed outline, trying to include the best and most relevant information that you have collected, along with your own ideas on the subject. Then, assess what you have. If it appears that you have evidence or examples to back up most of your assertions and that your final product will be complete, persuasive, and long enough to satisfy the assignment, you are ready to begin drafting your final paper or presentation. If not, pose your first, broad question about the topic to yourself again and identify parts of your answers that you did not include in your first attempt to create a working outline. Look at your notes again to determine what else you might introduce in your examination of the subject, and make a list of research questions you still need to answer. However, make certain that everything you decide to include answers your research question clearly.

When you have exhausted your imagination about your topic and the blank page or screen you started with is thoroughly messy and crowded with references to arguments, notes, examples, anecdotes, statistics, and personal details, you have a working outline. You may want to recopy it and attempt to establish divisions that group relevant information together. When you are confident that you have created at least a workable plan for the rough draft of your paper, weigh it carefully in your mind. It is easier to consider all of the parts of your product in outline form than to keep the full text of the whole thing in your head at once. Ask yourself whether it is balanced:

- Is there sufficient background or context so that your audience can appreciate the significance of the problem you will attempt to solve?

- Does your treatment of the subject accurately and adequately represent both sides of the argument, with the balance of proof demonstrating the greater strength of your position?

- Are rational, emotional, and ethical appeals used to support your claims?

- Are reliable facts, developed examples, and original ideas distributed throughout?

- Does each part of the working outline move logically and smoothly into the next?

Iron out problems in the design or organization of the paper or presentation now; don't expect brilliant writing to compensate for omissions or logical leaps in your outline. Make a logical working outline with sufficient notes and ideas to back up each assertion on it, so that you can concentrate on the finer points of writing as you compose your rough draft.

■ Kyle's Working Outline

Although it seems that many computer users must be familiar with the Internet and the World Wide Web by now, Kyle discovered in talking with friends in the dining hall that many had not shopped for consumer goods via computer. Some did not even know that it is possible. He decided, therefore, that his audience would include both novices and relative experts: people with essentially no Web surfing experience as well as a few who had made purchases on-line already. He also discovered that the computer science experts and professors he had spoken with were about equally divided over whether punching credit card numbers into a Web page is prudent, so he determined that his audience would include both supporters and skeptics.

To make a working outline, he looked back through his research journal and copied down some of the questions he had asked himself along the way. His first working outline is reproduced in Figure 10.2. Notice that it does not follow formal outline conventions concerning lettering, numbering, and indentation. Until you read the rough draft of his research paper, you may find

---

X How will the Internet change daily life for average Americans?
    E-mail
    International contact
    Immediate pictures and information
    News
    Travel
    Shopping
    Paranoia about access to private information
    Kids' access to pornography
    Make people want better and better companies

X How is on-line shopping nade possible?
    People want to have it.
    Merchants have to be willing.
        Microsoft technology
            (who is Bill Gates anyway?)
        Stores have to do it first.
            (Steve Coffey NPD Group quotation)

XX Why should people shop on line?
    Fun, exciting, convenient, flexible
    But why is it better than shopping on the phone?
    ????????

Figure 10.2 Kyle's Working Outline

some of the references on Kyle's working outline seem obscure or meaning-less. It is a personal guideline, an attempt to sort out his own thoughts on the subject and to organize a first attempt at writing his paper; it is not really in-tended for public scrutiny. Your own working outline may be more tradi-tional or even more free form than Kyle's.

■ Summing Up

Argumentation is a broad concept in contemporary society. The thesis, or main assertion, of your paper or presentation should be supported by the argu-ments, or minor assertions, that you construct. Each of these, in turn, should be backed up by rational proofs, emotional arguments, or ethical appeals.

Rational proofs are incontrovertible facts, such as statistics, scientific laws, historical certainties, and the testimony of expert witnesses. You proba-bly started out thinking of "research" only in terms of locating and reporting such hard-and-fast data. Rational proofs are the backbone of most re-searched writing, because they have the appearance of objectivity and an air of irrefutability. However, as you know, most "facts" are open to interpreta-tion. Rational proofs are often difficult to muster in discussing a truly contro-versial problem, and they are often not really conclusive. Although statistics reputedly don't lie, they can be manipulated to shade the truth.

Emotional arguments are sometimes referred to as "ploys" or "rhetoric" by persons who wish to discredit or dismiss them. Analogies, opinions, anec-dotes, and loaded language are examples of emotional, or persuasive, ele-ments that can be employed in a research project. Describing a situation from a victim's point of view or using biased language are persuasive argumenta-tive tactics. Although emotional arguments don't carry the esteem associated with rational proofs in academic writing, they may be more effective in prompting your readers to change their assumptions, attitudes, or actions.

Ethical appeals are arguments based on the authority of the person pre-senting them. If your own expertise with your topic does not enable you to make ethical appeals yourself, it is possible to import such authority by quot-ing experts who agree with you or by demonstrating that esteemed persons or agencies support your thesis.

It is possible and preferable to incorporate all three strategies—rational, emotional, and ethical arguments—into research projects on almost any topic. Since your audience is likely to be composed of persons who strongly agree with your main assertion, others who are apathetic toward it, and some who flatly disagree with your point of view, a mixture of rhetorical strategies will address your complete audience most successfully. You can also use deduction or induction to persuade your readers. A deductive argu-ment starts by presenting minor assertions, and attempting to convince the audience to accept them, before openly stating the more controversial major assertion. An inductive argument begins with a generally acceptable blanket statement, or main assertion, before carefully revealing the controversial assumptions or actions that undergird it.

Achieving an effective balance of rhetorical strategies and crafting a persuasive deductive or inductive argument require advance planning. Making a working outline before you begin to draft your paper or presentation will help you remember to include everything you want to say in a logical, persuasive order. It offers you a chance to plan your final product before you begin writing it. Like Kyle's, your working outline will not be for others to read and comprehend; it will be a list of arguments and sources that you hope to incorporate, and it will guide your writing process to ensure that the first draft of your research paper is coherent and complete.

Exercises: Sources and Strategies

1. Write a letter refuting your thesis in the voice of a person who is skeptical about what you are proposing. Alternately, if you can find an Internet mailing list on your topic, attempt to refute some of the arguments against your thesis offered by other list participants.

2. Make a copy of the chart printed below, and fill it in by classifying all of the evidence and examples presented in your proposed research project:

   Rational Proofs   Emotional Arguments   Ethical Appeals

3. Make a working outline for your research project.

Writing to Know

Closely analyze a published article about your topic that you believe is a well-written argument. (You might consider that article a model for your own research paper.) Start by outlining the article. What is its thesis? How does it begin? What are each of its author's main points or arguments? How is each of those proven? (For example, are primary sources or secondary sources cited? Are experts quoted? Are differing arguments refuted?) How does the author conclude? Write a rhetorical analysis (two or three pages) in which you look at *how* the writer of the article has presented and proven his or her main assertion. Which arguments are convincing? Which are you skeptical about? How are you affected by the essay overall?

Chapter Eleven

Incorporating Secondary Materials

You probably read many more research texts on a day-to-day basis than you realize. Most of your textbooks incorporate research, especially those for science, social science, business, and history classes. You almost certainly encounter research writing when you gather information for your own research projects. In addition, magazine and newspaper articles, how-to manuals, and television news shows incorporate both original research and secondary-source material in their reports. Think about how you read and respond to quoted materials in those media. If an expert is talking on television, don't you like to see that person's name and title displayed on the screen? When you encounter a long block quotation in a textbook, are you likely to scrutinize it, skim it, or skip it entirely? How often when reading a rather dry text have you realized at some point that for the last few pages you have been merely decoding words while mentally rummaging through your pockets, desk drawers, and wallet for enough money to order a pizza? Chances are, it was poorly integrated secondary-source material that drove you to your mental quest for pizza money.

Reading is a complex mental operation. This is something you knew when you were five or six and were first learning to master it, but you might have forgotten this fact now that you are able to decipher billboards at sixty-five miles per hour. Readers must translate letters into sounds, sounds into words, words into ideas, and ideas into arguments. Close readers savor the sounds of words as they decode them and test the reliability of ideas as they uncover them. As a reader yourself, you are familiar with the number of pages it takes to "get into" a text, and you know how confusing it can be when a writer merges his or her own style of expression with that of too many other contributors. When a reader encounters quotation marks or a long block quotation, a series of questions surges into the mix of mental operations that compose the act of reading: Who is being quoted? Why is this quoted here? How does this voice differ from the one I have gotten used to? What am I supposed to be looking for in this? These distractions constitute a significant set of hurdles for readers to clear.

Although you do not want your readers to stumble as they read your work, you can't complete a legitimate research paper without incorporating into it some of the evidence you have discovered in other sources. You consulted secondary sources to help defend your thesis, so naturally you will want to include some of that evidence in your final paper. However, secondary sources should not dominate the text you are drafting. Always think of your paper as discourse that *you* write, containing original ideas that are only reinforced and augmented, not defined, by secondary-source material. As the author of your work, you must maintain control over it and regulate the amount of outside information that gets in.

A good rule of thumb describing how much secondary-source material you should include in a research paper would be handy, but there isn't any such all-purpose guideline. A range of options awaits you. If your topic is largely unfamiliar to you when you begin, you may need to rely on secondary sources more than do writers who have firsthand experience or a long association with their subject. A controversial thesis will require more expert validation than will a self-evident one. You must use your own judgment in this matter, but if you imagine the skeptical readers of your text demanding corroboration from authorities and concrete proofs here and there, those are probably places where secondary-source materials are needed.

■ *Introducing the Work of Other Writers*

Let your readers know who and what you are inserting into your text. You are the host of the mix of sources and readers invited to participate in your discussion, so it is up to you to make the proper introductions. When you enter the work of another writer into the record for the first time (whether through summary, paraphrase, or direct quotation), clearly state his or her full name. If the person's job title is relevant to the information presented, include that too. The following sentences from Kyle's final research paper demonstrate this:

In a telephone interview with Mike Gelz, a senior Web site technical writer for Gateway 2000, I found that even though Gateway's home page does not support on-line purchasing, orders are taken on a limited basis.

In the mind of John Williams, chair and CEO of Computer Services, Inc., businesses have not taken full advantage of the opportunities available to securely hold on to the vital sixteen-digit credit card number.

According to David N. Bodley, who wrote an article on security at the South Florida Mall Web site, "there have been no major, consistent or organized reported thefts of funds transferred electronically."

Don't confuse readers by launching into quoted material without warning, and don't expect them to turn to your Works Cited page to figure out who is being summarized, paraphrased, or quoted. A text that is comprehensible in an oral medium as well (one delivered on audiotape or video tape, for example, or an oral presentation) will be easiest for readers to comprehend.

After you have introduced an outside speaker by his or her full name, refer to that speaker by his or her last name only throughout the rest of your discourse. Do not mention experts by their first names; that kind of familiarity is reserved for memoirs and autobiographies. Even if you personally know an authority you are citing in your paper or have been encouraged to call that person by his or her first name during an interview, always observe formal conventions on paper.

■ Exploring Contexts

Just as it is important to introduce the secondary-source material you cite in your work, it is often a good idea to follow up on it by explaining how it advances the argument you are making. In most cases, you will be removing source material from its context in a much larger discourse and inserting it into your own rhetorical structure, carefully juxtaposing certain ideas to support your arguments. Don't expect readers to connect the dots without your help. Provide some clues to the connections you are making, but do not restate the content of imported materials. Trust that the sources you employ make sense, that you have wisely included them in your work, and that your readers will peruse them carefully. Do not "translate" or reiterate material you include from secondary sources. Instead, tie comments from other writers into your text by building on them, and make careful transitions between quoted material and your own words. For example, the following passage occurs in Kyle's final research paper:

Dr. Paul Buis, an assistant professor in the Computer Science Department at Ball State University, believes "the technology is very complex, and the complexity is frightening. On the other hand, so is the technology in an automobile, the telephone, and an airplane." The complexities to which Dr. Buis refers are those which insure Internet Security, such as encryption.

Think of incorporating secondary-source material into your text as a landscaping problem. You wouldn't welcome the insertion of a stark new building into your neighborhood without some integrative elements to link it to the street and sidewalk, tie it in with the natural setting, or mask its rough edges with plants and decorations. Never just wedge secondary-source materials into your discourse and expect readers to adapt to them. Provide smooth transitions from your sentences to those written by others and back to the broader context of your paper.

Much of the persuasive information you will want to introduce in a research paper may come from secondary sources. Carefully deciding not only what to incorporate but also how to integrate it into your paper will determine whether secondary-source materials appear to dominate your text. Already you have read and listened to the maximum number of words allowable for your finished project many times over in the course of conducting your research, and now you must accurately communicate as much of that information as possible in as few words as possible. There are three basic ways to incorporate the many pages of secondary-source material you have consulted into your own final product: summarizing, paraphrasing, and quoting directly.

■ Summarizing

A summary is a very general statement, usually only one or two sentences, that condenses several paragraphs or pages into a very few words. Summaries are effective when you want to state another author's main assertion economically or you want to add the weight of a certain authority's credibility to your ethical appeals without reiterating that expert's whole argument. For instance, if you are writing about a consumer issue and you find that Ralph Nader or a high-ranking administrator at the Consumer Protection Agency has published an article advocating your position, you will want to call attention to that support briefly but conspicuously. Effective summaries are difficult to write, because you must take up into your head a whole passage, an entire chapter, or a complete discourse and decide what its one or two most powerful points are. Summaries are naturally reductive but must nevertheless faithfully represent the other author's complete argument or explanation, in one or two clearly written sentences. It is often wise to incorporate qualifying words in summaries, to say, for example, "Ralph Nader *seems* to agree in his recent article" or "It would *appear* that the Consumer Protection Agency is a key player in this movement." Always document summarized information as specifically as possible, indicating whether several pages, a whole article, or even a complete book is represented by your summary.

Summarizing is a useful technique for presenting complicated details or statistics, such as scientific data or survey results. You might use a summary to present detailed information or images that are useful to your readers but do not warrant extensive coverage in your discourse. For instance, one of Kyle's Web searches turned up the following passage from a graduate student paper posted to a site hosted by the Computer Science Department at the University of California at Davis. Written by Michael S. Borella, it offers two evocative comparisons, between cyberspace and its representations in the "cyberpunk" novels of William Gibson (such as *Neuromancer*) and between cyberspace and the physical world. Although he was charmed by Borella's definition of the illusive concept of the terrain around the information superhighway, Kyle knew he could not devote a full page of his final paper to such poetic rambling, especially since a discussion of cyberpunk novels was not really relevant to his thesis. So he decided to summarize Borella's comparisons in his notes. Here is the passage that caught Kyle's attention:

I: What Is Cyberspace?

Even after reading William Gibson's cyberpunk novels, one's conceptualization of cyberspace, the electronic world of computers and computer networks, can be insubstantial. Gibson describes cyberspace as a world of simulated stimulation that a computer feeds to a "jockey" (computer operator) via a "cyberspace deck" (human-computer interface). Explorers in Gibson's cyberspace often have difficulty telling what is real and what is not. Frequently in our world, the novice computer user has similar problems understanding how to use the potential wealth of information at their fingertips. In Gibson's uncharted future, people access computers by merging their thoughts with a database. Today we can "enter" cyberspace through a keyboard and modem. But what actually is cyberspace? Is it real? What does it look like? What are some of the personal and legal issues emerging from this vastly uncharted new frontier? This paper will answer those questions and more as we explore cyberspace, meet its frequenters, and discuss its increasing role in the life of every human being, not just those who actually use a computer.

Before we embark on our journey through the legal battles and rights issues regarding cyberspace, we need a working knowledge of what it is and how computer operators use it.

Envision a road map. Cities dot the otherwise sparse landscape and roads branch out in all directions, connecting every city. This network leaves no city without service. Although not every city is connected to every other, it is possible to reach any one city from any other. Like every other mass transit system, certain areas are more traveled than others. Some cities are larger than others and some stretches of road are more prone to traffic. The size and complexity of this road map defies the imagination—it encircles the world.

But the cities are not actual cities. They are computers or groups of computers. The roads are telephone lines or fiber-optic cable. The system surrounds the globe in an electronic web of data. The travelers on these "virtual" roads are packets of information which are sent from one city to another, perhaps to many. The road map is a worldwide computer "network." Each city is a depot or terminal for the packets, and is usually referred to as a "node." In reality they are mainframes owned by universities, companies, or groups of computer users. There are several worldwide computer networks currently in existence.

Before reading further, stop and write your own summary of this passage. What is the essence of Borella's two comparisons? How can you present one or both of them more generally and briefly without losing the basic elements? There are many versions possible. Kyle's paraphrase of Borella's comparison between cyberspace and the physical world is less poetic than the original but more efficient for his purposes:

Michael S. Borella, a graduate student in computer science at the University of California at Davis, likens the Internet to an inconceivably large public transportation system for transferring information cargo from computer to computer all around the world. Although most sites are not serviced by direct routes, it is possible to get information from any connected site to any other by means of transfers along the routes included in the infrastructure of the system.

Clearly, the ideas presented in Kyle's summary are Borella's, but Kyle has chosen the parts of the original source that best meet his readers' needs. Writing a summary is a highly individualistic process. You must attempt to extract those elements of the original text that are most applicable to your own project without minimizing them or contradicting other elements in the source. If you can mark up the sources you're reading (that is, if you're using photocopied articles or printouts of Web pages), highlight important passages and pay close attention to the text you have marked as you construct your summary. Or outline an article or passage briefly before writing your summary so that your synopsis will be faithful to the original.

■ Paraphrasing

Most of your references to secondary-source material in your final project will be in the form of paraphrases. Paraphrasing is like summarizing, except that instead of condensing a long passage, it transforms a much smaller excerpt—such as two or three sentences or a short, emphatic statement—into a differently worded passage of comparable length. Use a paraphrase when you want to incorporate a point from a secondary source into your discourse without interrupting the flow of your own prose. Because they are stated in your own words, paraphrases fit seamlessly into your text. Paraphrases are not set off by quotation marks, because they are not direct quotations, but they must be documented in exactly the same way as direct quotations.

When you come across a passage that you would like to paraphrase (in your paper or even just on a note card), read it over several times until you are certain that you understand and can remember every nuance of the author's intent. Put the original version away and think about it for a few minutes. If you were going to say that exact same thing, how would you phrase it? On a scrap of paper, write the same idea, in your own words. Then take out the original and compare the two. Determine how successful you have been. If key words or phrases from the original are included in your own version, or if you have unintentionally mimicked the other writer's sentence structure, you need to try again. Paraphrasing can be difficult, because it often seems that the original author of an idea has already said it in the best way possible, and it is hard to equal that.

Kyle went through this process. Figure 11.1 shows one of his note cards, containing a direct quotation from an e-mail written by a travel agent commenting on self-service on-line airline ticketing. Kyle wanted to acknowledge that on-line purchasing can be problematic for first-time users, and he wanted to draw on the ethical authority of the travel agent in making this point, but he did not want to use her e-mail's informal, conversational language in his paper. So he decided to paraphrase it instead of quote it; his attempt is shown immediately below the original quotation in Figure 11.1 What is wrong with his paraphrase?

As you can see, Kyle's "paraphrase" is unacceptable because it follows the exact sentence structure employed by the speaker of the original sentences. Each word is simply replaced by a synonym. It is a common misconception that effective paraphrases can be created by simply changing a few words from an original quotation. An appropriate paraphrase borrows only the ideas, not the language or sentence structure, from its source. The "paraphrase" above is not the travel agent's exact words, so it cannot be presented in quotation marks, but it maintains her language patterns, so it cannot be presented as Kyle's own work, either. It does not belong in an academic paper.

At the bottom of Figure 11.1 is an acceptable paraphrase of the travel agent's comments. Although the word *intended* is repeated from the original quotation, this paraphrase successfully restates the ideas of the source

Problems with online purchasing	12E

"...occasionally we get users who have tried to book plane tickets via ... a website. They have universally screwed up, so far. Typically a user will have unknowingly made multiple reservations (duplicates), or he will have booked a higher-than-intended fare, etc."

Figure 11.1   Kyle's Note Card and Attempted Paraphrase

material in the writer's own diction and syntax. Successful paraphrasing requires respect for the concept of intellectual ownership. Only when you can create passages that accurately reflect the originals yet are obviously your own—using your own diction and sentence structure—will you have mastered the art of paraphrasing. And even then, you still must acknowledge that the ideas you are paraphrasing are the property of another author, just as you do for summaries and direct quotations.

■ Quoting Directly

Direct quotations—someone else's exact words incorporated into your own text—are the most conspicuous type of outside evidence writers include in their research projects. They are the most cumbersome, disruptive, and troublesome elements of most research papers and presentations, and conversely, they can be the most entertaining, powerful, and memorable elements of a persuasive discourse. I apply the same rule to quotations that I employ with kitchen gadgets: if it's compact, sharp, and incredibly useful, keep it close at hand. In general, do not decide to include a direct quotation in your discourse unless it meets one of the following three criteria:

- It says exactly what you need to say, clearly and efficiently, to advance your argument at a particular point in your discourse, and you cannot improve on it. This is frequently the case with scientific data or statistics. Including such a quotation strengthens your rational appeals.

- It is memorable, forceful, or witty. For example, Picasso is reputed to have said, "Computers are useless. They can only give you answers." Such quotations strengthen your emotional appeals.

- It comes from a particularly respected or authoritative source, such as a widely recognized authority or an especially prestigious publication. Such quotations strengthen your ethical appeals.

Occasionally you will want to include a direct quotation that does not meet any of these criteria. Use your own judgment. Your final text is your own work, after all. Do not include most of your secondary-source information as direct quotations as a matter of course, however, no matter how attractive or convenient that might begin to look to you as you are sorting through your notes. Decide which direct quotes truly merit inclusion. Always know *why* you are choosing to insert someone else's words into your own discourse, and communicate your reasoning to your audience.

It is usually best for clarity and coherence if you can work directly quoted phrases and clauses into your own syntax rather than simply reproducing full sentences or paragraphs by other writers. Figure 11.2 (p. 190) shows a card containing a direct quotation from Kyle's notes:

Note that single quotations marks are used in this excerpt (from a 1995 *Computer World* article by Kim Nash) to denote a quotation within a quotation. That convention prevents confusion. If you quote one person who is

```
ENCRYPTION                                            27N

        "Earlier this year, on-line managers at
First Chicago began studying hacking methods,
encryption and other security issues. They soon
realized that 'there was a lot more complexity
there than meets the eye,' Heuberber said.
        "Not only are there nitty-gritty
technology issues to solve, but banks must meet
stringent federal and state regulations."
```

Figure 11.2   A Quote Within a Quote

quoting another person, place the whole quotation in standard quotation marks ("), and then place single quotation marks (') around the text quoted within the source you are quoting.

Block Quotations

The most obvious way to include a long quotation (like the one in Figure 11.2) in a research paper is to present it, in its entirety, as a block quotation. A block quotation is any uninterrupted quotation, including one containing ellipses, that fills four or more lines of your page. Some journals define block quotations as directly copied material of forty words or more. Choose a definition such as this and apply it consistently throughout your paper. Double-space all block quotations, just like the rest of your text, on your final copy, but indent them five spaces from the standard left-hand margin of your page. They are usually introduced by a colon. For instance, the quotation in Figure 11.2 could be introduced with the following sentence:

> Implementing Internet security measures requires more than just computer technology, as Chicago bankers discovered:

Block quotations make it very plain to readers that you are using outside sources in your text. For this reason (and others), it is a good idea to keep long quotations to a minimum. In a ten-page paper, one or two block quotations should be your limit. Few long quotations are worthy of being incorporated in their entirety in a final research paper.

A shorter version of the quotation in Figure 11.2 would be less disruptive to the discourse it supports. You can use ellipsis points to represent omitted words. Ellipsis points are series of three dots inserted into text to represent where words have been deleted from the middle of a sentence. Use four dots if the abridged passage makes a complete sentence on its own (see Figure 11.3). Brackets, the squared-off parentheses on your keyboard, can be used to enclose simple transitional words or changes in tense and number made to quoted passages to help them conform to surrounding text or main-

> "Managers at First Chicago . . . realized that . . . there was a lot more complexity [to computer security] than meets the eye. . . . [This is because] banks must meet stringent federal and state regulations" (Nash 70).

Figure 11.3

tain internal integrity. One possible way to abbreviate the quotation in Figure 11.2 is shown in Figure 11.3.

This version of the quotation is short enough to be run in with the regular text instead of being isolated as a block quotation, which makes it less obtrusive than the longer version.

Incorporating Quoted Material Within Sentences

There is an even better way to incorporate quotations into your text, and it is applicable about 85 percent of the time. If you work quoted material into your own sentence structures, your own voice will continue to come through in your prose. By combining paraphrasing and direct quotation in a single sentence, you can avoid distracting readers with a sentence in the voice of a secondary source's writer. It is not as complicated as it sounds. Figure 11.4 contains an example of one way to use both a paraphrase and a direct quotation to incorporate the above quotation into a research text.

Integrating secondary-source material into your own syntax in this way is often easier for you, and because it does not cause shifts in voice, it will make your text more accessible to your readers. In addition, it enhances your credibility to avoid drawing undue attention to directly quoted material. Summary, paraphrase, and direct quotation are choices that are available to you throughout your writing. You don't have to limit yourself to just one method of citing other works.

Double Quotations

When you find a quote-worthy passage that is itself quoted in a secondary source, it is often tempting to use those words or ideas yourself. Adding material that is quoted in another source into your own work is known as "double quoting" because it is, in effect, quoting a quotation. This practice is best avoided on the theory that it might cause misquoting. Remember the children's game called telephone, in which a whispered invitation ("Will you

> When a Chicago bank contemplated updating its on-line security, they discovered that "there was a lot more complexity there" than they had realized, including the need to "meet stringent federal and state regulations" (Nash 70).

Figure 11.4

come to my party?") gets passed around a circle until it takes on a distorted form ("Bill's pants are artsy")? The danger always exists that repeated information will be misrepresented, but since you are working with reputable sources for the most part, it is more likely that repeated quoting will simply remove the cited information farther and farther from its original context, perhaps unintentionally shading its meaning in ways that were never intended by its original author. It is best, then, to locate the original source and cite it directly.

Sometimes, though, the original source of cited material is unavailable. If, for instance, the author whose report you are reading or hearing draws on information gathered in an interview, you cannot turn back the clock and invite yourself to that appointment to hear the interview firsthand. Similarly, writers occasionally quote from rare manuscripts that you cannot obtain, obscure journals that your library does not carry, or books that are long out of print and unavailable. In such discouraging cases, it is permissible to double quote sparingly from a secondary source. If you use material that is cited by another author, follow the proper format for documenting information reported in another writer's text.

Incorporating Multimedia Materials into Your Project

Take a look at Figure 11.5. It is a photograph of my dog, Corbu, taken by an amateur photographer (K. S. Kirby 1994). It is another example of secondary-source material, and as such it must be documented when I insert it into my own work. I own a print of this photograph, but I still must acknowledge its source when I duplicate it privately, and I must obtain permission to reprint it in a published work (as it is here), because someone else took it. The same is true of tables, charts, graphics, photographs, computer screen captures, and so on that you include in your research project. You must properly cite not only words but also images that you borrow for use in your work.

Consider including such material in your work. Scanners and sound cards make it possible to include a wide range of visual and audio materials in your research projects. Even a traditional research paper can be enhanced with relevant photographs and graphics. Computer printers and color copiers produce photo-quality, full-color graphics inexpensively, and computers can be used to size and edit images to fit on your text pages. If you are permitted to turn in a final research paper on diskette, you can incorporate secondary sources ranging from "sound bites" to full-motion video.

Even if you don't discover graphics that appear to be ready-made for your research project, most word processing programs have chart- and table-creating features that will allow you to turn statistics, survey results, or chronological data into attractive, full-color presentations within your text. Remember, though, that the same rules for incorporating text-based secondary sources apply to using multimedia materials. Keep graphics to a minimum so as not to detract from your text. Only include multimedia files in your work if they are directly related to your subject and enhance the argu-

Figure 11.5   Corbu. Source: K.S. Kirby, 1984.

ments you are making. As glossy magazines, colorful newspaper pages, documentary films, television news programs, and radio reports demonstrate, however, almost any subject can be made more accessible with multimedia support.

Be creative in the presentation of evidence. Duplicating facilities have changed quite a bit since colleges invented the research paper, and your work should take advantage of contemporary capabilities.

■ *Avoiding Plagiarism*

Plagiarism, as you know, is the presentation of someone else's ideas or words as your own. Some students worry inordinately that they will accidentally plagiarize a secondary source by omitting a pair of quotation marks or inadvertently remembering something they have read or seen as their own thoughts or experience. In fact, such instances of accidental plagiarism are rare and inconsequential. If you have taken notes and written a preliminary draft as this book has suggested, there is little chance that you will commit egregious crimes in your final paper or presentation. Double-check your final draft by reading expressly to monitor your use of quotations and other secondary-source materials, and you can be reasonably certain that your work is entirely your own.

Writers who willfully lift text from a secondary source or even present as their own an entire discourse written by someone else can usually expect worse penalties than a failing grade. Research exercises usually fulfill several important learning objectives in college courses, and a student who ducks a research assignment in a course has not really completed the course. This means that submitting a paper written for a different course, even one you wrote yourself, is a form of self-plagiarism, and many instructors will not tolerate it.

It is fairly obvious to an instructor who has listened to a student speak or who has read any of his or her writing when the student tries to pass off text that is not original. Subtle clues in syntax and diction provide evidence of plagiarism when it occurs. Additionally, implied assumptions about a topic or audience can give away papers that were written with other course assignments in mind. Computerized bibliographies and Web search engines make it easier than ever for instructors to gather proof of plagiarism.

What to Document

Fear of committing plagiarism causes many students to overdocument their texts. If you feel like you will have to end nearly every sentence or paragraph by citing a secondary source, you are either relying too heavily on secondary sources or are erring on the side of caution in your documentation and creating distractions for your readers. It is true that you should document almost everything in your work that comes from another source, whether it is written, spoken, taped, illustrated, e-mailed, electronically published, or acted out. Some of what you have discovered, however, falls into the domain of public knowledge and does not need to be attributed to a specific source. The location and population of a country, for instance, although you will probably have to look them up in an encyclopedia, almanac, or atlas to obtain the exact details, are public knowledge, unless these facts are under dispute (for example, if a region disputes its census tallies, you should reveal who supplied variant figures). You may have to look in a history or reference book to recall that *Brown* v. *Board of Education of Topeka* was decided in 1954 and that the Court ruled that school segregation was unconstitutional and should be reversed "with all deliberate speed"; however, it is not necessary to cite that source of information, because these facts are part of our cultural literacy, or collective consciousness. The twenty-six amendments to the U.S. Constitution are common knowledge, although most American citizens would be hard-pressed to name even half of them. Popular quotations from Abraham Lincoln's "Gettysburg Address," Martin Luther King's "I Have a Dream" speech, John F. Kennedy's inaugural address, or other well-known fragments of the public record can be reprinted with the understanding that readers are familiar with them or know how to access copies of the original source. Sometimes these judgment calls are difficult to make. Conventional wisdom in these matters suggests that if you find the same information undocumented in three sources, it is probably available for you to use in the same way.

It is even more difficult to determine where to draw the line about documenting influences on your own ideas. In the course of researching your topic, you will come up with original ideas on your own, build on proposals you encounter in other texts, formulate solutions to problems yourself, and notice loopholes or problematic contingencies in suggestions offered by others. If the focus of your final project is reasonable, you should feel confident about presenting most of it as your own. If you are presenting your thoughts about the topic and supporting them with facts and opinions gathered from secondary sources, there should be plenty of sentences in your final discourse—at least two-thirds of it—that do not require citation. A research assignment asks *you* to prepare an opinion or analysis about a specific issue. Do not rely entirely on the words and ideas of others in your final product, and avoid giving the appearance of having done so by overdocumenting.

Undoubtedly, you have noticed that newspaper and magazine articles, television shows, documentary films, and many Web sites do not include the documentation necessary to receive a passing grade in an introductory level college composition course. That is one of the most noticeable differences between scholarly and popular publications. Professional journals nearly always present competent and complete documentation of sources, whereas television and newsstand publications hardly ever do. The popular press is casual with documentation for many reasons. Its deadlines are short, and so writers often don't have time to complete extensive research worthy of detailed documentation. In many cases, popular press writers don't want readers to know that they have neglected to examine landmark publications regarding their topics. Space in popular publications is at a premium; if you consider what a full page of advertisement costs in a for-profit magazine, you will see that omitting the Works Cited list from an article is a cost-effective sacrifice. Most of the audience for popular media does not use an academic library and would not pursue a list of sources cited if it were offered. Scholarly writing, however, firmly adheres to the convictions that researchers and writers should be credited for their work when it is reprinted and that readers should be given every opportunity to examine an article's original sources. The assignments that you are asked to complete in college generally are modeled after scholarly research, rather than popular press writing.

■ Summing Up

Your research project should be composed predominantly of your own ideas and opinions, supported by information you have collected from secondary sources. There are no hard-and-fast rules about how much secondary-source material you should include in your research project; a paper about a current event that has sparked lively debate in many periodicals may incorporate twice as many sources as it has pages, whereas a research project about a new or obscure medical procedure may rely on two or three detailed articles.

The introduction of others' voices into your text may be distracting or confusing to your readers if you do not carefully manage it. Always introduce quoted material by explaining who you will be quoting, establishing that person or agency's expertise with the topic, and telling what you hope readers will glean from the cited material. Follow up after secondary material is given in your text, too, by demonstrating how that borrowed information advances the point or assertion you are establishing. Use secondary sources to lend credibility and specificity to your research project, but do not allow them to dominate your work.

A combination of summarizing, paraphrasing, and directly quoting other writers works best in presenting a wealth of secondary source material in your own discourse. Summaries and paraphrases are especially useful because they follow your own language patterns and therefore do not confuse your audience with abrupt changes in voice. However, direct quotations are often the most memorable and persuasive elements in a research project. Try to use brief direct quotations instead of longer block quotations, which may cause some readers to lose concentration. Consider using computer capabilities to incorporate sound files, video clips, graphic images, tables, and charts into your finished product, but remember that the same criteria for evaluating the relevance of secondary source materials apply to audiovisual supplements to your work.

Report the contributions of others—writers, speakers, filmmakers, artists, and so on—to your research project conscientiously, and you will not have to worry about unintentionally committing plagiarism. Complete your work as assigned and on time to ensure that you will satisfy course objectives, including research and documentation requirements. Although careful documentation is not often modeled in the popular press, it is a mainstay of academic writing. A well-documented research project has credibility and can serve as a valuable secondary source to future researchers.

Exercises: Sources and Strategies

1. Conduct a survey of the documented sources in a research article or textbook chapter. How many sources are cited in total? How long is the document? How many summaries, paraphrases, and direct quotations are used? How many block quotations are included? Which article is cited most, and how many times is it cited? What can you infer about using the sources you have gathered from this analysis?

2. Write a brief but effective summary of one article or Web site you have discovered in your research, and explain why you might want to summarize it in your final project.

3. Construct a chart or graph that conveys statistical information you have gathered in the course of your research, or create a graphic and save it in a format that is compatible with the word-processing program you've used for your text, so you can import it into your final project.

Writing to Know

Photocopy or print out a newspaper article, magazine article, or Web page that you think contains secondary-source information but has no bibliography or Works Cited list. Underline or highlight material that you think is probably derived from a secondary source. Is the origin of that information explained in the context of the article? Make a list of sources acknowledged within the text. Is it essentially a complete Works Cited list for the article? If not, list information that is undocumented. Write a one-page analysis of the effectiveness of the article's documentation. Why do you think authors sometimes choose to document secondary sources within their texts when their articles will not be accompanied by Works Cited lists?

Chapter Twelve

Drafting and Revising the Final Project

Every whirlwind of social activity eventually leads to the tedious, rote task of writing thank-you notes: the parties surrounding graduation end, the honeymoon is over, the holiday season passes, and there you are, sitting at your desk or kitchen table, knowing exactly what you must say, and not feeling very enthusiastic about writing it all out. That is the way you might feel after the excitement of discovering information, meeting and talking to experts, visiting places important to your topic, and reviewing your notes. Now that the researching is over and you know what you want to say about your topic, it's hard to get back the energy that your searching and planning generated, and you wonder if you can find the strength to write a whole draft of a research paper.

Many writers are basically introverts who look forward to this solitary moment; some are extroverts who welcome the opportunity to begin communicating their findings to an audience. But pulling all of the elements of research together into final presentation form is daunting to most people. If you have a really clear idea of just what information your research project will contain and how you will present it, and you can't type fast enough to get it all onto paper, then you are incredibly lucky. Most writers are still a little confused at this stage. Many think their subject and the best approach to it will have become clear by the time they are ready to write their first draft. If you find that this is not the case (and you probably will), don't despair over how you can possibly answer all of the questions you've raised about your topic and fit in all of the information you've gathered together. Rather, concentrate on the information and material you have discovered that you really want to pass on to others. This may include some surprising statistics, a great anecdote, a description of something particularly interesting that you saw or heard during your researching process, or an idea that came to you as you investigated your topic. Think of that information as a gift you are giving to your readers. You could just hand it to them like it was nothing special, but that would minimize its importance, both to you and to them, and the effort you have put into procuring it. Instead, you should properly wrap your present so that your audience will anticipate and appreciate the surprise you have prepared for them. Once you know the main things you want to communicate to your audience and have answered your own questions about your topic, it is time to start wrapping your thesis in a suitable package.

■ *Writing Rituals*

Rituals are familiar tasks or procedures that people perform to put themselves into a proper frame of mind for certain thoughts or activities. You probably have evolved some writing rituals, or ways of preparing yourself to compose text, but you may not have thought about them as such. You might meditate or spend some time collecting your thoughts, for example. You might like to make yourself snug as you settle in for the long, lonely, sedentary activity of writing. Or you might even be the sort of person who seeks out hubbub and prefers to work in the midst of chaos. Whatever environment you prefer, before you begin preparing your paper or presentation, you should prepare yourself.

Pay attention to the things you prefer and require to help you accomplish your work. You need a custom set of tools, fuel, and even a suitable uniform to outfit yourself for bivouacking in research-writing territory. First, determine *where* and *when* you will write your paper. Some students like to write in the campus library, where sources are close at hand for checking, large tables are available for spreading materials out, and the environment is conducive to quick production without procrastination. If you want to write your rough draft in the library, campus study lounge, or computer lab, arrange to have plenty of time to perform your task during the hours that the facility is open. You also might want to pay attention to traffic and use patterns in the facility. Public spaces on most campuses tend to be less crowded during the early morning hours, so you might want to adjust your sleep schedule to take advantage of that.

Write When You Work Best

The majority of students I have asked about this (and I've asked a lot) prefer to write at home in their own room or apartment after the day's activities have subsided. Some like to start a project in the late afternoon, after their last class or work obligation for the day is completed. Others start even later, when most of their neighbors are sleeping and the possibility of interruptions and distractions is remote. You already know if you are a "morning person" or a "night owl," so plan to use your own biorhythms to your advantage. Write when your wits are at their sharpest, your threshold for frustration is highest, and your attention span is longest. Don't let poor planning, procrastination, or other demands on your time force you to draft your research paper between cat naps, in a caffeine-induced frenzy, or, worst of all, right up until the second it is due.

Write Where You Work Best

Make conscious choices about the environment in which you will write. Many writers I know confess to needing to clean and organize their space before embarking on a big project. Some like to create a big mess by piling reference books and notes within reach. Do you prefer background noise, such as music or television, or do you write best in complete silence?

Most books will tell you to write at a desk in a clean, well-lighted place that is as quiet as a monastery, but that does not work for everyone. The majority of students I know prefer to write while lying on the floor or across their beds in a semi-noisy environment. It is interesting to note that Kyle, a computer science major who uses his computer as an alarm clock, a radio, a television, an appointment calendar, and a telephone, prefers to hand-write the rough draft of his research papers with a roller-ball pen on white, legal-size, lined sheets of paper, front and back. If you do write at your computer, and it restricts you to your desk, make sure your keyboard cable is unobstructed so that you can pull it into your lap or onto the floor with you.

Take Breaks

Sustained writing requires incentives and fuel. This book hereby gives you permission to throw caution to the wind concerning calories and cavities while you are actively writing. If you write in a lounge or lab where refreshments are not allowed, plan regular breaks, and take time out to eat meals. Wear your favorite clothes. Most professional writers that I know well have confessed to a predilection for writing at home, where they can wear their pajamas.

Plan your time so that you can write a complete draft of your finished project in one session, but don't sit still throughout this entire period. Get away from your paper or screen from time to time. Take short walks; run up and down stairs; throw open a window and sing like an opera diva to amuse passersby. Whatever you do to facilitate writing your rough draft, make note of what is genuinely helpful and refreshing to you, and try to incorporate that into your personal writing rituals.

Drafting an Introduction

Answer each of the following questions to yourself, without doing any research:

- What assignments must you complete this week?

- How many school days until your next vacation?

- How many credits have you earned toward graduation?

- To whom do you owe e-mail or letters?

- Whose birthday or other anniversary is coming up next that you should try to remember?

These questions barely scuff the surface of the things you expect yourself to remember all of the time. Human beings tax their memories and attention every day with the business of conducting their personal lives. What this tells us is that our readers, the audience for the things we write, are similarly preoccupied with the business of getting along in life. The issues we choose to discuss and the positions we advocate may not predominate in their thoughts. The first duty of any text, then, is to wrest its readers' attention from their own troubles and delights and get them, for the duration of our discourse at least, to devote their full attention to the matter about which we have written. That is a tall order.

The introduction to any discourse must gain the audience's attention. It also must make honest claims about the importance of the topic it introduces, summarize the focus and span of the discussion to follow, and give an indication of the position or thesis its author intends to advocate or prove. The introduction of a presentation sets the parameters to which the remainder of the discourse will conform. It also establishes the voice of the author and the tone of the piece. We often think of the first paragraph of an essay or script as its introduction, but as you know, a complex text may require a longer introduction than that.

When you begin to draft your final research paper or presentation, spend time carefully crafting its introduction. Write and revise the first page or so of your text until you are completely satisfied with it. Read it aloud. Try to imagine it in the voice of a newscaster or as voice-over copy in a television ad. Work on it until it sounds exactly like *you* at your most confident and enthusiastic. Is it attention-getting, accurate, and interesting? Read it to someone else, and ask that person what expectations it creates. What will the finished product include? Does the listener want to hear more about the topic after hearing your introduction? If it were the first paragraphs of a newspaper or magazine article, would he or she turn the page to hear the rest of the story?

Write your introduction (and your whole rough draft, for that matter) in language that is comfortable for you. Establishing your authority does not mean writing over your own head or using jargon and obscure vocabulary. You will establish credibility by demonstrating that you know what you are talking about, not by showing that you know a lot of big words.

Rework your introduction until it appropriately emphasizes the importance of the issue you have researched, neatly summarizes what your paper or presentation will cover, and accurately reflects what the majority of your readers are likely to know and believe about the topic prior to encountering your work. Include documentation of sources as you write; it is much easier to incorporate references to other materials as you go along than it is to go back, track them all down, and fill them in later—in spite of what you might tell yourself when you actually begin drafting. You will be using the completed introduction to your paper as a benchmark throughout your drafting process. Whenever you feel at a loss for words or don't know how to incorporate part of your research into your draft, you can read back over the introduction to regain the sense of direction and tone that you started with. As you progress through the writing process, you don't have to give in to "writer's block." If you have a solid introduction, you can turn back to it and read it with satisfaction, letting it guide the organization of your draft.

■ Kyle's Introduction

When Kyle started to draft his research paper advocating on-line credit card purchasing, he was eager to startle his readers with the alarming statistics he had uncovered. The first draft of his introduction cut right to the chase, but it moved so quickly that bystanders couldn't even get the color of the car, let alone read the license plates. Here it is:

In the world today, it seems as though technological advances are made by leaps and bounds every minute of each passing day. A perfect example to illustrate this point is the unbelievable development and growth of commercial sites on the World Wide Web. The commercial domain on the Web—those addresses containing a ".com" URL—increased from 29,000 companies in December of 1994 to 170,892 in just over a year (Williams). Businesses have recognized the ever-increasing presence of people on the Internet, and they realized it was time to begin reaching those people with their products and services. As advertising teams and executives create new television commercials, one subtle change is made, and that change is the http address featured at the bottom of the television screen. Companies ranging from the obvious Internet contenders (Microsoft, Sony, and Gateway 2000) all the way to the not-so-obvious (Colgate, Pepsi, and Pizza Hut) are all attempting to reach the next generation of consumers.

Advertising is not all the new home pages of these companies are . . .

The home pages set up by these companies are not only advertising their products but also selling them.

As people are browsing, advertisements will not . . .

As people are visiting the various home pages of businesses and companies . . .

Companies such as Warner Brothers (www.studiostores. warnerbros.com/ssiol.html) and Universal Studios (www.mca.com/unicity/ store/store.html) have taken the idea of simply informing people about their products to a new height. The ability to purchase items and souvenirs on-line has found a home; its place is on their home pages. For instance, on the WB home page, the customers have the option to click on a link that takes them to various . . . jump to choose from one of six choices. The ability to browse through everything from "Friends" and "Batman" memorabilia on the WB home page to planning a vacation . . .

A portion of those companies venturing onto the Web with advertisements and product information are taking the simple notions to a whole new height. They have stepped up their involvement and taken the initiative to offer customers a new means by which they can shop and purchase. Now when customers find a product on one of the home pages, they can order it right from the comfort of their computer chairs.

Blah, blah, blah some more . . . Virtual malls such as eShop (http://eshop.com) combine various features four separate avenues of shopping for the customer to explore. From the main home page, a user can jump to Tower Records, Speigel, The Good Guys, or 1-800-Flowers, where ordering is reduced to pointing and clicking. Another storefront, Marketplace MCI (http://www2.pcy.mci.net/marketplace/ index.html), also allows users limited on-line shopping. Foot Locker, Champs Sports, and Lillian Vernon are not yet operational. They only provide product information and require the user to order via phone. One link, however, is set up to conduct on-line business—the X Files Store, which sports memorabilia from the hit show on the Fox Television network (4). The Universal Studios home page (http://www.mca.com/unicity/store/store.html) goes the extra mile, however. From its Web site it is possible for a person to set up an entire family vacation to the theme park, including the park tickets, hotel reservations, and plane tickets (2).

After writing this much, Kyle was confused and felt that his paper was veering out of control. He wanted to bring up everything he knew, all at once. Notice all of the false starts in his draft. By the time he was actually writing "Blah, blah, blah" on his paper, he knew he was in trouble. His introduction was not successful in getting readers' attention, because it did not provide enough background or context quickly enough to demonstrate how the issue of on-line purchasing affects average readers. Instead of establishing parameters for writing his paper— for the content it would contain—he had just launched right into it.

In the margin of the page, Kyle drew a series of three-dimensional cubes and wrote "WRITER'S BLOCK!" But this was a new kind of writer's block for him. Usually, having writer's block meant that he couldn't think of anything to say next. In this case, though, his brain was a gridlocked traffic jam of possible next sentences. So he started over, making cuts and inventing a scene to catch his readers' interest from the start. Here is his final rough draft introduction:

"Hey, Mom, can we use the computer now? Brad and I bought this cool new game, and we want to try it out."

"Hold on a minute; let me finish ordering dinner. What do you guys want on your pizza?"

"Where are you ordering it from?"

"The usual, Pizza Hut."

"Good. Can we see what that new triple-stuffed-crust or whatever looks like?"

"Okay, come look at the menu. Let's see, we just click on it . . . there it is."

"Yeah, that looks really good. Get it with, uh . . . sausage and pepperoni. Oh, click here to get extra cheese, too. Bread sticks would be nice, right Brad?"

"Uhh . . . good."

"I guess, since Brad is so adamant about it. Okay, just a couple more things to enter. There you go. Computer's all yours. You have about forty-five minutes to play before the pizza gets here."

"Thanks, Mom."

Whoa, wait a minute. What is going on? Can people really order pizza using the Internet?

Thanks to the current growth and development in today's on-line technology, the answer to that question is a resounding "yes." Computers are becoming an ever-present fixture in the households of America, and people are clamoring to partake in the lure and enticement of the new emerging frontier of cyberspace. The Internet is fast becoming a Mecca for the experienced Web surfer and "newbies" (amateur or beginning surfers) alike, who are part of the estimated 7.5 million households on-line (McLaughlin).

Growth in the domestic sector of the Internet has caused businesses to become major players in the increasing technology. They have recognized the phenomenal on-line interest of their customers, and they have reacted enthusiastically. As Steve Coffey, the vice president of NPD Group, a market research firm in New York, commented, "This is definitely the time for businesses to establish a presence online" (McLaughlin). Companies are listening, as the domain on the World Wide Web, which was created specifically for commercial sites, clearly shows. The domain—addresses ending with ".com" (i.e., http://www. <company name>.com),—increased from a mere 29,000 sites in December of 1994 to 170,892 in just over a year (Williams). In the few short months since the survey was taken, the number has jumped to 259,999 as of April 9, 1996

(OpenMarket, Inc.). Obvious Internet contenders such as Microsoft Corporation, Gateway 2000 (a mail order computer systems retailer), and Netscape Communications are all staking out their place in the realm of cyberspace. The surprise, however, is the growing number of the less Internet-driven businesses who are venturing on-line.

Companies, regardless of size, are beginning to take full advantage of the many benefits the Internet has to offer—twenty-four hours a day, seven days a week, worldwide access—to reach the next generation of consumers. A viable economic opportunity is lying in wait to exert its power. As advertising teams and executives create new commercials, one subtle change is added. Businesses and corporations such as AT&T, UPS, ESPN, and Toyota have all taken the step to include a simple World Wide Web address in their commercials or ads.

As the fictional narrative above about Pizza Hut illustrates, select companies are taking the notion of advertising on-line to the next level. Home pages containing rich and vibrant high-resolution graphics and information showcasing products are gaining a new component—the ability to purchase those featured items directly from the Web site. Now, when a person begins to do a little surfing, he or she could download shareware programs, read an article in his or her favorite magazine, or even purchase a new car.

Notice that many of the same facts and examples from the first draft remain in this version of Kyle's introduction. The fictional dialogue at the beginning of the introduction is designed to snag readers' attention with a kind of eavesdropping situation and to introduce them to the convenient possibilities for Internet shopping. The missing context has been supplied with a few quick details.

Revising an introduction is not as difficult or time-consuming as you might think. Missing details usually can be added with a sentence or a few words, and deleted text can often be moved to other parts of the discourse where it will be more relevant. Don't hesitate to start over or ruthlessly edit your first attempts at writing an introduction. Save your first attempts on disk, or keep the pages you've written around for a while, and experiment with various approaches to introducing your subject. It is worth the effort to start with a few paragraphs of text with which you are thoroughly satisfied, so you will have something to turn back to when the going gets tougher later on.

■ Drafting the Main Text

Some of the most efficient writers I know start generating text like a moon-landing mission. They just drop into the middle of things and begin collecting rocks and planting probes in all directions from a central spot. You might want to start right in the middle of things, with what you think will be the most interesting part of your project, but most of us want to begin at the beginning and write straight through to the end. Writing this way will help you judge whether you are making good transitions, including all relevant material, and steadily progressing from your introduction to your conclusion.

If you already have a working outline and a good introduction to guide you, you can spread your note cards out like bread crumbs along your path and run very little risk of getting lost in the woods. In fact, you may feel like you know what you want to say for the most part and that writing it out will be tedious. Unfortunately, you could be correct. Boredom is a serious threat to a research paper. Once the discovery stage is completed, you might wish you were just giving an oral report. It is much more fun to talk about your research than to write it out. You will find that it is difficult to find synonyms for *said* as you introduce quotations, that you have an almost irresistible urge to state your thesis point-blank at the end of every paragraph, that it takes too many words to explain the most complex points in your argument, and that making transitions between the subtopics listed on your outline is impossible or you have to reorganize as you go. These are not problems exclusive to beginning writers. Everyone who reports on research struggles with these difficulties. That is why you are writing a rough draft. No matter how bogged down or confused you become or how boring or repetitive your draft gets, keep slogging through the mire. It is much easier to eliminate superfluous words and information from your second draft than it is to fill in gaps. And remember, the next draft will be easier than the first.

Like an avalanche survivor, keep moving lest you succumb to hypothermia in the calm that follows the excitement. Keep your thoughts circulating and flowing out onto paper or into your computer. Write *something*, just to keep the process going; whatever you write can be edited, analyzed, or consulted later. Text of any quality is progress at this point.

If you are comfortable with leaving blank spaces where you don't know what to say, skip over parts of your rough draft and leave them for later—after you have checked out one last source, called back an authority, talked the issue over with a friend, met with your instructor, or consulted with a fellow student writer. If you are uncomfortable with leaving gaps in your rough draft, push on through with half-true or half-complete information and mark those passages so that you can find them easily as you revise. After you have gotten a whole rough draft down, it will be much easier to fix up those parts of your text.

Don't Fight the Process

Do not pretend that you can write a perfect draft that will require no revisions. Putting that kind of pressure on yourself will not save time or make a better product in the long run. Writing any text for an audience, especially a researched paper that incorporates various voices and points of view, is a complicated process. Writing a rough draft is a necessary step in synthesizing and refining your paper. Professional writers rely on drafting to help them craft a finished product. The writing process is a step-by-step job. You can't efficiently paint a house, run a marathon, or travel to another continent without adequate planning and preparation; the same is true of writing a research paper. Every mammoth project has a series of steps that, although invisible, nonetheless show up in the end result.

Writing is a recursive process. This means that even though the overall task moves forward in a single direction, from organizing to drafting to revising, the process often seems to double back on itself. A writer in the midst of putting the finishing touches on a text may suddenly realize that he or she needs to learn or tell more about one aspect of the topic. Be flexible about information gathering, drafting, and revising. Don't assume that once you have a rough draft on paper you are finished creating and can confine yourself to polishing what you have written. Word processing software makes text fluid and changeable up until you push the print button, and even after that it is not a huge undertaking to revise and reprint a research paper.

Don't be misled by the terms *rough draft* and *final copy*. Most research papers undergo many more revisions and reconsiderations than two. The first time you write all the way through your discourse, you will have a rough draft, and that will gradually evolve into a finished paper. You will probably generate several rough drafts. Sometimes you will make wholesale revisions; more frequently you will make small changes to localized parts of your text. The writing process is a constant state of motion; your rough draft morphs gradually into your finished product through a series of expansions and contractions. You don't simply write one draft, put it down, and then write the final one. You create a text, and then you begin editing, revising, and shaping it into a reasonably finished state. Often you cannot say exactly when your text ceases to be a "rough" draft and is in nearly final form. No one sits down to write a final version from beginning to end; the finished product is built slowly, the result of many large and small modifications over time.

Look at the credits that accompany your favorite music CDs. They have been mixed, engineered, remixed, and reengineered. In short, they have been revised. Each cut on an average CD has been recorded, rerecorded, and edited until it is as flawless and full-sounding as it can be. Even recordings of "live" performances undergo these revisions. Every creative or skillful endeavor is enhanced by the opportunity to make changes along the way. What would a baseball player give to replay errors? What basketball player wouldn't love to reshoot missed shots until they swish cleanly through the net or replay fouls to avoid a penalty? Constantly assess what you are doing as you assemble your paper. Take advantage of the opportunities that the writing process affords to rethink and rewrite your text. Indecision and experimentation are not signs of a lack of experience; on the contrary, they are necessary components of a refined and sophisticated writing process.

Avoid Sexist Language

While you are carefully considering which words to use to craft your arguments, make certain that you don't get your paper off to a bad start by using gender-specific pronouns or sexist terms. Languages evolve through use, creating new rules of usage to replace patterns that have become confusing or even offensive. You may have been told at some point that the word *man* refers to women, too, but your own usage probably proves otherwise. Try introducing your best female friend, your sister, or your mother to someone as a "man," and see how everyone involved (including yourself) responds. It just isn't true that *man* implies anything other than a male human being. When it would be convenient to use a word like *mankind*, you can try to pretend that it doesn't leave anyone out, but you know it isn't really fair to all of those kind human women out there.

Most of the time, gender bias in language is caused by long-standing cultural habits and deficiencies of the language. For example, consider what would be the best way to finish this sentence:

Every American should register and vote in elections, because it is ____ own voice heard nationally.

There doesn't seem to be an excellent choice, but here are some possibilities for filling in the blank in the sentence above—and a list of problems with each alternative:

his	Implies that this is not an important issue for women.
their	Ungrammatical; creates disagreement between a pronoun and its antecedent. *Every American* is singular, but *their* is plural; it says, in effect, that one equals many.
his or her	Becomes cumbersome if you keep it up over a few clauses; makes your text read like a multiple-choice test.
that person's	Implies that the voter and the person whose voice is heard are not the same individual.
each voter's	Redundant.
every American's	Redundant

With sentence constructions like this, you must make a compromise. One viable choice is to make the singular antecedent plural, allowing you to then use the plural pronoun *their* to refer to it (All Americans should register and vote in elections, because it is their own voices heard nationally). Most would argue that deleting the singular subject dilutes the point in this sentence, however. The lack of a singular pronoun that is gender-neutral and can be used to refer to people (unlike *it*) is a serious deficiency in the English language. It causes many experienced writers to struggle. Often you must choose a sentence that you know is flawed in some way (such as a redundant structure) to avoid one that is incorrect (for example, with pronoun-antecedent disagreement) or offensive (sexist).

Whenever possible—and it almost always is possible—choose a gender-neutral term or sentence structure. For example, write *congressional representative* instead of *congressman*, use *chair* instead of *chairman*, say *mail carrier* instead of *mailman*. Substituting *person* for *man* in compound words (for example, *congressperson, chairperson,* or *mailperson*) often just draws attention to the problem. And know when enough is enough: writing "cowperson boots" is going too far and makes a mockery of the whole matter.

Keep Your Own Voice Dominant

Do not resort, whether out of fatigue or laziness, to simply copying the contents of your note cards into your rough draft, one after another. If your final product is to be sustained by your own thoughts and ideas, you must generate those as part of the drafting process. Keep your own voice dominant in your prose. It is important that you try to write as good a rough draft as you can manage. It will help if you maintain interest in and enthusiasm for your topic as you write. If you communicate a genuine sense of excitement to your readers, you will find yourself enjoying this process and writing a better draft as a result. Think of it this way: if you are not paying attention to what you are saying or don't want to say it, how can you expect your readers to become engaged with it? Remember that although you know more about this topic than you can include in your paper, it is almost all new information to your readers. As you write, think about what intrigued you during the researching process, and re-create that sense of wonder and discovery in your text. Don't drop new information into your discourse haphazardly, without giving your readers some background on it, but don't belabor ideas either. This is not the time to worry about the length of your final paper. Just say what you must say in the most straightforward and engaging manner possible.

The best writers I know describe *hearing* their words as they write them, as if they are dictating their prose to themselves. For most, that phenomenon occurs when they are in their best "zone," or when their writing process really "clicks." If you start to hear yourself writing, don't tune it out. Trust it. It probably means that you are gaining some confidence and authority in your discussion of your topic. If it helps to pretend that you are delivering your text as a speech to a huge crowd, or just telling it to one close friend, imagine that situation as you write. Stop periodically and read over what you have written—aloud, if you are in a place where you can do it. Keep an audience in mind as you write your rough draft. Writing, however solitary and pointless it seems to the author of a half-finished rough draft, is communicating. It is conveying information to others. More importantly, in this case, it is *you* telling what you know to someone else.

Stay on Topic

If you find that you want to restate your thesis in every paragraph of your rough draft, go ahead and do it. You can revise it out later, and it probably means that you are doing a good job of staying on topic. If each of your paragraphs leads logically to your main assertion, you are probably staying on your topic. Pay attention to the transitions between paragraphs as you write. If your paragraphs don't lead smoothly into one another, you may need to reorganize your text according to a more workable outline, but that will not be as difficult as it seems. Once you have produced text following the outline you started with, it is like having the pieces of a jigsaw puzzle turned right-side up and sorted on a table in front of you. It will eventually fit together in a coherent sequence.

Don't discourage yourself by thinking that people who write well do it effortlessly. Watch a professional golf tournament on television sometime. Although great golfers can "drive for show and putt for dough," it is not easy for them. Observe the concentration and frustration in their faces. Sure, any of us would trade scores (and incomes) with them, but practice, although it has made them excel, has not made them perfect. Just as athletes develop "muscle memory" that facilitates execution of specific moves, you are cultivating mental habits that will make you a more astute critical thinker and a more fluid writer. Participants in any sport or profession work very hard at achieving and maintaining greatness, regardless of their proficiency, and even the best must ultimately struggle against the same challenges as amateurs do. If writing is difficult for you, it does not mean that you are not good at it. On the contrary: it probably means that you are getting better.

■ Drafting a Conclusion

You may have learned somewhere in the course of your education that a proper conclusion reviews all of the information reported in the preceding text and reiterates the thesis, but that strategy is probably unnecessary in a reasonably brief research paper, and it is potentially insulting to the audience. If your readers have been following your arguments closely and you have stated them clearly throughout your discourse, repeating them in simplified form at the end of your argument reduces your complex rhetorical strategy to a simple list of reasons to support your thesis. It is much more persuasive to leave your readers with a thought-provoking image or set of ideas to contemplate.

If you were leading a group on a hiking expedition and delivering a lecture on forestry or geology or pointing out rare indigenous flora and fauna along the way, you would want to end the hike with a spectacular, climactic sight: a dramatic waterfall, a breathtaking mountaintop view, a hidden swimming hole fed by a clear spring, or a field of flowers sheltered from strong winds. The trek would be anticlimactic if you simply wandered back into the parking lot where it began and said, "So, as I told you before we set out, hiking is a rewarding pastime." The same is true in a research paper or presentation. If you promise in your introduction to show why specific legislation is needed, for instance, simply asserting at the end that something needs to be done is dissatisfying. You should advance or develop your initial thesis in your conclusion. For example, you could suggest that readers support specific legislative initiatives and tell them how to write to the congressional representatives responsible for them.

If you began your introduction by stating a purpose for your research that would catch your readers' attention, win their initial agreement or consideration, and appear relevant to a wide audience, you probably started with a fairly broad treatment of your topic. By the end of your discourse, you have educated your readers considerably. They are more aware of arguments on all sides of the issues involved, they are familiar with some specific examples or case studies, and they have—vicariously, at least—consulted with authorities on the subject. If your work is informative, then you will be dealing with a more savvy audience at the end of your paper than you originally addressed in your introduction. Trust the information you have provided. Use it. Present, at the end of your research project, the conclusions that you have prepared your audience to contemplate.

■ Revising Your Draft

The revising process begins almost as soon as you begin writing your rough draft. You will fix problem paragraphs, tighten your language, adjust your usage, and make changes in organization and development as you read back over your work while you are drafting it. However, once you get a complete version of your discourse down on paper, your *real* revising process can begin. Aristotle suggested that writers put their rough drafts away for nine years. If after that cooling-off period they still thought them worthy of publication, he suggested then showing them to another person. You probably expect to receive a college degree in less than half of the time Aristotle recommended for retiring your prose, so you will have to step up the process somewhat.

As the author of your work, you are always responsible for its final form. You may choose to take or ignore the advice of others, and you should not abdicate important decisions or surrender control of your writing to anyone else. However, as you have probably noticed, it is nearly impossible to faultlessly proofread your own work. Sentences that sound perfectly natural and sensible to you may be difficult for others to comprehend. You always know just what you meant to say, so confusing syntax, misused terms, and misspellings escape your notice. You cannot even begin to guess every way that a myriad other readers will perceive your arguments, assertions, and assumptions. Therefore you should seek constructive criticism and advice from fellow students, writing tutors, or your instructor as part of your drafting process.

Most of us have a trusted reader, a friend or family member who reviews our rough drafts and offers suggestions for revisions. Even professional writers often try their work out on someone close to them before submitting it to a publisher or giving their consent to have it widely disseminated. Start your revising process by running your rough draft by a friend or support group. If your text is not so long that it might strain your personal relationship, I would suggest that you ask someone to read it aloud to you—cold. That way, you can hear how your words will sound to your readers, and you will quickly discover which sentences are cumbersome, which word choices are strained, where punctuation is needed, and whether your organizational pattern makes sense to another person.

Argument/Research Paper Editing Questionnaire

Your name _____ Author of paper _____

What is the topic of this paper?

What does the introduction of this paper make you think it will be about? What does it make you think the author believes about the topic? (Is this an inductive or deductive organizational strategy?)

What did you know about this topic before you read the paper?
What side of the argument were you on before you read the paper?

After reading the paper, what fact or statistic most stands out in your mind?

What questions do you still have about this topic? (Be specific; list at least two.)

What is the most interesting thing you learned from reading this paper?

In your opinion, is the paper mostly rational or emotional in its persuasive techniques?

Are the quotations in this paper smoothly included? List one that is adequately (or better) introduced and analyzed.

Take one long quotation from this paper and write your own summary of its contents on the back of this page.

Look at the sources used for this paper. Which would you most like to read or hear more about?

Check over the documentation (parenthetical notes and Works Cited List) of this paper. What, if any, problems do you find?

Figure 12.1 Editing Questionnaire

Get Feedback from Peers

If you have ever attempted to offer to others your opinions about their work, you know how difficult it can be to give honest feedback to a writer who has just completed an arduous project. A peer editor, after all, is usually a friend or colleague who does not share the writer's interest or background in the subject, is not familiar with all the nuances of the assignment for which the paper was written, and does not wish to take responsibility for the work or its final outcome.

There is much to be learned from closely analyzing a friend's writing, however. You might notice organizational patterns you haven't considered, discern new problem-solving methods, or acquire some new vocabulary words. You might begin to better appreciate the comments instructors have written on your own papers. It is difficult to see problems such as vagueness or abrupt transitions in your own writing, but identifying those kinds of errors in the work of others will help you diagnose them in your own writing in the future. Offer to trade papers with someone else in your class and edit one another's rough drafts. It should be a positive learning experience for both of you.

It is best to ask fellow students or friends to first simply outline or describe your paper for you. You will be surprised to learn, perhaps, that your readers discern a different focus, purpose, audience, or even thesis than you intended. Because most peer editors find it awkward or difficult to critique a friend or colleague's paper, it is a good idea to supply your reviewer with a list of considerations or editing tasks that you hope he or she will complete after reading your text. You could use an editing questionnaire like the one in Figure 12.1 to prompt your reviewers for specific information about your draft. You could copy it and ask a reader to fill it out and return it to you with your draft, or you might look it over and devise a questionnaire of your own that more specifically addresses your own concerns about your work in progress.

■ *Kyle's Rough Draft*

In writing his rough draft, Kyle has followed most of the advice given in this book. He has structured his argument inductively, reworked his introduction extensively, followed his outline reasonably closely, integrated brief quotations into his own syntax, made notes toward documenting his sources, and put his head down and ploughed on when the going got tough. As you will see, there are confusing passages, wordy sentence structures, poor transitions, and a weak conclusion in this draft. You will want to make many suggestions to Kyle as you read through this version of his paper. But remember, because he got all of this down on paper, you and he can imagine how to begin shaping it into final form. Kyle's work at this stage demonstrates why completing a rough draft is necessary to a writer and his or her peer editors. In reading Kyle's rough draft, you will probably learn things about Internet shopping and security, gain an interest in the topic and form an opinion about it, and observe that he has followed the processes outlined in this book. I think you will agree that he has done his homework thus far.

Research Paper Draft

"Hey, Mom, can we use the computer now? Brad and I bought this cool new game, and we want to try it out."

"Hold on a minute; let me finish ordering dinner. What do you guys want on your pizza?"

"Where are you ordering it from?"

"The usual, Pizza Hut."

"Good, can we see what that new triple-stuffed-crust or whatever looks like?"

"Okay, come look at the menu. Let's see, we just click on it . . . there it is."

"Yeah, that looks really good. Get it with, uh . . . sausage and pepperoni. Oh, click here to get extra cheese, too. Bread sticks would be nice, right Brad?"

"Uhh . . . good."

"I guess, since Brad is so adamant about it. Okay, just a couple more things to enter. There you go. Computer's all yours. You have about forty-five minutes to play before the pizza gets here."

"Thanks, Mom."

Whoa, wait a minute. What is going on? Can people really order pizza using the Internet? Thanks to the current growth and development in today's on-line technology, the answer to that question is a resounding "yes." Computers are becoming an ever-present fixture in the households of America, and people are clamoring to partake in the lure and enticement of the new emerging frontier of cyberspace. The Internet is fast becoming a Mecca for the experienced Web surfer and "newbies" (amateur or beginning surfers) alike who are part of the estimated 7.5 million households on-line (McLaughlin).

Growth in the domestic sector of the Internet has caused businesses to become major players in the increasing technology. They have recognized the phenomenal on-line interest of their customers, and they have reacted enthusiastically. As Steve Coffey, the vice president of NPD Group, a market research firm in New York, commented, "This is definitely the time for businesses to establish a presence online" (McLaughlin). Companies are listening, as the domain on the World Wide Web, which was created specifically for commercial sites, clearly shows. The domain—addresses ending with ".com" (i.e., http://www. <company name>.com)—increased from a mere 29,000 sites in December of 1994 to 170,892 in just over a year (Williams). In the few short months since the survey was taken, the number has jumped to 259,999 as of April 9, 1996 (OpenMarket, Inc.). Obvious Internet contenders such as Microsoft Corporation, Gateway 2000 (a mail order computer systems retailer), and Netscape Communications are all staking out their place in the realm of cyberspace. The surprise, however, is the growing number of the less Internet-driven businesses that are venturing on-line.

Companies, regardless of size, are beginning to take full advantage of the many benefits the Internet has to offer—twenty-four hours a day, seven days a week, worldwide access—to reach the next generation of consumers. A viable economic opportunity is lying in wait to exert its power. As advertising teams and executives create new commercials, one subtle change is added. Businesses and corporations such as AT&T, UPS, ESPN, and Toyota have all taken the step to include a simple World Wide Web address in their commercials or ads.

As the fictional Pizza Hut narrative above illustrates, select companies are taking the notion of advertising on-line to the next level. Home pages containing rich and vibrant high-resolution graphics and information showcasing products are gaining a new component—the ability to purchase those featured items directly from the Web site. Now, when a person begins to do a little surfing, he or she could download shareware programs, read an article in his or her favorite magazine, or even purchase a new car.

The basic design or setup of a virtual mall is simply a home page with links to various stores that are part of that mall. One in particular is eShop, and it allows a shopper to choose from six avenues of shopping. Tower Records, Speigel, The Good Guys, L'eggs, Insight, and 1-800-Flowers are all only a click away (Moeller). Another such location is Marketplace MCI, where Champs Sports, Lillian Vernon, an on-line X-Files Store, and Foot Locker are open to shoppers. However, of the four stores available, the X-Files Store is the only location where true on-line business takes place. The other locations require the shopper to print out an invoice and snail mail (post office delivery) it to the retailer.

Virtual malls are not the only home to businesses on-line; many are single sites featuring only a specific type of product. For example, at the Warner Brothers Studio Store, a customer can browse through an on-line catalog featuring Friends and Batman souvenirs and memorabilia and various works of art relating to the company's productions. Another page even allows someone to send a friend, family member, or loved one a virtual card from the Warner Bros. Post Office. Once the style is chosen and the information is entered, a message is sent via e-mail to the recipient, informing him or her of the delivery. All the person must do is visit the post office to pick up the card.

Ordering from a Web site is simplistic and user-friendly; once the customer has found the items he or she wishes to purchase, boxes next to the picture of the products are checked and everything is sent to a virtual shopping basket. Next, the customer clicks on a link to take him or her to the order form where the option to submit it electronically, over the phone, or by snail mail is available. If electronic submission is chosen, the customer enters all the pertinent information—name, address, credit card number, etc.—and e-mails the order to the retailer.

At this point in the process, concerns and questions begin to arise. Consumers have no problem browsing through the Web pages, viewing products and window shopping, but when it comes time to click on the "submit" button, a twinge of anxiety manifests itself. The reason behind the fear is the "public perception that the Internet is a dangerous place" (Weise 1), a place through which no vital information should pass. In the mind of John Williams, chair and CEO of Computer Services, Inc., businesses have not taken full advantage of the opportunities available to securely hold on to the vital sixteen-digit credit card number.

In a survey distributed to the users of two Internet service providers in southeastern Indiana (SEI Data), the question was raised as to how people felt when it came to sending their credit card number over the Net. Answers to the question were varied: some users will not, others are not sure where they stand, while others think it is the only way to conduct transactions. One user emphatically stated, "Never, I feel it would be a very stupid idea to use a credit card online; it is dangerous enough to just own [one]" (SEI Data). Michelle Kohorst, another respondent, was hesitant in her reply: "I actually don't know that the Internet is less secure, but it just has that feeling of being open and available to so many people with greater hacking abilities than I have." However, Josh Sherman felt "online [purchasing] is a preferred method for everything except special order items."

In comparing the opinions of the survey responses and articles I found on the Web, the views generally followed the same lines. A sense of faith and trust in the Internet and the companies who employ its powerful features is not present. All of the new technology is simply too much for the consumer to adjust to and feel comfortable with, and no one is totally sure where to stand. A major factor in feeling comfortable with on-line purchasing is merely taking the time to sort out all of the issues. At the present time, those issues are confusing and difficult for people to grasp. According to David N. Bodley, who wrote an article on security at the South Florida Mall Web site, "There have been no major, consistent or organized reported thefts of funds transferred electronically." The occasional media story about a "bored graduate student" stealing thousands of files containing credit card numbers discourages the already skeptical Web users (Weise). Bad press is not the only aspect that causes concern; the technical terms and concepts used when talking about the Internet are not exactly user-friendly.

Paul Buis, an assistant professor in the Computer Science Department at Ball State University, believes "the technology is very complex and the complexity is frightening. On the other hand, so is the technology in an automobile, the telephone, and an airplane." The complexity to which Dr. Buis refers are the facets that are needed to ensure security.

Along with Microsoft, VISA and MasterCard are assisting in the development of those facets to secure the transactions of customers who shop on-line. By implementing the Secured Transaction Technology (STT) developed by Microsoft, the two credit card companies hope to create a standard that companies such as Netscape and Mosaic can incorporate into their Internet browsers ("Microsoft's transactions . . ." 15). Browsers are the software programs that not only allow users to surf the Web but also are the tools by which the security methods must work through. Those methods are cryptography, the firewalls, and secured operating systems, which the average user is not well-versed in. The three components are necessary to ensure a secure transaction, and one weak link can disable the security of an entire system ("Internet Banking . . .").

The first piece of the security puzzle is cryptography. Basically, "cryptography ('hidden writing') involves the translation of a message in plain language into one in a secret language" (Stattler). Two types of encryption are used today to translate the credit card number and expiration date into meaningless zeros and ones: one is a public-key and the other is a symmetric-key encryption. In order to understand how the two differ, it is important to understand how encryption takes place.

In order to translate the message, one algorithmic key is used to encrypt (into the secret language) the data and another key is used to decrypt (into plain language) it. Symmetric-key cryptography requires the sender to encrypt the message with a key and then separately e-mail both the key and the message along to the recipient. A greater possibility of interception and eventual decryption exists with that method of cryptography. In contrast, public-key encryption, patented by RSA Data Security, relies on two separate keys to translate the message. Now, the sender only has to send an e-mail message and the recipient is able to decrypt it with a similar key ("Internet Banking . . .").

So, when a shopper finds an item (or items), he or she will enter all of the required data on the order form, and using an encryption method, either a part of the location or the e-mail program, the order form is encrypted and sent along to the merchant. Once the merchant receives the form, another key is used to decrypt the information, and the retailer checks to make sure the customer has the available credit. Finally, if the credit checks out, the order is processed and the transaction is over (Lane).

In a phone interview with Mike Gelz, a senior Web site technical writer for Gateway 2000, I found that even though Gateway's home page does not support on-line purchasing, orders are taken on a limited basis. Public transactions are not yet an available option, but about ten orders are taken per month from private institutions, such as the Federal Credit Union. Purchases are made via the company's experimental Stealth Division Web site, which allows for a secure transaction of funds and data. The method by which an order is taken is relatively similar to how other retailers conduct business. The order is made from a secure server (https rather than http), encrypted with a program called Pretty Good Privacy (PGP), and then is e-mailed to Mr. Geltz. From there, he decrypts the order form and sends the necessary information on to the shipping and ordering department. He said Gateway is in the process of hiring a gentleman from Switzerland to help develop security for the Web site, so one day, consumers will have the ability to purchase a system on-line. In a final question, I asked him about the security of the Internet and he said that no matter how much security is developed, it will never reach a level of ultimate security. Nothing is an absolute.

Of the three components, cryptography is the most important since it provides a secure transaction of valuable and important data. However, it does not keep unauthorized users from accessing the information once it reaches the server. At this point a firewall becomes very important. A firewall "controls traffic between outside and inside a network, providing a single choke point where access controls and auditing can be imposed" ("Internet Banking . . ."). In other words, imagine all the information a computer holds sitting behind a massive impregnable wall, with only a small, heavily guarded door for outsiders to enter through. When MCS/Universal Studios and First National Bank of Chicago first began to step into cyberspace, one of the biggest concerns they had was keeping external sites from breaking into the internal infrastructure of their computer systems, a situation in which a firewall was a necessity (Nash 70).

Finally, the third component, a secure operating system, picks up where the firewall leaves off. A firewall is excellent for controlling unauthorized external access, but it does not control against internal attacks. The UNIX operating system is where the Internet has its roots, but it is also the operating system that provides the feeling of openness that Ms. Kohorst earlier described. The entire system is centered on an omnipotent account, which if broken into, would grant the hacker uncontrollable access to all accounts ("Internet Banking . . ."). Microsoft is currently incorporating the existing security enhancements in the Windows NT operating system to act as a secure server operating system ("Microsoft Previews . . ."). Only the merchant, who will have a username and password, will have access to the secure areas of the information, such as credit card numbers ("Electronic Retailing . . .").

All the aspects covered in the previous paragraphs are necessary and vital to the security of on-line shopping. Despite all that the companies may implement, for some "the problem is entirely a perception of danger, not of reality" (Buis). Once that perception is dissolved, customers can begin to fully take advantage of all the amenities that businesses and corporations are merging into their Web projects. Of the participants in the on-line movement, Microsoft is leading the way in revolutionizing shopping on the Internet with the proposal of its electronic retailing strategy.

According to Bill Gates, chair and CEO, electronic retailing will include the "development of a compelling shopping experience, automatic order handling, payment security, tools for analyzing purchasing patterns and integration with a merchant's supply chain" ("Electronic Retailing . . ."). All aspects of the purchasing chain are represented with this plan. Customers are assured of a secure transaction, offered a new way of shopping, and given the opportunity to shop at whatever time is best for them. Down the road, Microsoft plans to include a shopping utility in the Windows operating system to allow the customer easy access to various on-line shopping locations. In turn, the merchants are able to increase revenues, lower costs, and create specialized custom home pages for the customers ("Microsoft Previews . . ."). The number of people who are on-line will greatly expand the market base retailers can reach with products and services. Also, with only a home page and the necessary links to upkeep, money will not have to go toward maintenance of a physical store location. The retailer will have the ability to cater to the individual preferences of the shopper by creating "communities of shared interest and customized one-on-one relationships with their customers" ("Electronic Retailing . . .").

Joining with Microsoft in the push to develop the on-line marketplace is the nation's largest retailer, Wal-Mart. David Glass, president and CEO of Wal-Mart Stores, Inc., stated, "Microsoft has a solid vision for solving the challenge of electronic retailing on the Internet and this is why we have chosen Microsoft technologies and products to expand our business and reach new customers through the Internet" ("Microsoft Previews . . ."). In the move to reach the new customers, the home page will feature thousands of products, ranging from computer software to gift items, with additional items appearing as the months pass (Letters to . . .).

Regardless of Microsoft's vigorous plan to offer advanced shopping features, a few universal advantages exist that every company and customer can benefit from. Shopping on-line provides customers with a wider selection of products and facilitates comparative shopping. Franc I??? believes, "in terms of comparison shopping, it is easier to 'compare specs' via computer and the variety increases everyday. I . . . have found higher quality and lower price[s] via online vendors as opposed to local electronics warehouses" (SEI Data). Ultimately, pricing will become more competitive since retailers will have to compete with a much larger market to attract customers to their cyberstore.

As on-line shopping becomes more widely used and accessed, the speed and effectiveness will increase to meet the demands of the customers more efficiently.

■ Summing Up

Beginning to write a draft of your researched paper requires energy and enthusiasm. You are finally starting to present the information you have gathered to the audience you have imagined throughout the researching process. However, initiating the reporting of your findings is not the close of one phase of the project and the opening of another; you are merely tapering off your reading and researching and starting to learn about your topic through writing about it. Don't think you have finished discovering information and now must simply record the things you have learned. Writing is a learning process, and you should keep your mind open and your interest in your topic engaged, because you will continue to invent good arguments and methods of presenting them as you write and revise.

Pay attention to your own preferences or "writing rituals." At what time of day do you write best? Do you think most clearly in an ambience of noise, music, or silence? Arrange your schedule and your working environment so that you can capitalize on routines and resources that stimulate your creativity and insight.

Start the drafting process by carefully crafting the introduction or some other key part of your text. Work on that fraction of the finished piece until you are reasonably satisfied with it. That section of the discourse can serve as a benchmark for you, a text you can reread to orient yourself to the tone, voice, and pace of the product you plan to produce. Whenever you are stuck or are returning to the task after a break, begin by looking at that strong section of your text. Try to stay on topic as you write, and keep your own voice dominant in your preliminary drafts.

Be persistent. The production of some text gives you material to work with in moving toward a final draft. Force yourself to put something on paper or disk, even if you know you will be changing it dramatically before you are willing to let others read it. Recognize that writing is a slow—but continuous—process. You will add to and amend your rough draft many times before it becomes a public document. Do not take the terms *rough draft* and *final copy* too literally. Your rough draft will gradually become, through reconsideration and rewriting, the paper you will submit to fulfill your assignment.

Consult with fellow students and friends as you write. Peer review can net you some good advice and a fresh perspective to advance your own writing process, and you can learn from reading others' works in progress as well. Examine Kyle's rough draft reprinted in this chapter. He has managed to include most of the information that he wants to cover in his finished project, but parts of the text are wordy and cumbersome. As you can see, he has a good start, and he can use it to prompt himself to continue thinking about his topic and refining both his message and the ways in which he presents it.

1. Write two introductions for your research project: one presenting your topic in a fairly straightforward manner and one that uses a narrative or anecdote to get your readers' attention. Decide which will work best for your project.

2. Using the editing questionnaire in this chapter (Figure 12.1), review Kyle's rough draft. What strengths or problem areas do you notice? Do you see any of these in your own writing?

3. Give yourself thirty minutes (set an alarm clock) to produce a very rough draft of your research paper. Write in incomplete sentences, and leave blank spaces where quotations will be incorporated later. It is okay if the result resembles an outline more than a finished paper. When the alarm sounds, give yourself a few minutes away from your writing project to compensate for the quick work you have just accomplished. Then read through the document you have just created to determine whether it provides a solid structure for your first serious rough draft.

Writing to Know

Write a complete rough draft of your paper, attempting to follow the advice in this chapter. You may want to post it on a Web site and invite comments from classmates and other interested readers to gather suggestions for revisions.

Chapter Thirteen

APA Format and Scientific and Technical Documentation Styles

Although there are several other documentation styles currently in use, most college teachers and publishers in the United States require either the format used by the American Psychological Association (APA) or that of the Modern Language Association (MLA). Two other styles, that advocated by the Council of Biology Editors (CBE) and the Chicago Style are also popular. This chapter looks at APA guidelines for presenting professional discourse, as described in the *Publication Manual of the American Psychological Association*, fourth edition, published by the APA (Washington, D.C.) in 1994, and the CBE Style as described in *Scientific Style and Format: The CBE Manual for Authors, Editors, and Publishers*, 6th ed., 1994. APA and CBE guidelines are frequently used by writers in the sciences and social sciences. Chapter Fourteen covers MLA and Chicago styles, which are often used by writers in the arts and humanities. Most likely, your instructor will tell you which format to use. If he or she leaves it up to you to decide, choose one style and stick with it consistently.

Each of the various bibliographic sources that you consulted while constructing your working bibliography provided the necessary information to help you locate the sources you used. You may have noticed that practically every bibliographical index uses its own formula for reporting publication data for the items it lists. Some, such as *Dissertation Abstracts International* and the ERIC database, employ a complex cross-referencing formula based on their own numbering system. Others, such as the *Reader's Guide to Periodical Literature* and Infotrac, provide abbreviated periodical titles with dates and volume, issue, and page numbers within the citation, enabling you to go directly to the sources you seek. You may have found it disconcerting to have to decipher a new system with each bibliographic source you consulted, but since you'd logged on or opened the volume to use it, you persevered and learned to crack its code.

Now imagine that the writer of every article, researched paper, book, and so on invented his or her own idiosyncratic method for listing bibliographic information. Documentation would become meaningless pretty quickly, and readers would not even attempt to evaluate the sources used in constructing a particular discourse. To make documentation instantaneously decipherable and uniform, a few professional societies have published guidelines for citing information in scholarly texts within their disciplines. Most professional journals adhere to the documentation system that is most widely recognized in their field. Students are taught to use one or two of those systems because they provide reliable, thorough documentation of secondary sources that is easy to read and helps readers easily locate sources they wish to evaluate.

Some of these societies go further than advising writers how to credit secondary sources; they also provide models for how researched texts should be presented on paper or computer disk. They offer specific guidelines for how articles should be titled, how wide page margins should be, and which extraneous elements (such as title pages, outlines, abstracts, and appendixes) should be included. Although such guidelines may seem elitist or "stuffy" and "picky" to you at first, they are really very egalitarian—they ensure that a first-year college student's ideas will be presented in the same way as a postdoctoral fellow's research findings. By conforming to these models, you will be publishing your work in the style expected of practitioners in the field you are studying, and you will be demonstrating that you have learned the least of your lessons about writing in that discipline. You will use these documentation and formatting guidelines well beyond your college composition assignments; they will likely become the mode of communication you use in your career as well.

Once you are familiar with professional formats, they will become second nature to you, like writing a letter or addressing an envelope. Although you need to follow the guidelines you use carefully, you need not commit them to memory. That would be like memorizing the addresses of everyone to whom you would ever want to send correspondence. When you want to mail a letter or a package, you probably pull out your address book or some other reference and copy the necessary information onto an address label or envelope. Just as you keep some kind of print or electronic database for addresses, you should own a copy, for example, of the *Publication Manual of the American Psychological Association* if you will be using APA format in the future, so that you can refer to it whenever you need to document text. By copying the models from a style guide, you can be assured that your work conforms to professional standards.

■ Printing Your Paper

Use high-quality (16, 20, or 24 lb.), $8\frac{1}{2}$ x 11 inch, white paper for work that is to be submitted for a grade or publication. If your printer uses perforated, continuous-form pages, separate them and stack them in the correct order before submitting your work. Print text so that a one-inch margin is preserved at the top, at the bottom, and on both the left and right sides of the page; only page numbers should violate these margins. If you're using a word processor, choose a font (typeface) that is clear and readable—such as Courier, which looks like traditional typewriter text—and size it at 10 or 12 points, so that roughly fifteen to twenty words fit on a line. Do not use a script or art font. Print text in black ink, using a "high" print-quality setting. If possible, use a laser printer or other high-quality printer for your final copy. Justify (align) the text of your document on the left margin. That will result in a page of text with an even left edge and a ragged, or varied, right edge. Do not use "full" justification, because it is difficult for readers' eyes to find their way back to the start of the next line when both the right and left margins are exactly even throughout. Indent the start of each paragraph one-half inch, or five spaces, from the left margin. The whole document should be double-spaced entirely, including quotations, footnotes, end notes, and the Works Cited list. Do not include extra spaces between paragraphs or between items in the end notes or on the Works Cited list. Print on only one side of each page. Do not ornament the pages of a researched paper with watermarks, borders, enders, lines, or other drawings. Present your work so that physical aspects of the text do not compete with its content for your readers' attention.

Page Numbering and Fastening

Always number your pages, and label each page with an abbreviated version of your title in case pages get separated during grading or review. Pages should be numbered consecutively, beginning with the first full page of the essay itself (do not include a title page or outline in the same numbering sequence). Place page numbers one-half inch from the top of the page, flush with the right margin. Use the header feature in your word processing program to include a much-shortened version of the title just before the page number, without any intervening punctuation. (Do not print "p." before a page number or add a comma, dash, or anything else between the title and the page number.) Begin numbering pages with the title page, and show page numbers on every sheet of the text.

Fasten all the pages together with a single paper clip; do not use staples or binders. Make it convenient for your instructor or editor to detach pages to write comments on them and reassemble the document afterward. Remember that even the final copy of your paper is not meant to be a bound publication; it should be presented as a final *draft*.

Title and Title Page

Choose a title for your research paper carefully, to reflect the thesis. Avoid using obvious phrases such as "an investigation into" or "research regarding" in your title. This does not mean that your title must be clinical sounding or bland, by any means. Be creative in the titling of your work. In accordance with APA documentation standards, a formal title page and abstract are required. The title page should contain five elements:

- Page number and header

- The running head that would appear at the top of every page if your article were published in a journal

- The full title of the discourse

- Your name

- Your academic or professional affiliation

The header and running head are located at the top of the page; the full title, your name, and your affiliation are centered in the middle of the page. The full title of the paper is repeated at the top of the first page of text also.

Remember that every element in an APA-formatted paper must be double-spaced. That means you must double-space between the items on the title page and between the title and the first line of text. Items in tables must be double-spaced as well, as must be the items in your Works Cited list at the end of the paper. See Kyle's final research paper, at the end of this chapter (pages 242–252) for an example of these conventions in practical use.

Abstracts

An abstract is a brief statement that summarizes the important points of your research paper. Abstracts in the APA style are strictly limited to between 75 and 120 words. They must be able to stand alone, apart from the body of the paper, as a summary of it; therefore, you must define any abbreviations you use in the abstract, and it should not contain any information that your paper does not include. An abstract should explain the purpose and scope of your work to let readers know whether it is applicable to their own research. Thus it should be neutral, describing your *topic* rather than your conclusions. The most difficult thing about writing an abstract is accomplishing all of that in a readable, coherent single paragraph. It is a challenge.

Headings

The outline in an APA-styled paper is embedded in the text as subject headings. Headings should follow the conventions appropriate to outlines in general. Items of the same importance should share the same heading style. Subheadings should be used for lesser or subsumed topics, and you should not use a single subheading without a parallel one following it within the same section. Just as you do not use an (a) on an outline unless it is continued with a point labeled (b), do not subhead a point if it is not part of a series of points. Do not number or label the headings in your text. The introduction of a paper is not subheaded "Introduction" because readers assume that the first part of a text is its introduction.

The American Psychological Association recognizes five styles of headings for inclusion in scholarly text, but in a short paper you may need only one or two. The APA heading styles are as follows:

CENTERED UPPERCASE HEADING
Centered Uppercase-Lowercase Heading
Centered, Underlined, Uppercase-Lowercase Heading
Flush Left, Underlined, Uppercase-Lowercase Heading
    Indented, underlined, lowercase paragraph heading ending with a period.

When only one heading style is required in a text, use centered uppercase-lowercase headings. If a second level of heading is needed, use flush left, underlined, uppercase-lowercase headings.

Graphics, Tables, and Charts

As you know from reading magazine articles, pictures and charts that are printed as closely as possible to the text that refers to them are the most useful. Try to include compact graphics in your text. Photographs, tables, and charts that are relegated to an appendix (a collection of useful supporting materials attached to the end of a researched project) will not receive as much attention as those embedded in the text itself. If you can quickly and reasonably learn to insert graphic materials into your text with the word processing software you are using, use that method of including visual aids in your work. If your software prohibits that, leave space in the text where you can paste in the graphic element and photocopy that page for inclusion in your researched paper's final version.

It is tempting in scientific writing to include too many tables. Remember that tables should augment and support information reported in your text, not duplicate it. Do not include more information in your tables than readers need; include only that portion of data that relates directly to your text. There should be sufficient text between tables to preserve the author's voice in the discourse and to facilitate typesetting. A page containing a table should be the exception, rather than the norm, in your document.

The conventional APA method of labeling graphic elements in texts is to call charts and tables "Table 1," "Table 2," and so on and to label photographs, color plates, and other picture-type inclusions "Figure 1," "Figure 2," and so on. Do not use suffix numbers or letters (such as "5.a"), but number all tables consecutively in whole numbers. Give tables brief, descriptive titles that summarize their focus or contents.

■ Correcting Errors

Inevitably, just as you are ready to turn in the meticulously prepared and endlessly proofread copy of your final researched paper, you will spot a typographical error, a missing word, a homonym that your spell checker missed (such as *hear* instead of *here* or *to* in place of *too*), a paragraph that mysteriously reformatted itself with a column of white space down its center, or a line or two of text that your printer seems to have ignored. There are many products on the market for painting and pasting over errors in finished copy, but none is quite so handy or unobtrusive as a plain black-ink pen and careful lettering. If there are only one or two very small errors in your work, correct them efficiently in ink. If there are more, consider fixing them on disk and reprinting your text.

■ APA Parenthetical Citation

Parenthetical citation is the method required by the APA for acknowledging secondary sources used in research. The idea behind parenthetical citation is to place in parentheses the absolute minimum amount of information necessary to direct readers to the appropriate source in the Works Cited list, which provides complete publication information so readers can locate original sources if desired. The system is very clear and logical. The basic formula consists of the last name of the author or authors of the cited source, plus the year in which the source was published. This makes it easy to quickly locate a source on the Works Cited list, because in the APA format this list is arranged alphabetically by authors' names and chronologically for authors with more than one work listed. And because the date of scientific theories and discoveries is important in judging their relevance, it is helpful to have the publication dates of secondary sources identified within the text. As an example, a parenthetical citation of neuropsychologists Judith Hooper and Dick Teresi's 1986 book *The 3-Pound Universe* would appear as (Hooper and Teresi, 1986). All of the information necessary for readers to locate a copy of that book would then be included in the corresponding Works Cited entry.

Notice that the basic parenthetical citation is simple; a comma separates the authors' names and the year their work was published. Page numbers are required for direct quotations; they are not mandatory, but are preferred, in documenting summaries or paraphrases.

Despite its sparseness, sometimes even this basic formula can introduce redundancies. For instance, if your discourse has already named the author of a source you are citing, there is little reason to spell it out again in the parenthetical citation; this only creates an unnecessary distraction for your readers. In such cases, you need only mention the publication year and (if required or desired) the page number where the information can be found in the original source. For example:

> Neuropsychologists Hooper and Teresi note that violence is a natural function of the human brain. Throughout history, violent thoughts and actions have characterized our race (1986, p. 162).

Conversely, sometimes the information offered in a basic parenthetical citation is not adequate for identifying the documented item in the References list. Usually, the date will help distinguish between source material written by the same author or authors. For instance, Hooper and Teresi jointly published an article in *Health* magazine, but it came out in 1989, so the date in a note citing that article would distinguish it from their 1986 book. Occasionally you will cite works by different authors with the same surname. For example, Scott L. Hooper is another prominent neuropsychologist. If his single-authored work in a 1994 volume of *Science* and Judith Hooper's article from a 1996 issue of *Time* both appeared on your References list, you would cite a quotation from Judith Hooper's text as (Hooper, J., 1996, p. 46) and a quotation from Scott L. Hooper's work as: (Hooper, 1994, p. 117). Use first initials only with the source that appears first on your References list.

Because multiple authorship is common in scientific writing, the APA format is very specific in its treatment of such sources. For a source with two authors, name both authors every time you cite the source in your paper. If a source has three to five authors, list each author's last name the first time you cite that source, but include only the first author's last name, followed by the Latin abbreviation "et al.," in subsequent citations of that source. If a cited source has six or more authors, name only the first author, followed by "et al.," unless the first author is also the first author of another source with six or more authors, and the list of authors of the second source differs from that of the first; in that case, list as many of the authors as necessary to show the difference between the two sources. For example, consider the following groups of authors:

Washington, G.	Washington, G.
Adams, J.	Adams, J.
Jefferson, T.	Jefferson, T.
Madison, J.	Van Buren, M.
Monroe, J.	Harrison, W.
Adams, J. Q.	Adams, J. Q.
Jackson, A.	

You would cite the first source as (Washington, Adams, Jefferson, and Madison, et al., 1751) and the second one as (Washington, Adams, Jefferson, and Van Buren, et. al., 1782). Always keep the names of authors in the same order that they are presented in the source material.

If you are citing a document with an unnamed author, your parenthetical note should begin with a fragment of the title. For instance, the periodical *FDA Consumer* ran an article called "Committee Advises FDA on Antidepressants" in its December 1991 issue, and the article was unsigned. A parenthetical note citing that would look like this: ("Committee," 1991, p. 5).

If you are confused by these formulas, just remember that the objective of a parenthetical citation is to direct readers to the corresponding complete entry describing the source in your References list, to indicate the original source from which summarized, paraphrased, or quoted information is taken. This purpose is very simple, and the format reflects that simplicity.

■ Footnotes and End Notes

Under current APA guidelines, footnotes or end notes are not used for documentation, except to express that permission to reprint something commercially has been granted. However, they still provide opportunities for writers to include brief tangential notes without disrupting the flow of their discourse. For example, if you were writing about physical aspects of the brain and wished to mention that "modern" brain surgery began in 1920 with the work of Harvey Cushing, you could relegate that tidbit of trivia to a footnote or an endnote. As their names suggest, footnotes are printed at the bottom of the page bearing reference to them, and end notes are listed consecutively on a page at the end of the paper. They are meant to be very brief. If you find yourself writing a paragraph or more, you should include that information in an appendix, rather than as a note.

To include a footnote or an end note, place a superscript cardinal number in the text where the information would be relevant (for example, "to jokingly refer to all difficult tasks as 'brain surgery' has become commonplace [1] among . . ."). The corresponding note is then identified with the same number (also a superscript) at the bottom of the page or the end of the paper. Number footnotes or end notes consecutively throughout your text. If you are using parenthetical citation (and you should be), you can produce a text without any footnotes or end notes.

■ Reference List

A References list begins taking shape from the very beginning of a research project. Items that start as part of your working bibliography or crop up during your investigation and eventually become useful sources in your research will be included on your References list. A list of references is simply a highly organized, alphabetized, uniform summary of all of the secondary sources upon which you have built your final researched paper. Its purposes are to acknowledge the contributions of predecessors to your research, to provide readers with information that will help them locate your original sources for their inspection, and to serve as a guide for future researchers working on the same topic. Your bibliography cards or notes serve as a make-shift References list during your drafting process, and it is from them that you will take the necessary information for your parenthetical citations. When it is time to assemble your final Reference list, there are specific models that you should follow in the APA format.

An APA References (or Works Cited) list is double-spaced in its entirety. The list is included after the last text page of your paper. It is numbered along with the text but is not usually counted in a page-limited assignment. For instance, if you were asked to write a ten-page paper, your References list should begin on page 11.

Most of the items on your list will probably begin with authors' last names or the first words of titles. Alphabetize all entries by the first word, regardless of what it represents (for example, "Hanson" precedes "History," which precedes "Holhman," and so on). If two or more works by the same author appear on your list, enter the name at the start of each item. Single-author entries are listed before multiple-author entries beginning with the same name. Articles with the same authorship are presented in chronological order. Do not number, bullet, or otherwise label the items on your References list. Indent the first line of each item five spaces, or one-half inch, from the left margin. Some listed items will be longer than a single typewritten line; print second (and subsequent) lines of a single entry even with the left margin.

The following sections provide examples of APA Works Cited list format for some common secondary sources.

Books

Because printed works make up most of the secondary sources cited in researched work, there are strict guidelines for how to list them as references. A basic book reference in APA style should include the following:

- The author's last name and initials.

- The publication date of the book.

- The book's title, underlined or in italics. Capitalize the first letter and all proper nouns; leave the rest in lowercase.

- The city and state or country where the book was published. If several cities are listed on the book's title page, choose the first one listed or the city where the publisher's home office is located. Omit the state or country for very well known cities such as New York, San Francisco, and London.

- The publisher.

If there is more than one author or editor, list them in the order in which they appear on the book's title page. When listing multiple writers, use an ampersand (&) before the last name on the list.

Unnecessary words in publishers' names are eliminated; therefore Charles Scribner's Sons Publishing Company would be listed as simply "Scribner." However, the words *Books* and *Press* are conventionally retained. The abbreviation "ed." is used for *editor* and *edited*, and the Latin abbreviation "et al." (meaning "and others") is used in listings of multiple authors or editors.

APA formatting is strictly followed for conventional sources such as books, journals, magazines, and newspapers. You will not find variations in the way these sources are described in legitimately documented texts, and you should take pains to follow these formulas exactly.

A Book with a Single Author

Goodwin, D. K. (1997). <u>Wait till next year: A memoir.</u> New York: Simon and Schuster.

A Compilation with an Editor

Jackson, K. T. (Ed.). (1995). <u>The encyclopedia of New York City.</u> New Haven: Yale University Press.

A Book with Two or Three Authors

Kelly, A. H., Harbison, W. A., & Belz, H. (1983). <u>The American constitution: Its origins and development.</u> New York: Norton.

A Book with Three or More Editors or Authors

Wolfinger, D., Knable, P., Richards, H. L., & Silberger R. (1990). <u>The chronically unemployed.</u> New York: Berman Press.

Two or More Books by the Same Author

Goodwin, D. K. (1994). <u>No ordinary time: Franklin and Eleanor Roosevelt: The home front in WW II.</u> New York: Simon and Schuster.

Goodwin, D. K. (1997). Wait till next year: A memoir. New York: Simon and Schuster.

A Single Work from an Anthology

Lloyd, G. E. R. (1981). Science and mathematics. In M. Finley (Ed.), <u>The legacy of Greece</u> (pp. 256–300). New York: Oxford University Press.

A Book by a Corporate Author

Boston Women's Health Collective. (1986). <u>Our bodies, ourselves.</u> New York: Simon and Schuster.

An Introduction, a Preface, a Foreword, or an Afterword

Boaz, F. (1959). Introduction. In R. Benedict, <u>Patterns of culture.</u> Boston: Houghton Mifflin.

Government Publications

National Science Foundation. (1998). <u>Relative density in quarks and black holes</u> (DHHS Publication No. ADM 98-1959). Washington, DC: U.S. Government Printing Office.

An Unpublished Dissertation

Sakala, C. (1993). <u>Maternity care policy in the United States: Toward a more rational and effective system.</u> Unpublished doctoral dissertation, Boston University.

An Abstract in **Dissertations Abstracts International**

Mead, D. G. (1975). E. E. Cummings: The meaning of the sonnets (Doctoral dissertation, University of Michigan, Ann Arbor, 1975). Dissertation Abstracts International, 36, 8062A.

Periodical Articles

A basic journal, magazine, or newspaper article reference contains five parts:

- The author's last name and initials.

- The publication date.

- The article title. Capitalize only the first word of the title (and subtitle, if there is one) and any proper nouns. Do not enclose in quotation marks.

- The periodical title. Type the journal title in "headline style," capitalizing the first and last words and all words in between except for prepositions, articles, and coordinating conjunctions. Underline the periodical title or set it in italics. For newspapers, add the city in brackets if it's not part of the title (for example, *Freeman Journal* [Webster City, Iowa]).

- Publication information, including volume and issue numbers and page numbers.

See the following examples for the various conventions for reporting volume and issue numbers and dates. Underline or italicize volume numbers. Include issue numbers for journals and magazines that use them (not all do). All entries end in periods. Most, but not all, journals are paginated continuously, which means that the first issue of the year begins on page 1 and all subsequent issues in that year (or volume) begin where the previous issue left off. Magazines are usually paginated separately, which means that every issue begins with page 1. List all of the page numbers for periodical articles, even if you did not use the whole article.

An Article in a Journal That Pages Each Issue Separately

Friedman, N. (1988). A new encyclopedia entry on Cummings. Spring: The Journal of the E. E. Cummings Society, 8, 2–11.

An Article in a Newspaper

Poore, C. (1962, September 4), Too good to be obvious. The New York Times, p. B33.

An Article in a Magazine

Balf, T. (1988, January/February). He's back and he's pissed. Bicycling, pp. 52–55.

An Unsigned Article

Soviet television. (1990, December 13). <u>Los Angeles Times,</u> pp. B3, B5.

An Article from an Information Service

Breland, H. Assessing writing skill. <u>ERIC; ED,</u> 1994, Abstract No. 286 920.

A Review

Goodwin, D. K. (1990). Gay soldiers: They watched their step [Review of
the book <u>Coming Out Under Fire: The History of Gay Men and
Women in World War Two.</u>] <u>New York Times Review of Books,</u> p. 9.

An Editorial, Advertisement, Letter to the Editor

Kennedy, J. (1997, November). A mother like no other [Editorial].<u> George,</u>
pp. 23–24.

Pain may be eliminated for millions. (1998, January 8). [Advertisement].
<u>The Muncie Star Press,</u> p, 2B.

Balliett, W. (1997, September 15). [Letter to the editor]. <u>The New Yorker,</u>
p. 6.

Archived Items

The variety of objects housed in archives makes them especially challenging
to document. You must essentially describe material you have seen and tell
where you saw it. Because archived articles do not circulate, you do not need
to include catalog numbers or specific information that one would use to request such pieces.

A Work of Art

DuChamp, M. (1912). Nude descending a staircase, number 2. [Painting].
Philadelphia Museum of Art, Philadelphia.

A Map

The Aran Islands. (1975). [Map]. Dublin, Ireland: Ordinance Survey.

Private Correspondence

Cummings, E. E. (1924, May 7). [Letter to Scofield Thayer]. Houghton
Library, Boston.

Manuscript

Eliot, T. S. (1910). Fourth caprice in Montparnasse. [Poem]. [Holograph
edition]. New York Public Library, New York.

Electronic Media

Documenting electronic media involves a complex group of tasks. Some electronic works change daily or even more often than that (Web sites, for example), and some combine the work of many contributors that cannot be separated (for example, the ad-libbed performance of a blues standard). Some events captured electronically are here and gone so quickly that it is impossible to gather all the information about them that you would choose to cite (for example, the words of a bystander overheard during a live remote news broadcast, or a comment heard on a radio program *after* the speaker has already been identified). This is where documentation conventions give out and integrity must take over. Try to tell as much about the source you are describing as is reasonable to credit its owners and to prove to readers that it exists or existed. Rely on generalizations that you can make from more established forms. For instance, you can essentially follow the format for a similar periodical article when citing part of a periodically published, physically distributed electronic source (a microfilm, CD-ROM, computer disk), and you can follow the format for a similar type of book (that is, a book by a single author, an anthology with an editor, and so on) when citing a nonperiodical, physically distributed electronic publication, but add information describing the source you are using (title of the product; media through which it is distributed; edition, release, or version).

Audiovisual Sources   Audiovisual productions include many elements that you may wish to emphasize in your documentation. Most are the result of the work of many different professionals. For instance, you must decide whether you are citing an actor's performance, a director's influence, or a screenwriter's text when you document a film, or a singer's or musician's performance, an arranger's version, or the lyricist's words when you document a sound recording. Illustrating this are the two variant, yet acceptable, citations for Orson Welles's original broadcast of *The War of the Worlds* shown in the following examples. It is impossible to anticipate every documentation scenario, and some forms must simply be improvised.

Internet Sources   Undoubtedly, the greatest challenge yet to time-honored styles of documentation are publications found on the Internet. Offering documentation for material viewed on the World Wide Web can be like citing a declaration written in sand during yesterday's low tide or advising a lost traveler to proceed to the corner where a dog was standing one day last week. Because Web sites are written over and revised almost constantly, you cannot be assured that you are directing readers back to the same information you accessed earlier. When you use information from a source on the World Wide Web, you are probably creating one of the few permanent records of its existence and content. Right now, the trend is toward giving as much publication information as you can discern about a Web site, so that you can demonstrate the currency and reliability of the source and prove as convincingly as possible that the information you are reporting was posted at that site on the day you accessed it. The first date in most Web citations, then, is the date of the text's last reported revision (if that is available), and the second date (usually in parentheses) is the date you saw it.

Other important information for Web site documentation includes the name of its author, the title of the page the information is on, the title over the complete site or home page name, and the complete URL for the cited page. As the use of Web resources in researched writing becomes more common, uniform documentation forms will evolve, and reputable sources will respond by offering relevant information. Now, however, it is often difficult to discern who authored information on the Web and when it was written, so some documentation styles include only a page title, URL, and access date. Precise documentation of Internet sources increases their acceptance in academic circles. You can advance on-line research and its documentation by providing reliable, useful descriptions of the Internet sources you cite.

Interviews Interviews, e-mail correspondence, and comments posted to Internet mailing lists are not included on reference lists in APA style because, as private conversation or correspondence, they generally cannot be accessed by readers. Instead, document such sources in your text: "In an interview in August 1998, J. Scherschel, biochemist with the Centers for Disease Control in Atlanta, said that . . . "

An Article in a Microform Collection

Michelson, D. (1998, May 29). "Lightning speed: New CD-ROMs even faster." Technology Times, 13, p. 37. Microfiche article in Industry Standard: Business Reports, fiche 3, grids B11–14.

A Periodically Published CD-ROM

Russo, M. C. (1992). Recovering from bibliographic instruction blahs. RQ: Reference Quarterly, 32, pp. 178–83. [CD-ROM]. Infotrac: Magazine Index Plus, 1993.

A Nonperiodical Publication on CD-ROM or Diskette

Ellison, Ralph. (1991). [CD-ROM]. Disklit: American Authors Diskette, Boston: Hall.

A Television or Radio Program

Welles, O. (Producer). (1938, October 30). The war of the worlds. New York: Columbia Broadcasting Service.

Wells, H. G. (1938). The war of the worlds. [Performed by O. Welles]. [Adapted by Howard Koch]. Mercury Theatre on the Air, New York: WCBS.

Sound Recordings

Dylan, B. (1997). Time out of mind. "Starting in the Doorway." [CD]. New York: Sony Music Entertainment.

Gershwin, G. & Gershwin, I. (1955). Love is here to stay. [Recorded by F. Sinatra]. [Arranged by N. Riddle]. On Songs for Swingin' Lovers [CD]. New York: Chappell Music.

Film

Capra, F. (director). (1946). It's a Wonderful Life. [performed by James Stewart, Donna Reed, Lionel Barrymore, & Thomas Mitchell]. RKO.

Welles, O. (Producer). (1941). Citizen Kane. RKO.

FTP (File Transfer Protocol) Sites Available for Downloading

Scherl, R., & Levesque, H. (1996, December 4). The frame problem and knowledge producing actions. Commentary on cognitive robotics problem-solving. FTP: University of Toronto: Ftp://ftp.cs.toronto.edu/pub/corob/README.html (8 January 1998).

WWW (World Wide Web) Sites

Associated Press. (1997, October 9). Researchers note increase of diabetes in overweight kids. Results of quantitative study. USA Today, Retrieved January 8, 1998 from the World Wide Web: http://www.usatoday.com/life/health/general/diabetes/hdgio14.htm

Florida's manatees. (1996-97). Information about species. Manatee Snorkel Tours. Retrieved January 9, 1998 from the World Wide Web: http://www.xtalwind.net/~/bird/tips.html

Human Genome Project. (1997, October). Human genome project frequently asked questions. Human Genome Project Information. Retrieved January 10, 1998 from the World Wide Web: http://www.oml.gov/TechResources/Human_Genome/faq'faq1.html

Irmer, T. An interview with Leslie Marmon Silko. Reported conversation with Native American writer. Alt-X Online Publishing Network. Retrieved January 8,1998 from the World Wide Web: http://www.altx.com/interviews/silko.html

Silk, J. (1993). Dark matter. Discussion of particle physics issues. Center for Particle Astrophysics/NSF Science and Technology Center. Retrieved January 12, 1998 from the World Wide Web:http://physics7.berkeley.edu/darkmat/reading.html

CBE Style

Once you fully understand the APA style, it is not hard to grasp the gist of the Council of Biology Editors (CBE) system as described in *Style and Format: The CBE Manual for Authors, Editors, and Publishers* (6th edition, 1994) by the Council of Biology Editors. Also used for writing in the sciences, the CBE style is much like the APA style in its formulas for listing items on a Reference page. Probably the most noticeable difference between CBE and other styles is that book and periodical titles reported in CBE styles are not set off by italic or underlining; the entire citation is printed in the same font as the rest of the document.

CBE N-Y System

Actually, there are two CBE styles, the Name-Year (N-Y) system and the Citation-Sequence (C-S) System. The Name-Year system is almost identical to APA style. A parenthetical citation in the N-Y system is nearly indistinguishable from one in APA. Simply enclose the author's name and the year the cited material was published in parentheses at relevant points in your text. Notice that in APA format, a comma separates the author's name from the page number, but in CBE style no punctuation intervenes.

Citing Books in CBE style

Similarly, References list citations in the CBE style are very similar to those in the APA format. For example, in citing a book with a single author in a CBE-formatted research paper, you should include the same information as in APA style with one addition. The last item in a CBE book entry to a References list is the total number of pages contained in the volume. CBE style uses periods to separate items in each entry, as opposed to parentheses in the APA style. When citing multiple authors in CBE style, do not separate last names and initials with commas, but place commas between names of authors. Below are examples of CBE-style references to books.

A Book with a Single Author

Goodwin, D.K. 1997. Wait till next year: a memoir. New York: Simon and
    Schuster. 336 p.

A Book with Two or More Authors

Kelly A. H., Harbison W.A., Belz, H. 1983. The American constitution: Its
    Origins and development. New York: Norton. 350 p.

A Book with an Editor

Jackson K. T., editor. 1995. The encyclopedia of New York City. New
    Haven: Yale University Press, 1350 p.

A Book by a Corporate Author

Boston Women's Health Collective. 1986. Our bodies, ourselves. New York:
    Simon and Schuster. 752 p.

Citing Periodicals in CBE Style

As with book titles in CBE N-Y style, capitalize only the first word of the title, and do not capitalize the first word of subtitles. CBE N-Y periodical citations are much like those in APA style, except numbers are listed differently and periodical titles are often abbreviated. In CBE N-Y style, publication year is listed after the periodical title; furthermore, a semicolon separates publication year from volume numbers, and a colon separates volume numbers from page numbers. Periodical titles a single word long are not abbreviated, but longer titles and words are shortened, usually by leaving off some of the last letters (e.g., "Technical" or "Technology" becomes simply "Tech"). Common words in titles are always abbreviated (e.g., "Journal" becomes "J," and "Association" becomes "Assoc"). The following are examples of journal citations for a References list compiled in CBE N-Y style:

An Article in a Journal That Pages Each Issue Separately

Friedman N. A new encyclopedia entry on Cummings. Spring: J of the E.E.
Cummings Soc1988: 8: 2-11.

An Article in a Newspaper

Poore C. Too good to be obvious. New York Times 1962 Sept 4; Sect B:33
(col 1).

An Article in a Magazine

Balf T: He's back and he's pissed. Bicycling 1990 December 13: 52-55.

An Unsigned Article

Soviet television. Los Angeles Times 1990 Dec 13; See B: 3, 5.

CBE C-S System

CBE Citation-Sequence (C-S) system, as its name implies, differs from the CBE Name-Year (N-Y) system in the ordering of citations on the References list and the method by which those are documented in the text of a research paper. The format for Individual References Cited list entries is essentially the same in both CBE styles, but the method of identifying them in the text is different.

Providing Internal Documentation in CBE C-S Style

Instead of a parenthetical reference system, as used in APA and CBE N-Y systems, the CBE C-S system uses superscript reference numbers in the text of the paper that correspond with superscript numbers on the References Cited list. For example, the first reference to a secondary source in Kyle's research paper, as cited in the CBE C-S system, would look like this:

> The Internet is fast becoming a Mecca for the experienced web surfer and for "newbies"—amateur or beginning "surfers"—alike, who are a part of the estimated 7.5 million households on-line[1].

Citations in the text of a CBE C-S style documented paper are numbered chronologically throughout the text. (The next, different source to which

Kyle refers would be numbered [2], the next would be [3], and so on.) When a secondary source is cited a second time, the same number it was assigned originally is used again and in all subsequent citations. For instance, whenever Kyle cites the *PCWorld* article by Laurianne McLaughlin, which is represented by the superscript number [1] above, he will number it [1] again.

Compiling a References Cited List in CBE C-S Style

As you can guess, the items on a References Cited list in CBE C-S style are not alphabetized. Instead, they are listed in the order in which they appear in the text of the paper, and each is numbered with the same symbol it is assigned in the paper's text. Therefore, Kyle's References Cited list in CBE C-S style would begin with the following entries, as determined by their positioning in his paper.

References Cited

1. McLaughlin L. Microsoft previews electronic retailing strategy and technology to world's leading retailers. Press release regarding intentions to collaborate with Wal-Mart in devising Internet security measures. 1996. Retrieved 12 Feb 1996: http://www.microsoft.com.

2. Openmarket Inc. Results of a survey tabulating number of commercial sites on the World Wide Web 1996. Retrieved 15 March 1996: http//www.directory.net/dir/statistics.html.

3. Moeller M. Let's hang out at the E-mall: eShop opens its doors to Tower Records, Spiegel on the web 1995 Nov 6: 3-4.

4. Weise E. Experts: internet purchases safe as mail ordering. Ball State Daily News 1996 Jan. 22: 1 (col 1).

■ Kyle's Final Draft

During the process of revising his researched paper, Kyle actually cut back on the amount of information he was providing his readers, to spend more time defining technical terms associated with encryption. Since his most up-to-date sources on Internet security were World Wide Web postings, a heavy proportion of his Works Cited list is electronic materials, which is a weakness in his final project. Kyle is a good writer, however, and he has managed to pull his many meager sources together into an informative and compelling argument paper.

Notice that documentation formats for on-line sources have changed considerably in the few months since Kyle finished this paper. He wanted to go back and look for posting or revision dates, but many of his sources had vanished into cyberspace, and he decided to keep his documentation style consistent by not altering those for which additional information could be found. The vagueness of his Internet documentation does demonstrate why changes are needed, but nothing will prevent on-line sources from vanishing before readers have the chance to peruse them.

ON-LINE PURCHASING IN THE COMPUTER AGE

Let Your Mouse Do the Shopping: On-line Purchasing
in the Computer Age

Kyle Parker
Ball State University

Abstract

Computers are becoming a fixture in American households. Growth in the domestic sector of the Internet has caused businesses to become major players in technology marketing. Retailers have recognized the interest of customers. Companies are beginning to take advantage of the benefits of the Internet. Ordering from a Web site is simple and user-friendly. Consumers browse through Web pages, viewing products, but when it comes time to click the "submit" icon, a twinge of anxiety manifests itself. The reason for fear is the "public perception that the Internet is a dangerous place" (Weise, 1996, p. 1). Many consumers express ignorance about on-line shopping options. Microsoft, VISA, and MasterCard are assisting in the development of technology that secures the transactions of customers who shop on-line. By implementing Secured Transaction Technology (STT), developed by Microsoft, credit card companies hope to create a standard that companies such as Netscape and Mosaic can incorporate into their Internet browsers (Microsoft's transactions, 1995). Browsers are not only the software programs that allow users to surf the Web but are also the same tools through which security measures must be implemented. Those measures include cryptography, firewalls, and secured operating systems.

"Hey, Mom, can we use the computer now? Marcia and I bought this cool new game, and we want to try it out."

"Hold on a minute. Let me finish ordering dinner. What do you guys want on your pizza?'

"Uhm, where's it coming from?"

"The usual, Pizza Hut."

"Good. Can we see what that new triple-stuffed crust thing looks like?"

"Okay, let me just click on the menu here. Hold it. Let's see; I just click here, and . . . there it is."

"Yeah. That looks pretty good. Look at all that cheese. I can taste it already. Get it with sausage and pepperoni, and, can we have extra cheese like that? Bread sticks, too. Right Marcia?"

"I dunno."

"Well, I guess since Marcia is so adamant about it. Okay, just a couple more things to enter, and . . . there. It's all yours. You've got about forty-five minutes to play until the pizza gets here. Have fun."

"Thanks, Mom."

Wait a minute. What's going on here? This isn't <u>The Brady Bunch.</u> Can people in the 1990s really order pizza using the Internet?

Internet growth

Thanks to the current growth and development of on-line technology, pizza is only one thing that consumers can buy with a click of the mouse. Computers are becoming an ever-present fixture in the households of America, and people are clamoring to partake in the lure of the emerging frontier called cyberspace. The Internet is fast becoming a Mecca for the experienced Web surfer and for "newbies"—amateur or beginning "surfers"—alike, who are part of the estimated 7.5 million households on-line (McLaughlin, 1996). Growth in the domestic sector of the Internet has caused businesses to become major players in the technology marketing scene. Progressive retailers have recognized the phenomenal on-line interest of customers, and they have reacted with equal enthusiasm. As Steve Coffey, vice president of NPD Group, a market research firm in New York, commented, "this is definitely the time for businesses to establish a presence online" (McLaughlin, 1996). Companies are watching as the domain on the World Wide Web, which was created specifically for commercial sites on the Internet, expands. The domain, which includes all Internet addresses ending in a ".com" phrase (e.g. http://www.<company name>.com) increased from a mere 29,000 sites in December of 1994 to 170,892 in just over a year, according to John Williams, an Internet marketing specialist with whom I spoke via telephone. A few months after Williams's survey was taken, the number had jumped to 259,999, with 975 sites opening in the week ending on April 8, 1996 (Open-Market, Inc., 1996). Obvious Internet contenders such as Microsoft Corporation, Gateway 2000, and Netscape Communications are staking out their claims in the realm of cyberspace. The surprise, however, is the growing number of the less Internet-driven businesses that are venturing on-line.

ON-LINE PURCHASING IN THE COMPUTER AGE

On-line businesses

Companies, regardless of size, are beginning to take advantage of the benefits of the Internet—twenty-four-hour a day, seven days a week, worldwide access—reaching the next generation of consumers. A viable economic opportunity is beginning to exert its influence on consumers. As advertising teams and executives create new commercials for companies such as AT&T, UPS, ESPN, and Toyota, all have created links to the World Wide Web and include a cyberspace address (URL) in their conventional media advertisements.

As the Pizza Hut narrative illustrates, select companies are taking the notion of on-line advertising to its next logical step: on-line purchasing. Home pages containing rich and vibrant high-resolution graphics convey information about the product and electronic alternatives for ordering through the computer. Now, when a person does a little Web surfing, he might bring home a catch—downloaded shareware programs, a print-out of a magazine article, or even a new car.

Many electronic storefronts are linked together to form virtual malls. The basic design of a virtual mall is the same as any home page; its hypertext links connect users to various stores that are part of the mall. One such virtual mall is eShop, which allows shoppers to choose from six avenues of storefronts. Tower Records, Spiegel, The Good Guys, L'eggs, Insight, and 1-800-Flowers are only a click away (Moeller, 1995, p.34). Another such location is marketplaceMCI, where Champs Sports, Lillian Vernon, an X-Files Store, and Foot Locker are open for business all day and all night. However, of the four stores in marketplaceMCI, only the X-Files boutique and Foot Locker are equipped to make on-line sales. The other locations require shoppers to print out invoices and surface-mail them to the retailers.

Just as there are malls and stand-alone stores along your local state route, the information superhighway sports shopping centers and single business sites, too. For example, at the Warner Brothers Studio Store, a customer can browse through an on-line catalog featuring Friends and Batman souvenirs and various products relating to the company's many television and movie productions. You can send a virtual postcard from the Warner Bros. site. Once the card is selected and information composed and entered, a message is sent via e-mail to the card's recipient, who can claim his or her mail by visiting the Warner Bros. site.

ON-LINE PURCHASING IN THE COMPUTER AGE

On-line purchasing procedures

Ordering from a Web site is simple and user-friendly. At most on-line stores, once the customers find the items they wish to purchase, they click on them and the products are sent to a virtual shopping basket. Customers click on links that take them to the order form, where they can choose between submitting their order electronically, over the phone, or via surface mail. If they choose electronic ordering, they must enter pertinent information, such as name, address, credit card number and expiration date, etc., all of which is e-mailed to the retailer.

Many buyers balk at the last steps in this process. Consumers have no problem browsing through the Web pages, viewing products and window shopping, but when it comes time to click the "submit" icon, a twinge of anxiety manifests itself. The reason for fear is the "public perception that the Internet is a dangerous place" (Weise, 1996, p.1), a place through which vital information should not pass. In the mind of John Williams, chair and CEO of Computer Services, Inc., businesses have not taken full advantage of the opportunities available to securely hold on to the valuable sixteen-digit credit card numbers that buyers submit.

On-line purchasing drawbacks

A question about confidence in Internet credit card security posted to two listserves got sixteen responses about how people felt when it came time to send their credit card numbers over the Internet. Answers to the question were varied: some users will not enter banking data, others are not certain whether they can adapt to this new form of ordering goods, and some believe it is the optimal way to conduct transactions. One user emphatically stated in e-mail to the author, "Never. I feel it is a very stupid idea to use a credit card online. It is dangerous." Michelle Kohorst, responding to the on-line posting, was hesitant: "I actually don't know that the Internet is less secure than in-person transactions, but it just gives the appearance of being open and available to anyone with hacking abilities." However, Josh Sherman disagreed, saying, "online [purchasing] is a preferred method of buying everything except special order goods."

The views reflected above generally mirror the national attitude toward on-line purchasing. A sense of faith and trust in the Internet and the companies that employ its powerful marketing features is missing. All of the new technology is simply overwhelming for consumers, and no one is sure about it. A major factor in feeling comfortable with on-line purchasing is merely taking the time to sort out the issues. Many consumers express ignorance about on-line shopping options. At the present time, there are no solid reassurances for consumers. Even those who hasten to ensure buyers that this new medium is safe seem to overqualify their claims. David N. Bodley, who wrote an article on security at the South Florida Mall Web site, writes that "there have been no major, consistent or organized reported thefts of funds transferred electronically." Then, too, the occasional news story about a "bored graduate student" stealing thousands of files containing credit card numbers discourages the already skeptical Web user (Weise, 1996, p. 1). Bad press is not the only deterrent to on-line sales; the technical terms and concepts used to describe Internet security are not exactly user-friendly or trust-inspiring.

Cryptography

Dr. Paul Buis, an assistant professor in the computer science department at Ball State University, believes that "[computer] technology is very complex, and that complexity is frightening. On the other hand, so is the technology in an automobile, the telephone, and an airplane." The complexities to which Dr. Buis refers include the intricate facets involved in ensuring computer security.

Microsoft, VISA, and MasterCard are assisting in the development of technology that secures the transactions of customers who shop on-line. By implementing the Secured Transaction Technology (STT), developed by Microsoft, the two credit card companies hope to create a standard that companies such as Netscape and Mosaic can incorporate into their Internet browsers (Microsoft's transactions, 1995). Browsers are not only the software programs that allow users to surf the Web but also the same tools through which security measures must be implemented. Those measures include cryptography, firewalls, and secured operating systems—all of which are still alien to most computer users. The three components are necessary, however, to ensure a secure transaction, and one weak link can disable the security of an entire system (Five Paces, 1996).

The first piece of the security puzzle is cryptography. Basically, "cryptography ('hidden writing') involves the translation of a message in plain language into one in a secret language" (Sattler, 1995). Two types of encryption are used today to translate the credit card number and expiration date into meaningless zeros and ones: one is public-key and the other is symmetric-key encryption. In order to understand how the two differ, it is important to understand how encryption takes place.

In translating a message, one algorithmic key is used to encrypt (into the secret language) the data, and another key is used to decrypt it (into plain language). Symmetric-key cryptography requires the sender to encrypt the message with a key and then separately e-mail both the key and the message along to the recipient. A greater possibility of interception and eventual decryption exists with that method of encoding text. In contrast, public-key encryption, patented by RSA Data Security, relies on two separate keys to translate the message. The sender only has to e-mail a message, and the recipient is able to decrypt it with a similar key at hand (Five Paces, 1996).

When a shopper finds an item (or items), he or she enters all of the required data on the order form, and using an encryption method that is incorporated as part of the Web site or the e-mail program, the order form is encrypted and sent along to the merchant. Once the merchant receives the order form, a key is used to decrypt the information, and the retailer checks to make sure the customer has the available credit. Finally, if the credit checks out, the order is processed, the account is billed, and the transaction is over (Lane, 1996).

In a telephone interview with Mike Geltz, a senior Web site technical writer for Gateway 2000, I found that even though Gateway's home page does not support on-line purchases, orders are taken on a limited basis. Public transactions are not yet an option, but about ten orders are taken each month from private institutions, such as the Federal Credit Union. Purchases are made via the company's experimental Stealth Division Web site, which allows for a secure transaction of funds and data. The method by which an order is taken is relatively similar to how other retailers conduct business. The order is made from a secure server (https, rather than http), encrypted with a program called Pretty Good Privacy (PGP), and then it is e-mailed to Geltz. From there, he decrypts the order form and sends the necessary information on to the shipping and billing departments. He said Gateway is in the process of hiring a man from Switzerland who will develop security for its Web site. Someday, consumers will have the ability to use their old computer system to order its replacement. When I asked Geltz about the security of the Internet in general, he said that no matter how much security is developed, it will never reach a level of ultimate perfection. Nothing is an absolute.

Firewalls

Of the three components of secure technology, cryptography is the most important, since it provides the secure transaction of valuable data. However, it does not keep unauthorized users from accessing the information once it reaches its destination server. At that point, a firewall becomes necessary. A firewall "controls traffic between outside and inside a network, providing a single choke point where access controls and auditing can be imposed" (Five Paces, 1996). In other words, imagine all the information a computer holds sitting behind a massive, impregnable wall, with only a small, heavily guarded door for outsiders to enter. When MCS/Universal Studios and First National Bank of Chicago first began to enter cyberspace, one of their biggest concerns was keeping external sites from breaking into the internal infrastructure of their computer systems. A firewall was needed (Nash, 1995, p. 70).

UNIX systems

Finally, the third component, a secure operating system, picks up where the firewall leaves off. A firewall is excellent for controlling unauthorized access, but it does not eliminate internal attacks. The UNIX operating system supports the roots of the Internet, and it is also the operating system that creates the sense of openness that worries users like Ms. Kohorst (quoted earlier). The entire Internet system is centered on an omnipotent account, which, if broken into, would grant the hacker uncontrollable access to all accounts (Five Paces, 1996). Microsoft is currently working on incorporating the existing security enhancements in the Windows NT operating system into the UNIX system to act as a secure location for data (Microsoft Corporation, Microsoft Previews, 1996). Only the merchant, who would have a username and password, would have access to the secure areas of information, such as credit card number lists (Microsoft Corporation, Electronic Retailing).

All of the aspects of electronic security covered so far in this paper are necessary and indispensable to the security of on-line shopping. Despite all that the companies may implement, for some "the problem is entirely a perception of danger, not of reality." Once that perception is dissolved, customers can fully realize the advantages of the World Wide Web. Of the participants in the on-line marketing movement, Microsoft is leading the way in revolutionizing shopping in the world with its designs for electronic retailing strategies.

Developments at Microsoft and Wal-Mart

According to Bill Gates, chair and CEO of Microsoft, electronic retailing will include the "development of a compelling shopping experience, automatic order handling, payment security, tools for analyzing purchasing patterns, and integration with a merchant's supply chain" (Microsoft Corporation, Electronic retailing). All links in the purchasing chain are represented in Microsoft's plan. Customers are assured of a secure transaction, offered a new method of shopping, and given the opportunity to shop at any time they wish. Down the road, Microsoft plans to include a shopping utility in the Windows operating system that will allow customers easy access to various on-line shopping locations. In turn, the merchants will increase revenues, lower costs, and create specialized markets via customized home pages for customers (Microsoft Corporation, Microsoft previews, 1996). The number of people who are on-line will greatly expand the market base retailers can reach with products and services. Also, with only a home page and the necessary links to keep up, money will not go toward maintenance of physical store locations. The retailer will have the ability to cater to the individual preferences of shoppers by creating "communities of shared interest and customized one-on-one relationships with customers" (Microsoft, Electronic retailing).

Joining Microsoft in the push to develop the on-line marketplace is the nation's largest retailer, Wal-Mart. David Glass, president and CEO of Wal-Mart, Inc., stated, "Microsoft has a solid vision for solving the challenge of electronic retailing on the Internet, and this is why we have chosen Microsoft technologies and products to expand our business and reach new customers through the Internet" (Microsoft Corporation, Microsoft previews, 1996). In the race to reach new customers, the Wal-Mart home page will feature thousands of products, ranging from computer software to gift items, with additional items appearing as the months pass.

Reasons to make on-line purchases

Regardless of Microsoft's vigorous plan to offer advanced shopping features, a few universal advantages exist from which every company and customer can benefit. Shopping on-line provides customers with a wider selection of products and facilitates comparative shopping. One on-line buyer claims in e-mail correspondence that "in terms of comparison shopping, it is easier to 'compare specs' via computer, and the variety increases everyday. I . . . have found higher quality and lower price[s] via on-line vendors as opposed to local electronics warehouses." Ultimately, pricing will become more competitive, since retailers will have to compete with a much larger market in cyberspace. As on-line shopping becomes more widely used, its speed and effectiveness will increase to meet the demands of customers. And if customers are dissatisfied with service at one site, the next is only a second away.

Internet purchasing is a widespread economic boon. First of all, customers will need a means of accessing the Web. Internet service providers, such as America Online, Prodigy, CompuServe, and the Microsoft Network, along with local direct access providers and cable carriers will become as essential to the economy as regular telephone lines are today. Delivery services, likewise, will proliferate and prosper.

When the projected on-line shopping movement is in full swing, the resulting economic growth will be staggering. According to a survey conducted by ActivMedia, an on-line analysis group that specializes in quantitative studies of on-line marketing, the future of on-line shopping looks promising. One survey indicated that "sales generated by the Web are expected to grow from $436 million in 1995 to nearly $46 billion by 1998" (ActivMedia, 1996). The predicted growth is in part due to the ever-increasing attention the on-line market is receiving. Such a medium gives the small and mid-sized marketers a chance to compete on-line and receive the overall revenue increase.

The marketplace of the future is becoming more geographically diverse (ActivMedia, 1996). Profits are already noticeable in a variety of on-line markets, including "computer-related hardware, software, and other high-tech equipment, travel services, investments, training, boilerplate legal services, prestige real estate, male-orientated luxury goods, specialty hobbies and crafts, technical employment services, audio recordings and consumer electronics" (ActivMedia, 1996). Regardless of growth, ActivMedia believes businesses will continue to experiment and test the Web. As we reach the next millennium, every major company around the globe will find its business has been altered because of the World Wide Web (ActivMedia, 1996).

Does this mean that instead of families' packing into the sedan to go to the mall they will simply huddle around the computer? Will physical stores go the way of Green Stamps? Probably not. Conventional shopping is not going to come to an abrupt halt; people will still go to malls and use catalogs and will still call Pizza Hut and drive over to the restaurant to pick up their own pizzas. Cyberspace is not going to replace the physical realm, after all.

References

ActivMedia, Inc. Trends in the World Wide Web marketplace. Market survey results and predictions for Internet marketing growth. Retrieved 26 April 1996 from the World Wide Web: http://www.activmedia.com.

Bodley, D. N. South Florida mall: Commercial and credit card security on the Internet. Description of security measures in use by Florida Internet retailers. Retrieved 14 April 1996 from the World Wide Web: Http://sf-mall.com.

Five Paces Software, Inc. Internet banking security. Description of security measures in use by a Chicago banking firm on the Internet. Retrieved 20 April 1996 from the World Wide Web: http://www.fivepaces.com.

Lane, H. Internet security hinders cyber-shopping growth. Retrieved 24 February 1996 from the World Wide Web. Available via e-mail at: Hillary@dash.com.

McLaughlin, L. (1996, March 30). Survey says: Growing but still small population using the Web. PCWorld Online. http://www.pcworld.com.

Microsoft Corporation. (n.d.). Electronic retailing-FAQ. Answers frequently asked questions about on-line purchasing. Retrieved from the World Wide Web: www.microsoft.com.

Microsoft Corporation. (1996). Microsoft previews electronic retailing strategy and technology to world's leading retailers. Press release regarding intentions to collaborate with Wal-Mart in devising Internet security measures. Retrieved on February 12, 1996 from the World Wide Web: http://www.microsoft.com.

Microsoft's transaction technology on way to ubiquity. (1995). Windows Watcher, September 1995, p. 15.

Moeller, M. (1995). Let's hang out at the E-mall: eShop opens its doors to Tower Records, Spiegel on the Web. PC Week, 6 Nov. 1995, p. 34.

Nash, K. S. (1995). Firms learn 'net security lessons. Computer World, 29, p. 70.

OpenMarket, Inc. Results of a survey tabulating number of commercial sites on the World Wide Web. Retrieved on March 15, 1996 from the World Wide Web: http://www.directory.net/dir/statstics.html.

Sattler, M. (1995, November 13). Basic issues and concepts in privacy and cryptography. Discussion of Internet security measures and their effectiveness. Available through e-mail at: Webmaster@jungle.com.

Weise, E. (1996, 22 January). Experts: Internet purchases safe as mail ordering. The Ball State Daily News, p. 1.

■ Summing Up

As your forays into various indexes have revealed, there are many possible ways to document, or describe the location of, articles and other secondary-source materials. In most disciplines, professional societies and leading journals have agreed on standard documentation styles for their field. The American Psychological Association (APA) and Council of Biology Editors (CBE) documentation styles are widespread, accepted formats, used predominantly in the sciences and the social sciences.

The *Publication Manual of the American Psychological Association,* fourth edition, published by the association in Washington, D.C., in 1994, contains a complete, detailed explanation of APA documentation style. It dictates how to cite sources within the text of a paper, as well as how to format the entries in a reference list at the end of the work. Examples demonstrate how to cite secondary sources such as books, articles by single or multiple authors, government publications, private correspondence, Internet postings, and interviews. The manual also prescribes how abstracts, margins, page numbers, notes, titles, graphs, and tables should be presented in papers in the sciences. Similarly, *Scientific Style and Format: The CBE Manual for Authors, Editors, and Publishers,* Sixth Edition describes CBE style.

Memorizing all of the conventions listed in the APA or CBE manual is unnecessary. The systems are logical, and the examples in the manual are straightforward. Keep a copy of the manual you are using on hand and consult it while you are preparing your final draft. Correctly using the APA or CBE format will make your work readily accessible to readers and give it the same professional appearance as articles in respected journals and books.

Exercises: Sources and Strategies

1. Compile a final Works Cited list for your research paper, and exchange it with a classmate. Try to name the *kind* of source (for example, a book by a single author, an article in a journal that numbers pages consecutively) represented by each item on your peer's list.

2. Review your own Works Cited list, and categorize the kinds of sources you have used. What does this teach you about your research strategies and the types of evidence you have chosen to use?

3. Try to locate full copies of a dozen or so of the items cited in the published articles you have read during your researching process. How many of the items cited in your most useful source can you find in your own library? What does that demonstrate about the kinds of sources used by professional writers?

Writing to Know

Complete the final version of your researched paper, and write your own evaluation of your work. What would you do differently or the same if you had the project to do over again?

Chapter Fourteen

MLA Format and Arts and Humanities Documentation Styles

Although there are several other documentation styles currently in use, most college teachers and publishers in the United States require either the format used by the American Psychological Association (APA) or that of the Modern Language Association (MLA). This chapter looks at the MLA guidelines for presenting professional discourse, as described in the *MLA Handbook for Writers of Research Papers,* fourth edition, edited by Joseph Gibaldi and published by the Modern Language Association (New York City) in 1995 and at the Chicago Style as described in the *Chicago Manual of Style* (1993). MLA guidelines are frequently used by writers in the arts and humanities. Chapter Thirteen covers APA and documentation styles for scientific and technical writing. Most likely, your instructor will tell you which format to use. If he or she leaves it up to you to decide, choose one style and stick with it consistently.

Each of the various bibliographic sources that you consulted while constructing your working bibliography provided the necessary information to help you locate the sources you used. You may have noticed that practically every bibliographical index uses its own formula for reporting publication data for the items it lists. Some, such as *Dissertation Abstracts International* and the ERIC database, employ a complex cross-referencing formula based on their own numbering system. Others, such as the *Reader's Guide to Periodical Literature* and *Infotrac,* provide abbreviated periodical titles with dates and volume, issue, and page numbers within the citation, enabling you to go directly to the sources you seek. You may have found it disconcerting to have to decipher a new system with each bibliographic source you consulted, but since you'd logged on or opened the volume to use it, you persevered and learned to crack its code.

Now imagine that the writer of every article, research paper, book, and so on invented his or her own idiosyncratic method for listing bibliographic information. Documentation would become meaningless pretty quickly, and readers would not even attempt to evaluate the sources used in constructing a particular discourse. To make documentation instantaneously decipherable and uniform, a few professional societies have published guidelines for citing information in scholarly texts within their disciplines. Most professional journals adhere to the documentation system that is most widely recognized in their field. Students are taught to use one or two of those systems because they provide reliable, thorough documentation of secondary sources that is easy to read and helps readers easily locate sources they wish to evaluate.

Some of these societies go further than advising writers how to credit secondary sources; they also provide models for how researched texts should be presented on paper or computer disk. They offer specific guidelines for how articles should be titled, how wide page margins should be, and which extraneous elements (such as title pages, outlines, abstracts, and appendixes) should be included. Although such guidelines may seem elitist or "stuffy" and "picky" to you at first, they are really very egalitarian—they ensure that a first-year college student's ideas will be presented in the same way as a postdoctoral fellow's research findings. By conforming to these models, you will be publishing your work in the style expected of practitioners in the field you are studying, and you will be demonstrating that you have learned the least of your lessons about writing in that discipline. You will use these documentation and formatting guidelines well beyond your college composition assignments; they will likely become the mode of communication you use in your career as well.

Once you are familiar with professional formats, they will become second nature to you, like writing a letter or addressing an envelope. Although you need to follow the MLA or APA guidelines carefully, you need not commit them to memory. That would be like memorizing the address of everyone to whom you would ever want to send correspondence. When you want to mail a letter or a package, you probably pull out your address book or some other reference and copy the necessary information onto an address label or envelope.

Just as you keep some kind of print or electronic database for addresses, you should own a copy of the *MLA Handbook for Writers of Research Papers* if you will be using MLA format in the future, so that you can refer to it whenever you need to document text. By copying the models from a style guide, you can be assured that your work conforms to professional standards.

■ Printing Your Paper

Use high-quality (16, 20, or 24 lb.), 8½ x 11 inch, white paper for work that is to be submitted for a grade or publication. If your printer uses perforated, continuous-form pages, separate them and stack them in the correct order before submitting your work. Print text so that a one-inch margin is preserved at the top, at the bottom, and on both the left and right sides of the page; only page numbers should violate these margins. If you're using a word processor, choose a font (typeface) that is clear and readable—such as Courier, which looks like traditional typewriter text—and size it at 10 or 12 points, so that roughly fifteen to twenty words fit on a line. Do not use a script or art font. Print text in black ink, using a "high" print-quality setting. If possible, use a laser printer or other high-quality printer for your final copy. Justify (align) the text of your document on the left margin. That will result in a page of text with an even left edge and a ragged, or varied, right edge. Do not use "full" justification, because it is difficult for readers' eyes to find their way back to the start of the next line when both the right and left margins are exactly even throughout. Indent the start of each paragraph one-half inch, or five spaces, from the left margin. The whole document should be double-spaced entirely, including quotations, footnotes, end notes, and the Works Cited list. Do not include extra spaces between paragraphs or between items in the end notes or on the Works Cited list. Print on only one side of each page. Do not ornament the pages of a research paper with watermarks, borders, enders, lines, or other drawings. Present your work so that physical aspects of the text do not compete with its content for your readers' attention.

Page Numbering and Fastening

Always number your pages, and label each page with your name in case pages get separated during grading or review. Pages should be numbered consecutively, beginning with the first full page of the essay itself (do not include a title page or outline in the same numbering sequence). Place page numbers one-half inch from the top of the page, flush with the right margin. Use the header feature in your word processing program to print your name on the same line, right before the page number, without any intervening punctuation. (Do not print "p." before a page number or add a comma, dash, or anything else between your name and the page number.) Suppress (that is, do not print) the page number and any headers on the very first page of text, but count that as page number 1.

Fasten all the pages together with a single paper clip; do not use staples or binders. Make it convenient for your instructor or editor to detach pages to write comments on them and reassemble the document afterward. Remember that even the final copy of your paper is not meant to be a bound publication; it should be presented as a final *draft*.

Endorsement and Title

A formal title page is optional unless a final outline is submitted with the paper, in which case it is mandatory. If you will not be including a formal outline with your final draft, include an endorsement in the upper left-hand corner of the first page, consisting of your name, your professor's name, the name of the course for which you wrote the paper, and the date you will be submitting it, each on its own line in a double-spaced text block at the left margin, one inch from the top of the page. Center the title under that. The title may be printed in boldface type, as the following example from Kyle's paper demonstrates:

Kyle Parker
Professor Peterson
English 114/02
24 April 1998

Let Your Mouse Do the Shopping:
On-line Purchasing in a Computer Age

"Hey, Mom, can we use the computer now? Brad and I bought this cool new game and we want to try it out."
Hold on a minute, let me finish ordering dinner. What do you guys want on your pizza?"

Remember that every element in an MLA-formatted research paper must be double-spaced. That means you must double-space between the items in the endorsement, between the endorsement and the title, and between the title and the first line of text. In most cases, your text will begin 3 1/3 inches from the top of your first page.

If your final submission will include a formal outline, you must make a title page to cover your final draft. Center the title of your paper on the page. Underneath that, print your name, as author of the text. One inch from the bottom of the page, center the remaining lines of the endorsement (professor's name, course title, submission date). See Kyle's title page on his final research paper at the end of this chapter.

Formal Outlines

Up until now in this process, you have made outlines as you pleased, because *you* were the audience for them. Working outlines can be as disheveled as you want them to be, but a final outline is a formal one, and so, predictably, there are rules to follow in constructing one. Your instructor may require you to submit a final outline with the last draft of your work, or you may choose to provide one for the convenience of your readers and yourself. A final outline serves as a table of contents for your research paper. It makes it possible for your audience to quickly scan and preview or review the arguments or ideas you have assembled in your discourse. Place it before your text, just behind the cover sheet, and number the pages of the outline in lowercase Roman numerals (i, ii, iii, iv, v, and so on). Because every serious research project contains some kind of "introduction," "body," and "conclusion," never just list those headings on a final outline. Instead, a final outline should be a detailed summary of the paper it describes. It is usually most efficient to construct a final outline after you've finished writing the paper.

The MLA prescribes the following format for a formal outline:

   I. Bicycles

      A. Off-road

          1. Mountain bikes

            a. All-terrain

               (1) Aluminum

                   (a) Shock forks

                   (b) Full suspension

               (2) Steel

            b. Downhill

          2. Hybrid bikes

      B. Road

  II. Sleds

As this example demonstrates, parallel categories are numbered consecutively, using Roman numerals, and subordinate information is arranged beneath it in a logical manner, using capital and lowercased letters and cardinal numbers in parentheses or followed by periods. In the example outline fragment, *Bicycles* and *Sleds* are the main topics, and *Off-road* and *Road* are parallel subtopics, as are *Aluminum* and *Steel,* and *Shock forks* and *Full suspension.* If a topic has no parallel counterpart, then it is not numbered or lettered on the outline. If, for instance, hybrid bikes were covered elsewhere in the outline, there would be no letter preceding the Mountain bike heading. Don't use a "1" or "A" or "(a)" if there is no "2" or "B" or "(b)" to follow it, because there is no sense in using a complicated labeling system to keep one item straight. The MLA documentation and presentation formats are quite logical and straightforward, which makes them easy to learn and implement.

Graphics, Tables, and Charts

As you know from reading magazine articles, pictures and charts that are printed as closely as possible to the text that refers to them are the most useful. Try to include compact graphics in your text. Photographs, tables, and charts that are relegated to an appendix (a collection of useful supporting materials attached to the end of a research project) will not receive as much attention as those embedded in the text itself. If you can quickly and reasonably learn to insert graphic materials into your text with the word processing software you are using, prefer that method of including visual aids in your work. If the graphic or the software you are using prohibits that, leave space in the text where you can paste in the graphic element, and photocopy that page for inclusion in your research paper's final version.

The conventional MLA method of labeling graphic elements in texts is to call charts and tables "Table 1," "Table 2," and so on and to label photographs, color plates, and other picture-type inclusions "Figure 1," "Figure 2,"and so on. If you have few tables and figures, or you do not refer to them in your text frequently, you may want to give graphic elements more descriptive titles that describe the information or images they convey.

■ Correcting Errors

Inevitably, just as you are ready to turn in the meticulously prepared and endlessly proofread copy of your final research paper, you will spot a typographical error, a missing word, a homonym that your spell checker missed (such as *hear* instead of *here* or *to* in place of *too*), a paragraph that mysteriously reformatted itself with a column of white space down its center, or a line or two of text that your printer seems to have ignored. There are many products on the market for painting and pasting over errors in finished copy, but none is quite so handy or unobtrusive as a plain black-ink pen and careful lettering. If there are only one or two very small errors in your work, correct them efficiently in ink. If there are more, consider fixing them on disk and reprinting your text.

■ MLA Parenthetical Citation

Parenthetical citation is the method required by the MLA for acknowledging sources used in research. The idea behind parenthetical citation is to place in parentheses the absolute minimum amount of information necessary to direct readers to the appropriate source in the Works Cited list, which provides complete publication information so readers can locate original sources if desired. The system is very clear and logical. The basic formula consists of the last name of the author or authors of the cited source, plus the page number where the cited information was printed in that source. This makes it easy to quickly locate a source on the Works Cited list, because in the MLA format this list is arranged alphabetically by authors' names. The page number of cited material is given in the parenthetical notation because that is the most efficient way to direct readers to the exact page numbers where pertinent information can be found. Thus, a parenthetical citation of information reported by historian Doris Kearns Goodwin on page 385 of her book *No Ordinary Time: Franklin and Eleanor Roosevelt: The Home Front in World War II*, would appear simply as (Goodwin 385). All of the information necessary for readers to discover which Goodwin book is quoted (including which author named *Goodwin* it is) and how to locate a copy of that book will be included in the corresponding Works Cited entry.

Notice that the basic parenthetical citation in MLA style is as simple as it can get: there is no intervening punctuation between the author's name and page number, and no *p.*, even, to indicate what the number means. It creates the least possible interruption in the text with its minimal content. Frequent users of the MLA documentation style recognize it immediately, and so it requires no embellishment for its audience. Don't be tempted to add punctuation or extraneous information to your parenthetical notes. Trust the system.

Despite its sparseness, however, sometimes even this basic formula can introduce redundancies. For instance, if your discourse has already named the author of a source you are citing, there is little reason to spell it out again in the parenthetical citation; this only creates an unnecessary distraction for your readers. In such cases, you need only mention the page number where the information can be found in the original source. For example:

> Popular historian Doris Kearns Goodwin reveals that FDR named his cabin in the Maryland woods "Shangri-la" because it was a relaxing haven at which he could escape the pressures of the presidency (385).

Conversely, sometimes the information offered in a basic parenthetical citation is not adequate for identifying the documented item in the Works Cited list. Obviously, if you have referred to more than one work by the same author in your research paper, noting that last name only in your parenthetical citations could lead to some confusion about which work is being cited in a specific instance. This is a fairly common difficulty in research writing because many professionals acquire the status of expert in their field by writing several articles or books on related topics. So if your research led you to the Doris Kearns Goodwin book mentioned earlier, for instance, it might also have turned up her *Newsweek* article "Echoes of FDR: What Today's Roosevelt Wanna-bes Should Learn from His Legacy." And if you wanted to use both of these sources in your paper, citing Goodwin's ideas would become a bit more complicated than it would if you used only one of them. If you are documenting two or more texts by the same author in your paper, include a fragment of the titles of the cited works in your parenthetical notes for that author's materials only. Thus the parenthetical notes for the two Goodwin sources would be something like this: (Goodwin, *No Ordinary* 385) and (Goodwin, "Echoes" 9). Present just enough of the titles so that readers will be able to easily identify the appropriate source on your Works Cited list for each parenthetical citation. Notice that title fragments in parenthetical notes are punctuated and styled as their full versions would be; for books and long manuscripts they are underlined, and for shorter works they are presented in quotation marks. Although your word processor undoubtedly has the ability to print in italics, the MLA still prefers that writers use underlining to designate titles, because underlining is easier to see than italics in some fonts. A comma separates an author's last name from the abbreviated title of his or her work, but no other punctuation is included in the extended version of a parenthetical notation.

Similarly, if you are citing a document whose author is unnamed, your parenthetical note should begin with a fragment of the title. For instance, the *Washington Post* ran a one-page article on April 27, 1992, called "Remembering Franklin Delano Roosevelt" that was unsigned. A parenthetical note citing that would look like this: ("Remembering" A:22). Similarly, if you just happen to have two or three authors named "Gupta," "Jones," "Smith," or "Wu," you will need to distinguish between them by using first initials in your parenthetical notes.

If you are confused by these formulas, just remember that the objective of a parenthetical citation is to direct readers to the corresponding complete entry describing the source in your Works Cited list and to indicate the exact page of the original source where the summarized, paraphrased, or quoted information you are using was printed. This purpose is very simple, and the format reflects that.

■ Footnotes and End Notes

Under current MLA guidelines, footnotes or end notes are not used for documentation. However, they still provide opportunities for writers to include tangential information without disrupting the flow of their discourse. For example, if you were writing about FDR's retreats to his cabin "Shangri-la" and wished to mention that *Shangri-la* is the name James Hilton invented for the hidden Buddhist lama paradise in his 1933 novel *Lost Horizon*, you could relegate that information to a footnote or an end note. Footnotes and end notes are also used to add concurrent documentation to a parenthetical note. For example, if you quote a specific author as the source of information that is available in several different places, you can list other locations for that information in a note. As their names suggest, footnotes are printed at the foot of the page bearing reference to them, and end notes are listed consecutively on a page at the end of the paper. If you decide to use notes in your research project, choose between footnotes and end notes, and use that format consistently throughout it.

To include a footnote or an end note, place a superscript cardinal number in the text where the information would be relevant (for example, "in the Maryland woods 'Shangri-la'[1] because"). The corresponding note is then identified with the same number (also a superscript) at the bottom of the page or the end of the paper. Number footnotes or end notes consecutively throughout your text. If you are using parenthetical citation (and you should be), you can produce a text without any footnotes or end notes.

■ Works Cited List

A Works Cited list begins taking shape from the very beginning of a research project. Items that start as part of your working bibliography or crop up during your investigation and eventually become useful sources in your research will be included on your Works Cited list. A Works Cited list is simply a highly organized, alphabetized, uniform summary of all of the secondary sources upon which you have built your final research paper. Its purposes are to acknowledge the contributions of predecessors to your research, to provide readers with information that will help them locate your original sources for their inspection, and to serve as a guide for future researchers working on the same topic. Your bibliography cards or notes serve as a make-shift Works Cited list during your drafting process, and it is from them that you will take the necessary information for your parenthetical citations. Only items that are actually cited in your text should be included on the Works Cited list. When it is time to assemble your final Works Cited list, there are specific models that you should follow in the MLA format.

An MLA Works Cited list is double-spaced in its entirety. Older versions of the MLA style guide called for single-spacing of listed items, but that has gone the way of the manual typewriter and its carriage return lever. If the guide you are using shows a single-spaced Works Cited list, it is probably out of date in other areas (such as documentation of on-line sources) as well, and you should replace it with the current edition.

Include your Works Cited list as the last text page of your paper. Although you should number the pages of a Works Cited list along with the rest of the text, you do not usually count these as part of your paper in a page-limited assignment. That is, if you were asked to write a ten-page paper, your Works Cited list should begin on page 11.

Most of the items on your Works Cited list will probably begin with authors' last names or the first words of titles. Alphabetize all entries by the first word, regardless of what it represents (for example, "Hanson" precedes "History," which precedes "Holhman," and so on). If two or more works by the same author appear on your list, replace the author's name in second and subsequent citations with three spaced dashes (- - -). Do not number, bullet, or otherwise label the items on your Works Cited list. Some listed items will be longer than a single typewritten line; indent second (and subsequent) lines of a single entry one-half inch, or five spaces, from the left margin. Following are example MLA Works Cited list entries for some common types of secondary sources.

Citing Books

Because printed works make up most of the secondary sources cited in researched work, there are strict guidelines for how to list them as references. A basic book reference in MLA style should include the following:

- The author's name (last name first, then the first and any subsequent names, in order, separated from the last name by a comma)

- The book's title

- The name of the city where it was published

- The name of the publisher

- The year of the book's most recent copyright

All entries end with a period. If more than one author or editor is named, they are listed in the order in which they appear on the title page of the original source. Only the first author named is presented in the last-name-first manner. Names of subsequent authors are printed conventionally, with first names first.

The words *University Press* are abbreviated "U" and "P." Unnecessary words in publisher's names are eliminated; therefore Charles Scribner's Sons Publishing Company is called simply "Scribner." The U.S. Government Printing Office is listed simply as "GPO." The abbreviation "ed." is used to represent the words *editor* and *edited*, and the Latin abbreviation "et al." ("and others") is used in listings of four or more authors or editors.

MLA formatting must be strictly adhered to with conventional sources, such as books, journals, magazines, and newspapers. You will not find variations in the way these sources are described in legitimately documented texts, and you should take pains to follow these formulas exactly.

A Book with a Single Author

Goodwin, Doris Kearns. <u>Wait till Next Year: A Memoir</u>. New York: Simon
    and Schuster, 1997.

A Compilation with an Editor

Jackson, Kenneth T., ed. <u>The Encyclopedia of New York City</u>. New Haven:
    Yale UP, 1995.

A Book with Two or Three Authors

Kelly, Alfred H., Winfred A Harbison, and Herman Belz. <u>The American</u>
    <u>Constitution: Its Origins and Development</u>. New York: Norton, 1983.

A Book with Three or More Editors or Authors

Anderson, Judith H., et al., eds. <u>Spenser's Life and the Subject of</u>
    <u>Biography</u>. Amherst: U of Massachusetts P, 1996.

Moore, Mark H., et al. <u>Dangerous Offenders: The Elusive Target of Justice</u>.
    Cambridge: Harvard UP, 1984.

Two or More Books by the Same Author

Goodwin, Doris Kearns. <u>No Ordinary Time: Franklin and Eleanor Roosevelt:</u>
    <u>The Home Front in WW II</u>. New York: Simon and Schuster, 1994.

- - -. <u>Wait till Next Year: A Memoir</u>. New York: Simon and Schuster, 1997.

A Single Work from an Anthology

Lloyd, G. E. R. "Science and Mathematics." <u>The Legacy of Greece</u>. Ed.
    Moses Finley. New York: Oxford UP, 1981. 256–300.

A Book by a Corporate Author

The Boston Women's Health Collective. <u>Our Bodies, Ourselves</u>. New York: Simon and Schuster, 1986.

An Introduction, a Preface, a Foreword, or an Afterword

Boaz, Frank. Introduction. <u>Patterns of Culture</u>. By Ruth Benedict. 1934. Boston: Houghton Mifflin, 1959.

Government Publications

United States. Cong. House. Committee on the Judiciary. <u>Immigration and Nationality with Amendments and Notes on Related Law</u>. 7th ed. Washington: GPO, 1980.

An Unpublished Dissertation

Sakala, Carol. "Maternity Care Policy in the United States: Toward a More Rational and Effective System." Diss. Boston U, 1993.

An Abstract in **Dissertations Abstracts International**

Mead, David Goddard. "E. E. Cummings: The Meaning of the Sonnets." <u>DAI</u> 36 (1975): 8062A.

Periodical Articles

A basic journal, magazine, or newspaper article Works Cited entry contains four parts:

- The author's name (last name first, and so on)
- The article title, in quotation marks
- The periodical title, underlined
- Publication information (including volume and issue numbers, dates, and page numbers)

Omit introductory elements in periodical titles (for example, list *The New York Times* as *New York Times*). If a newspaper's name does not indicate its city of origin, add that in brackets (e.g., *Freeman Journal* [Webster City, Iowa]). No punctuation intervenes between periodical titles and volume numbers.

See the following examples for the various conventions for reporting volume and issue numbers versus dates. Issue numbers are not used by all journals and magazines. Do not report volume and issue numbers if they are assigned by newspapers, but do indicate edition names (for example, city edition, late edition), because the various editions of a newspaper actually contain different information. Enclose dates in parentheses. Separate page numbers from the rest of the entry with a colon. End all entries in periods.

Most, but not all, journals are paginated continuously, which means that the first issue of the year begins on page 1, and all subsequent issues in that year begin where the previous issue left off. Magazines are usually paginated separately, which means that every issue begins with page 1. List all of the page numbers for periodical articles, even if you did not use the whole article. If an article is continued throughout a magazine, not on consecutive pages, list only its first page number, followed by a plus sign (for example, 21+).

An Article in a Journal That Pages Each Issue Separately

Friedman, Norman. "A New Encyclopedia Entry on Cummings." Spring:
    The Journal of the E. E. Cummings Society 8.2 (1988): 2–11.

An Article in a Journal That Uses Only Issue Numbers

Garfinkel, Alan. "A Mathematics for Physiology." American Journal of
    Physiology 245 (1984): 145–53.

An Article in a Newspaper

Poore, Charles. "Too Good to Be Obvious." New York Times 4 Sept. 1962,
    late ed., sec. 2: 33.

An Article in a Magazine

Balf, Todd. "He's Back and He's Pissed." Bicycling Jan./Feb. 1998: 52–55.

An Unsigned Article

"Soviet Television." Los Angeles Times 13 Dec. 1990, sec. 2: 3+.

An Article from an Information Service

Breland, Hunter. Assessing Writing Skill. ERIC ED 286 920.

A Review, Editorial, Advertisement, Letter to the Editor

Goodwin, Doris Kearns. Rev. of Coming Out Under Fire: The History of Gay
    Men and Women in World War Two. by Allan Berube. New York
    Times Review of Books 8 April 1990: 9.
Kennedy, John. "A Mother Like No Other." Editorial. George Nov. 1997: 23–4.
"Pain may be eliminated for millions." Advertisement. Muncie Star Press 8
    January 1998: 2B.
Balliet, Whitney. Letter. New Yorker 15 Sept. 1997: 6.

Archived Items

The variety of objects housed in archives makes them especially challenging to document. You must essentially describe material you have seen and tell where you saw it. Because archived articles do not circulate, you do not need to include catalog numbers or specific information that one would use to request such pieces.

A Work of Art

DuChamp, Marcel. <u>Nude Descending a Staircase</u>, No. 2. Philadelphia
   Museum of Art, Philadelphia.

A Map

<u>The Aran Islands</u>. Map. Dublin, Ireland: Ordinance Survey, 1975.

Private Correspondence

Cummings, E. E. Letter to Scofield Thayer. 7 May 1924. Houghton Library,
   Boston.

Manuscript

Eliot, Thomas Stearns. "Fourth Caprice in Montparnasse." Poem.
   Holograph edition. 1910. New York Public Library, New York.

Electronic Media

Documenting electronic media inolves a complex group of tasks. Some electronic works change daily or even more often than that (Web sites, for example), and some combine the work of many contributors that cannot be separated (for example, the ad-libbed performance of a blues standard). Some events captured electronically are here and gone so quickly that it is impossible to gather all the information about them that you would choose to cite (for example, the words of a bystander overheard during a live remote news broadcast, or a comment heard on a radio program *after* the speaker has already been identified). This is where documentation conventions give out and integrity must take over. Try to tell as much about the source you are describing as is reasonable to credit its owners and to prove to readers that it exists or existed. Rely on generalizations that you can make from more established forms. For instance, you can essentially follow the format for a similar periodical article when citing part of a periodically published, physically distributed electronic source (a microfilm, CD-ROM, computer disk), and you can follow the format for a similar type of book (that is, a book by a single author, an anthology with an editor, and so on) when citing a nonperiodical, physically distributed electronic publication, but add information describing the source you are using (title of the product; media through which it is distributed; edition, release, or version).

Audiovisual Sources Audiovisual productions include many elements that you may wish to emphasize in your documentation. Most are the result of the work of many different professionals. For instance, you must decide whether you are citing an actor's performance, a director's influence, or a screenwriter's text when you document a film, or a singer's or musician's performance, an arranger's version, or the lyricist's words when you document a sound recording. Illustrating this are the two variant, yet acceptable, citations for Orson Welles's original broadcast of *The War of the Worlds* shown in the following examples. It is impossible to anticipate every documentation scenario, and some forms must simply be improvised.

Internet Sources Undoubtedly, the greatest challenge yet to our time-honored styles of documentation are publications found on the Internet. Offering documentation for material viewed on the World Wide Web can be like citing a declaration written in sand during yesterday's low tide or advising a lost traveler to proceed to the corner where a dog was standing one day last week. Because Web sites are written over and revised almost constantly, you cannot be assured that you are directing readers back to the same information you accessed earlier. When you use information from a source on the World Wide Web, you are probably creating one of the few permanent records of its existence and content. Right now, the trend is toward giving as much publication information as you can discern about a Web site, so that you can demonstrate the currency and reliability of the source and prove as convincingly as possible that the information you are reporting was posted at that site on the day you accessed it. The first date in most Web citations, then, is the date of the text's last reported revision (if that is available), and the second date (usually in parentheses) is the date you saw it.

Other important information for Web site documentation includes the name of its author, the title of the page the information is on, the title over the complete site or home page name, and the complete URL for the cited page. As the use of Web resources in research writing becomes more common, uniform documentation forms will evolve, and reputable sources will respond by offering relevant information. Now, however, it is often difficult to discern who authored information on the Web and when it was written, so some documentation styles include only a page title, URL, and access date. Precise documentation of Internet sources increases their acceptance in academic circles. You can advance on-line research and its documentation by providing reliable, useful descriptions of the Internet sources you cite.

Interviews

Walker, Alice. Personal interview. 4 December 1995.

Vonnegut, Kurt, Jr. Telephone interview. 17 November 1996.

Updike, John. On-line interview. 23 October 1997.

An Article in a Microfilm Collection

Michelson, Daniel. "Lightning Speed: New CD-ROMs Even Faster."
Technology Times 29 May 1998: 37. Industry Standard: Business
Reports 12 (1998): fiche 3, grids B11–14.

A Periodically Published CD-ROM

Russo, Michelle Cash. "Recovering from Bibliographic Instruction Blahs." RQ: Reference Quarterly 32 (1992): 178–83. Infotrac: Magazine Index Plus. CD-ROM. Information Access. Dec. 1993.

A Nonperiodical Publication on CD-ROM or Diskette

"Ellison, Ralph." Disklit: American Authors. Diskette. Boston: Hall, 1991.

A Television or Radio Program

"War of the Worlds." Writ. H. G. Wells. Perf. Orson Welles. Columbia Broadcasting Network, New York. 30 Oct. 1938.

Welles, Orson, dir. "The War of the Worlds." By H. G. Wells. Adapt. Howard Koch. Mercury Theatre on the Air. CBS Radio. WCBS, New York 30 Oct. 1938.

Sound Recordings

Dylan, Bob. Time Out of Mind. Sony Music Entertainment, 1997.

Gershwin, George and Ira Gershwin. "Love Is Here to Stay." Perf. Frank Sinatra. Arr. Nelson Riddle. Chappell Music, 1955. Rpt. Songs for Swingin' Lovers. Capitol Records, 1987.

Film

It's a Wonderful Life. Dir. Frank Capra. Perf. James Stewart, Donna Reed, Lionel Barrymore, and Thomas Mitchell. RKO, 1946.

Welles, Orson, dir. Citizen Kane. RKO, 1941.

FTP (File Transfer Protocol) Sites Available for Downloading

Scherl, Reynald and Henri Levesque. "The Frame Problem and Knowledge Producing Actions." Cognitive Robotics Department, University of Toronto 4 Dec.1996. Ftp://ftp.cs.toronto.edu/pub/corob/README.html (8 January 1998).

WWW (World Wide Web) sites

Associated Press. "Researchers note increase of diabetes in overweight kids." USA Today 9 Oct. 1997. http://www.usatoday.com/life/health/general/diabetes/hdgio14.htm (8 Jan. 1998).

"Florida's Manatees." Manatee Snorkel Tours 1996–97. http://www.xtalwind.net/~/bird/tips.html (8 Jan. 1998).

Human Genome Project. "Human Genome Project Frequently Asked Questions." Human Genome Project Information Oct. 1997.

http://www.oml.gov/TechResources/Human_Genome/faq'faq1.html
(8 Jan. 1998).

Irmer, Thomas. "An Interview with Leslie Marmon Silko." <u>Alt-X Online
Publishing Network</u>. http://www.altx.com/interviews/silko.html
(8 Jan. 1998).

Silk, Joe. "Dark Matter." <u>Center for Particle Astrophysics/NSF Science and
Technology Center 1993</u>. http://physics7.berkeley.edu/darkmat/
reading.html (8 Jan. 1998).

Chicago Style

Once you fully understand the MLA style, it is not hard to grasp the gist of the Chicago Style system as described in the *Chicago Manual of Style* (14th edition, 1993). Also used for writing in the arts and humanities, the Chicago Style is much like the MLA style in its formulas for listing items; however, the Chicago Style uses full footnotes or endnotes and no Works Cited list, so, in practice, it is quite different to use.

Chicago Style Notes Instead of the parenthetical citations used in text documented in the MLA style, the Chicago Style relies upon superscripted numbers (like those used in the CBE Citation-Sequence system), which refer to end notes or footnotes that contain full bibliographic citations for the documented material. As their names indicate, "end notes" are a list of sources printed on a separate page after the conclusion of your research paper, and "footnotes" are citations printed at the bottom of the page upon which they occur. Most word processing programs will help you compile end notes or footnotes, and if you are documenting your paper in the Chicago Style, it is well worth your effort to run a tutorial or take time learning how to use that feature of your software.

Documentation in the Chicago Style has essentially two parts: the superscripted numbers in your text and the notes to which they refer. For example, the first reference to a secondary source in Kyle's research paper, as cited in the Chicago Style system, would look like this:

> The Internet is fast becoming a Mecca for the experienced web surfer and for "newbies"—amateur or beginning "surfers"—alike, who are a part of the estimated 7.5 million households on line[1].

The superscripted number in Kyle's text ([1]) refers to an end note or footnote describing the *PCWorld* article by Laurianne McLaughlin from which the statistics he reports are taken. Notes are numbered with the same digit as the citation in the text, but it is not superscripted in the notes. The Chicago Style note for that information would look like this:

1. Laurianne McLaughlin, "Microsoft Previews Electronic Retailing Strategy and Technology to World's Leading Retailers" [database online] (Microsoft Press Release, 1996, [cited 12 Feb 1996]), http://www.microsoft.com.

Notice that citations in the Chicago Style do not invert author's first and last names because they are not alphabetized entries. Also, titles in the Chicago Style are capitalized traditionally; major words start with capital letters. Finally, items in each citation are separated by commas, as opposed to the periods used in many other documentation formats.

Numbering Items in Chicago Style   Cited items are numbered consecutively in the Chicago Style system. When the same source is cited later in a research paper, it is given—not the same number it was assigned the first time, but—the next consecutive number. Thus, in Kyle's paper the second citation is again a reference to the McLaughlin article. His third reference to a secondary source is credited to an interview with John Williams. Hence, the first three items on endnotes for Kyle's paper would appear as follows:

1. Laurianne McLaughlin, "Microsoft Previews Electronic Retailing Strategy and Technology to World's Leading Retailers" [database online] (Microsoft Press Release, 1996, [cited 12 Feb 1996]), http://www.microsoft.com.

2. Laurianne McLaughlin, "Microsoft Previews Electronic Retailing Strategy and Technology to World's Leading Retailers" [database online] (Microsoft Press Release, 1996, [cited 12 Feb 1996]), http://www.microsoft.com.

3. John Williams, telephone interview, 25 March 1996.

Latin Terminology in Chicago Style   Although the most recent guidebook to the Chicago Style discourages the use of Latin terms Loc. cit. and Op. cit. to refer to items previous listed (with intervening sources), it does allow the use of Ibid. to denote consecutively repeated sources. It is permissible, then, to list the above three sources in end notes or footnotes as follows:

1. Laurianne McLaughlin, "Microsoft Previews Electronic Retailing Strategy and Technology to World's Leading Retailers" [database online] (Microsoft Press Release, 1996, [cited 12 Feb 1996]), http://www .microsoft.com.

2. Ibid.

3. John Williams, telephone interview, 25 March 1996.

Citing Books and Periodicals in Chicago Style   Because the citation formats for end notes and footnotes in the Chicago   Style are essentially complete bibliographic references, a Works Cited list is unnecessary is this documentation system. The end notes or footnotes themselves comprise a complete references list. Below are given sample citations formulas for the Chicago Style. Notice that cited page numbers are included in the entries.

A Book with a Single Author

4. Doris K. Goodwin, Wait till Next Year: A Memoir (New York: Simon and Schuster, 1997), 112.

A Book with More than Three Authors

5. Judith H. Anderson, et al., Spenser's Life and the Subject of Biography (Amherst: University of Massachusetts Press, 1996), 32.

A Book with an Editor

6. Kenneth T. Jackson, ed. The Encyclopedia of New York City (New Haven: Yale University Press, 1995), 1016.

A Book by a Corporate Author

7. Boston Women's Health Collective, Our Bodies, Ourselves (New York: Simon and Schuster, 1986), 659.

A Journal Article

8. Alan Garkinkel, "A Mathematics for Physiology," American Journal of Physiology 245 (Spring 1984): 147.

A Newspaper Article

9. Charles Poore, "Too Good to Be Obvious," New York Times, 4 Sept. 1962, late ed., sec 2, 33.

A Magazine Article

10. Todd Balf, "He's Back and He's Pissed," Bicycling, Jan./Feb. 1998, 54.

An Unsigned Article

11. "Soviet Television," Los Angeles Times, 13 Dec. 1990, sec 2, 3.

Bibliography   Writers using the Chicago Style may wish to append a Bibliography at the end of their papers, to direct readers to other sources of interest on their topics that were not cited in the paper's end notes or footnotes. Essentially, a Bibliography is a list of supplemental readings—texts that the paper's author found interesting although they were not used directly in the presentation of the preceding manuscript.

In preparing a Bibliography page for a paper documented in the Chicago Style, some differences between the end or footnote citations must be observed. Most noticeably, sources on a Bibliography list are not numbered, but alphabetized by their authors' last names (or first available information). Therefore, authors' names are inverted in a Bibliography list citation. Below is a brief comparison of note and bibliography form examples in the Chicago Style.

Notes

7. Boston Women's Health Collective, <u>Our Bodies, Ourselves</u> (New York: Simon and Schuster, 1986), 659.

8. Alan Garfinkel, "A Mathematics for Physiology," <u>American Journal of Physiology</u> 245 (Spring 1984): 147.

Bibliography

Boston Women's Health Collective. <u>Our Bodies, Ourselves</u>. New York: Simon and Schuster, 1986.

Garfinkel, Alan. "A Mathematics for Physiology," <u>American Journal of Physiology</u> 245 (Spring 1984): 145–53.

■ Kyle's Final Draft

In revising his research paper, Kyle actually cut back on the amount of information he was providing his readers, to spend more time defining technical terms associated with encryption. Since his most up-to-date sources on Internet security were World Wide Web postings, a heavy proportion of his Works Cited list is electronic materials, which is a weakness in his final project. Kyle is a good writer, however, and he has managed to pull his many meager sources together into an informative and compelling argument paper.

Notice that documentation formats for on-line sources have changed considerably in the few months since Kyle finished this paper. He wanted to go back and look for posting or revision dates, but many of his sources had vanished into cyberspace, and he decided to keep his documentation style consistent by not altering those for which additional information could be found. The vagueness of his Internet documentation does demonstrate why changes are needed, but nothing will prevent on-line sources from vanishing before readers have the chance to peruse them.

Let Your Mouse Do the Shopping: On-line Purchasing

in the Computer Age

submitted by

Kyle Parker

Professor Peterson

English 114/02

April 24, 1997

Outline

I. Narrative about on-line pizza ordering

II. Establishing the importance of the issue
   A. Internet growth
   B. Examples of on-line businesses
      virtual malls

III. Explaining the on-line purchasing process
   A. Procedures
   B. Drawbacks
      1. Imagined risks
      2. Real security problems

IV. Solutions to Internet security problems
   A. Cryptography
      1. Encryption types
      2. Gateway example
   B. Firewalls
   C. Operating systems
      1. UNIX
      2. Windows NT

V. Future developments
   Microsoft/Wal-Mart

VI. Reasons to make on-line purchases
   A. Lower prices
   B. Comparison shopping
   C. Convenience
   D. Customer attention

VII. Benefits to peripheral businesses
   A. Computer retailers
   B. Internet providers
   C. Delivery services
   D. National economy
      projected sales growth

VIII. Impact on physical realm
   A. Family life
   B. Retailing

"Hey, Mom, can we use the computer now? Marcia and I bought this cool new game, and we want to try it out."

"Hold on a minute. Let me finish ordering dinner. What do you guys want on your pizza?'

"Uhm, where's it coming from?"

"The usual, Pizza Hut."

"Good. Can we see what that new triple-stuffed crust thing looks like?"

"Okay, let me just click on the menu here. Hold it. Let's see; I just click here, and ... there it is."

"Yeah. That looks pretty good. Look at all that cheese. I can taste it already. Get it with sausage and pepperoni, and, can we have extra cheese like that? Bread sticks, too. Right Marcia?"

"I dunno."

"Well, I guess since Marcia is so adamant about it. Okay, just a couple more things to enter, and ... there. It's all yours. You've got about forty-five minutes to play until the pizza gets here. Have fun."

"Thanks, Mom."

Wait a minute. What's going on here? This isn't <u>The Brady Bunch</u>. Can people in the 1990s really order pizza using the Internet?

Thanks to the current growth and development of on-line technology, pizza is only one thing that consumers can buy with a click of the mouse. Computers are becoming an ever-present fixture in the households of America, and people are clamoring to partake in the lure of the emerging frontier called cyberspace. The Internet is fast becoming a Mecca for the experienced Web surfer and for "newbies" —amateur or beginning "surfers" —alike, who are part of the estimated 7.5 million households on-line (McLaughlin).

Growth in the domestic sector of the Internet has caused businesses to become major players in the technology marketing scene. Progressive retailers have recognized the phenomenal on-line interest of customers, and they have reacted with equal enthusiasm. As Steve Coffey, vice president of NPD Group, a market research firm in New York, commented, "this is definitely the time for businesses to establish a presence online" (McLaughlin). Companies are watching as the domain on the World Wide Web, which was created specifically for commercial sites on the Internet, expands. The domain, which includes all Internet addresses ending in a ".com" phrase (e.g., <u>http://www.<company name>.com</u>) increased from a mere 29,000 sites in December of 1994 to 170,892 in just over a year (Williams). A few months after that survey was taken, the number had jumped to 259,999, with 975 sites opening in the week ending on April 8, 1996 (OpenMarket, Inc.). Obvious Internet contenders such as Microsoft Corporation, Gateway 2000, and Netscape Communications are staking out their claims in the realm of cyberspace. The surprise, however, is the growing number of the less Internet-driven businesses who are venturing on-line.

Companies, regardless of size, are beginning to take advantage of the benefits of the Internet—twenty-four-hour a day, seven days a week, worldwide access—reaching the next generation of consumers. A viable economic opportunity is beginning to exert its influence on consumers. As advertising teams and executives create new commercials for companies such as AT&T, UPS, ESPN, and Toyota, all have created links to the World Wide Web and include a cyberspace address (URL) in their conventional media advertisements.

As the Pizza Hut narrative illustrates, select companies are taking the notion of on-line advertising to its next logical step: on-line purchasing. Home pages containing rich and vibrant high-resolution graphics convey information about the product and electronic alternatives for ordering through the computer. Now, when a person does a little Web surfing, he might bring home a catch—downloaded shareware programs, a print-out of a magazine article, or even a new car.

Many electronic storefronts are linked together to form virtual malls. The basic design of a virtual mall is the same as any home page; its hypertext links connect users to various stores that are part of the mall. One such virtual mall is eShop, which allows shoppers to choose from six avenues of storefronts. Tower Records, Spiegel, The Good Guys, L'eggs, Insight, and 1–800-Flowers are only a click away (Moeller 34). Another such location is marketplaceMCI, where Champs Sports, Lillian Vernon, an X-Files Store, and Foot Locker are open for business all day and all night. However, of the four stores in marketplaceMCI, only the X-Files boutique and Foot Locker are equipped to make on-line sales. The other locations require shoppers to print out invoices and surface-mail them to the retailers.

Just as there are malls and stand-alone stores along your local state route, the information superhighway sports shopping centers and single business sites, too. For example, at the Warner Brothers Studio Store, a customer can browse through an on-line catalog featuring <u>Friends</u> and <u>Batman</u> souvenirs and various products relating to the company's many television and movie productions. You can send a virtual postcard from the Warner Bros. site. Once the card is selected and information composed and entered, a message is sent via e-mail to the card's recipient, who can claim his or her mail by visiting the Warner Bros. site.

Ordering from a Web site is simple and user-friendly. At most on-line stores, once the customers find the items they wish to purchase, they click on them and the products are sent to a virtual shopping basket. Customers click on links that take them to the order form, where they can choose between submitting their order electronically, over the phone, or via surface mail. If they choose electronic ordering, they must enter pertinent information, such as name, address, credit card number and expiration date, etc., all of which is e-mailed to the retailer.

Many buyers balk at the last steps in this process. Consumers have no problem browsing through the Web pages, viewing products and window shopping, but when it comes time to click the "submit" icon, a twinge of anxiety manifests itself. The reason for fear is the "public perception that the Internet is a dangerous place" (Weise 1), a place through which vital information should not pass. In the mind of John Williams, chair and CEO of Computer Services, Inc., businesses have not taken full advantage of the opportunities available to securely hold on to the valuable sixteen-digit credit card numbers that buyers submit.

A question about confidence in Internet credit card security posted to two listserves got sixteen responses about how people felt when it came time to send their credit card numbers over the Internet. Answers to the question were varied: some users will not enter banking data, others are not certain whether they can adapt to this new form of ordering goods, and some believe it is the optimal way to conduct transactions. One user emphatically stated, "Never. I feel it is a very stupid idea to use a credit card online. It is dangerous." (Crowe). Michelle Kohorst, responding to the on-line posting, was hesitant: "I actually don't know that the Internet is less secure than in-person transactions, but it just gives the appearance of being open and available to anyone with hacking abilities." However, Josh Sherman disagreed, saying, "online [purchasing] is a preferred method of buying everything except special order goods."

The views reflected above generally mirror the national attitude toward on-line purchasing. A sense of faith and trust in the Internet and the companies that employ its powerful marketing features is missing. All of the new technology is simply overwhelming for consumers, and no one is sure about it. A major factor in feeling comfortable with on-line purchasing is merely taking the time to sort out the issues. Many consumers express ignorance about on-line shopping options. At the present time, there are no solid reassurances for consumers. Even those who hasten to ensure buyers that this new medium is safe seem to overqualify their claims. David N. Bodley, who wrote an article on security at the South Florida Mall Web site, writes that "there have been no major, consistent or organized reported thefts of funds transferred electronically." Then, too, the occasional news story about a "bored graduate student" stealing thousands of files containing credit card numbers discourages the already skeptical Web user (Weise 1). Bad press is not the only deterrent to on-line sales; the technical terms and concepts used to describe Internet security are not exactly user-friendly or trust-inspiring.

Dr. Paul Buis, an assistant professor in the computer science department at Ball State University, believes that "[computer] technology is very complex, and that complexity is frightening. On the other hand, so is the technology in an automobile, the telephone, and an airplane." The complexities to which Dr. Buis refers include the intricate facets involved in ensuring computer security.

Microsoft, VISA, and MasterCard are assisting in the development of technology that secures the transactions of customers who shop on-line. By implementing the Secured Transaction Technology (STT), developed by Microsoft, the two credit card companies hope to create a standard that companies such as Netscape and Mosaic can incorporate into their Internet browsers ("Microsoft's transactions" 15). Browsers are not only the software programs that allow users to surf the Web but also the same tools through which security measures must be implemented. Those measures include cryptography, firewalls, and secured operating systems—all of which are still alien to most computer users. The three components are necessary, however, to ensure a secure transaction, and one weak link can disable the security of an entire system (Five Paces).

The first piece of the security puzzle is cryptography. Basically, "cryptography ('hidden writing') involves the translation of a message in plain language into one in a secret language" (Sattler). Two types of encryption are used today to translate the credit card number and expiration date into meaningless zeros and ones: one is public-key and the other is symmetric-key encryption. In order to understand how the two differ, it is important to understand how encryption takes place.

In translating a message, one algorithmic key is used to encrypt (into the secret language) the data, and another key is used to decrypt it (into plain language). Symmetric-key cryptography requires the sender to encrypt the message with a key and then separately e-mail both the key and the message along to the recipient. A greater possibility of interception and eventual decryption exists with that method of encoding text. In contrast, public-key encryption, patented by RSA Data Security, relies on two separate keys to translate the message. The sender only has to e-mail a message, and the recipient is able to decrypt it with a similar key at hand (Five Paces).

When a shopper finds an item (or items), he or she enters all of the required data on the order form, and using an encryption method that is incorporated as part of the Web site or the e-mail program, the order form is encrypted and sent along to the merchant. Once the merchant receives the order form, a key is used to decrypt the information, and the retailer checks to make sure the customer has the available credit. Finally, if the credit checks out, the order is processed, the account is billed, and the transaction is over (Lane).

In a telephone interview with Mike Geltz, a senior Web site technical writer for Gateway 2000, I found that even though Gateway's home page does not support on-line purchases, orders are taken on a limited basis. Public transactions are not yet an option, but about ten orders are taken each month from private institutions, such as the Federal Credit Union. Purchases are made via the company's experimental Stealth Division Web site, which allows for a secure transaction of funds and data. The method by which an order is taken is relatively similar to how other retailers conduct business. The order is made from a secure server (https, rather than http), encrypted with a program called Pretty Good Privacy (PGP), and then it is e-mailed to Geltz. From there, he decrypts the order form and sends the necessary information on to the shipping and billing departments. He said Gateway is in the process of hiring a man from Switzerland who will develop security for its Web site. Someday, consumers will have the ability to use their old computer system to order its replacement. When I asked Geltz about the security of the Internet in general, he said that no matter how much security is developed, it will never reach a level of ultimate perfection. Nothing is an absolute.

Of the three components of secure technology, cryptography is the most important, since it provides the secure transaction of valuable data. However, it does not keep unauthorized users from accessing the information once it reaches its destination server. At that point, a firewall becomes necessary. A firewall "controls traffic between outside and inside a network, providing a single choke point where access controls and auditing can be imposed" (Five Paces). In other words, imagine all the information a computer holds sitting behind a massive, impregnable wall, with only a small, heavily guarded door for outsiders to enter. When MCS/Universal Studios and First National Bank of Chicago first began to enter cyberspace, one of their biggest concerns was keeping external sites from breaking into the internal infrastructure of their computer systems. A firewall was needed (Nash 70).

Finally, the third component, a secure operating system, picks up where the firewall leaves off. A firewall is excellent for controlling unauthorized access, but it does not eliminate internal attacks. The UNIX operating system supports the roots of the Internet, and it is also the operating system that creates the sense of openness that worries users like Ms. Kohorst (quoted earlier). The entire Internet system is centered on an omnipotent account, which, if broken into, would grant the hacker uncontrollable access to all accounts (Five Paces). Microsoft is currently working on incorporating the existing security enhancements in the Windows NT operating system into the UNIX system to act as a secure location for data (Microsoft, "Microsoft Previews"). Only the merchant, who would have a username and password, would have access to the secure areas of information, such as credit card number lists (Microsoft, "Electronic Retailing").

All of the aspects of electronic security covered so far in this paper are necessary and indispensable to the security of online shopping. Despite all that the companies may implement, for some "the problem is entirely a perception of danger, not of reality" (Buis). Once that perception is dissolved, customers can fully realize the advantages of the World Wide Web. Of the participants in the on-line marketing movement, Microsoft is leading the way in revolutionizing shopping in the world with its designs for electronic retailing strategies.

According to Bill Gates, chair and CEO of Microsoft, electronic retailing will include the "development of a compelling shopping experience, automatic order handling, payment security, tools for analyzing purchasing patterns, and integration with a merchant's supply chain" (Microsoft, "Electronic Retailing"). All links in the purchasing chain are represented in Microsoft's plan. Customers are assured of a secure transaction, offered a new method of shopping, and given the opportunity to shop at any time they wish. Down the road, Microsoft plans to include a shopping utility in the Windows operating system that will allow customers easy access to various on-line shopping locations. In turn, the merchants will increase revenues, lower costs, and create specialized markets vis customized home pages for customers (Microsoft, "Microsoft Previews"). The number of people who are on-line will greatly expand the market base retailers can reach with products and services. Also, with only a home page and the necessary links to keep up, money will not go toward maintenance of physical store locations. The retailer will have the ability to cater to the individual preferences of shoppers by creating "communities of shared interest and customized one-on-one relationships with customers" (Microsoft, "Electronic Retailing").

Joining Microsoft in the push to develop the on-line marketplace is the nation's largest retailer, Wal-Mart. David Glass, president and CEO of Wal-Mart, Inc., stated, "Microsoft has a solid vision for solving the challenge of electronic retailing on the Internet, and this is why we have chosen Microsoft technologies and products to expand our business and reach new customers through the Internet" (Microsoft, "Microsoft Previews"). In the race to reach new customers, the Wal-Mart home page will feature thousands of products ranging from computer software to gift items, with additional items appearing as the months pass ("Letters to").

Regardless of Microsoft's vigorous plan to offer advanced shopping features, a few universal advantages exist from which every company and customer can benefit. Shopping on-line provides customers with a wider selection of products and facilitates comparative shopping. One on-line buyer claims that "in terms of comparison shopping, it is easier to 'compare specs' via computer, and the variety increases everyday. I ... have found higher quality and lower price[s] via on-line vendors as opposed to local electronics warehouses" (Franc). Ultimately, pricing will become more competitive, since retailers will have to compete with a much larger market in cyberspace. As on-line shopping becomes more widely used, its speed and effectiveness will increase to meet the demands of customers. And if customers are dissatisfied with service at one site, the next is only a second away.

Internet purchasing is a widespread economic boon. First of all, customers will need a means of accessing the Web. Internet service providers, such as America Online, Prodigy, CompuServe, and the Microsoft Network, along with local direct access providers, and cable carriers will become as essential to the economy as regular telephone lines are today. Delivery services, likewise, will proliferate and prosper.

When the projected on-line shopping movement is in full swing, the resulting economic growth will be staggering. According to a survey conducted by ActivMedia, an on-line analysis group that specializes in quantitative studies of on-line marketing, the future of on-line shopping looks promising. One survey indicated that "sales generated by the Web are expected to grow from $436 million in 1995 to nearly $46 billion by 1998" ("Sales Trends"). The predicted growth is in part due to the ever-increasing attention the on-line market is receiving. Such a medium gives the small and mid-sized marketers a chance to compete on-line and receive the overall revenue increase.

The marketplace of the future is becoming more geographically diverse ("Sales Trends"). Profits are already noticeable in a variety of online markets, including "computer-related hardware, software, and other high-tech equipment, travel services, investments, training, boilerplate legal services, prestige real estate, male-orientated luxury goods, specialty hobbies and crafts, technical employment services, audio recordings and consumer electronics" (ActivMedia, "Trends"). Regardless of growth, ActivMedia believes businesses will continue to experiment and test the Web. As we reach the next millennium, every major company around the globe will find its business has been altered because of the World Wide Web (ActivMedia, "The Future").

Does this mean that instead of families' packing into the sedan to go to the mall they will simply huddle around the computer? Will physical stores go the way of Green Stamps? Probably not. Conventional shopping is not going to come to an abrupt halt; people will still go to malls and use catalogs and will still call Pizza Hut and drive over to the restaurant to pick up their own pizzas. Cyberspace is not going to replace the physical realm, after all.

Works Cited

ActivMedia, Inc. "Trends in the World Wide Web Marketplace." http:// www.activmedia.com. 29 April 1996.

Bodley, David N. "South Florida Mall: Commercial and Credit Card Security on the Internet." http://sf-mall.com. 14 April 1996.

Buis, Paul. E-mail interview. 29 March 1996.

Crowe, Cheryl. "RE: In Need of Some Opinions." E-mail to Kyle Parker. 21 Feb. 1996.

Five Paces Software, Inc. "Internet Banking Security." http://www .fivepaces.com. 20 April 1996.

Franc. "RE: In Need of Some Opinions." E-mail to Kyle Parker. 22 Feb. 1996.

Geltz, Mike. Telephone Interview. 19 Feb. 1996.

Kohorst, Michelle. "RE: In Need of Some Opinions" E-mail to Kyle Parker. 22 Feb. 1996.

Lane, Hillary. "Internet Security Hinders Cyber-shopping Growth." Hillary@dash.com. 24 Feb. 1996.

McLaughlin. Laurianne. "Survey Says: Growing but Still Small Population Using the Web."

Microsoft Corporation. "Electronic Retailing-FAQ." www.microsoft.com.

- - -. "Microsoft Previews Electronic Retailing Strategy and Technology to World's Leading Retailers." http://www.microsoft.com. 12 Feb. 1996.

"Microsoft's Transaction Technology on Way to Ubiquity." Windows Watcher. (Sept. 1995): 15.

Moeller, Michael. "Let's Hang Out at the E-mall: eShop Opens Its Doors to Tower Records, Spiegel on the Web." PC Week (6 Nov. 1995): 34.

Nash, Kim S. "Firms Learn 'Net Security Lessons." Computer World 29 (1995): 70.

OpenMarket, Inc. http://www.directory.net/dir/statstics.html. 15 March 1996.

PCWorld Online. http://www.pcworld.com. 30 March 1996.

Sattler, Michael. "Basic Issues and Concepts in Privacy and Cryptography." Webmaster@jungle.com. 13 Nov. 1995.

Sherman, Josh. "RE: In Need of Some Opinions." E-mail to Kyle Parker. 20 Feb. 1996.

Wal-Mart, Inc. "Letters to the President." E-mail to Kyle Parker. 19 Feb. 1996.

Weise, Elizabeth. "Experts: Internet Purchases Safe as Mail Ordering." <u>The Ball State Daily News</u> 22 Jan. 1996: 1.

Williams, John. Telephone interview. 25 March 1996.

■ Summing Up

As your forays into various indexes have revealed, there are many possible ways to document, or describe the location of articles and other secondary-source materials. In most disciplines, professional societies and leading journals have agreed on standard documentation styles for their field. The Modern Language Association (MLA) and Chicago Style documentation systems are widespread, accepted formats, used predominantly in the arts and humanities.

The *MLA Handbook for Writers of Research Papers,* fourth edition, edited by Joseph Gibaldi and published in New York City by the Modern Language Association in 1995, contains a complete, detailed explanation of that arts and humanities documentation style. The *Chicago Manual of Style,* 14th ed., 1993, describes Chicago Style. It dictates how to cite sources within the text of a paper, as well as how to format the entries in a Works Cited list at the end of the work or in footnotes and endnotes. Examples demonstrate how to cite secondary sources such as books, articles by single or multiple authors, government publications, private correspondence, Internet postings, and interviews. The handbooks also prescribe how outlines, margins, page numbers, notes, titles, graphs, and tables should be presented in papers in the arts and humanities.

Memorizing all of the conventions listed in the MLA or Chicago Style handbooks is unnecessary. The systems are logical, and the examples in the handbook are straightforward. Keep a copy of the handbook you are using on hand and consult it while you are preparing your final draft. Correctly using the MLA or Chicago Style format will make your work readily accessible to readers and give it the same professional appearance as articles in respected journals and books.

Exercises: Sources and Strategies

1. Compile a final Works Cited list for your research paper, and exchange it with a classmate. Try to name the *kind* of source (for example, a book by a single author, an article in a journal that numbers pages consecutively) represented by each item on your peer's list.

2. Review your own Works Cited list, and categorize the kinds of sources you have used. What does this teach you about your research strategies and the types of evidence you have chosen to use?

3. Try to locate full copies of a dozen or so of the items cited in the published articles you have read during your researching process. How many of the items cited in your most useful source can you find in your own library? What does that demonstrate about the kinds of sources used by professional writers?

Writing to Know

Complete the final version of your researched paper, and write your own evaluation of your work. What would you do differently or the same if you had the project to do over again?

Chapter Fifteen

Creating Alternative Media Presentations

R esearch is like gossip: sooner or later you'll have learned enough fascinating details and fit enough mysterious bits of information together
that you'll just have to tell it all to someone else. You could talk obsessively
about your subject among your friends and family, trying always to steer the
topic of conversation back to euthanasia, seat belt laws, landfill regulations,
the human genome project, or whatever, or you could present your findings
in a format that will encourage people who are genuinely interested in your
topic to hear what you have to say about it. There are many ways to present
your research findings to a wide audience, and several alternative media provide opportunities for your findings to be seen by many more people than
just the instructor who will grade your work. Although most college writing
classes require a standard, ten- to twenty-page research paper as the final
product of a research assignment, your instructor may ask you to present
your project in another, more widely accessible medium as well, such as

   a public presentation,

   a storyboard or poster session,

   a World Wide Web site devoted to your topic, or

   a videotaped documentary.

   If you are interested in creative writing, public speaking, computer-
based design, or telecommunications, you may be able to combine skills in
one of those areas with your researching abilities to create a finished product that is as exciting to complete as it was to contemplate. Don't think,
though, that presenting your research findings in a format other than the
usual research paper will require less writing or planning. In all cases, some
kind of script or text is required, and considerations of other elements (such
as graphic design, computer proficiency, and so on) are added to the job.
Alternative media presentations usually require more time, effort, writing,
planning, and last-minute crises than the standard research paper assignment creates.

◼ Public Presentations

There is no better way to measure public reaction to your ideas than to clearly state them in front of an attentive audience. Giving a conference paper or public lecture is perhaps the most immediate way to gauge audience receptiveness to your ideas and to gain immediate feedback about your proposals. Preparing a public presentation of your research also increases your awareness of your audience. A wide range of responses is possible from an audience, and you will almost certainly be speaking both to people who agree with you and to people who disagree with you. You may choose to enhance your presentation with handouts, computer graphic "slides," charts, photographs, film clips, audio recordings, or other media that are accessible to twenty or thirty viewers or listeners at once. Distribute a copy of your Works Cited list to your audience along with any illustrations or other handouts that you plan to circulate, so your listeners can see the range of background work you have accomplished and examine any of your source materials firsthand if they wish.

Your class can stage its own conference by grouping papers on similar topics together and scheduling time for several students to read or lecture on their research. Because you probably feel comfortable in front of your classmates by now, it is a good idea to invite some outsiders to join your classroom conference audience. That way you will be "on the spot" somewhat and prompted to do your best. Consider inviting local authorities whom you have consulted during your research or faculty and students from a related academic discipline. Or arrange to present your final research project in front of a different class than the one for which you prepared it. Many advanced college courses and professional jobs require presentations as a way of communicating ideas and information. You can use this classroom experience to help shape your style and determine a process by which you will prepare for presentations.

◼ Poster Sessions

If your group is short on class time in which to stage an extended conference, you could host an information fair instead, with each student contributing a storyboard or poster session or presentation. These are graphic and textual presentations set up on tables or in small booths, consisting of one to three 2- to 3-foot posters or storyboards. You might be able to conduct such a fair in a hallway one afternoon by attaching your posters to the walls. Invite interested faculty and students from other writing classes to attend, and elicit their responses to your presentation. You can distribute copies of your outline, Works Cited list, or entire paper to interested visitors.

Think of a poster session project in terms of your thesis and main arguments, like an outline. Communicate as much as you can about your topic with graphics, and reduce the text on your posters to essential elements of your research project. Because your topic is probably too complex for you to fully explain it and persuasively argue your thesis on three posters, you may want to gear your session toward convincing spectators to take a copy of your paper away with them and read it. You should plan to be present for the duration of your class's information fair so that you can answer questions and engage visitors in conversation about your topic. It is usually pleasant to meet people and guide them through an issue with the aid of graphic illustrations and text on boards, because it creates a focused conversation about a commonly held interest. Poster sessions are a relatively low-stress method of making public presentations.

■ World Wide Web Sites

A Web site on your topic is only a scanner and some Hypertext Mark-Up Language (HTML) away from a poster session. A Web page can be like a virtual poster session, with the potential for an enormous audience. If you post your paper on the Web, make sure you put it in some context by including it as part of your personal Web page or linking it to a college or class site. If you have a Web page of your own, you could attach it to that site and explain that it is a research paper prepared for a writing course. Include a link to your e-mail address, and invite readers to contact you directly with questions or comments.

If your instructor or class maintains a Web site containing the course syllabus, handouts, and chat rooms for class discussions, you may be able to append your research projects to that site. If everyone in the class does not have Web design experience, students could pool their skills (typing, graphic design, proofreading, Web publishing, source checking, and so on) and construct a common Web site posting all students' research projects. Or use your research skills and get onto the Web yourself to download shareware that enables you to write in Java script or some other Web-compatible format. Seek help from on-line sources and campus consultants. If you have text on disk in a common word processing format, you should be able to put it up on the World Wide Web without even retyping it.

Although graphics are not mandatory on Web pages, many sites make use of the Web's graphic capabilities and are illustrated or even animated. You can scan in images that you would include in a poster session or as part of your text, or, using your Web browser, you can download free graphics from other sites. (Make sure that any graphics you download are not copyrighted and that the site owner has explicitly given his or her permission for you to take graphics from the site.) Spend some time designing your Web site thoughtfully, so that incorporated graphics and hyperlinks enhance the persuasive power of your text. Remember that if text is too long, too dense, too small, hard to decipher, or difficult to concentrate on on a computer screen, it will not be read on the Web.

Publication on the World Wide Web is just that (publication), and you must ensure that you have not violated any copyright laws in the presentation of your manuscript. Include your Works Cited list as part of your text. If you cited other Web sites in your research project, you can hyperlink entries in your Works Cited list to those URLs for your readers' convenience. The Web is massive, and most users are "surfers," or casual browsers, so although your site may get several "hits," you might not get much feedback in the initial days after posting. It provides a real-world test for beginning researchers, however, because it takes their work out of the supportive confines of academia and puts it right out there to compete side by side with commercial sites and the work of professional writers. Be prepared for a wide range of responses to research projects posted to the Web: everything from no response at all to vociferous criticism is possible.

■ *Video*

Why not make a movie about your topic? Your school probably has video equipment that students can borrow for use in class projects. Think about how parts of your research could be dramatized or your text could be used as voice-over with archival footage (available in your library's audiovisual department) or original footage. Watch television news and magazine shows carefully to see how video clips are structured and used. You could follow a documentary format or pattern your production after political roundtable debate shows or news presentations. Enlist your classmates and friends as actors and cinematographers, and start shooting. If you make your video for classroom use only, you can recruit friends to impersonate authorities and the authors of source material and have them actually *say* the quotations you want to include. As long as you don't misrepresent anything or anyone in the video version of your research project, you could offer it to the local-access cable channel in your area for possible screening on television.

Video production is extremely time-consuming. Whether you use one camera or two, built-in microphones or microphones mounted on booms or clips, natural or artificial light, studio sets or actual locations, your work will require a lot of repetition to compensate for human and mechanical errors. You usually don't know that a shot hasn't worked until you've folded up all of the equipment and released all of the actors for the day, so sometimes you will have to retrace your steps. Later, you'll discover that editing videotape is intense work, requiring patience and diligence. Professional video editors estimate that it takes about thirty minutes to process one minute of finished footage—and that is after it has made it into the editing bay. You may have to edit your tapes with a makeshift system consisting of two VCRs, but even if your school can loan you state-of-the-art editing tools, the results you get probably won't be equal to the video footage you are used to seeing on television. Don't be discouraged by this—there is a reason that film school admissions are so competitive. Knowing that your video production will not meet professional cinematography standards, you can and should concentrate your efforts primarily on the script.

Making a video version of your research project is an exciting and enjoyable way to learn about pacing, tone, and organization—which are elements of all narrative media, including research papers. Video production is, by necessity, group work, and it is a lot less lonely than the solitary task of typing a research paper until dawn. It requires collaborative writing and planning, and you may be surprised at how creative you and your friends can be with the equipment you are issued and a shoestring budget. You have probably grown up with television as part of your everyday information-rich milieu. It is a lot of fun to begin creating in the media that has been a large part of your life.

■ Kyle's Web Page

Kyle considered posting a draft of his research paper to his personal World Wide Web page, but he decided it was "too dry and way too technical" to keep the interest of Web surfers. However, he felt strongly that consumers should be encouraged to make purchases on-line, so that retailers will be encouraged to offer more goods and services on-line. Kyle believes that on-line shopping increases convenience, facilitates customer service, and will simplify the lives of consumers and retailers. Since virtual stores require no parking lots, no strip mall developments, and no unattractive signs on the horizon, and customers don't need to drive anywhere to visit them, Kyle

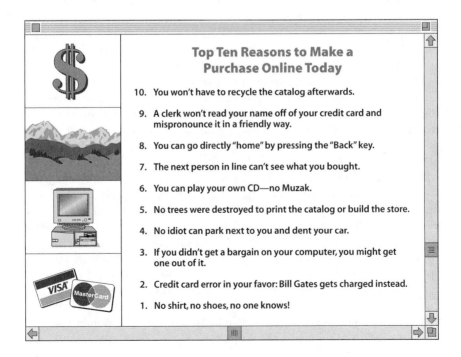

Top Ten Reasons to Make a Purchase Online Today

10. You won't have to recycle the catalog afterwards.

9. A clerk won't read your name off of your credit card and mispronounce it in a friendly way.

8. You can go directly "home" by pressing the "Back" key.

7. The next person in line can't see what you bought.

6. You can play your own CD—no Muzak.

5. No trees were destroyed to print the catalog or build the store.

4. No idiot can park next to you and dent your car.

3. If you didn't get a bargain on your computer, you might get one out of it.

2. Credit card error in your favor: Bill Gates gets charged instead.

1. No shirt, no shoes, no one knows!

thinks they will be good for the environment, too. He wanted to get this message out to Web surfers, the people who are in a position to make purchases on-line. Although his research paper provided a medium for in-depth exploration of various issues surrounding credit card use on the Internet, including such technical topics as encryption, he thought that most visitors to his Web site would appreciate a lighter treatment of the topic. Therefore he posted the following "Top Ten" list on his personal Web site and followed it up with hyperlinks to retail sites equipped to process credit card sales as well as to a draft of his research paper.

■ Summing Up

Most college writing courses will require you to submit your final research project as a traditional paper, but the information you have collected can be presented using a variety of media. You or your instructor might want the information you have amassed to be showcased in a public presentation, in a poster session, on a World Wide Web site, or in a videotaped "show." All of these alternative media are fun and challenging formats, but be prepared that they will probably require a greater commitment of time and effort than a traditional paper usually does. In addition to organizing and presenting your arguments, you will also have to master some new skills, ranging from public speaking to graphic illustration and video editing. In return for the extra effort required, these alternative media can reach a wide audience—anywhere from a roomful of people to the whole world of the Internet. Thus they can be a very effective way to get your point across.

Creating alternative media presentations may utilize skills you have honed in other courses (such as speech, computer science, art, or theater classes), and they may require you to seek the cooperation and assistance of others, both fellow students in your course and people with specific expertise needed for your project. Even if the results you get are not as professional looking or sounding as you hoped, you will learn valuable lessons about the constraints and possibilities inherent in presenting research in another medium besides a written paper.

Exercises: Sources and Strategies

1. Make an outline of your research project that you could use to talk through the subject in a conference presentation.

2. Design and make posters that clearly communicate your thesis. Scan the posters and upload them to a class or personal Web site.

3. Using desktop publishing software, create a newsletter or brochure version of your research paper. Break the essay down into several smaller

articles, and give "chunks" of information bold headings. Use color, graphics, and photographs to make the pages attractive and inviting. Do you prefer this kind of design-intensive format to the traditional research paper look?

Writing to Know

Write a script for a video documentary about your research topic. List the visuals you want to use and the text that will accompany them. Include music and camera angles in your script notations.

PART THREE

Student Researchers

*U*ndoubtedly, your own experiences in researching, drafting, and revising a research paper has sometimes coincided with as well as differed from that of Kyle Parker as described in this book. One of the great things about research paper assignments is the individuality they permit, giving students freedom to explore topics they are curious about and to develop their own style as researchers. Depending on the resources around you, you may have found your best data in your library's reference or bound periodicals sections, or you might have uncovered some amazing evidence from a primary source. It isn't necessary, or even preferable, to incorporate all of the kinds of sources covered in this book in a single college research paper. For virtually any topic, there exists a multitude of research possibilities, and no researcher or paper could possibly encompass them all.

The papers written by the student researchers described here use a variety of sources. Some depend heavily on library research, others on the World Wide Web, and still others on personal experience and primary research. Each of the writers represented here has made choices about how to define, focus, research, and present his or her topic. As you read through these papers, you will see both work that you admire and instances where you could have done a better job. Each paper has strong points and elements that would benefit from another revision. These papers are "model essays" only in the sense that they are examples supplied for study. They are not uniformly exemplary work or "models" in the sense of setting a standard for others to emulate. All of the writers are undergraduate students, and these papers were prepared for ordinary college composition courses. Close reading of these papers should give you some ideas about how to conduct and present your own research. Talking about these examples with your classmates, teachers, and friends will help you see the results of choices researchers and writers make.

The first two examples here are formatted according to APA guidelines, but notice that there are variations within that style. Brian Seelig's paper uses the References list format for papers that will be submitted to professional scientific journals, indenting the first lines of each item on the list. Carole Kirsch's paper omits subheadings, which is permissible in a brief paper. It conforms closely to the APA style proscribed for college course assignments.

The last three examples in Part Three are presented in the MLA style, with permissible variations. Cathy Bennett's paper contains a formal outline, so it begins with a cover page. Sean Slagle's and Tim Peters's essays include the traditional cover sheet information in a text block in the upper left-hand corner of the first page of text, as is recommended for college research papers printed in the MLA style.

As you now know, research papers must conform to rigorous guidelines, but much flexibility and room for creativity remains. Notice, for instance, that Brian's essay contains a pie chart that he constructed using his word processing program's tables and charts function. As computer hard drives get larger and artwork becomes easier to import, graphic images will be even easier to add to text. The research projects that you prepare in the future will undoubtedly differ from the ones you have completed this semester, but you have learned the basics on which you will continue to build and experiment.

■ Student Researcher: Brian Seelig

Brian Seelig's research paper about interstellar travel could easily have ventured into outer space itself. Propulsion physics is a complicated subject that can quickly become incomprehensible to those outside the scientific community. In this paper, Brian has worked to keep his subject accessible to a wide variety of readers. He avoids using scientific jargon as much as possible, and he defines terms such as *BPP* and *annihilation* when he uses them.

An on-line interview with physicist Lawrence Krauss gives depth to his paper because Krauss is ambivalent about funding interstellar travel research. He calls the BPP "a waste of money," yet concedes that the study of propulsion physics is "a good idea." Brian's paper may seem a bit confusing and wishy-washy, because the scientists who comment on the issue are dubiously supportive of the project, and although the author is enthusiastic about the idea, as a beginning college student he is respectful of the experts' skepticism.

Brian believes that the BPP should be funded so that scientists will be poised to take advantage of it when a breakthrough making interstellar travel a real possibility occurs. In his paper's conclusion, however, he argues for the NASA program for more middle-of-the-road reasons: because possible spin-offs from the research will benefit mankind on Earth.

Notice that Brian has indented the items on his References list seemingly unconventionally. Actually the APA recommends indenting the first line of each item (instead of using hanging indents for subsequent lines of each item) on papers that will be sent to scientific journals. It is conventional for typesetters to reverse the indentation of references items when the article is formatted for publication. He does not plan to submit this paper to a professional journal, but he is training himself now in the habits of a research scientist.

Interstellar Travel: Searching for a Breakthrough

Submitted by

Brian Seelig

Dr. Rai Peterson

English 103

July 24, 1998

Abstract

Interstellar travel has captured people's imaginations through fiction for a long time, but it is still impossible in reality. The problems are the great distance between stars and man's current inability to exceed the speed of light. It is currently impossible to equip a rocket ship with enough fuel to complete an interstellar mission.

Notable physicists Alcubierre and Lagoute have worked out warp theory, but a breakthrough in space travel is needed to realize their plans. NASA currently has a Breakthrough Propulsion Physics (BPP) program, but it is in danger of losing its funding because of detractors in the scientific community. Many peripheral gains could be made if the program were expanded. Man will probably not travel to other galaxies in our lifetime, but we should act now so that our descendents will be prepared when the breakthrough occurs.

From the Evening Inter-planetary News Report: "Today the interplanetary research spaceship, Warp 182, successfully landed on a new planet near the Epsilon Eridani star. Scientists hope to discover life-supporting conditions and observe the galaxy surrounding the planet. In other news, a recent census shows colonies near Tau Ceti have almost doubled since last year. A marketing director from Boeing suggests the increase is because of advancements in interstellar travel."

Interstellar travel

Although the above newscast is fiction, many scientists are working on projects that could make such ideas reality. The main reasons traveling to stars is so difficult is because they are so far away. Even the closest star is over 25 trillion miles from Earth. In order to make a trip to a star or galaxy in a reasonable amount of time—say, in a human lifetime—one would require a ship that could travel at or beyond the speed of light. Two major obstacles exist for traveling at the speed of light. One, the amount of propellant required to accelerate a ship to light speed is unimaginable. Second, "special relativity, formulated by Albert Einstein ... forbids it" (Greenwald, 1998).

A decade ago scientists believed science fiction stories like Star Trek and Star Wars would remain fiction. A number of recent papers in journals and speeches, however, have sparked an interest in interstellar travel research. In 1994, an astrophysicist named Miguel Alcubierre published a paper on warp drives. Alcubierre explains how rapid speeds can be obtained by warping space-time. In theory, warp drives will work. Humans will not be warping anytime soon, though. Currently, nothing is capable of generating the amount of energy needed to warp (1994). A recent paper published in the American Journal of Physics provides formulae for interstellar travel. The authors admit the necessary technology is not yet available. Although the formulae are of no use today, when the technology is ready, scientists will have the necessary information (Lagoute, 1995).

Breakthroughs needed

The universe holds many mysteries. If scientists could get closer to the stars and other galaxies, numerous mysteries could be solved. The installation of a telescope in a remote area could provide scientists with information for charting the universe (Guterl, 1995). Life on Earth will not last forever. Space explorers could discover a planet, similar to Earth, where humanity could settle some day.

A breakthrough in propulsion physics would make such exploration possible. Currently, the main technology used for sending objects into space is large rockets filled with chemical propellants. Rockets are sufficient for launching objects into space, but the energy required to travel to even the nearest galaxy will require a new technology. Technologies such as nuclear and fusion propulsion were considered, but these are difficult to control under high temperatures (Guterl, 1995).

NASA's program

Realizing the need for a breakthrough, NASA created a program to make progress in the area of propulsion physics. In 1996, NASA established the Breakthrough Propulsion Physics (BPP) program at the Lewis Research Center (LeRC) in Cleveland, Ohio. Marc Millis, a rocket scientist at LeRc, heads the program. As explained on the BPP Web site, the program has three goals: "(1) Discover new propulsion methods that eliminate or dramatically reduce the need for propellant.... (2) Discover how to attain the ultimate achievable transit speeds to dramatically reduce travel times.... (3) Discover fundamentally new on-board energy production methods to power propulsion devices" (1998). The BPP program hosts workshops for brainstorming ideas, reviewing papers, and examining new technologies. Attendance is by invitation only. Eighty-four of ninety people attended the last workshop, and many ideas were introduced. Even if an idea becomes a working project, it may never be finished. Each project "must be of relatively short duration (1–3 [years]) and modest cost ($50–150 [thousand])" ("Soliciting," 1998).

Threats to interstellar travel programs

Skeptical scientists responded negatively to the program. One argument is that too much is unknown about the universe. Gravity and the makeup of the universe still remain a mystery. Until scientists know more about physics, interstellar travel will be very difficult. Modern technology is another problem. No practical applications exist for moving through space at rapid speeds. Scientists also fear criticism from employers and colleagues. Interstellar travel is still only possible in movies and books. Many of the ideas currently being researched are very complex concepts. Physicists must ignore the absence of adequate technology and focus on their theories. For example, in Alcubierre's proof about warp drives, he ignores the absence of energy required to power the vehicle.

Well-known physicist Lawrence Krauss believes the BPP program "is a waste of money." Krauss was one of the fourteen physicists invited to the BPP workshop to give a presentation. In a recent interview with Wired, Krauss admits that, besides all the study on ideas like wormholes, the program is "a good idea" (1998). In a recent survey conducted by MSNBC, 2,228 people were asked

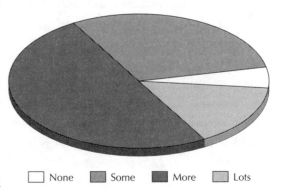

☐ None   ▨ Some   ▩ More   ▨ Lots

questions related to interstellar travel. Figure 1 is a graphical representation of one of the responses MSNBC received to the question, "How much attention should researchers devote to faster-than-light travel and anomalous physics" ("Science," 1998)? Although the survey included any visitor on MSNBC's Web site, it reveals interesting results. Seventy-six percent of the people polled believe interstellar travel will be possible in the next 200 years. Only two percent believe it is impossible. Most scientists agree that interstellar travel will not be possible in the foreseeable future. Research should begin today, however, or we will be stuck on Earth forever and much of the universe will remain a mystery. Another interesting statistic from the MSNBS survey revealed that 69% of the people polled believe that more scientific research should be conducted in the area of interstellar travel ("Science," 1998). Of the fourteen keynote speakers at the BPP workshop, only two voiced negative thoughts toward the program.

Resolving the question

After a breakthrough discovery is made, a technology will be engineered. Research must begin at some point, and now is a good time to start. Lately scientists have published numerous papers and conducted a lot of research on interstellar travel. Perhaps the most amazing thing about research on interstellar travel is not all the dead ends researchers have encountered but how close they have come to discovering a breakthrough. Raymond Chiao, a popular theorist, has successfully accelerated photons beyond the speed of light. No technology is able to control when a photon exceeds light speed, though. Gerald Smith has conducted extensive research and experiments on antimatter. Antimatter is a negative form of matter. When antimatter collides with normal matter (annihilation), a larger amount of energy is released. Although scientists have produced antimatter, they cannot produce large quantities of it in a reasonable amount of time (Guterl, 1995). A light sail is another possible candidate for distant space travel. The light sail method works by focusing the sun's light on a thin metallic sail. The sail would weigh nearly a ton and stretch approximately a mile.

Even though scientists' research may not be used for interstellar travel, it could be used for practical applications here on Earth. Trains, jets, or portable computers could use antimatter annihilation as a source of energy. Even the theories proven wrong broaden scientists' perspective on physics.

Student Researcher: Brian Seelig   **301**

A breakthrough will not happen anytime soon—at least for three decades or so—according to Millis' observations. Even when a breakthrough is discovered, it may take more than a decade before technology is fully developed. Krauss does not believe a breakthrough will happen in our lifetime (Greenwald, 1998). Millis strongly believes, however, that research must begin now, or we may never explore the stars.

Scientists may not visit the stars and other galaxies in my lifetime, but scientists should begin searching for a breakthrough now. Millis coments on his Web page (in response to a question about how long until a breakthrough is found) that "we, as a society, will gain far more from trying to make such breakthroughs happen than if we didn't" (1998). I believe many interesting ideas, proofs, and technologies will be gained from the BPP program. Scientific breakthroughs, like the transistor, do not occur often. I believe, as do many scientists, that the government should continue funding the BPP program so that it can reach its full potential. Not only should government funding continue, but NASA should enlarge the program and its funds.

References

Alcubierre, M. (1994). The warp drive: hyper-fast travel within general relativity. Unpublished doctoral dissertation, Wales University, U.K.

Davoust, E., & Lagoute, C. (1995). The interstellar traveler. American Journal of Physics, 63, 221–27.

Greenwald, J. (1998, July). To infinity and beyond. Wired, 90–97.

Guterl, F. (1995, October). A small problem of propulsion. Discover, 100–09.

Millis, M. (1998). Warp drive, when? FAQ. Lewis Research Center. Retrieved July 18 from the World Wide Web: http://www.lerc.nasa.gov/WWW/PAO/html/warp/warpfaq.htm

MSNBC Space News. (1998) Science fiction or fact? MSNBC. Retrieved July 18,1998 from the World Wide Web: http://www.msnbc.com/modules/FlexSurvey/physics.asp

Naeye, Robert. (1996, August). Journey to the outer limits. Astronomy 36–44. Soliciting and supporting research tasks. Lewis Research Center. Retrieved July 21,1998 from the World Wide Web: http://www.lerc.nasa.gov/WWW/bpp/bpp_RESEARCH_TASKS.htm

■ Student Researcher: Carole Kirsch

Carole Kirsch's research paper is an example of an excellent choice of topic. A great deal of press is devoted to promoting organ donation, but very little is said against it publicly. This paper was difficult for Carole to write. She had kept her thoughts about organ donation to herself at work and, consequently, kept them from herself as well. As her readers, we can only guess what a watershed this assignment was for her. Although this research paper is not perfect, it stands out as a very memorable one because of the effectiveness of its imagery and the veracity of its voice. In researching this paper, Carole discovered not only what others had said about the issues but also what *she* wanted to say.

One of the strengths of Carole's paper is that she uses rational, persuasive, and ethical appeals to excellent effect. Also, since most of the rhetoric that those of us outside of the medical professions routinely encounter on this subject is in favor of organ donation, Carole's perspective is startling. Yet she manages to write a convincing paper with an inductive organizational pattern (telling her thesis at the outset).

This paper uses very few sources, and it depends too heavily on the evidence presented in *60 Minutes*, a show that is usually considered confrontational and sensational in its rhetorical strategies. The two print sources that Carole uses are from respected professional journals, and she augments those articles with a personal interview. Carole's own ethical credibility is considerable, and so she also uses her own experience as a source. Although this paper cites few print sources, Carole's firsthand knowledge of the topic is extensive. The result is a very persuasive paper that is hard to forget or refute.

Organ Donation: To Sign or Not to Sign

Carole Kirsch

Parkview Hospital

Abstract

The author is a surgery room nurse who has participated in organ harvesting operations and become disaffected with the process because of its inherent carnage and potential for corruption and contradiction of the Hippocratic Oath.

Pending legislation that would compensate surviving family members for donated organs will further jeopardize the integrity of the system. Financial compensation would create a market for human body parts and cast suspicion on an altruistic act.

Examples from television's <u>60 Minutes</u> suggest that patients suffer until their organs are taken and that organ harvests have been the cause of death in others. The author argues that organ transplantation has received positive press coverage, but no one ever talks about the negative aspects of organ harvests.

Organ Donation: To Sign or Not to Sign

Organ procurement (or donating an individual's organs after his/her death) is not a topic about which friends and family sit around the dinner table and talk. More than likely the subject isn't brought up until the need arises. The family is in a crisis period, hardly a time to be discussing and second-guessing what the deceased would want. I have performed my fair share of "harvests," or procurements, during my nursing career. I will in no way have this act of violence (as I view it) happen to me, and I will strongly discourage my family members from giving consent to donate their organs.

Treatment of Donors

An article in <u>Canadian Nurse</u> notes that significant barriers to organ procurement start with the nurses and physicians (Molzahn, 1996). I know from my experience that this is true. My strong feelings stem from the perspective as an operating room nurse helping to perform the harvests. There appears to be little, if any, respect for the donor on the operating table or for the personnel in the room. A chaotic four to six hours leaves me to clean up with what I view as a carcass that vultures have finished with. The idea is pretty graphic, but true. Molzahn writes about a study performed in Canada. One thousand two hundred thirty-nine nurses responded to questions regarding organ donations. Over half of the nurses reported that they do not like to become involved. Nearly a quarter did not like the time involvement, and 45.8 percent saw organ donation as a conflict of interest. Sixty-nine percent of these nurses reported that organ donation was emotionally demanding (1996). The last statistic is very accurate. When I finish with an organ harvest I want a chaplain in the room. Not for the donor's benefit, albeit he/she is dead, but for the operating room personnel. Depending on how the donor became brain dead, the story of his/her death could easily send me into tears.

Molzahn found that positive follow-up after a harvest had a positive effect on personal attitudes. This isn't true for me. Our hospital will receive a follow-up letter from the procurement agency revealing where the organs went and the success of the transplant. That's all fine and good, but where were they when I was pulling invasive lines from the body, putting on dressings to stop oozing bodily fluids, cleaning the body with cold water, applying the toe tag, and positioning the body in preparation for rigor mortis? In addition, Molzahn found some of the nurses had a hard time accepting that a brain-dead person no longer existed. The nurses believed it was preferable to let a patient die peacefully, rather than to "make everyone hang on while the donor process goes on" (1996). I couldn't agree with this more. There can be many hours lapsed between the time the physician declares brain death and the actual harvesting of organs begins.

I interviewed Lynn Driver, the clinical coordinator for the Indiana Organ Procurement Organization, more commonly known as IOPO. He was taken aback as I explained to him my feelings about procurements. However, he was willing to do his best to help me. As our discussion ensued, I realized that the main reasons for not becoming an organ donor are ethical and financial.

Reasons against organ donation

Driver mentioned several different reasons families did not care to donate a loved one's organs. Not all of the reasons reflect my views;

however, those reasons are meaningful to some other people. There is a delay in funeral arrangements. Families don't want to see the loved one suffer any longer, and they can't be guaranteed the organs are going to a recipient they would choose. The organs go to the sickest on the waiting list. Driver mentioned that families of different ethnic origins or religious backgrounds often do not want the organs of their loved ones to be transplanted to someone different from themselves.

Driver said that everyone in the system makes money from organ-procurement except the family of the deceased. The procuring and transplanting hospitals, the surgeons, the anesthesiologist, and the IOPO all benefit financially for procuring and transplanting. Medicare financially guarantees payment to these participants. There is legislative action pending that would award approximately $1,500 toward funeral expenses of organ donors. While I believe this is long overdue, there are people in the world who would be forced or coerced, by financial incentives, to make decisions they normally would not make. I believe that if the donor family is unable to make their decision from the heart, the proposed financial rewards could result in some selfish organ trade. It boils down to selling a loved one's body. I believe that is a repulsive business.

Financial incentives

DePalma and Townsend revealed in an article regarding the proposed financial incentives for organ donorship that altruistic donations are not keeping pace with the need for organs (1996). They note several possible ways to stimulate organ donation. These might include insurance money for funeral expenses available only to organ donors, reduced estate taxes, or free medical care. I still believe that if money prompts the decision to donate, it is being done for the wrong reasons. DePalma and Townsend list oppositions to incentives as follows: altruism becomes questionable, financially strapped families can be coerced, donor families are denied the therapeutic benefits of voluntary donation, and an atmosphere of bargaining for organs may develop (1996). The basic problem with financial incentives comes down to these questions: is it ethically correct to put dollar values on organ donations, and is it ethically correct to discuss financial incentives with grieving families? These may be tough questions for some, but my answers come with ease. Many families may or may not be informed that one financial incentive is already in place. As soon as the families agree to donate and the patient is declared brain dead, then any expenses incurred from that point on are billed to the local organ procurement organization.

Financial incentives are the devil in disguise. DePalma and Townsend agree that some will see financial incentives as bargaining over organs, and others will perceive the program as creating a fair market for a commodity. Neither reason would make me sign an organ donor's agreement.

Establishing legal death

A new twist regarding organ donation was brought to my attention very recently. Organ procurements are being performed on patients who are brain damaged and not legally brain dead. 60 Minutes recently aired a program entitled "Not Quite Dead." This broadcast cemented my feelings toward organ procurement. Mike Wallace conducted excellent interviews with many people directly involved. One case came to light in Ohio, concerning a young lady who was shot in the head by an intruder. She did not die immediately. When the attorney who prosecuted the intruder read the coroner's report, he discovered that the patient's time of death was virtually the same minute her heart was procured. The attorney reached a disturbing conclusion: it was the act of organ harvesting that killed the victim, not the bullet. The attorney, Dave Williams, felt the real problem in the case was that the victim never had a chance to survive. Physicians prolonged her life for purposes of organ donation, rather than treating her as a neurosurgical patient. Even the neuropathologist, Dr. Jas Leestma, concurred that the victim's brain looked startlingly normal. It was a lower-grade brain injury, which the doctor would expect the patient to survive. Wallace contacted the hospital involved in the incident; their spokesperson insisted the patient was dead prior to the removal of her organs. Interestingly enough, the prosecutor dropped aggravated murder charges against the intruder who fired the bullet, allowing him to plead guilty to a lesser charge. Williams, the attorney, said it alarmed him that a person who was not fatally injured could wind up on the operating table, having his or her organs harvested.

That tragic story made a deep impression on me. I've helped with multiple organ procurements, but never would I knowingly be in a harvest involving a patient who was brain-damaged but not brain dead. Mike

Wallace contends that doctors have begun aggressively taking organs in situations that distinguished doctors and medical ethicists say are highly improper and possibly illegal.

Wallace adds that when seriously injured patients are not yet brain dead, doctors have to use an older, less precise method of declaring death: the absence of a heartbeat. Dr. Norman Paradis is a researcher who has studied this method of declaring death. He states it's much more complex and difficult to diagnose. Doctors can think the heart has stopped when it hasn't. My impression of this situation makes me wonder whether nurses and doctors are always acting as patient advocates. Dr. Arthur Caplan, a medical ethicist, stated, "If you have a heart that might resuscitate... even if it's stopped, even if it's not working right now, you don't want to say someone is dead" ("Not," 1997). My gut feeling allows me to believe the physician may be looking at the potential income and notoriety associated with transplantation instead of the rights of the person on the table. This is a "God-like" role to which many physicians succumb.

Dr. Caplan, medical ethicist, added that if we make people wonder if a patient is "dead enough," or "sort of dead," or "kind of dead," or "close enough," because the organs are needed, and that's what's driving the determination of death, that isn't good policy. I believe this is an understatement.

Dangerous drugs

Mike Wallace uncovers other atrocities committed against brain-damaged patients. Physicians can administer medications (Regitene and Heparin) that don't benefit the patient, just the donor organs. Regitene helps keep the organs healthy, but it also blocks the body's automatic release of adrenaline, which in a critically injured patient helps the body fight off death. Heparin helps the organs, but in brain-damaged patients it could increase the possibility of bleeding inside the brain, killing them.

Mike Wallace points out that one hospital actually has a policy for pain-relieving medications to be given to organ donors if there is any doubt the patient might experience pain. Dr. Caplan responds to such a policy by arguing that if pain-relieving medications are still needed, it's a clear sign that the patient has not succumbed to death.

Organic Donation

Making a choice

The two hospitals cited in this edition of <u>60 Minutes</u> are the Cleveland Clinic and the University of Wisconsin. Ironically, these are two of the teams that have performed harvests when I was on duty. I no longer work in surgery. I now find the business end of nursing a better choice.

When you renew your driver's license or attend a health fair at your local mall and someone asks you if you want to be an organ donor, think about what your answer will be. Don't be swayed by the happy endings you usually hear about. Remember to tell your family your wishes. There is more than one side to organ transplantation, and procurement is the other.

References

DePalma, J. A., & Townsend, R. (1996, May). Ethical issues in organ donations and transplantations: Are we helping a few at the expense of many? <u>Critical Care Nursing Quarterly</u>, 1–9.

Molzahn, A. (1996, October). Organ donation: What do nurses know and believe? <u>Canadian Nurse</u>, 25–30.

Wallace, M. (Reporter). (1997, April 13). 60 Minutes: Not quite dead. New York: Columbia Broadcasting Service.

■ Student Researcher: Cathy Bennett

It won't surprise readers of Cathy Bennett's research paper to learn that she worked at a social service agency that provided health care to low-income citizens. Cathy has developed a very professional-sounding voice, and she advocates awareness and health care reform like a veteran lobbyist. Cathy's interest in the subject of HIV infection in women grew out of her concern for the rising number of AIDS-infected females who visited the clinic where she worked. Her employer encouraged her to learn more about the particular problems of women with the disease so that their agency could better serve that population.

To preserve client confidentiality, Cathy draws all of her anecdotes from published sources, rather than writing about the people she knows who are infected with the AIDS virus. However, she consults with two local physicians (one who preferred not to be identified, and one who agreed to be included on her Works Cited list) to give her research paper some primary materials. She consulted a wide variety of secondary sources in her preparation of this paper, and she synthesizes those capably, incorporating them reasonably inconspicuously throughout her text.

Cathy's main assertion is that women and men's experience with HIV infection differ more than most people would guess. From the way they are diagnosed and treated to their attitudes about health care, the rise in infection of females represents some specific challenges to the medical community and society at large. She argues that women must take a more proactive stance in seeking treatment early and that medical doctors must educate themselves on women's experience with the disease. Cathy concludes that mandatory, confidential testing in clinics would address both of these problems.

Women and HIV/AIDS: Should Testing Be Mandatory?

Submitted by

Cathy Bennett

Professor Peterson

English 103

Second Summer Session

Outline

I. HIV/AIDS

    A. Definition

    B. Transmission

    C. Statistics

II. Social Stigma of HIV

    A. Morley discussion of article

III. Awareness of HIV

    A. Physicians

    B. Patient

IV. Testing

V. Diagnosis of HIV in women

    A. Symptoms

    B. Gender-related issues of HIV

VI. Prevention

    A. Education

    B. Awareness

Is HIV/AIDS a homosexual disease? Do only promiscuous women or men contract HIV/AIDS? Are they all using IV drugs? These are all common misconceptions about HIV/AIDS (human immunodeficiency virus/acquired immune deficiency syndrome). The difference between HIV and AIDS is that HIV breaks down the body's immune system while AIDS is actually the life-threatening complications of the HIV infection (Zylstra 182).

Since ninety percent of all new HIV cases being reported are indicating that transmission has occurred through sexual intercourse of one kind or another, no one wants to talk about it. However, this is not the only way it can be transmitted. It can be transmitted by sharing or reusing needles, through blood transfusions, or through the mother during pregnancy to an unborn child (Berer 6).

The statistics reported to the Indiana Department of Health from the United States CDC (Center for Disease Control and Prevention) lead me to believe this could be the single largest mistake a woman can make when it comes to personal health care. The report indicated that the number of women infected between 1991 and 1995 was up sixty-three percent. The method of transmission was highest in women in heterosexual relationships between the ages of 25 and 44 (Whortley 911). This is rather ironic because typically heterosexual women do not feel they are at risk as long as they do not use intravenous drugs and are not currently behaving in a promiscuous manner.

Catherine Wyatt-Morley is one of those women who did not believe she was at risk. Morley states, "experience has taught me that this is a fatal assumption." Morley was a middle-class married mother of three who found out in 1994 she was not immune to HIV. Her husband had not been faithful and had used intravenous drugs, leaving her very much at risk. In her recent article "AIDS: A Straight Woman's Health Crisis" published in the Los Angeles Times (October 8, 1997), Morley addresses the anger she felt when she was diagnosed with HIV and just how vulnerable she believes women are to this deadly virus.

Women tend to put everyone else's needs first. Whether this is a child, spouse, boyfriend, mother, grandmother, or neighbor is quite irrelevant. We are trained to take care of others. Even if you make a conscious effort to change this thought pattern it will take generations. The reason for this is that subconsciously we learn what we live. Our mothers' caregiving to other family members trained us that caregiving is expected. Typically women are looked at as being self-centered if they even begin to put themselves before home and family obligations. Society shapes women to be submissive. Women are typically more sensitive; therefore, it is easier to make us feel guilty. Families know just what to do or say to pull a woman's chain. Men, also, tend to look at our roles as caregivers not only to them but to their mothers, children, or anyone they may be obligated to take care of. This type of thinking makes it uncomfortable for women to protect themselves against HIV.

Women and HIV/AIDS: Should Testing Be Mandatory?

Women are not the only ones uncomfortable talking about HIV. Many physicians also find it a difficult subject to discuss with patients. Due to the social stigma that HIV is only contracted through women who are selling sex or by homosexuals, doctors tend to ask the general questions but nothing specific. Therefore, women are not being diagnosed until they are well into the disease.

While visiting with a local physician, who doesn't wish to be identified, I found he is not currently aware that any of his patients are HIV positive. He addressed the issue I am confident many doctors face: not enough hours in the day. It would appear to be a waste of time for a physician to study the latest treatment or the latest symptoms of any one particular disease if they did not have anyone suffering with it. The feedback from this physician was identical to the material I found in Ann Kurth's article "Clinical and Psychosocial Needs of HIV-Positive Women Living Outside Epicenters" (Kurth 21). The main problem with this line of thinking is, until tests are administered on a more regular basis, how could a physician know if a patient had HIV or not?

It only makes sense to test individuals at risk. Dr. Robert Joseph, critical care internal medicine specialist, addresses this as I am sitting in his exam room: "Everyone who has ever had sexual intercourse with more than one partner in the course of their life is at risk. This disease does not discriminate." There are, of course, certain groups of people for whom the disease may be more common, such as women between the ages of 25 and 44 (Whortley 911) and homosexual men. With this in mind it would appear that doctors would want to take a stand on what becomes standard practice when working with these patients.

Women's health care has come a great distance over the last several years. For the most part women are taking an active role in their personal health and wellness. The problem with HIV in women is that it has been a very quiet epidemic. The technology and medicine have all been geared towards men, due to the stigma that HIV carries. Basically, no one has been watching as the disease rages out of control in women. In 1994, the CDC report shows AIDS as the leading cause of death in women 25–44 (Whortley 911). All of a sudden it's a women's health issue.

Even though it has been recognized as a women's health issue, clinics are still not including women in their HIV testing (Smith 7). There appear to be many reasons for this. As caregivers many women have sole custody of their children and do not have the resources for a baby sitter and are not comfortable taking a child to a doctor's visit of this nature. Another reason women are not included in many clinical trials is due to the late diagnosis of the disease. Clinics need to study the manifestation of the disease and the medications' response for the duration of the entire disease in order to observe reactions.

There are many symptoms physicians commonly overlook in women with HIV because they are common problems found in women's health care in general. The most common is a recurrent yeast infection. While this does not seem to be important, it may very well be the very first sign of HIV. Other symptoms include enlarged lymph glands in the neck, armpit, or groin, severe tiredness, unexplained weight loss, fever lasting more than a month, skin rash, joint pain, nausea, shingles, and viral infections on the tongue (Berer 17).

Once a woman has been diagnosed with HIV it is typically less than two years when the first signs of AIDS appear (Kurth 18). This would mean the woman has been living with this disease for several years without treatment. At this point the disease becomes more difficult to treat, and there is less time to combat it.

Women also deal with issues men do not. Cervical cancer is one of the main gender-specific differences with HIV. Like most everything else, cervical cancer is more difficult to treat in an HIV-positive patient than in a patient who tests negative for HIV. Also, because HIV infection usually happens to people in their childbearing years, many questions arise. Does a woman have a baby or not? What happens if she does and leaves an orphan? What are the health risks to the mother? What are the health risks to her unborn child? These questions require the advice of a professional counselor who can help women make decisions that they will live with for the rest of their lives. The decisions a woman makes will determine how much additional support she might need.

Typically, especially in rural areas, women with HIV have a hard time finding support and friends. Wellness groups are usually formed for people suffering with HIV/AIDS, but they usually are made up of men. Women tend not to talk freely in front of men, so such support groups may not benefit women much.

While there seem to be many obstacles for a woman with HIV, it's time to quit taking the role of the victim and take action. Women as well as men need to be more involved and take responsibility for their actions. At the same time, we need physicians to make testing their priority. For example, when a woman goes in for her annual examination, she generally does not have a choice as to which tests will be performed. Why can't the HIV test become part of this ritual? It is very relevant to what she is already at the doctor for, whether it be family planning, pregnancy, contraceptives, or STDs (sexually transmitted diseases). It seems to be a constant problem for the Indiana Department of Health to keep a full staff to ensure testing at high-risk health care centers. Women need to urge all physicians to make testing their priority. We are all at high risk.

With all of these things to consider, education and testing are the two most important issues at hand. Physicians need to be required to have specialized training for HIV, regardless of the status of their current patients. Women need to demand that local, state, and federal government representatives know HIV is a "women's health issue" and that we are dying at alarming rates from this disease. Testing in clinics and physicians' offices needs to be made easier for the patient. We need doctors to be familiar with the different symptoms of HIV and to become more comfortable talking about it with patients. In addition to this, office staff in all health care facilities need to be properly trained, not only in blood pathogen training but in HIV/AIDS as well. This would help with many of the misconceptions of how HIV/AIDS can be transmitted such as through a sneeze by touching the HIV-infected person, and even by working in the same office. These sound absurd to an individual with training, but to a common person they are real fears.

Once these issues have been addressed, we can move forward. Until then, we all have a responsibility to educate whomever we come in contact with about the HIV/AIDS disease and hope they, too, will spread the word.

Works Cited

Arno, Janet N., M.D. "HIV Infection and Women." The Health Monograph Series. 14: 1 (1996): 7–9.

Berer, Marge, Sunandra Ray. Women and HIV/AIDS—An International Resource Book. Hammersmith: Pandora Press, 1993.

Jenkins, Sharon Rae, Helen L. Coons. "Psychosocial Stress and Adaptation Processes for Women Coping with HIV/AIDS." Women and AIDS: Coping and Caring. Ed. Ann O'Leary and Loretta Sweet Jemmott. New York: Plenum Press, 1996. 33–8.

Joseph, Robert. Personal Interview. 9 July 1998.

Kurth, Ann. "Clinical and Psychosocial Needs of HIV-Positive Women Living Outside Epicenters." The Health Monograph Series 14: 1 (1996): 16–22.

Smith, Dawn K., Janet S. Moore. "Epidemiology, Manifestations, and Treatment of HIV in Women." Women and AIDS: Coping and Caring. Ed. Ann O'Leary and Loretta Sweet Jemmott. New York: Plenum Press, 1996. 1–32.

Wortley, Pascale M. M.D., Patricia L. Fleming, PhD. "AIDS in the United States." JAMA—Journal of the American Medical Association 278 (1997): 911–916.

Wyatt-Morley, Catherine. "AIDS: A Straight Woman's Health Crisis." Los Angeles Times 8 October 1997, 116:312 C3.

Zylstra, Mignon M., David Biebel. When AIDS Comes Home. Nashville: Thomas Nelson Publishers, 1996.

■ Student Researcher: Sean Slagle

Research papers about literature are difficult to read, because their writers generally must assume that their audience is familiar with the texts under discussion. In this paper, however, Sean Slagle guesses that many of his readers read Lewis Carroll's *Alice's Adventures in Wonderland* (or had it read to them) long ago and will remember the scenes he is describing if he deftly sketches them from a few details. The result is a very readable paper—even for those who never read Carroll's book.

Readers familiar with the critical controversies surrounding Carroll's text will see that Sean has taken a stronger thesis in his paper than meets the eye. Some critics maintain that *Alice's Adventures in Wonderland* is a simple child's story, and attempts to read some political or social message into the text are misguided. Sean's paper begins with the assumption that the book is an example of political satire, and his explication of various scenes from the book are his arguments in support of that assertion.

The sources on Sean's Works Cited list are excellent ones; the three secondary sources that he cites are all sophisticated and intended for literary scholars. Because Sean's thesis is very close to that of Daniel Bivona's article from *Nineteenth Century Literature*, he depends too heavily on that source, especially toward the end of his paper. Parts of Sean's essay are essentially paraphrases of Bivona's work.

Sean wisely decided he could not learn everything necessary to prove his original thesis: that *Alice's Adventures in Wonderland* is a thinly-veiled indictment of imperialism. However, he might have interviewed a colonial literature or colonial history professor to add credence to the hurriedly made allegations in his conclusion. His observations about the primary text are well supported with quotations and specific examples, however.

Sean Slagle

English 104

Literary Analysis

7/24/98

Victorian Culture vs. Wonderland Culture:

A Study in the Lack of Understanding

In a discussion of African literature, Anthony Appiah said that readers must not be asked "to understand Africa by embedding it in European
culture" (Gates 174). I believe Lewis Carroll is saying a similar thing in <u>Al-
ice's Adventures in Wonderland</u>. Carroll is telling readers that Wonderland
cannot be understood by embedding it in Victorian culture. However, Alice
tries to understand the Wonderland culture by applying the rules of regulation of Victorian culture. By looking at Alice's encounter with the mice and
birds, caucus race, caterpillar, and croquet game, one can see that <u>Alice's
Adventures in Wonderland</u> is a story about the inability to understand one
culture by embedding it in another.

The first cultural conflict Alice encounters is with the mouse and the
birds. To Alice, Dinah "is such a dear quiet thing ... and she sits by the fire,
licking her paws and washing her face—and she is such a nice soft thing to
nurse" (Carroll 11). According to Victorian culture, Dinah succeeds at one
of the main things a cat does, catching mice and birds. In the Wonderland
culture, this success brings disgust and terror. To the mouse, cats are
"nasty, low, vulgar things" (Carroll 12). When the birds learn that Dinah is
a cat, they quickly leave.

Some critics believe that the way the mouse and the birds refute Alice's talk about Dinah displays "the higher levels of Wonderland (read Victorian) society, where the forms of etiquette are used to dissemble and
even to excuse rudeness" (Matthews 112). These critics make the same
mistake as Alice. They try to place Wonderland within the context of Victorian England. Wonderland has its own culture, which is different from England. If Wonderland were like Victorian England, there would be no cultural
conflict, nor much of a story.

Another source of cultural conflict is the caucus race. This Wonderland race is different than any race Alice has seen. The shape of the race
course does not matter. Everyone jumps into the circle and runs around
however each likes. They start when they want and go until someone calls
out, "The race is over!" Then everyone is declared a winner and a loser.

However, in Wonderland culture, games include everyone equally. In fact, the Wonderland culture respects the true meaning of <u>caucus.</u> Caucus "carries the implication of a meeting to iron our differences in order to present a united front for exerting political pressure, a local game of political accommodation within a larger adversarial context, rather than a contest of winners and losers" (Bivona 147). The Victorian culture values winning. The Wonderland culture values accommodation.

Alice's conversation with the caterpillar clearly reflects cultural differences. First of all, the caterpillar is smoking a hookah. "The hookah, itself a stock 'orientalization' feature, highlights the caterpillar's foreignness" (Bivona 151). However, I would ask this critic who the foreigner really is: the caterpillar or Alice? Secondly, Alice finds the caterpillar to be rude. The first thing the caterpillar says to Alice is, "Who are you?" Immediately, Alice assigns her cultural values to the caterpillar by saying to herself, "This was not an encouraging opening for a conversation" (Carroll 27).

Once Alice and the caterpillar begin their conversation, the caterpillar refuses to let Alice assume she knows how it feels. The caterpillar answers everything the opposite of what she expects; for example:

"I ca'n't explain <u>myself</u>, I'm afraid, Sir," said Alice, "because I'm not myself, you see."

"I don't see," said the Caterpillar.

"I'm afraid I ca'n't put it more clearly," Alice replied, very politely, "for I ca'n't understand it myself, to begin with; and being so many different sizes in a day is very confusing."

"It isn't," said the Caterpillar.

"Well, perhaps you haven't found it so yet," said Alice, "but when you have to turn into a chrysalis—you will some day, you know—and then after that a butterfly, I should think you'll feel it a little queer, wo'n't you?"

"Not a bit," said the Caterpillar (Carroll 28).

Alice is assuming that because she feels a certain way, the caterpillar should, too. This is not the case. In Wonderland, it is not queer for the caterpillar to change shapes. The caterpillar does not fit into the Victorian mold for polite conversation, so Alice denounces the caterpillar and walks away.

The best example of cultural conflict is on the croquet grounds. From the beginning Alice follows Victorian rules, instead of taking the example

Student Researcher: Sean Slagle   **319**

put forth by the others in Wonderland. For instance, look at what happens with the King and Queen's procession:

> Alice was rather doubtful whether she ought to lie down on her face like the three gardeners, but she could not remember ever having heard of such a rule at processions, "and besides, what would be the use of a procession," she thought, "if people had all to lie down on their faces, so that they couldn't see it?" So she stood where she was, and waited. (Carroll 52)

Because Alice does not follow the social norms of Wonderland, she draws attention to herself. The King and Queen stop the procession and look at her. Alice is quickly sentenced to be beheaded, which brings about another cultural conflict. Where Alice comes from, a queen's order to be beheaded meant a public display which resulted in a head being cut off. Alice later learns that no one gets beheaded in Wonderland. In Wonderland, the decree is only symbolic of the queen's power.

The next mistake Alice makes is assuming that she knows how to play croquet. She knows how to play the English version of the game, not the Wonderland version.

> Alice thought she had never seen such a curious croquet-ground in all her life: it was all ridges and furrows; the croquet balls were live hedgehogs, and the mallets live flamingoes, and soldiers had to double themselves up and stand on their hands and feet, to make arches (Carroll 55).

Instead of seeing this as a new cultural experience, Alice sees the game as a perverted version of the English game. She tells the Cheshire cat,

> "I don't think they play at all fairly ... and they all quarrel so dreadfully one can't hear oneself speak—and they don't seem to have any rules in particular; at least, if there are, no body attends to them—and you've no idea how confusing it is all the things being alive" (Carroll 56).

Also, Alice fails to see that the queen is supposed to win. Like the caucus race, Alice sees the croquet match as being competitive with a winner and a loser. This assumption points to Alice's own "ethnocentrism" (Bivona 150). She is unable to put aside her own beliefs about the world and open up to the world of others.

Alice's inability to accept the other culture as being different carries over into the trial of the knave. She tries to apply the rules of Victorian court to the Wonderland court. When Alice cannot take it anymore, she interrupts the proceedings by saying, "It doesn't prove anything of the sort! ... Why you don't even know what they're about" (Carroll 81). Alice ends up making "herself the center rather than the periphery of the action: another solipsistic recentering, which ultimately appoints this rather limited little girl as judge, jury, and executioner of all the 'creatures'" (Bivona 166).

Ultimately Alice is unable to comprehend the Wonderland culture. She tries to place Victorian rules out of context. Victorian rules and values do not belong in Wonderland any more than Alice does. Perhaps author Lewis Carroll wanted readers to see what was happening when England encountered the many cultures of its empire. A village in South Africa should not be expected to follow the rules governing the English culture. Perhaps the South Africans have races without definite courses. Perhaps the games in Australia are meant for accommodation, not winning. Perhaps the hookah smokers in India do not wish to be understood by Victorians and, ultimately, changed by them. Perhaps there are croquet games in Canada that bear little resemblance to the English version. Perhaps we are all like Alice, applying our cultural assumptions in the context of others' cultures.

Works Cited

Bivona, Daniel. "Alice the Child-Imperialist and the Games of Wonderland." Nineteenth Century Literature. 41 (1986): 143–71.

Carroll, Lewis. Alice's Adventures in Wonderland. New York: Dover, 1993.

Gates, Henry Lewis, Jr. "Canon-Formation, Literary History, and the Afro-American Tradition." In Falling into Theory: Conflicting Views on Reading Literature. Ed. David Richter. Boston: Bedford, 1994. 173–80.

Matthews, Charles. "Satire in the Alice Books." Criticism 12 (1970): 105–19.

■ Student Researcher: Tim Peters

You can tell by reading his research paper that Tim Peters takes a personal interest in his argument in favor of a school voucher system. A father who is facing a decision about where to school his child, he is frustrated and angry. The result is an essay with a strong voice and lots of emotional or persuasive appeals but few logical or rational arguments. This paper is close to being full-fledged ceremonial discourse. In it, Tim invokes the founding fathers, freedom, and parental duties.

Tim's paper demonstrates why analogy is considered an emotional rather than a rational appeal. His extended comparison between parents whose tax dollars are automatically distributed to public schools and the early American colonists who protested "taxation without representation" is moving, but not entirely logical. American taxpayers do have the vote, which is representation. They have the opportunity to elect politicians who will advance their cause.

Tim does a good job of refuting one argument that is continually used against his cause. Many people oppose school vouchers because they believe that funding religious private schools violates constitutional law. This paper demonstrates that many American's understanding of the "separation between church and state" is based on erroneous information.

A commuting student with little opportunity to visit the campus library, Tim depended heavily on the holdings of his small-town public library for the sources for this paper. Notice that six of his seven secondary sources are books, and the remaining document is a magazine article. In addition, many of the texts Tim relies on are biased products from self-interested publishing houses. Had he consulted more reputable sources, his research paper probably would have been more objective.

The strength of this paper is its voice. A forceful and dramatic argument such as this won't win many converts to its position, but it is a rousing battle cry for those who already agree.

School Vouchers

Tim Peters

English 103/01

Dr. Peterson

Ball State University

20 June 1997

School Vouchers

"The educational system is in trouble."

"SAT scores are continually dropping."

"Violence and drugs plague our schools."

"Our children are graduating and can't even read."

"Teachers are being physically attacked by students."

"Parents don't care."

"Teachers don't care."

These statements, and many others similar to them, are echoed daily in homes, schools, newspapers, television shows, and government agencies. In fact, they are so commonplace that most Americans have heard them, regardless of their concern for or knowledge about education. To quote SAT score statistics, juvenile crime statistics, or other thought-provoking data is unnecessary in America today. Everyone has heard it all before.

There are as many ideas about how to fix the problems in education as there are people who are concerned about it. And to allow trial and error solutions as presented by experts would only benefit the nay-sayers and statisticians as the system continues to erode. While the different sides square off, another class graduates; as the mud slinging continues, someone's five-year-old starts kindergarten; and as legislation is debated, parents become more confused and less interested. Ultimately, what is at stake is the parents' control over the educational system and their right to choose what is best for their children. Thus, the most heated debate in educational policy issues right now is parental choice through the use of school vouchers.

The school voucher program gives all parents financial freedom of choice because it allows the tax dollars for education to go to the school a family chooses. It is easy to see why the debate is so hotly contested if you look at the dollars spent on education. "The National Center for Education

Statistics estimated nationwide spending for elementary and secondary education in 1993–94 was $5,920.00 per student" (Harmer 38). That is money that is being spent on administration and programs that do not benefit students. "As a major contributor of tax dollars to public education, corporate America is getting a lousy return on its investment" (Perry 70). And it is this tax investment that many families would like to invest at their discretion.

It is this same "taxation without representation" that led our founding fathers to stand up and voice their concerns and issue ultimatums that cost many of them their families, their homes, and even their lives, yet gave us the freedom to form a republic-based government of the people and for the people. From 1763 until 1765 under the rule of King George III, those who lived in the thirteen colonies were subjected to trade and tax regulations that benefited only England. The colonists were unable to buy land west of the Appalachian Mountains or trade with the Indians who lived there without purchasing a permit. They were forced to house and feed soldiers and then pay England for its unwanted governance. They were unable to have their own currency. They were taxed heavily on imports, sugar, and stamps—all without representation. Finally, fed up with regulation without a voice, Patrick Henry ended a speech given to the Virginia House of Burgesses on March 28, 1775, saying the famous words, "I know not what course others may take; but as for me, give me liberty, or give me death" (Lowman, Thompson, and Grussendorf 95).

It was to this end that a committee led by Thomas Jefferson introduced a document to the Continental Congress on July 4, 1776, which started, "When, in the course of human events, it becomes necessary for one people to dissolve political bands which have connected them with another.... (103). The Declaration of Independence was unanimously adopted not because the people wanted war, nor because everyone in the thirteen colonies wanted to be separated. They did, however, want representation in determining their taxes.

The same desire for independence is felt by many families in America now. We are being denied representation in the matter of raising our own children. It is one of the "courses of human events." We have the right to choose the best education for our families in this free country. It seems strange that we live in a society based upon "choice," yet the issue of school vouchers is contested. We can choose the occupations we desire, the churches we attend, or whether to abort an unborn baby. But it is not feasible for us to decide where a child goes to school once we "choose" to let him live. The issue in both cases is not merely choice, but money.

The opponents of parental choice have made the issue a religious one, stating that school vouchers would create a violation of the separation of church and state clause in the American Constitution. "In the words of Thomas Jefferson, the prohibition against establishment of religion by law was intended to erect 'a wall of separation between church and state'" (Doerr 39). The problem with that reasoning is two-fold. First, there are many private schools that are not religious in nature, and parents are currently denied the choice to divert their tax dollars to those institutions. Second is the myth that the "separation of church and state" is a law. The First Amendment to the Constitution of the United States says, "Congress shall make no law respecting an establishment of religion, or prohibiting the free exercise thereof" (Lowman, Thompson, and Grussendorf 69). In other words, the people who live in the United States would no longer have to worship the way that was once required by the Church of England.

The association of a speech made by Thomas Jefferson and Constitutional law is a fallacy that has been brought to the attention of the American public before. The letter, which was written on January 1, 1802, was addressed to the Danbury Baptist Association, calming their fears that Congress was going to choose a single religious denomination for the whole country. Jefferson borrowed a phrase from the colonial minister Roger Williams who said, "The hedge or wall of separation between the garden of the church and the wilderness of the world, God hath ever broke down the wall." Jefferson's letter included the following:

Believing with you that religion is a matter which lies solely between man and his God, that he owes account to none other for faith or his worship, that the legislative powers of government reach actions only, and not opinions, I contemplate with solemn reverence that act of the whole American people which declared that their legislature should "make no law respecting an establishment of religion, or prohibiting the free exercise thereof," thus building a wall of separation between Church and State. (Federer 325)

Thomas Jefferson did not sign the Constitution, nor was he present at the Constitutional Convention in 1787. He also was not present when the First Amendment was being debated in 1789, as he was in France as a

School Vouchers

U.S. Minister. The letter to the Danbury Baptist Association was written thirteen years after the First Amendment. There is a saying that goes, "If you repeat a lie often enough, people will come to believe it." Such is the case with the "law" separating church and state.

The issue is not a failing public school system vs. the successful private educational enterprises in America, but whether a parent has a right to choose which system is best for his or her child. "To compare the effectiveness of the two without regard to their very different missions could lead to the conclusion that public schools are less effective when they are actually doing different things" (Haetrel 51). What is the mission of public education? Should parents have the right to choose which public or private school system they agree with, or should they quietly accept their "only" option? When the Soviet Union tried this approach, its whole government failed.

At present, parents in most states may choose where they want to send their children to school, but their tax dollars remain in the public school district where they reside. There are parents who would like to place their children in private schools but cannot because of financial limitations. Under a government that supports people who are unable to find employment, buy food, afford housing, or go to college, it seems unbelievable that we cannot help families send their children to the school of their choice. All American parents should have the opportunity to select schools that reflect their values.

Do educators believe the public school systems are the best? "In cities around the nation—in Albuquerque, Houston, Los Angeles, Long Beach, Memphis, Milwaukee, New Orleans, San Francisco, and Seattle—20–50% of children of public school teachers attend private schools" (Henderson 3). Are they afraid of "skimming the cream from the top," or of having only the "undesirables" left in public education? Is the issue of parental choice stalled by statistics and surveys? Or could the government be shielding its $5,920.00 per student?

"The ultimate test of a school's quality is whether parents from outside that school district want to send their children to that district" (Henderson 11). Taxation without representation will take people under tyranny from discouragement to rebellion. The tax money for public education should no longer be used to buoy a sinking system, but rather should be the tax dollars of the people, tax dollars by the people, and tax dollars for the people. Put into the hands of taxpayers their education vouchers! Give parents of the United States of America freedom of choice.

Works Cited

Doerr, Edd, Elbert J. Menendez, and John M. Swomley. The Case Against School Vouchers. New York: Prometheus, 1995.

Federer, William J. America's God and Country Encyclopedia of Quotations. Texas: Fame, 1996.

Haetrel, Edward H., Thomas James, and Henry M. Levine. Comparing Public and Private Schools. New York: Falmer, 1987.

Harmer, David. School Choice: Why You Need It—How You Get It. Washington, D.C.: Cato Institute, 1994.

Henderson, David R. The Case for School Choice. Stanford: Hoover Institution, 1993.

Lawman, Michael R., George Thompson, and Kurt Grussendorf. United States History: Heritage of Freedom. Florida: Beka, 1996.

Perry, Nancy J. The Educational Crisis: What Business Can Do." Fortune 118 (1988): 70–81.

■ Summing Up

There is no correct way to conduct research or write an essay. Neither is there a certain number of sources required of a well-supported research paper. Collecting and organizing research are intricate tasks, and you must use your "professional judgment" to determine when you have accumulated enough information, whether you have consulted the best sources, if you have focused your topic adequately, and whether you have placed it in context to a sufficient degree to allow your readers to understand your thesis. One purpose of this book is to make explicit the complexity of the researching process so that you will make informed choices on future research projects. Just as the various student papers in this part of the book are all different from one another, so will the essays you write in the future differ from one another, depending on the topic, the available resources, and the audience and purpose for your text.

Exercises: Sources and Strategies

1. Read each of the student researchers' papers carefully and determine which one you believe is best. For your next class meeting, be prepared to explain why you have chosen that one.

2. Pretend that you are editing a student magazine, and all of the papers in Part Three have been submitted to you for publication. Choose one that you think has potential but needs improvement, and write a letter to its author suggesting changes that will improve its chance of being published.

3. Write a rebuttal to one of the papers in Part Three, disagreeing with its thesis or some of its arguments. Use secondary sources to support your arguments if necessary.

Writing to Know

Write a "literacy autobiography." Tell about the significant events in your life that shaped the way you learn, think, read, and write. What comes to mind as you contemplate the importance of language and writing in your personal and academic life? Were language skills and literary arts valued in your home? Think about instances when your language was criticized or praised. What were your proudest achievements in school? What are your strengths today as a writer? How have the values and occurrences of your past shaped the writer that you are today?

PART FOUR

Researching an Internship

*M*ost people use the same skills necessary for writing research papers in their careers. As the researcher profiles in Part One suggest, almost every profession involves gathering data, deciding which sources are reliable, synthesizing a plethora of information, organizing findings, and passing those on (along with authoritative recommendations) to supervisors or clients. Research skills are also crucial to finding a job or internship and to persuading an employer that you are capable of filling a particular position. Not surprisingly, since most of the jobs sought by college-educated persons involve research, candidates with good research skills are most successful in securing jobs. The same sources and strategies that you have been practicing in this course to produce research projects can help you get a good job.

People have probably been asking you what you want to be when you grow up ever since you were old enough to wield a baby rattle or to speak, and even then you knew that clichéd answers such as "cowboy" and "fireman" were just the things you were supposed to say until you were old enough to consider becoming an account executive or systems analyst. You've probably heard many warnings about the "changing marketplace" and that choosing a career isn't what it once was. In industries such as manufacturing that fluctuate with supply and demand, people are changing jobs and relocating more than during previous generations. In others, such as teaching and government work, where the number of jobs remains relatively finite or "downsizing" has reduced available opportunities, people are staying in their initial positions or locales more than before. Generalizations about the job market reflect worldwide trends that may or may not affect your specific situation. Don't be dismayed by doomsayers' talk about the state of the job market. There has always been grousing and apprehension about the economy, and the world still produces ideas and inventions that exceed the output of the halcyon days of the past.

■ Considering an Internship

If the prospect of finding a job seems overwhelming, consider for a minute all of the evidence of people's work that you see in the world around you every day. There is nothing in society or the natural environment that is not the product of someone's labor, the source of someone's capital, or the target of someone's economic ambition. What can you find that is not a testament to labor and commerce? Even the skies above us represent a work environment, for meteorologists, pilots, physicists, and communications engineers, among others. There is lots of work to be done in the world, and you, like most people before you and around you, will find something to do. You know it will take some planning and preparation to obtain a position that gives you the level of rewards to which you aspire. If, for example, there are very few jobs in your field, that means you must compete in a buyer's market, one where you need employers more than they need you.

In this course you have learned many of the skills necessary for searching for an occupation. The methods you use to find your next job and the kind of success you have at that task will probably influence your willingness and ability to do it again, and again, as necessary. You will almost certainly seek more than one professional position in your lifetime, but your career will evolve one task, one project, one job at a time. Most people's career paths are not linear and may not even appear logical to outside observers.

You can't plan your whole life from where you stand today. An internship provides an opportunity for you to explore the working world without much risk. Internships are a kind of apprenticeship for college students. They offer students the chance to observe and work in their intended profession for a specified amount of time (usually six weeks to four months) as part of their academic experience. Internships give students the chance to learn in the working environment without the pressures and all of the responsibilities of a professional position. The job you are seeking now should fit your needs at present and hold some potential for future growth, but look for a role that you believe you desire and are able to perform. Success in the future depends on success today.

Thinking About an Internship Now

Although the prospect of finding a fulfilling job with a good salary might have been one of the reasons you decided to attend college in the first place, it probably seems a bit premature to start trolling the job market now. After all, another popular reason for going to college is to avoid the rat race for four or five years, and being a student may feel enough like a job already. However, education and work aren't the separate domains they once were; many students intern or work cooperatively to gain experience, make extra money, or earn college credit, and long-time members of the work force commonly return to campus for retraining or to gain additional certification, even in areas where they have considerable work experience.

Even students who are quite certain about what they want to do after graduation experience some apprehension about actually taking on the job they desire. Prospective teachers often worry that they won't like their students or vice versa. Nurses in training wonder if they will have the emotional stamina to face illness every day. Chemists and engineers suspect it may be a long time before they get to direct projects and put their best ideas to the test. Many students fear they won't be ready to settle into a desk job when it is time to leave school; you may question whether you can happily submit to the forty- to sixty-hour work week that is common in most professions and if two weeks of vacation will feel like sufficient reward after fifty weeks of toil. Ever mindful of the proverb "be careful what you wish for," many students are afraid they won't like the careers they have spent time and money training to enter. An internship in your chosen field, completed as early as your second or third year in college, may confirm or allay such misgivings. If you discover that you love working, you can return to school with renewed vigor and the desire to complete your studies quickly and well in order to get back to the rewards of the job. If any of your apprehensions are confirmed, then you might want to modify your course of study or your career goals as you see fit.

Every major and college degree prepares its graduates for a range of first jobs, and more than one of those may seem attractive to you. Most everyone must decide whether to work for a large or small employer in an urban or rural setting, near or far from home. One or two internships, undertaken while you are still a student, will help you decide how and where to focus your job search in the future. Even if you think you know exactly the sort of job you will seek upon graduation, it is a good idea to intern in a different sort of business or position. You may be surprised at the range of placements you would enjoy or the kinds of situations in which your skills are appreciated. Internships provide the opportunity to explore the latitude your degree permits.

Generally, internships are regarded as a civic contribution to education and an investment in each intern's future, but they also make it possible for students to make a difference in their adopted workplaces and home academic departments. As an intern, you can bring new ideas, technological skills, and innovative practices to the businesses where you apprentice, and you can carry the changes and concerns of the marketplace back to campus. Employers who take on interns have the opportunity to test prospective employees without extending the benefits or commitment of a full-fledged job contract. They can also shape the way future employees are trained by teaching them vital skills and making them understand problems that the universities are well equipped to solve. Commerce between colleges and the working world for which they prepare students is crucial to the growth and advancement of both.

Some students find that an off-campus internship provides welcome relief from school. If you would rather spend your time working than contemplating it, an internship will provide a respite from the campus atmosphere. If taking tests makes you nervous but demonstrating your competence practically does not, an internship might make your four- or five-year hitch at school more tolerable. An internship won't get you out of school altogether, though. Most companies that offer internships require participants to return to school the following semester. Reputable companies will not permanently hire interns who have not yet finished their degrees. An internship is not a fast-track to professional employment that circumvents formal education. No one profits in the long run when an intern quits school.

Some companies provide financial incentives for interns to finish their degrees. Financial compensation for interns ranges from nothing to nearly $1,000 per week, depending on the discretion of the company offering the position. Cooperative work programs, or "co-ops," offer alternate semesters of work and full-time schooling or a combination of part-time employment and part-time schooling. Co-ops give students the opportunity to gain hands-on work experience while banking money for college tuition and living expenses. Some employers regard internships as private financial aid packages, enabling qualified students to continue their education and perhaps return to work for their benefactors after graduating. Others pay only in practical experience. Also, internships in fields where such experience is commonly required for graduation or where internships are highly competitive (such as architecture, telecommunications, and political science) include no stipends. Generally, internships that involve close observation of a professional at work, or "job shadowing" stints, are unpaid. The opportunity to work with celebrities in sports or entertainment comes, almost always, at the student's own expense. Most not-for-profit organizations cannot offer to pay interns either. However, it is often possible to receive student financial aid while interning, and some schools offer scholarships or stipends to students while they are engaged at unpaid internships. If you can intern near school or home, it may be possible to accept a part-time, unpaid internship without incurring any extra expenses in the process.

Whether you are paid for your work as an intern or not, the salary or compensation for those hours is only the beginning of the benefits you can realize from your internship. As a long-time student, you may be growing weary of doing things because they are "good for you," but taking an internship now may pay dividends in the future. Even if your temporary position doesn't turn into a more permanent offer upon graduation, you will learn what to look for in your first full-time professional appointment. You will learn the answers to important career-related questions, such as the following:

- Are you the kind of person who needs support and feedback from your supervisor?

- Do you like a highly social and informal office atmosphere?

- Do you work best when informed of deadlines long in advance?

- Can you cooperate well in collaborative situations?

- Do you need direct access to production workers, or can you communicate satisfactorily through others?

- Are you amenable to the standard 8:00 A.M. to 5:00 P.M. work day, or are you interested in a position that offers "flex time" or compensation for early-morning or late-evening hours?

- Is salary or independence more important to you?

- Is the mission statement of the company more important to you than its bottom line?

- Would you rather face the public or work behind a closed office door?

- Do you prefer certain management structures, performance review methods, or inter-office networking software?

You might think that you can answer all of these questions based on your self-awareness and experience as a student, but your performance and preferences in the workplace might surprise you. Even if the office where you intern is incompatible with your personal style, you will learn about how the business of your intended profession is conducted, and you will undoubtedly meet some people whom you admire.

In some academic fields, internships are required of students. One or a series of successful internship experiences suggests to employers that you are willing to work, dependable, reliable, personable, and aware of the demands of the workaday world. Nearly every working professional interviewed in the course of compiling information for this book said that he or she had served in a similar capacity as an intern, and all recommended internships as a way to round out an undergraduate education and find satisfactory employment upon graduation.

■ Discovering Internship Opportunities

You are probably the person who will benefit the most from your internship experience, but others stand to gain from it, too, and they are ready and willing to help you get started. Your college gains prestige by placing strong students in visible positions, and your eventual long-term job placement reflects well on your school, too. Your school's placement or career services personnel are experts in finding internship opportunities and can help you apply for those. Additionally, your academic department or school advising office may have an internship specialist on staff. Seek help from college personnel who can help you identify internship opportunities, prepare resumes and cover letters, and arrange mock interviews so that you can practice your internship-seeking skills. They will be familiar with openings in your area and can arrange for you to talk with students who have already interned in the areas you seek. Businesses, too, enjoy rewards as a result of offering internship positions, and many large companies that offer several such opportunities employ internship coordinators to help students apply. Employers who are seeking interns routinely notify college placement personnel about openings and desired qualifications for applicants.

You may walk past hundreds of notices about internships every day. Somewhere on your campus, there are probably physical or virtual bulletin boards covered with advertisements for internships. If the career placement department at your school has a Web page, check it for leads about internships, or stop by their offices and look for posted notices. Some large companies that employ many interns send representatives to college campuses periodically, seeking internship candidates. A few of those will place ads in the campus newspaper, but most will depend on campus internship advisers to get the word out. Similarly, a very small percentage of offices offering internships will advertise in your college paper or in magazines that are popular among college students, but the majority will go through academic channels to get the word out.

Several commercial guides to internship opportunities are published annually, and your campus library probably subscribes to a few of them. For instance, one of the most popular is the *Princeton Review Student Access Guide to America's Top Internships,* edited by Mark Oldman and Samer Hamaden. Such directories list and sometimes rate internship opportunities with nationally prominent agencies. Some include only internships in certain fields, such as nursing, government, management, and education. Most describe the kinds of work available, provide rough figures for compensation, describe prerequisites for applicants, and detail the application procedures. Internships listed in commercial guides are highly competitive, simply because the "inside advice" offered in such catalogs is widely available. There may be as many as one hundred applicants per position for such widely publicized internships.

Your internship choices are not limited to those agencies that advertise on your campus. If you know of an employer you would like to work for temporarily, you or an official from your school may be able to set up an internship program for you there. Or, if you can imagine and describe the kind of internship you want but don't know where to find such a position, it may be within your reach. Once you decide to seek an internship, start telling your friends, classmates, teachers, and family about what you hope to achieve. Everyone knows people in a variety of jobs, and it is quite possible that someone you already know can be instrumental in setting up your ideal internship situation. The same kinds of research that lead to factual information can result in employment opportunities. Start asking around. On a college campus, you are surrounded by hundreds of acquaintances from diverse backgrounds; some networking can have far-reaching effects.

If you know the kind of place in which you'd like to intern and have a geographical region in mind (near campus or near home or in some attractive locale where you have always hoped to live, for instance), an ordinary telephone directory may prove to be a valuable research tool. Your campus library probably has an extensive collection of phone books in single volumes or collected on microfiche. Yellow Pages directories on the World Wide Web are helpful as well. Start by looking up the kinds of businesses where you hope to intern in a regional directory. Collect the names of potential employers, as well as their addresses and telephone numbers. You might also seek out possible situations by searching the World Wide Web at large. Enter a search string consisting of the type of employment you want, the name of a city where you hope to work, and the word *intern* (for example, "metallurgy and Atlanta and intern"). With some luck, that will suggest a few potential employers as well. For example, a search for information about "forestry and Colorado and intern" turned up the Access Colorado Library and Information Network Site (http://www.aclin.org), which lists over fifty internships and summer jobs for students in that state. You can also write to the chambers of commerce in cities where you would like to work, asking for lists of potential employers.

If you know which company you'd like to work for, check to see if it has a Web site. Many corporations' Web sites include an employment page that advertises job and internship opportunities and application procedures. Large, highly competitive corporations make it possible to apply for internships directly through their Web sites. The leading U.S. auto manufacturers, for example, all have on-line internship application capabilities. The World Wide Web is becoming a great place to look for employment. However, it has its drawbacks as a search tool. For example, it is virtually impossible to screen out information about medical residencies and internships (the kind that medical school graduates pursue) when using a search string including the word *intern*.

Use the reference section of your library. Popular reference books list internship opportunities by industry, such as health care, education, publishing, and telecommunications. Your library will also have directories of potential employers, such as the American Hospital Association Guide, the Glass Factory Directory, and the National Wildlife Refuge and Fish Hatcheries Guide. Once you have learned about an interesting agency or company, you can find out with a quick telephone call whether it offers internships.

Researching Potential Employers

Do your research before you contact potential employers to ask for an internship. If you write up a generic resume and letter of application and send it to one hundred companies that might offer an internship, you are unlikely to recoup the money you spend on postage. No one wants to hire an employee simply because that person desires experience or a salary. Employers are looking for employees who will fill a need. They look for genuine expertise and enthusiasm, for the people who will be most likely to advance projects and products of importance to their organization or their customers. If your band needed a bass player, would you prefer to audition someone who merely claimed to be interested in music or someone with actual experience as a bass player? If that person came seeking inclusion in your group, wouldn't you be more inclined to listen if he or she had heard your band perform? What if he or she could offer specific additions to your repertoire? Even when hiring interns, employers want people who can make an effective contribution to the existing group.

Approach each internship application as a separate research project. Single out ten or fewer potential employers, and market yourself to each one individually. Learn what each prospective employer does, some examples of recent projects, and the names of key persons you should contact, so that you can present yourself as a knowledgeable person with admiration for and an interest in the ongoing projects of the company or agency. The research skills you have been practicing will make this a fairly easy process. Read and discover everything you can find about potential employers before contacting them or beginning to prepare your application materials.

As mentioned previously, you can use the World Wide Web to begin your investigation of potential employers. One or two searches will determine whether the agency or business you are interested in has a Web site of its own. You might also turn up information about some of the company's recent projects. If the company has a Web site, check to see if it lists job openings and internships and whether job descriptions for interns are included. Take down the name, address, telephone number, and e-mail address of the human resources contact person.

Don't stop with Web information about an employer, however. Search periodicals in your library to discover journal and newspaper articles about accomplishments of your potential employer. Look for good news—a product launching, a grant awarded for research, an honorary citation for environmental protection, or a charitable contribution to the community. Request annual reports from any corporations where you are considering applying for an internship and read them to learn what those companies perceive to be their strengths and most promising future projects. Contact trade associations and the Better Business Bureau to request further information about employers. Ask professors and fellow students in your academic department what they know about the agencies and businesses you have identified as potential internship sites. If possible, obtain interviews with current employees who are familiar with the kinds of work you are interested in doing. Learn as much as you can about the places where you hope to apply for internships, so that you can accurately describe the reasons you are interested in working there and the contributions you expect to make.

Writing Letters of Application

A letter of application is sometimes referred to as a "cover letter" because it is the front page, or "cover" of your application materials. This letter is a routine piece of correspondence, but a very important representation of yourself. In it, you must introduce yourself to your potential employer, indicate your interest in an internship, and demonstrate that you are a good candidate for the position. Remember, however, that the letter's purpose is only to get you an interview, not to land the job. You don't want or need to tell everything about yourself in your cover letter. You don't need to anticipate all of the questions your potential employer might ask of you, and you don't need to prove that you have absolutely every qualification needed for the job. Most letters of application are just three or four short paragraphs long, pointing out the relevant and interesting parts of your previous experience and explaining why you are eager for the opportunity to talk more about the position.

Always address your letters of application to real people. Generic letters sent to an anonymous director of human resources or job search committee chair do not receive the same attention as those addressed to the actual person who will read the letter and make a hiring decision. You know from your own experience that bulk mail addressed to "occupant" or "resident" is not as ardently scrutinized as letters bearing postage stamps and personal addresses. Use your researching skills to discover the name and correct job title of the person who should receive your application materials. Look in corporate directories on Web sites or in the library, ask the career counselors on your campus to help you locate contact names, or—as a last resort—telephone the office where you plan to send your application and ask to whom it should be addressed.

In your opening paragraph, make clear for which internship you are applying. Indicate the period for which it is advertised and in which department or area it is offered. Tell how you learned about the opportunity, and if you have any contacts inside the agency who have given you permission to mention their names, do so. Set a proper tone: be businesslike and efficient. Don't attempt to show enthusiasm with informal remarks or exclamation points. Remember that this is business correspondence, and the people who will read your letter have not yet met you. Approach them on paper as you would in person; be straightforward and reverent.

The middle one or two paragraphs of your cover letter should establish that you possess the necessary skills to succeed in the position. If the internship has prerequisites, show that you have met them. For instance, if only accounting majors are encouraged to apply, explain how far along you are toward completing your accounting degree. If the internship position requires special skills (such as dealing with the public or computer literacy), mention any relevant experience that demonstrates your abilities (for example, working in a sales position or successfully completing computer courses). Avoid making apologies; don't start sentences with words or phrases like *Although* or *In spite of* (for example, "Although I am not an accounting major, I have taken several mathematics courses" or "In spite of my lack of previous work experience, I am looking forward to a career in sales"). Be positive and sincere, and stress those areas in which you are knowledgeable.

If you were able to learn about any specific projects at the company that are related to your interests or experience, a third paragraph, stating that you are applying for the position in the hope of working on a certain project, may be helpful. Indicate why you believe you are the best candidate for the company's or agency's purposes, not why the internship would be beneficial to you. For example, if an applicant for an internship at a theater with a renowned children's theater department had previously worked in a day care center, he would want to mention his experiences with entertaining and educating preschool children.

Finally, ask the employer for the opportunity to talk further about the position. Occasionally applicants close by telling the recipients of their letters that they will telephone them in two weeks to inquire about a possible interview, but it is important to remember that the job is being offered by the employer on their time table and at their convenience. Most employers with a position to fill want to do so as soon as possible with the most qualified candidate available. It is better to simply indicate your desire to speak further and leave it at that. When employers decide to consider you for a position, they will usually contact you promptly.

QUYEN (QUINN) LOI NGUYEN
1422 NE 57th St., Apt. No. 18 • Seattle, WA 98105 • 206.282.5938

7 March 2000

Mr. E. Arnold Hanson
U.S. Forest Service
Department of Agriculture
Region One Headquarters
Missoula, MT 59801

Dear Mr. Hanson:

My Environmental Geology professor, Dr. Harold Roepke, has spoken with you about my interning in your office this summer, and I am writing to inquire about the possibility of that. I am a first-year geology major at the University of Washington in Seattle, and I am interested in human safety and environmental issues related to outdoor recreation in our nation's parks.

As my enclosed resume indicates, I have worked during weekends for the past two winters as a ski lift attendant at Snoqualmie Pass Recreational Area. There, I had the opportunity to meet Mr. Mark Wodecki, who is a geologist with the United States Department of Agriculture, when he consulted on the creation of new ski runs and the installation of snow machines. His work in avalanche prediction got me interested in the subject of geology.

I am aware that your staff is currently involved in the design of new ski runs at Snow Bowl, and I am eager to participate in that project. As an intern with your office, I would uphold the Forest Service's commitment to understanding ecosystems and promoting safe interaction between people and natural resources.

I look forward to the opportunity to talk with you and learn more about your involvement with the Snow Bowl design and other current projects underway in your office. Please contact me at the address or phone number listed above.

Sincerely,

Quinn Nguyen

Quinn Nguyen

A sample letter of application, for an internship with the U.S. Forest Service, appears above. Notice that the applicant, Quinn Nguyen, is applying for an unadvertised internship position. She learned about Mr. Hanson and the work of the U.S. Forest Service in Missoula through her geology professor at the University of Washington. Because the position was not advertised, it has no prerequisites or formal job description. Quinn chooses to describe her qualifications for the job: her college major in geology, her experience at a local recreational area, and her familiarity with the work of a government geologist. She demonstrates that she has learned about the work of the

Missoula Forest Service office and that she is interested in helping to advance that work. In her closing she indicates her willingness to learn about other projects under way at the agency. Although this is a brief letter, a positive picture of Quinn begins to emerge from it. Her resume, to which she has skillfully alluded in her letter, will tell more about her.

Compiling a Resume

Quick! In sixty seconds, summarize your job skills. It sounds difficult, but that is the challenge that a resume must rise to meet. A resume is a brief (usually one- or two-page) document that attempts to describe one's educational history and employment qualifications at a glance. Essentially an advertisement for yourself, your resume is a carefully designed descriptive tool. Your letters of application present you as an articulate, well-informed, enthusiastic job candidate, and your resume serves as proof of that. It details your educational achievements, employment history, and related personal accomplishments in a reasonably standard format that allows employers to compare your qualifications with those of other candidates.

All resumes start with the same information: the candidate's name (usually in a larger, bolder font than the rest of the text), followed by information about how to contact that person (an address, phone number, fax number, and e-mail address). If you are living at a temporary, school address—an apartment or residence hall room away from your permanent address—give both addresses at the top of your resume, and indicate the dates at which you will be living at each.

Some people put the word *Resume* or *Vita* (which means life) at the top of the first page, but that is unnecessary. Since a resume is designed to be deciphered at a glance, it is recognizable without a heading.

The design of your resume is a personal issue. This says a lot about you. Experiment with graphic elements such as boldface type, italics, spacing, margins, ornamental lines, and type fonts. Resumes, like cover letters, tend to be formal and traditional; even restrained graphic elements may become a distraction. Very subtle touches give a resume its "customized" appearance. The purpose of a resume is to convey standard information clearly, so every mark on the page should aid the reader in quickly gathering the facts. Do not include illustrations or pictures on your resume. Even resumes posted on the World Wide Web, a medium designed to facilitate incorporation of graphic elements, should be devoid of gratuitous artwork.

Do not include any information on your resume that explicitly identifies you by gender or race. Never put a photograph of yourself on your resume, and do not reveal your marital status or age. Government guidelines for nondiscriminatory employment practices prohibit persons directly involved in hiring from asking for such information, and many employers fear that the voluntary revelation of personal data might prejudice their decisions. Resumes that are too revealing are often discarded without serious consideration.

Information on a resume is summarized in reverse chronological order. Put the most recent experiences first, and work backwards, so that readers can quickly see what you have accomplished so far in life and the steps you took to get to that point. For example, list your education, starting with where you are in school now, followed by any colleges you have previously attended, and end with your high school record. If you have graduated from college once before, list that, and do not include information about your high school attendance. Use dates to make the chronology of your experiences apparent.

For a college student seeking an internship, the most important part of a resume is the Education section. Give the name of your college and the major and minors you are pursuing. Include the date you plan to graduate, preceded by the word *expected* or the abbreviation *exp.* If you are enrolled in a special program, such as an honors college, identify that on your resume. You may wish to reveal your grade point average, if it is very good; simply introduce it as "GPA" and identify the scale used to calculate it (for example, GPA: 3.86 on a 4.0 scale). However, since most internship committees request copies of students' transcripts (the official list of courses you have taken and grades you have received, available from the registrar's office at your school), indicating your GPA on your resume is redundant. The most up-to-date information on your earned credit hours and grade point average are included on your transcript.

Devise a special paragraph or text block to contain all of the information you want to communicate about your current educational experience, and follow that format as closely as possible when listing past educational achievements. Throughout your resume, group similar items and present them in parallel structures to facilitate easy comprehension. Rely on what you have learned about constructing formal outlines in planning your resume. Use a consistent formula for indenting blocks of information and presenting main headings in larger fonts or boldface type. Balance each page so that design elements are distributed throughout the document.

Another important element of most resumes is the Experience section, where current and previous jobs are described. Try to include between two and four examples of work experience, or evidence that you have assumed responsibilities in your life. If you have never worked at a formal job, consider listing offices you have held in school or clubs and organizations, leadership roles on sports teams, and other duties that attest to your trustworthiness. As a student, you are not expected to have held many jobs before, but you should be able to supply some evidence of punctuality, responsibility, or civic awareness.

The focus of the Experience section of your resume should be on what you have actually accomplished, not merely the job titles you have held. Describe your responsibilities in each position briefly and concisely. Start your list of responsibilities with verbs, such as *supervised, developed, wrote, drove, made, delivered, taught, programmed, managed,* and so on. Always be sure to emphasize the responsibility you shouldered by indicating if you were in charge of a group of workers or accountable for meeting deadlines or ensuring customer satisfaction.

Don't pad or stretch the evidence on your resume. If you have experience as a babysitter, don't try to pass it off as running a day care center or teaching early childhood education. If you were a cashier at a gas station, don't imply that you were a mechanic. No rational employer will fault you for having experience commensurate with your age. Your resume is as much about your personality and character as it is about your past achievements. Be honest and straightforward about your accomplishments so that you won't be embarrassed or discredited if you are asked about the items on your resume later in an interview.

Other categories on a resume, such as Skills, Awards and Honors, and Activities, are optional. If you have two or more relevant and impressive items with which to create such a category, include it. A Skills category might encompass abilities with various computer software, fluency in other languages, maintenance of a pilot's license, certification in basic life support or First Aid, or proficiency in sign language. Awards and Honors include things such as winning academic prizes or scholarships, gaining distinction in an intellectual pursuit (for example, winning a chess championship or speech contest), being named to the honor roll, or winning election to an honor society or to an office in a civic organization. Activities are honors won in less academic pursuits, such as athletic participation, volunteer work, being a mentor for a Big Brother or Big Sister organization, or membership in professional organizations. Do not list activities on your resume that are essentially hobbies or forms of relaxation.

A final item you might choose to include as part of your resume is a References section. Most internship applications ask for three to five references. These should be people who have supervised you as an employee, volunteer, or student. If you list a current job on your resume, be certain to include your direct supervisor as a reference. As a student, you should also list one or two of your college professors, and at least one of them should teach a subject related to the job for which you are applying or the subject in which you are majoring. Don't include "character witnesses." Because your resume is a professional document, choose persons who can recommend you on the basis of their familiarity with your academic and vocational performance.

Always ask people for permission before you give their names as references, and tell them about the positions for which you are applying so that they will be prepared to give relevant information. It is a good idea to give your resume to people who agree to act as references for you, so that they are reminded of your accomplishments when they write or speak on your behalf. If there is not room on a one- or two-page resume to list your references, create a separate References page to send to employers who require it. In some cases, potential employers will expect you to request letters of reference yourself and instruct writers to mail them directly to the hiring committee. Occasionally, however, employers will want to speak directly with the people you have identified. If it is acceptable to those individuals, include their telephone numbers and e-mail addresses on your references list.

Quinn Nguyen's resume is reproduced on page 344. It is an all-purpose resume. She does not have a variety of vocational or academic experiences; she has held two jobs and attended one college so far. Because she is applying for an internship, she decided to list her employment experience first. Notice that her references are people who are prepared to address her current job performance and her current and past academic record. Quinn plans to send this resume as part of each of her internship applications.

If you have abundant potential resume material from which to choose, you might decide to write a custom resume for each specific internship you are seeking. On page 345 is an individualized resume prepared by David Meeker, a student who is seeking a second cooperative internship with a software development company. He indicates this goal clearly in the Objective section at the top of the first page and reinforces his image as an accomplished computer programmer and designer throughout the resume.

As you can see, David has taken some liberties with the traditional resume design. He includes only an e-mail address, since he knows that employers in the computer software industry prefer using the Internet. The heavy lines that separate the sections on his resume and the bullets that punctuate the individual items within each category are striking but not overwhelming. The design is also well suited to posting the resume on David's Web site, which he does and invites potential employers to view it there and print it out for themselves. Another version of his resume is focused on his skills as a Web site designer. The URL that he includes in his (usually e-mailed) cover letters determines which version of his resume potential employers will see.

Brainstorm a comprehensive list of the experiences, accomplishments, skills, activities, and honors that you have amassed during your lifetime. Using this list, create two or three different versions of your resume, each subtly emphasizing a different aspect of your background. You will probably want to include different people as references, depending on the focus of each resume. Most professionals have not a single resume but a variety of different ones suitable for use in different situations. Your resume will always be changing, especially when it is successful in gaining another job, internship, or honor to be added to its contents.

Preparing for an Internship Interview

As you are preparing for an internship interview, think about what you want as an interviewer when you are conducting research. You hope to learn specific information. You try to learn about your subject and interviewee in advance to appear prepared and interested in the encounter. You hope to make your

interaction pleasant, enjoyable, and informative. Although prospective employers are in a much different situation than students or reporters seeking information from an authority, they want much the same to occur during an interview.
If your application is chosen for the next step in the intern selection process, you
will be contacted and asked to participate in an interview, either in person or
over the telephone. Let the person you will be meeting with choose the time
and place for your interview.

It should help you in preparing to be interviewed to remember your own
experiences as an interviewer. You know that an interview is, essentially, a brief

DAVID MEEKER   dfm@po.cwru.edu

OBJECTIVE   A Cooperative Education position in Software Development for the period of
                 January through August, 1999.

EDUCATION   CASE WESTERN RESERVE UNIVERSITY, CLEVELAND, OHIO
                 • Pursuing a B.A. in Computer Science, minors in Art and Artificial Intelligence
                 • National Merit Scholarship, Presidential Scholar, Dean's High Honors List
                 • Grade Point Average: 3.6/4.0 (3.75/4/0 within major)
                 • Rank as a Senior, will graduate in spring 2000 with 4 semesters co-op
                 • Related Coursework:
                     • Software Engineering   • Object-Oriented Programming
                     • Operating Systems   • Database Systems
                     • Data Structures   • Algorithms
                     • Microprocessor Design   • Autonomous Robotics

EXPERIENCE   NETSCAPE COMMUNICATIONS CORPORATION (MOUNTAIN VIEW, CA)
                 COOPERATIVE EDUCATION INTERN (JANUARY 1998—AUGUST 1998)
                 Developed new features for the 5.0 version of Netscape's popular Internet client
                 software. Worked in a large, dynamic team development environment on an evolving
                 product. Participated in the product management process for features. Developed
                 cross-platform C and C++ code.

                 DIGITAL GELATIN (CLEVELAND, OH)
                 SENIOR PARTNER (MAY 1996– DECEMBER 1997)
                 Established Internet design and consulting firm. Developed custom applications in
                 Java and C++, created numerous web sites tailored to meet the needs of our clients,
                 solved problems through consulting services. Client list includes Turner Network
                 Television, the Cleveland Clinic, Charter One Financial, Industry Week.

                 NEW RIDERS PUBLISHING (INDIANAPOLIS, IN)
                 CO-AUTHOR (JANUARY 1996–FEBRUARY 1996)
                 Authored chapter of *Webmaster's Professional Reference* (ISBN: 1562054732)
                 on how to select software, hardware, and networks in order to maximize usefulness
                 and minimize cost when establishing a web site.

                 UNIVERSITY COMPUTING SERVICES, BALL STATE UNIVERSITY (MUNCIE, IN)
                 STUDENT INTERN (AUGUST 1995– AUGUST 1996)
                 Occupied positions of both systems analyst and applications programmer.
                 Developed numerous applications to specifications, performed configuration and
                 tuning of mainframe systems serving 23,000 users.

conversation between two people for the purpose of frankly sharing information. Don't think of an internship interview as a trial or a test you must pass to
get the job you desire. Focus on the interview as it occurs, not on the outcome of
it. Instead of trying to win the internship, enjoy the opportunity to meet someone who is accomplished in a field that interests you, to find out more about a
position that you think you would enjoy, and to discuss your career plans with a
knowledgeable, attentive listener. Think of your interview as a conversation
rather than an interrogation. You will have some opportunities to ask questions
of your own and to respond to the things your interviewer tells you.

PROFICIENCIES & SKILLS	COMPUTER PROGRAMMING
	C/C++, Java, Pascal/Turbo Pascal
	Microsoft Windows programming with MFC and Windows API
	Network Programming (TCP, UDP, Client/Server, Peer-to-Peer)
	Graphics and custom interface componentry under Java
	Event-based programming
	Object-oriented programming
	COMPUTER GRAPHICS
	Design and Layout (Web and General)
	Interface Design
	3D Modelling
	Computer Animation
	GRAPHIC DESIGN
	Print Ad Design
	Art Direction
	Logo/Identity Design
	SOFTWARE PROFICIENCIES
	Microsoft Visual C++ 5.0, Sun Workshop, Irix Visual Debugger
	Rational Quantify, Purify
	Unix (Linux, Solaris/SunOS, HP-UX, Irix, Aix)
	Windows 95/NT, Mac OS, Open VMS

ACTIVITIES

- Weatherhead Entrepreneurial Society
- Salvation Army Volunteer
- Kiwanis Volunteer
- Spring Olympics Indoor Soccer
- IM Indoor Soccer

AWARDS & HONORS

- Presidential Scholarship, Case Western Reserve University. (1996–Present)
- National Merit Scholar, Case Western Reserve University. (1996–Present)
- Golden Key National Honor Society Member. (1998– Present)
- Deans High Honors, Case Western Reserve University. (Fall 1996)
- Deans Honors, Case Western Reserve University. (Spring 1997–Present)
- Tandy Technology Scholar. (1996)
- Outstanding Achievement Award for Excellence in Mathematics. (1996)
- Purdue University Junior Scholar in Mathematics. (1995)
- Participant, Richard Lugar's Symposium for Tomorrow's Leaders. (1994)

Although you will already have completed some research about the agency or company, you will need to conduct more in-depth research once you are invited to interview. Just as when you are conducting interviews for research purposes, don't waste valuable meeting time asking questions that can be answered elsewhere. For instance, learn what the company with which you are interviewing does at all of its locations and offices. Study recent press releases about staff members.

Your interview probably will last about an hour, but you must demonstrate in that time that you are professional and capable of being trusted with your employer's work and image. Dress professionally. Make eye contact with everyone in the room. Sit up straight, and gesture naturally with your hands. Smile when you are introduced to others. Shake hands upon entering and exiting. Keep your answers to questions brief and to the point. Remember that the person who requests an interview is responsible for its content and pacing. Follow your interviewer's lead in choosing topics and asking questions. Try to appear as relaxed and enthused about the situation as possible. Ask your own questions as they occur to you. The interview is your opportunity to find out about the job for which you have applied and the atmosphere in which you will work. An internship interview helps you discover more about your potential employer as much as it allows them to learn more about you. Both you and the interviewer want a good job match, a work experience from which all will profit.

As with interviews for research projects, face-to-face meetings are preferable but not always practical. Especially if you are interviewing for an internship a long way from where you live, you may be asked to interview over the telephone. Consciously project a professional image. You might want to record a simple, direct, but friendly message on your answering machine whenever you are expecting calls from potential employers. Take care to answer your phone politely and clearly whenever a prospective employer might call. Listen carefully to questions as they are posed during a telephone interview. Since you won't be able to make eye contact with your interviewers, you will want to be certain that you are "connecting" with them verbally by answering their questions exactly. Keep your answers brief and direct. Avoid the temptation to ask for verbal feedback in the absence of visual cues. Don't end your answers by asking "Do you know what I mean?" or "Is that okay?" Try to sound confident and friendly.

Be polite and circumspect in all dealings with potential employers. Job or internship applications are formal social situations. At the conclusion of the interview, thank everyone for taking the time to talk with you and tell you about their business. After the interview is over, write a brief letter to the person responsible for conducting your interview, expressing your continued interest in the position and thanking that person for showing an interest in your career and taking the time to speak with you about it. Once you have been offered and have accepted an internship position, write letters to the people who served as references for you, telling them about the job you have taken and thanking them for their role in helping you secure it. Most professional disciplines are surprisingly small, and the people involved in them are well connected. By seeking to enter the working world through an internship, you have begun to make a reputation for yourself in that community. Your profession has started. The researching and writing strategies that you are practicing in your college classes are the beginning of your career.

■ Summing Up

The researching skills that you have been learning in this course will serve you well throughout your career. Of course, sources and strategies will change over time, but the methods of investigation you have learned will help you adapt. Most of the jobs sought by college graduates involve research and the ability to adapt to new methods and technology. A few years ago, the Internet did not exist, but accomplished researchers caused it to proliferate vigorously. Similarly, you will participate in advancing future research materials and methods.

You may be eager to begin participating in professional work, or you may be apprehensive about your first job. In either case, an internship is a great way to learn more about your own future and contribute to your academic field and your education. An internship may be a summer- or semester-long trial employment period. It may involve actually working in your chosen field of study or observing established professionals closely at work. It might pay a stipend or a salary, or its dividends may be experience only. Most school-sanctioned internships earn college credit as well.

Because you will likely want to intern during your second or third year of college, it is not too early to begin researching and planning for it. Talk to the internship specialists in your school's placement office for advice. Using the Internet, government publications, library reference materials, and networking among your professors and friends, you should be able to discover several internship opportunities in your academic field. Once you have found a few positions that sound promising, you can use your research skills to learn more about your potential employers and determine whether you want to pursue those leads with applications.

Read about employers in periodicals, request annual reports, check out their Web sites, and interview working professionals about the places where you plan to apply for internships. For each position you apply for, you will need to compose a letter of application that demonstrates that you know something about the job you want and the agency or company offering it. The techniques for persuasive writing that you have practiced in this class will aid you in that task. You will also need to compose a resume that demonstrates a correlation between your previous experience and education and the position you are seeking. Your skills with gathering and organizing data and your ability to outline information will come in handy as you write your resume. Finally, experience with interviewing others to gather information will help you understand and negotiate job and internship interviews. You will find that the work you have been completing for this course has been part of the real world all along.

Exercises: Sources and Strategies

1. Search the World Wide Web and internship directories in your campus library, and talk to career specialists and faculty members to learn about

internships for which you might be qualified. Make a list of the top three internships for which you would like to apply, and annotate it with the application procedures for each.

2. Write a letter of application for each of the internship positions you have identified as being interesting to you. Ask a professor or someone from your campus placement office to edit it and return it to you for revisions.

3. Make a list of your vocational and educational achievements and experiences. Be comprehensive. Include honors, awards, and any specialized skills that you possess. Edit and arrange your list into a resume.

Writing to Know

Write a short (five- to eight-page) description of yourself ten years from now, as you hope to be. What professional and personal goals will you have attained? Where will you live? What will your job be? Who will live with you? What will your hobbies be? Who will your friends be? What goals will still be in progress? Be as sincere or fantastic as you want to be with this assignment. Sometimes even people's wildest dreams do come true.

Index

351

Burns, Ken, 69
Busi, 25

Card catalogs, 27
Cataloging systems, 128
CBE C-S System, 239–241
CBE-N-Y System, 239
CBE style, 224
CD-ROM indexes, 135
Census Bureau documents, 61
Ceremonial discourse, 172
Charts, 228
"Checkers" speech, 167
Chicago Manual of Style (University of
        Chicago), 255, 269
Chicago Style, 255
    bibliographies in, 272
    citing books and periodicals in,
        271–272
    description of, 269–270
    documentation in, 270
    Latin terminology in, 271
    numbering items in, 270–271
Child Protective Services, 64
City recorder's office, 64
Closed stacks, 23
Collections
    libraries with special, 26–27
    in Library of Congress, 31
    purpose of, 59–60
Collections development librarians, 29
College libraries. *See* Research libraries
Computerized card catalogs, 27
Computers. *See also* Electronic catalogs;
        Electronic resources; Internet;
        World Wide Web
    incorporating multimedia material
        using, 192
    in public libraries, 21
Computer Select, 141
Conclusions, 210–211
Congressional Record, 61
Connotations, 170
Connotative meaning of words, 170
Cooperative work programs, 332–333
Corporations
    advertising and public relations docu-
        ments from, 71–72
    annual reports of, 70–71
    Web sites for, 335–336
Costs, search parameters and, 131
Council of Biology Editors (CBE), 224.
        See also CBE style
County clerk's office, 63–64

County recorder's office, 64
Courier, 226, 257
Curators, 66–67

Databases, on-line, 134
Deduction, 174–175
Defense Department documents, 61
Denotative meaning of words, 170
Department of Labor documents, 61
Descriptors
    description of, 127
    finding information on Web by using,
        137
    process of finding, 127–129
    refining search by adding, 134
Dictionaries, 126
Direct quotations
    block, 190–191
    criteria for use of, 189
    double, 191–192
    guidelines for using, 155–156
    integration of, 183–184
    punctuation for, 155–156, 189, 190
    within sentences, 191
Dissertation Abstracts International, 224,
        255
Dissertation citations, 234
Diversity University, 45
Docents, 66–67
Double quotations, 191–192
Drafts
    of conclusion, 210–211
    examples of, 202–205, 214–221
    of introductions, 200–202
    of main text, 205–210
    revising, 211
    writing provisional, 123–124

Education Resources Information Center
        (ERIC), 134, 255
Electronic catalogs
    benefits of, 28, 38
    description of, 27–28
    searching holdings of world-wide
        libraries with, 28
Electronic Library, 48
Electronic media
    APA style for, 236–238
    MLA style for, 267–269
Electronic resources, 27–28, 38
Ellipses, 155–156, 190
E-mail (electronic mail). *See also* Mailing
        lists (Internet)
    description of, 38

Interview formats (*cont.*)
    first-person narrative, 98
    first-person quotation, 96–98
    methods for integrating, 98
    paraphrase, 97, 98
    question and answer, 95–96
Interviews
    APA style for citations for, 237
    compiling questions for, 85, 87–88
    finding people for, 80–82
    internship, 343–346
    interpreting nonverbal cues during, 90
    maintaining your interest level during, 91–92
    methods for ending, 92–93
    methods for requesting, 82–84
    overview of, 80
    preparing for, 84–85
    process for conducting, 88–90
    source information for, 149
    tape-recording, 91
    writing up notes following, 93
Introductions
    drafts of, 200–202
    example of, 202–205
IRC (Internet Relay Chat), 44–45

Jefferson, Thomas, 31
Journals
    biographical statements about contributors to, 150
    distinguishing between magazines and, 151–153
    documentation of sources by, 195
    source information for articles in, 149

Key, Francis Scott, 171
Kirsch, Carole, 303–309

Latin terminology, 271
Letters of application
    example of, 339
    for internships, 337–338, 340
Librarians
    description of, 28
    reference, 29–30
    subject matter specialist, 28–29
Libraries
    cataloging systems in, 27–28
    college or research, 21–24, 26–30 (*See also* research libraries)
    nature of, 17–18
    public, 18–19, 21, 30

researching internships in, 336
    school, 18
Library of Congress
    cataloging system of, 128
    description of, 30
    special collections and archives in, 31
    visiting and using, 30–31
Library support staff, 28
The Library of Congress Subject Headings Index, 127, 128
Local government
    assistance agencies and, 64–65
    county clerk's office and, 63–64
    recorder's office and, 64
    records of, 63
LookSmart, 48
Lurkers, 42
Lycos, 48

Magazines
    biographical statements about contributors to, 150
    distinguishing between magazines and, 151–153
    documentation of sources by, 195
    source information for articles in, 149
    types of, 152
Mailing lists (Internet)
    description of, 41
    finding relevant, 43
    lurking and listening on, 42–43
    subscribing and unsubscribing to, 41–42
Main text
    avoiding sexist language in, 207–209
    getting started on, 205–207
    keeping voice dominant in, 209
    staying on topic in, 209–210
Margins, 226
McIntosh, Elizabeth, 33–35, 94, 96
Media center, 21
Melder, Keith, 75–79, 95, 98
MLA Handbook for Writers of Research Papers (Modern Language Association), 255
MLA style
    correcting errors and, 260
    endorsement and title and, 257–258
    footnotes and end notes and, 262
    page numbering and fastening and, 257
    parenthetical citations and, 260–262
    preferences for, 255
    printing papers and, 256–257